A History of Aristotle's *Rhetoric*

with a bibliography of early printings

by

PAUL D. BRANDES

The Scarecrow Press, Inc.
Metuchen, N.J., & London
1989

British Library Cataloguing-in-Publication data available.

Library of Congress Cataloging-in-Publication Data

Brandes, Paul D. (Paul Dickerson), 1920
  A history of Aristotle's Rhetoric, with a bibliography of early printings.

    Bibliography: p.
    Includes index.
    1. Aristotle. Rhetoric. 2. Aristotle. Rhetoric--Bibliography.
3. Rhetoric, Ancient. 4. Rhetoric, Ancient--Bibliography. 5. Bibliography--Early printed books--16th century. 6. Incunabula--Bibliography.
  I. Title.
PN173.A73B73 1989   808.5   88-33713
ISBN 0-8108-1952-X

Copyright © 1989 by Paul D. Brandes
Manufactured in the United States of America

This book is respectfully dedicated to the following persons who have been most helpful to the author, not only in this research but in his lifetime career:

his seven buddies from World War II:
Bing Bingham* of Seattle, Washington
Tom and Clare Gartley of Secaucus, New Jersey
Fred Heil* of Nutley, New Jersey
Rocky Horne* of San Francisco, California
Matt and Pat Mahoney of Beverly, Massachusetts
Don* and Millie Morehouse of Gowanda, New York
Tom Samples of Clinton, Tennessee

his foreign friends from World War II and his German relatives
Robert & Georgette* Marcouf and their children, Michel and Brigitte of Rueil-Malmaison, France and LaRogue sur Pernes
Claudine Levergeois Rieu, Jean Rieu, and their children, Anne Julia and Jean Manuel of Châtenay-Malabry, France
Gabrielle Desmier* and Suzette Jullien* of Avranches, France
Jean and Yvette Osmond of Avranches, France, and their children Philippe, Dominique, Laurence, Thierry and their respective spouses Lucie, Caroline, Jean-Marie and Dominique
Clotilde and Jean Chéron of Le Mans, France
Gunter and Gerda Brandes of Herrenberg, Germany
Folker and Sigrid Brandes and their children Hilke and Fion of Heiligkreuzsteinach, Germany
Wulf and Uta Brandes of Mannheim, Germany
Gordon and Flo Nendick and their children and spouses Paul and Margo, Phillip and Wendy, Rob and Bronwen, and John and Raeleen of Perth, Australia
Vera and William* Nendick of Perth, Australia
Robert Marchand* of Paris, France

*deceased

TABLE OF CONTENTS

Preface i

Chapter One: The Composition & Preservation of Aristotle's *Rhetoric* 1

Chapter Two: The Greek & Latin Manuscripts of Aristotle's *Rhetoric*
That Emerged during the Renaissance 9

      Plate One: an Abridgement of Kassel's *schema* 10
      Plate Two: folio 120r of Parisinus Grec 1741 12
      Plate Three A: folio 3r of Cambrigiensis Ff.5.8 18
      Plate Three B: folio 108v of Cambrigiensis Ff.5.8 19
      Plate Four: the beginning of the fragment of Marcianus 214 21
      Plate Five: excerpts from Monacensis Graec 313 22
      Plate Six: folio 1r of Monacensis Graec 90 26
      Plate Seven: folio 1r of Monacensis Graec 176 27
      Plate Eight: folio 4r of Marcianus Grec 200 30
      Plate Nine: folio 154r of Marcianus Grec 200 31

Chapter Three: The Fifteenth & Sixteenth Century Greek & Latin
Printings of Aristotle's *Rhetoric* 42

      Plate Ten: working draft of Trapezuntius' translation 44
      Plate Eleven: folio 1r of Parisinus Latin 1876 46
      Plate Twelve: folio 1v of Parisinus Latin 1876 47
      Plate Thirteen: folio 2r of Parisinus Latin 1876 48
      Plate Fourteen: initial folio of 1515 Venice edition 49
      Plate Fifteen: folio 2v of Parisinus Latin 1876 50
      Plate Sixteen: second folio of 1515 Venice edition 51
      Plate Seventeen: first folio of Victorius' copy of the 1508 Aldine *Poetics* 52
      Plate Eighteen: first folio of Victorius' copy of the the 1508 Aldine *Rhetoric* 53
      Plate Nineteen: second folio of Victorius' copy of the 1508 Aldine *Rhetoric* 54
      Plate Twenty: third folio of Victorius' copy of the 1508 Aldine *Rhetoric* 55
      Plate Twenty-One: fourth folio of Victorius' copy of the 1508 Aldine *Rhetoric* 56
      Plate Twenty-Two: engraving of Erasmus 58
      Plate Twenty-Three: beginning of Book Two of the 1536 Trincavelli edition 59
      Plate Twenty-Four: continuation of Book Two of the 1536 Trincavelli edition 60
      Plate Twenty-Five: continuation of Book Two of the 1536 Trincavelli edition 61
      Plate Twenty-Six: beginning of Book Two of the 1546 Isingrinius edition 62
      Plate Twenty-Seven: continuation of Book Two of the 1546 Isingrinius edition 63
      Plate Twenty-Eight: continuation of Book Two of the 1546 Isingrinius edition 64
      Plate Twenty-Nine: title page of Victorius 1548 65
      Plate Thirty: title page of Victorius 1549 66
      Plate Thirty-One: title page of Victorius 1579 67
      Plate Thirty-Two: title page of Barbaro 1544 Venice 68
      Plate Thirty-Three: Victorius 1508 copy showing clipped pages 70
      Plate Thirty-Four: folio 1r of Monacensis Graec 175 71
      Plate Thirty-Five: folio 3r of Monacensis Graec 175 72
      Plate Thirty-Six: folio 4r of Monacensis Graec 175 73
      Plate Thirty-Seven A: Victorius' bookmark 75
      Plate Thirty-Seven B: Victorius' medallions 76
      Plate Thirty-Eight: etching of Maioragius 77

Plate Thirty-Nine: title page of Sigonio 1577 78

Table One: Greek Printings of the *Rhetoric* between 1508 & 1599 86
Table Two: Latin Printings of the *Rhetoric* between 1475 & 1599 88
Table Three: Annotated Bibliography of the Printings of Aristotle's
    Rhetoric between 1477 & 1599 90

Plate Forty: first two folios, c.1477 edition 91
Plate Forty-One: handwritten title page, c.1477 92
Plate Forty-Two: title page, 1499 Leipsig 95
Plate Forty-Three: colophon, 1499 Leipsig 96
Plate Forty-Four: colophon, 1515 Paris 97
Plate Forty-Five: 1st page *Rhetoric*, 1531 Basel 100
Plate Forty-Six: title page, 1531 Basel 101
Plate Forty-Seven A: 1st page, 1548 Victorius 108
Plate Forty-Seven B: 1st page, 1549 Victorius 109
Plate Forty-Eight: title page, 1550 Basel 112
Plate Forty-Nine: title page, 1558 Paris 115
Plate Fifty: title page, 1561 Vincentius, I 118
Plate Fifty-One: title page, 1561 Vincentius, II 119
Plate Fifty-Two: title page, 1561 Frellonius, II 120
Plate Fifty-Three: title page, 1577 Rostock 124
Plate Fifty-Four: first page, Victorius 1579 125
Plate Fifty-Five: title page, I, 1581 Honoratus 127
Plate Fifty-Six: title page, II, 1581 Honoratus 128
Plate Fifty-Seven: title page, II, 1581 Michaelis 129
Plate Fifty-Eight: title page, 1584 Sylburg 131
Plate Fifty-Nine: title page, 1590 I Laemarius 134
Plate Sixty: title page, 1590 II Laemarius 135
Plate Sixty-One: title page, 1590 I Bubonius 136
Plate Sixty-Two: Latin Riccobono in II 1590 137
Plate Sixty-Three: title page, 1592 Pomeranian 139
Plate Sixty-Four: title page, 1575 Maioragius 145
Plate Sixty-Five: title page, 1575 Maioragius 146
Plate Sixty-Six: title page, 1575 Muret 150

List of Libraries Indexed in Table III 154

Bibliography of Sources concerning Medieval & Renaissance Scholars 158

Chapter Four: Improvements in the Greek Text during the Nineteenth and Twentieth Centuries 161
    Table One: Relationship between Selected Indexes and Editions 174
    Table Two: The Development of Subdividing the Text of the *Rhetoric*
        into Chapters and of Developing Numbering Systems to Indicate
        Sections or Lines of the Text 175

Chapter Five: Perspectives on a New Translation of Aristotle's *Rhetoric* 178
    Passage from 1376a6-1376a33 Translated to Emphasize the
    Legal Aspects of Aristotle 196

PREFACE

It is commonly said that scholarship is not dull, but that scholars are. We do not wish to be dull if we can help it. Therefore, to maintain the exhilaration of the research process, we have retained what many scholars would advise us to omit, e.g., brief sketches of the lives of some of the translators, descriptions of some of the Aristotelian manuscripts, and other human interest material that may bring to the readers some of the excitement that the researcher maintained as he gathered the material and wrote the book.

We would like to call the reader's attention to the following:

a. Because spelling in Latin was fluid during the Renaissance period, there are Latin spellings that do not conform to classical Latin. We have tried to maintain what was printed when the translations were made. This policy has sometimes resulted in multiple spellings of the names of some authors and puzzling abbreviations used by scribes. Multiple spellings are coordinated in the index.

b. We worked in at least six languages: Greek, Latin, Italian, German, French and English, as well as consulting catalogues in libraries where Hungarian, Polish, and Czech were the prevailing languages. The spelling of the name of a publisher or author may vary widely within any one of those languages, and among the languages. Our procedure was to adopt a spelling that most nearly represented the person being discussed and to use it unless another spelling was preferable in a given context, e.g., Muret is called Muret and not Mureto because he was of French birth. Some of these spellings may not be the spellings that the reader has customarily seen. We ask the readers to role play with us as we went through the card catalogues of the foreign libraries, trying to find under what variant spelling a particular author had been catalogued. The spellings often seemed infinite.

c. In the period of the early printings, editors often changed aspects of their editions with no warning. Titles, authors, publishers and texts were modified from printing to printing. Therefore, if the version offered here is not exactly what the reader finds in a given copy, it may be that the reader's copy and those copies consulted by this researcher varied because of abrupt modifications of the printer.

We wish to offer our particular thanks for the cooperation of the following persons, either in assisting us to locate materials or in editing the manuscript. However, whatever errors in composition or language may occur are totally our responsibility.

The University Research Committee of the University of North Carolina for its repeated support of the project

The University of North Carolina Computation Center and in particular Dan Wingate, Mike Padrick and Tom Rutledge

Roger Deese of the University of North Carolina Printing Department

Scott Madry, my son-in-law, for contributing his expertise in computers and my daughter Sarah for being patient with both of us

John Kirby of Smith College for offering suggestions about the manuscript

Peter Smith of the University of North Carolina for assistance with selected passages of the Greek

Richard Enos of the University of Pittsburgh for offering suggestions about Chapter Five

Antonio Tovar of Madrid

André Wartelle of the Institute Catholique in Paris

Andrew Becker of the University of North Carolina for helping to edit the Greek and Latin entries

Manuel Lopez of the University of North Carolina for assisting with the Spanish translations

Bob Peoples and John Hauser of the University of North Carolina for assisting with the German translations

David Eckerman of the Department of Psychology of the University of North Carolina for generously allowing us to use a Spinwriter printer to generate the tables

Landon Whitt of the Department of Psychology of the University of North Carolina for assisting us in using the Spinwriter

Dr. Dóra Csanak, Director of the Magyar Tudományos Akadémia Könyvtára, Budapest

Kálmán Benda, Director, Református Egyházkerület Raday Gyüjteményc, Budapest

Dr. Agnes Wojtilla-Salgó, Assistant Director, Országos Széchényi Könyvtár, Budapest

Lidia Ferenczy, Director, Országos Széchényi Könyvtár, Budapest

Dr. Marion Zwiercan, Deputy Director, Universytet Jagielloński Biblioteka, Krakow

Andrzej Lechowski, Director of Incunabula, Uniwersytet Jagielloński, Krakow

The Honorable Andrzej Dobrzynski, First Secretary for Press Cultural Affairs, Polish Embassy, Washington, D.C. for his assistance in obtaining the holdings at the libraries in Wroclaw

S. Ferguson, Rare Book Room Librarian, Princeton University

Dr. Peter Voit, Director, Abteilung der Manuskripte und Wiegendrucke, Státní Knihovna C.S.R.

Marie Nadvornikova, Director, Bibliotheksamtmann, Státní Vedecka Khinovna, Olomouc

Dr. Dietrich Grobe and Dr. Klaus Haenel of the Universitäts Bibliothek, Göttingen

Dr. Ursula Altmann, Abteilungs Direktor, Deutsche Staatsbibliothek, E. Berlin

Hans Kasper, Direktor der Benbutzungsabteilung, Deutsche Staatsbibliothek, E. Berlin

Fred Nash and Mary Ceibert, Rare Book Librarians, University of Illinois at Champaign-Urbana

Maria Sicco of the Instituto Centrale per il Catalogo Unico delle Biblioteche Italiane

R. Russell Maylone, Curator, Special Collections, Northwestern University

Frau Reder of the Bayerische Staatsbibliothek, Munich

In addition to the acknowledgements made on the pages featuring the plates, the author wishes to thank the following for permission to reproduce materials, either in part or in the whole: Walter de Gruyter Co. for permission to reproduce in whole and in part schemata from Rudolf Kassel's "Der Text der Aristotelischen Rhetorik" and from Bernd Schneider's "Die Mittelalterlichen Griechisch-Lateinischen Ubersetzungen der Aristotelischen Rhetorik" and to the Speech Communication Association for using parts of two articles by Paul Brandes: "The Composition and Preservation of Aristotle's *Rhetoric*," 35, 482-491 and "Printings of Aristotle's *Rhetoric* during the Fifteenth and Sixteenth Centuries," 52, 63-69. Our special thanks go to Dr. Lucretia O. Kinney who assisted nobly in researching, assembling, and editing the manuscript, and to my wife, Melba Brandes, whose patience and proof-reading were of invaluable assistance. Without their help, the project could not have been completed.

The import of Aristotle's *Rhetoric* has been well expressed by Solmsen in the conclusion to his preface to his 1929 essays:

As a whole, the Aristotelian Rhetorik presents itself to us the result of an inclusive and penetrating order in the Greek intellectual possession. In the newly erected structure in which Platonic, Isocratic and sophistic ideas were gathered together, an Aristotelian organizational capacity was required to put all in its place. This accomplishment is Aristotle's real work, an eminent intellectual philosophical treatise.

As Bonitz said in his introduction to his *Index*, "if our critics be just," we ask them to remember that this is but "a" history of Aristotle's *Rhetoric* and not "the" history of Aristotle's *Rhetoric*. There is much left to be said, and much more that we ourselves would like to cover in future research. However, the work presented here is in our opinion sufficiently extensive to warrant publication. It answers for us, and we hope it will answer for others, many questions that we raised when we were studying and teaching the *Rhetoric*, answers that we were not able to find elsewhere and so set about to find them ourselves. Whatever errors it entails, we regret and look forward to correcting them and expanding the entries in a second edition. With all of its travails, the work has been a pleasure to produce, and we trust it will serve as a pleasure to its readers.

Paul D. Brandes, Professor
University of North Carolina

CHAPTER ONE

THE COMPOSITION AND PRESERVATION OF ARISTOTLE'S RHETORIC

Although Aristotle's *Rhetoric* has served as the basis for an incalculable amount of experimental and critical research in communication, it is often forgot that the "book" we read today is at best an imperfect statement of Aristotle's rhetorical concepts. This first chapter reminds us of the facts and speculations that help to clarify, in so far as possible, what may be the origins of the *Rhetoric*.

What follows, therefore, is a collation and interpretation of research and hypotheses concerning (a) when Aristotle's *Rhetoric* was written, (b) how it was written, and (c) how it was preserved during the Greek and Roman periods. The exposition draws upon scholarship extending across a century and a half and is offered to encourage a realistic contemporary treatment of the *Rhetoric* as a source of hypotheses and critical postulates useful to the contemporary study of rhetorical discourse.

THE DATE OF THE RHETORIC

The evidence to establish a date for the *Rhetoric* is meager, but there are indications that three periods of Aristotle's life may have figured in its composition. During his first residence in Athens (c. 367-347 B.C.), Aristotle set up a school in competition with Isocrates (Cope, 1867, 39-40) and so had need for some guide in his teaching. Cope pointed to the evidence of jealousy between the two rhetoricians, and, since Isocrates died in 338 B.C., more than two years before the beginning of Aristotle's second residence in Athens, the date of this rivalry must fall within the first period of Aristotle's residence in Athens. Cope remarked "...it may naturally be inferred that this was the period in which Aristotle's attention was first directed to the study of rhetoric, and that the indignation which he felt at the undeserved popularity of Isocrates whom he looked upon as the perverter and corruptor of the genuine study of rhetoric...induced him to set up a rival school in which rhetoric should be philosophically and systematically treated, for the use of which he may have drawn up a body of rules and precepts taking the form of an art of rhetoric." (1867, 40) Düring was more certain: "It by no means follows that Aristotle started lecturing and writing books...only after Plato's death. Certainly," continued Düring, "we must imagine that he had the place of a teacher in the Academy for ten years at least. We may be sure that he taught there logic and rhetoric, and that in these years he wrote the *Topics* and an important part of his book on rhetoric." (1960, 253) That Aristotle was proud of the place that rhetoric played in Athenian life is demonstrated by his comment in the *Politics* [1305a11-13] that the development of the art of rhetoric had made such progress that it was the orators and not the demagogues who led the people. Such an attitude by Aristotle would have encouraged him to treat rhetoric seriously and to begin his treatise early in his teaching career.

What part was played by Aristotle's residence in Asia Minor that Burnet referred to as the most important years of the philosopher's life? (1924, 117) Lee (1946), Thompson (1910, vii) and Louis (1948, 91-95) have argued that Aristotle's studies in natural history were conducted largely during his exile from Athens. Zeller assigned the treatise known as the Θεοδέκτεια, which may have been written by Aristotle, to Aristotle's residence in Asia Minor. (1897, 73,n.2) Can the same be said of the *Rhetoric?*

Two passages make it appear that Aristotle was writing the *Rhetoric* when living elsewhere than Athens. (1481a29-30 and 1413b1) Therefore Sandys said: "Aristotle may possibly have begun the *Rhetoric* before his second residence in Athens. The reference to 'the Attic orators' and to the 'orators at Athens' prompts the suspicion that these passages were written while the author was still absent from Athens, but they are also consistent with the sense of aloofness from Athenian politics which was natural in a Macedonian resident at Athens." (1909, xix) However, Sandys concluded that "as a whole, the work is best assigned to the period of his second residence." (1909, xix) Yet Burnet said: "Most of the best of what we have belongs to the time when he [Aristotle] was not at Athens..." (1924, 123) and Jaeger agreed that Aristotle's most productive period was during his interim absence from Athens. (1934, 124) Zeller concluded that Aristotle probably continued his literary activity at Atarneus, at Mitylene, and in Macedonia. (1897, 154) If he had gathered notes for a rhetoric during his first stay in Athens, he would have had, if he had so chosen, an excellent opportunity to polish them while at the court of his friend, Hermeias, and later, at Mitylene.

A discussion of a possible date for the *Rhetoric*, with references to the studies of Schmidt and Brandis and to the works of Spengel, Stahr and others, is found in Cope, who was of the opinion that evidence in the work itself established conclusively that the *Rhetoric* was formulated during one of the two periods of residence in Athens. (1867, 36 ff.) Cope declined to choose between the two episodes of Aristotle's residency, but said: "It seems equally certain that the final publication of the work did not take place till the second residence of the author at Athens." (1867, 38) It is difficult to know just what Cope meant by "publication." Did he mean that a central manuscript became available from which scribes might make copies? It seems wiser to say that the work may have achieved its final form during the second residence, a form that would permit its being used as a guide to teaching.

On Aristotle's return to Athens, he established a school, the Lyceum, which, for twelve to thirteen years, according to McKeon, was devoted to "a program of investigation and speculation in almost every branch of inquiry" and where he composed many of his writings, particularly those of a more scientific nature. (1941, xiv) The stimulus of such a school could have caused the philosopher to continue work on an art of rhetoric or to begin organizing his notes in earnest, whichever the case required. Moraux is positive that Aristotle formulated the treatise during the second residence. "The Rhetoric," he said, "is posterior to 338 and must have been composed during the first years of his second sojourn in Athens." (1951, 317) Havet pointed out that there are references in the *Rhetoric* to both the *Analytics* and the *Topics*, and that, since both of these were composed late in Aristotle's career, the *Rhetoric* must also have been a late composition. (1846, 2) Havet interpreted a letter of Dionysius of Halicarnassus to the effect that the *Rhetoric* was written between 334 B.C. and 324 B.C. (1846, 2) Dionysius devoted his first letter to Ammaeus to prove that the great contemporary of Aristotle, the orator Demosthenes, owed nothing of his greatness in speaking to Aristotle's *Rhetoric* and furthermore Dionysius observed "that, at the time when Aristotle wrote his *Rhetoric*, Demosthenes was already at the height of his public career...." (Roberts, 1901, 57) Dionysius held that it was absurd to say that Aristotle wrote the *Rhetoric* while still a disciple at Plato's school, and referred to Book III, Chapter 10, that alludes to the Olynthiac war, to prove that the *Rhetoric* must have been written after 348 B.C. Dionysius concluded that the work was composed in Aristotle's prime of life, after he had published his treatises on the *Topics*, the *Analytics* and the *Methodics*. (Roberts, 1901, 63)

The relationship between the *Rhetoric* and Demosthenes is problematic. A Demosthenes is mentioned three times in the *Rhetoric*. The first instance, in Book Two, Chapter 23, probably refers to another Demosthenes. The second instance, in Book Two, Chapter 24, refers to Demosthenes only indirectly. The third instance, in Book Three, Chapter 4, cites a metaphor by a Demosthenes, but Cope was inclined to believe that the reference is not to the orator. (1867, 46) Nowhere is Demosthenes quoted to exemplify effective oratory. There were, of course, no organized media to preserve the statements of an orator such as Demosthenes to provide Aristotle with a ready source that he could quote. Still it seems improbable that a scholar as curious as Aristotle should not have taken the opportunity to investigate Demosthenes for himself and to include selections from his speeches in the *Rhetoric*, if he thought them worth quoting.

METHOD OF COMPOSITION

A question has been lurking behind this discussion that is more important than establishing a specific date for the *Rhetoric*. Was the treatise formulated from a first sketch that received annotations and corrections as Aristotle progressed in his teaching, or was it the summation of the thoughts of a mature teacher, composed within a relatively short period of time? The former appears the more probable. Cope pointed out that Aristotle is certain to have written two other works on rhetoric and that, to him, the evidence in support of a third is conclusive. Those works are a history of rhetoric, the Συναγωγὴ τεχνῶν, that appears to antedate the *Rhetoric*; a dialogue named after Xenophon's son, Gryllus, the Γρῖλλος; and the Θεοδέκτεια, referred to in the *Rhetoric* itself in Book III, Chapter 9. Sandys

(1909, xviii) and Zeller (1897, 72, n.2) allowed the Theodectea, and Cope assigned that work to Aristotle's first period of residence in Athens:

> ...I infer from the passage of the *Rhetoric*, that Aristotle in the early part of his career, probably whilst he was still carrying on his rhetorical school, composed a work upon this subject, mainly devoted to style and composition, and arrangement, the contents "in extenso" of the third book on his extant *Rhetoric*, to which therefore the matter would naturally refer for fuller details...and to this he gave the name of his friend Theodectes, himself a proficient in the art, and also the author of a treatise on it. (1867, 57)

Shute, on the other hand, was doubtful, holding that the work was probably non-Aristotelian and that the reference to the *Theodectea* in Book III was inserted into the manuscript at a later date. (1888, 100-101) It is therefore possible, but not certain, that there was an earlier Aristotelian manuscript that might have been expanded into the *Rhetoric*. It is reasonably certain that the *Rhetoric* we have was not its author's only work on the subject.

Even if there was no earlier composition available for direct revision, evidence in the *Rhetoric* suggests that it was under revision over a long period of time. Scholars are divided on the point, but, generally, recent opinions encourage the generic view, i.e., that the work was the product of several writings, in contrast to the systematic view that makes Aristotle's work into a planned unity executed to provide an integrated solution to philosophical and moral problems. The generic theory was acknowledged as early as 1873 by Niebuhr who said: "...Aristotle has evidently enlarged his *Rhetoric*, which in its first sketch was one of his earlier works, with additions till toward the close of his life." (1873-1874, 1, 39)[1] Cope observed that Niebuhr gave no reason for his position, but that it was perhaps a conclusion drawn from the knowledge that Aristotle set up a school in competition with Isocrates and probably composed a treatise and revised it as his teaching progressed. (1867, 40) Cope himself was inclined to agree with Brandis who stated in 1849: "By closer inspection, I cannot find in the substance of the *Rhetoric* anything that is based on an early version and cannot include it, likewise, in the completed works which one can assume Aristotle kept by him for personal revision." (1849, 4, 9) Whereas Brandis did not deny that certain of Aristotle's compositions were developed genetically, he excluded the *Rhetoric* from those that were progressively developed.

But Brandis seems not to have considered the distracting organization of the treatise, an organization that seems more the result of evolution than of uninterrupted, methodical composition. Cope grumbled that the order Aristotle promised in Chapter 3 of Book One is not followed, pointing out that one would expect the κοινοὶ τόποι and the enthymemes to begin Book Two. (1867, 245) Ross agreed saying: "Instead of proceeding, as might be expected, to the 'commonplaces' of argument, he now turns to the other main persuasives...we do not reach the commonplaces till ch. 18." (1964, 273) And, drawing upon his own research and that of Jaeger and others, Solmsen (1954, xx) concluded that "...the Rhetoric was not a 'book' intended for publication but rather something like a professor's lecture notes which Aristotle used not once or twice but a good number of times and kept revising ...." Hill concluded that "probably the most credible theory about the composition of these works is that they are Aristotle's own lecture notes, revised several times in the course of years of teaching." (1972, 20) This, thought Solmsen, accounted for the alternations between high philosophical and moral tone and eminently practical considerations. (1954, xx) After studying Solmsen's support for the generic theory, Hill concluded that, instead of one point of view, Aristotle partially developed two or more positions on different subjects at different periods in his life and that he did not ever reconcile his somewhat contrasting viewpoints. Hill concluded that, "despite his grasping for universal statements, Aristotle never purported to give the final answers to any of these problems." (1963, 199)[2] Aristotle was a seeker after the truth, proposed Hill, drawing upon his predecessors in an effort to develop a philosophy of rhetoric. Corbett concurred with Hill, saying that "since the extant text of the *Rhetoric* creates the impression of being a tentative, unfinished set of lecture notes, it seems likely that Aristotle had incorporated some, if not most, of the notes he used in the elementary lectures that he was delivering in the years 360-353." (1984, x)

Tovar is the most positive of all of the scholars that "the *Rhetoric* that we are reading now is clearly the final product of a long evolution that began during Plato's lifetime." (1953, xxvi) At present, said Tovar, we are at opposite poles to what Brandis proposed a century ago when he saw the work "aus einem Güsse." Tovar (1953, xxvi), pointing out that he differed from Dufour, concluded that the *Rhetoric* was, in its present form, written after 338 B.C., or even after 335, and was therefore completed during the first years of Aristotle's final residence in Athens. Solmsen (1975, 208), referring to the Göttingen dissertation by Kantelhardt, noted that lines 1354a11-1355b23, consisting of Aristotle's polemic against previous rhetorics, "were singled out by Kantelhardt as a complex which was distinct in its basis from subsequent parts." It is possible, therefore, that this section of the *Rhetoric* had been written by Aristotle for another work or for another purpose, and was incorporated into the *Rhetoric* at a later date. If we end what may be the separately composed polemic with 1355b21 instead of Kantelharddt's citation of 1355b23, we can speculate that Aristotle composed a short paragraph [1355b22-1355b25] to serve as a transition between his previously composed material and the body of his work on rhetoric. The generic theory then is predominant today and the one adopted in this book.

As was implied earlier, the generic theory is convincingly supported by the structure of the *Rhetoric* that shows numerous instances of a confused organization. Book Two begins with an unsatisfactory transitional statement on ethos (Chapter 1), moves abruptly to pathos (Chapter 2-11), returns to ethos (Chapters 12-17), and finally discusses the τόποι beginning with Chapter 18. A second example of the confusion in organization will suffice. If Aristotle's comments early in Book One were to be prophetic of order, we would expect ethical proof to be discussed first, followed by pathetic proof, and finally by logical proof. But such is not the case. The special topics take up most of Book One; then the treatise shifts to the confusion at the beginning of Chapter 2 as discussed above; finally, the general topics are given their treatment. Hill concerned himself with those portions of the *Rhetoric* that can be assigned to later additions. (1963, 152-180) Hill's observations, based on the generic theory, attempted to explain why there is such confusion in the organizational structure of the *Rhetoric*. Tovar's observation that Aristotle felt under no pressure to produce a finished product, because the treatise was not to be "published," reinforced Hill's conclusions about the lack of unity in the treatise.

Other contemporary scholars have reached the same conclusions that Solmsen reached, i.e., that what we now know as the *Rhetoric* was in Aristotle's time a set of lecture notes. Burnet observed that "what are now called the works of Aristotle are, in the main, his own personal manuscripts which he used as a foundation for his lectures." (1924-1925, 109) Ross concurred: "The composition of the lectures of which Aristotle's extant works are the notes probably belongs in the main to the twelve or thirteen years of his headship of the Lyceum..." (1964, 6), adding subsequently: "Aristotle may have written out his lectures complete before delivering them, and the written works may be his lectures in this sense: but it seems likely that he lectured more freely than this, and that the books as we have them were written down subsequently by him as memoranda to show to those who had missed the lectures, and by way of having a more accurate record of his views than the memory or the notes of his students could provide." (1964, 17) Zeller reasoned that the *Rhetoric* was never "published" and was only used among Aristotle's pupils and for his lecturing, therefore being subject to revision, because the *Rhetoric* includes a reference to the *Politics*, a work generally considered incomplete at Aristotle's death. (1897, 127)

The clear thrust of internal evidence and scholarly speculation favors the position that the *Rhetoric* was not a "book" in the usual sense, but was a set of lecture notes subjected to a series of revisions, not always systematic. It follows, then, that the work cannot be dated by any particular historical reference, as Dufour proposed. (1932, 14-16)[3] Tovar pointed out that "for ancient writers, that which had not an artistic form and was not a 'finished product'—like a Platonic dialogue—did not need to conform to the formalities imposed by custom, formalities that would have resulted in artificiality and would have marred the liveliness of thought." (1953, xxvi) As he was not developing a completed work, Aristotle was not under pressure to formalize his treatise and make it into a coordinated, internally consistent whole.

THE PRESERVATION OF THE RHETORIC

Considerable opportunity for distortion of the manuscripts of the *Rhetoric* developed after Aristotle's death. Taylor said: "Aristotle's books have almost wholly been lost, but we possess many of his lectures. The 'works' of Aristotle praised by Cicero for their eloquence were philosophical dialogues.... None of them have survived....That our 'works' are actually the MSS. of a lecturer posthumously edited by his pupils seems clear from external as well as from internal evidence." (1955, 13) Shute set forth a view of the way these "works" came into existence, a view still generally accepted. Shute supposed that only a few of Aristotle's writings were widely distributed during the author's lifetime or in the years immediately after his death. For the bulk of them "...there was certainly no other publication than the public reading of such of them as may be considered representing courses of lectures." (1888, 19) After Aristotle's death the peripatetic school at the Lyceum was maintained and the master's writings continued in use. In Shute's opinion, the continued use of the manuscripts proceeded as follows:

> The notes on Aristotle's lectures, whether his own or those taken by his former pupils, were

read out to the class, who, as I believe, could not otherwise easily obtain access to copies of them. Occasional notes and criticisms were interpolated by the lecturer, who probably did not always warn his hearers as to what was interpretation and what was text. Only on this supposition can the repetition of the whole, or nearly the whole, of the Aristotelian titles in the works ascribed to Eudemus, Theophrastus, and later, Straton, be explained. (1888, 26)

Shute envisioned "each lecturer giving his own version of Aristotelian doctrine, and each probably believing and trying to get his pupils to believe that his was the most correct version of the master's thought, or at all events that it differed only from that thought by reason of certain valuable additions and corrections by the teacher's own invention." (1888, 33)[4]

Assuming that the lectures continued in use at the Lyceum, what happened to the rather remarkable library of his notes and other material that Aristotle had developed? Of the seven texts that de Vleeschauwer (1957, 1-14) examined concerning the disposition of Aristotle's library, three are of primary importance: Strabo's *Geography* (1929, VI, 109-113; Book 13, I, 53-55), the *Deipnosophists* by Athenaeus (1927, 1, 11 & 2, 471; Book I, 3 and Book V, 214), and Plutarch's sketch of Sulla (1914-1926, 4, 407; Sulla, xxvi, 1-2). Strabo proposed that Aristotle left his library to Theophrastus who in turn willed it to Neleus, a pupil of Aristotle and Theophrastus. It must be assumed that Aristotle's library included Aristotle's own manuscripts, in whatever condition they were at his death. When Neleus was not named director of the school following the death of Theophrastus, he left Athens and took the library with him to his native Skepsis. According to Strabo, Neleus' descendants were ordinary people who kept the scrolls locked up and not even carefully stored. However, by secreting the library in some sort of trench, they kept it from being confiscated by the kings of Asia Minor. Later, Neleus' descendents sold the library to Apellicon of Teos, for a large sum of money. Apellicon was more librarian than philosopher, so his efforts to restore the ravages of dampness and insects may have done more harm than good. His new copies, which he "published," were faulty. After Apellicon died, Sulla took the library off to Rome where Tyrannion the grammarian, a contemporary of Strabo, gained access to it by paying court to the librarian to whom the scrolls had been enstrusted. Tyrannion attempted to establish an authentic text of Aristotle. Plutarch stated that Andronikos of Rhodes, who revived peripatetic philosophy in Rome, had Tyrannion's edition "published." Thus, versions of Aristotle's works, taken in some fashion from the library, became known to the Roman world. However, Strabo recorded that other booksellers "who used bad copyists and would not collate the texts" also had access to Apellicon's library. Thus several versions of Aristotle's work were seemingly available.[5]

Exactly what Tyrannion had to work with in preparing his editions of Aristotle's works is not clear. He had Apellicon's versions, possibly the manuscripts from Skepsis also. If he had the manuscripts, it is still not known whether these included single or multiple versions of individual works.

Athenaeus' account of Aristotle's library differs somewhat from Strabo's. At one point Athenaeus reported that Neleus sold the library to the Ptolemys for the collection at Alexandria, but later in the same work Athenaeus supported the story that Sulla seized the library of Apellicon "in which were most of the treatises of Aristotle and Theophrastus, at that time not yet well known to the public." (1927, x, xx) Both Shute and de Vleechauwer have sought to reconcile Athenaeus' two accounts. Neleus could have sold to the ambassasdors of Ptolemy those works of Aristotle that were already widely distributed. This would have satisfied the thirst of the Egyptian librarians without handicapping the school at Athens and without endangering the value of Neleus' collection. Later, the heirs of Neleus could have sold the uniquely Aristotelian materials to Apellicon.

While the manuscripts were secreted at Skepsis, versions of the *Rhetoric*, derived from the Lyceum lectures or from other sources, appear to have retained considerable popularity. For example, Cicero was acquainted with the *Rhetoric*. (1939, lvii, 194; xxvii, 94; xxxii, 114, lvii, 192; lxiii, 214; and 1942, II, xxxviii, 160.) As Shute pointed out, Cicero's source was substantially the same as ours, "but I am inclined to think," said Shute, "that in some cases at least the MS. which Cicero uses is not the corrected text by Tyrannion, but the corrupted recension which that correct text supplanted." (1888, 49) More recently Randall has pointed out that Cicero referred to Aristotle's works as commentaria or notebooks, some apparently Aristotle's own outlines and others, notes of students. (1960, 25)

Once the edition of Andronikos of Rhodes had been issued, the Roman world had access to the majority of Aristotle's works. But the *Rhetoric* we know surely differs in some details from those available to the Romans. Extant Greek MSS are almost certainly copies, or copies of copies.[6] The earliest Greek version of the *Rhetoric* is Parisinus Grec 1741, that was "assigned on palaeographical evidence to the end of the tenth century." (Lobel, 1933, 6) Chapter Two will discuss in some detail the manuscripts of the *Rhetoric* that emerged during the Renaissance, and will clarify what is known of the transition between the Roman period and the revival of learning.

SUMMARY

Because the date of the *Rhetoric* cannot be established, because it is almost certain that Aristotle revised his treatise over a long period without always integrating his revisions with the previous text, and because it is certain that whatever was originally Aristotelian passed through numerous versions and even translations, considerable care must be taken before anyone can draw highly positive conclusions from the position of a chapter or a turn of a sentence in the *Rhetoric*. Randall said: "The Aristotelian documents are fragmentary, and frequently break off; they are repetitious, and often display little clear order in their parts. Still more, they exhibit manifest contradictions, of approach, of mood, of theory, even of fundamental position and 'doctrine.'" (1960, 23) Randall continued by saying that obviously the text now available is considerably different from the one left by Aristotle. Grayeff concluded: "The Corpus Aristotelicum that we possess was edited about three centuries after Aristotle's death, and, indeed, after the peripatetic school had suffered a long eclipse, during which time all peripatetic writings had been in the hands of people who, to say the least, did not bestow on them the care and attention which was given e.g. to Plato's work." (1956, 108) It is with these decided cautions in mind that the *Rhetoric* must be examined.

Solmsen [1975 (1929), 229] summarized for us the value of the *Rhetoric*. "In its entirety," said Solmsen, "the Aristotelian *Rhetoric* presents to us the results of a comprehensive and penetrating ordering of the Greek intellectual endowment." Aristotle, said Solmsen, used his powers of organization to integrate the ideas of Plato, Isocrates, and the sophists. "This accomplishment," Solmsen noted, "is the true value of Aristotle's treatise, an eminent intellectual and philosophical work."

NOTES

1. In the English translation of Niebuhr's work by W. Smith and Leonard Schmitz (London, 1842), note 30 falls on pp. 15-16 rather than page 39. Evidently the paginations of the index for the translation were not changed to conform to the new page numbers of the English version.
2. Hill expressed indebtedness to the two German scholars whose commentaries on Aristotle's *Rhetoric* have promoted the generic theory: Jaeger's *Aristotle* (1934) and Friedrich Solmsen's *Die Entwicklung der Aristotelischen Logik und Rhetorik* (Berlin, 1929).
3. Therefore Dufour's rather meticulous attempt to establish the date of the *Rhetoric* by internal evidence between 339 to 338 B.C. becomes less valuable. See Dufour (1932), 14-16.
4. For additional information concerning the history of Aristotle's library, see the references cited by Lynch (1972, 147, n. 20).
5. Grayeff's position that the account by Strabo arose largely in order to "give authenticity to the new edition of Aristotle's works prepared in Rome at first by Tyrannion and then by Andronikos of Rhodes" appears somewhat strained. See Grayeff (1936), 106-108.
6. The evidence presented in Chapter Two makes it unlikely that anything earlier than the tenth century would appear. From the Greek period itself, there is nothing. For example, Kenyon's work on the Greek Papyri in the British Museum lists only one entry for Aristotle, and it is for the *Politics*.

BIBLIOGRAPHY

Athenaeus. (1927). *The Deipnosophists*, tr. C.B. Gulick, New York.

Bekker, Immanuel & C.A. Brandis, eds. (1831-1870). *Aristotelis Opera*, 5 vols, Academia Regia Borussica, Berlin.

Brandes, Paul. (1966). "The Composition and Preservation of Aristotle's *Rhetoric*," *Speech Monographs* 35, #4, 482-91.

Brandis, C.A. (1849). "Über Aristoteles' Rhetorik und die Griechischen auslegen Derselben," in *Philologus Zeitschrift für das Klassische Alterthum*, ed. F.W. Schneidewin, Göttingen, 1-47.

Burnet, John. (1924). "Aristotle," in *Proceedings of the British Academy*, London, 109-124.

Cicero. (1939). *Orator*, tr. H.M. Hubbell, Cambridge, Mass.

Cicero. (1942). *De Oratore*, tr. E.W. Sutton, Cambridge, Mass.

Cope, E.M. (1867). *An Introduction to Aristotle's 'Rhetoric'*, London.

Corbett, P.J. (1984). "Introduction," *Aristotle's Rhetoric*, tr. W.R. Roberts, New York, v-xxvi.

de Vleeschauwer, H.J. (1957). *L'Odyssée de la Bibliothèque d'Aristote et ses Répercussions Philosophiques*, Pretoria.

Dufour, Médéric. (1932). *Rhétorique*, 3 vols, Paris.

Düring, Ingemar. (1960). *Aristotle & Plato in the Mid-fourth Century*, Goteborg.

Gaisford, Thomas, ed. (1820). *Aristotelis de Rhetoric Libri Tres, ad fidem Manuscriptorum Recogniti*, 2 vols, Oxford.

Grayeff, Félix. (1956). "The Problem of the Genesis of Aristotle's Text," *Phronesis* I, #2, 106-8.

Havet, Ernest. (1846). *Étude sur la Rhétorique d'Aristote*, Paris.

Hill, F.I. (1963). "The Generic Method in Recent Criticism on the *Rhetoric* of Aristotle," unpubl. diss. Cornell.

Hill, F.I. (1972). "The *Rhetoric* of Aristotle," in *A Synoptic History of Classical 'Rhetoric'*, ed. J. Murphy, New York, 19-76.

Jaeger, Werner. (1934). *Aristotle, Fundamentals of the History of His Development*, tr. Richard Robinson, Oxford.

Kenyon, F.G. (1895). *Greek Papyri in the British Museum*, ed. F.G. Kenyon, London.

Lee, M.H.D.P. (1946). "Place Names and the Date of Aristotle's Biological Works," paper delivered on November 28, 1946, to the Philological Society of Cambridge.

Lobel, Edgar. (1933). *The Greek Manuscripts of Aristotle's 'Poetics'*, Oxford.

Louis, Pièrre. (1948). "Sur la Chronologie des Oeuvres d'Aristote," *Bulletin de l'Association Guillaume Budé*, new series, 5, 91-95.

Lynch, John P. (1972). *Aristotle's School*, Berkeley.

McKeon, Richard. (1941). *The Basic Works of Aristotle*, New York.

Moraux, Paul. (1951). *Les Listes Anciennes des Ouvrages d'Aristote*, Louvain.

Niebuhr, B.G. (1873-74). *Romische Geschichte*, new ed., ed. M. Isler, Berlin.

Plutarch. (1914-1926). "Sulla," tr. Bernadotte Perrin in *Plutarch's Lives*, London, 324-445.

Randall, J.H. (1960). *Aristotle*, New York.

Roberts, W.R., ed. & tr. (1901). *Dionysius of Halicarnassus: The Three Literary Letters*, Cambridge, England.

Roemer, Adolphus, ed. (1898). *Aristotelis Ars Rhetorica* Leipsig.

Ross, W.D., ed. (1959). *Aristoteles Ars Rhetorica*, Oxford.

Ross, W.D. (1964). *Aristotle*, New York.

Sandys, J.E. (1909). "Introduction," *The 'Rhetoric' of Aristotle*, tr. R.C. Jebb, Cambridge, England.

Shute, Richard. (1888). *On the History of the Process by Which the Aristotelian Writings Arrived at Their Present Form*, Oxford.

Solmsen, Friedrich. (1975). *Die Entwicklung der Aristotelischen Logik und Rhetorik*, Wiedmann, W. Berlin. Originally published in 1929 from the dissertation that appeared in 1928.

Solmsen, Friedrich. (1954). "Introduction," in *Aristotle's Rhetoric and Poetics*, tr. Rhys Roberts, New York.

Spengel, Leonard, ed. (1967). *Aristotelis Ars Rhetorica*, 2 vols, Leipsig.

Strabo. (1929). *Geography*, tr. H.L. Jones, New York.

Taylor, A.E. (1955). *Aristotle*, rev. ed., New York.

Thompson, d'Arcy. (1910). *Historia Animalium*, vol. 4 of *The Works of Aristotle*, eds. J.A. Smith and W.D. Ross, Oxford.

Zeller, Eduard. (1897). *Aristotle and the Earlier Peripatetics*, tr. B.F. Costelloe & J.H. Muirhead, New York.

CHAPTER TWO

THE GREEK AND LATIN MANUSCRIPTS OF ARISTOTLE'S RHETORIC THAT EMERGED DURING THE RENAISSANCE

The scholar who wishes to appreciate fully what may be the significances of Aristotle's *Rhetoric* should be aware of the antecedents upon which the text rests. In Chaper One we explored three questions that helped to clarify that appreciation: (a) what may be the date of the composition of the *Rhetoric*; (b) what may be the method by which Aristotle composed the *Rhetoric*; and (c) how the *Rhetoric* was preserved during the Greek and Roman period leading to its rediscovery during the Renaissance. Chapter Two explores the manner in which the *Rhetoric* became available to scholars in manuscript form during the Medieval and Renaissance periods. The remaining chapters will discuss how the printed editions replaced the manuscripts, how the definitive Greek editions of the *Rhetoric* were established by nineteenth and twentieth century scholars, and what sort of translation should be made of those definitive Greek editions keeping in mind that Aristotle was both a teacher of rhetoric and a man well versed in Greek law and methods of pleading.

In this discussion of the manuscripts of the *Rhetoric*, paleographical terminology will appear only when necessary. Therefore, the rather recent distinction between parchment, as derived from sheep-skin, and vellum, as derived from calf-skin, will not be stressed. In general, manuscripts will be referred to as parchments, which was the custom until a very late period. (Christopher, 1938, 24) All of the MSS. examined for this study except one papyrus were codices, i.e., the folded form of parchments that replaced the scroll and that gave us the model for the contemporary bound book.

It is hoped that among our readers will be students and scholars of the *Rhetoric* who are not acquainted with the specifics of paleography and who would be unnecessarily confused by the use of technical terms where their use is not needed. Perhaps in taking this position, we have been influenced by the recent movement to simplify legal language, a movement of which we approve. The practicality of such simplification is only emphasized by the opposition of the recalcitrants who seem not to wish to communicate except to their brethren in law. As Uriah Heep said in *David Copperfield,* he had been initiated by "going through Tidd's practice." Uriah continued later in the novel by saying to David, "There are expressions, you see, Master Copperfield—Latin words and terms—in Mr. Tidd that are trying to a reader of my humble attainments." We do not need Heep's false humility to avoid trying the reader with paleographical terms that are unnecessarily complex. For specific details on the Greek manuscripts examined, we refer the reader to Wartelle's *Inventaire des Manuscrits Grecs d' Aristotle et de Ses Commentateurs* (1963) and to volume one of Paul Moraux's *Aristoteles Graecus.* (1976) Unfortunately the death of Moraux may delay indefinitely the publication of volume two. For specifics on the Latin manuscripts, readers are referred to the two volumes of *Aristoteles Latinus,* edited by Lacombe. (1939 & 1955)

HOW DID THE RHETORIC SURVIVE THE TRANSITION BETWEEN THE CLASSICAL & RENAISSANCE PERIODS?

As might be predicted, scholars are not certain of the exact manner in which the *Rhetoric* escaped destruction. Eisenstein (1983, 46) observed that "many valued texts were barely preserved from extinction; untold numbers failed to survive." The *Rhetoric* may have been preserved through the efforts of a particular scholar who made his own transcription. Where there *was* one lone parchment copy in existence, it could so easily be lost. The period between the end of Roman learning and the Renaissance was therefore a precarious period for the works of antiquity. As Chapter One pointed out, other works on rhetoric by Aristotle have not survived. The *Rhetoric* has. During the early Medieval period, one or more copies of the *Rhetoric* must have been preserved, probably in a monastery library or in a private collection. Where did this surviving version come from?

Of the two routes by which most classical texts survived, i.e., the route through Arabic-Hebraic culture and the route through Graeco-Roman culture, the former so far has played only a minor role in the preservation of the *Rhetoric*. According to Boggess (1968, 227-350), there were Arabic versions of the *Rhetoric* circulating in Spain in the thirteenth century. The Latin translation of one of these is discussed in Chapter Three. Unfortunately, what has survived from the Latin version by Hermannus Alemannus is not of sufficient exactitude to assist materially in developing a definitive Greek text.[1]

There does exist, however, in the *Bibliothèque Nationale*, Parisinus 2346 [ancien fonds Arabe 882 A]. Although Kassel investigated this MS. and had provided to him a German translation of the first book and of parts of Books Two and Three, he was not satisfied that his knowledge of the Arabic MS. was sufficiently clear for him to evaluate altogether what might be its contribution. (Kassel, 1971, 88-92)

Margoliouth (1897), after having examined the Paris MS., concluded that an anonymous translation (from Greek? or Syrian? into Arabic) was made in A.D. 1016 and collated with other manuscripts in 1027. Apparently, the copyist had two Arabic manuscripts before him, one of which the copyist considered faulty and the other "fairly correct." (Margoliouth, 376) He also had available a Syriac original. The translator developed from these three sources his own version which is Parisinus 2346. Margoliouth speculated that *marginalia* by Ibn al-Samh in one of the manuscripts collated dates the Arabic copies as early as 900 A.D., while the Syriac copy available to the translator "probably takes us back a century earlier; and the underlying Greek copy to a yet earlier date." (1897, 376-377) Although Margoliouth does present some isolated comparisons between the Greek and the Arabic, his work is not extensive enough to make a substantial contribution to the Greek text.

Stern (1956) disagreed with the date assigned by Margoliouth to Ibn al-Samh, placing his death in 1027. Stern agreed that the MSS. was copied from one by Ibn al-Samh, but he cannot determine whether it was written while Ibn was alive or after he had died. Unfortunately Stern did not concern himself sufficiently with translating the Arabic text to allow his work to be helpful in determining the contribution of the Arabic text.

The well-known scholar of the *Poetics* (1928), Tkatsch, also undertook, said Kassel, a translation of the Arabic version of the *Rhetoric*, which was left unfinished at Tkatsch's death. Kassel's efforts to locate the notes left by Tkatsch proved unsuccessful. (1971, 89)

The Arabic text was printed in 1959 in Cairo by A. Badawi. Kassel's investigations led him to conclude the the reprint was unreliable. (1971, 90).

Although Kassel was unsatisfied with his complete assessment of the contribution that might be made by Parisinus 2346, Kassel was able to determine that its text had the same *lacuna* in Book III as is found in the Greek and Latin MSS. Therefore, it was derived, at least to some extent, from the same archetype as were the Greek and Latin MSS. to be discussed in this chapter.

The full extent of the contribution of this Arabic MS. must wait until a rhetorical scholar can lift the veil that Kassel found still blocked his clear vision to the significance of the MS. If the MS. could be painstakingly collated with the Greek text and an edition published that placed the Arabic and the Greek side by side, the MS. could be accurately evaluated for its ability to shed further light on Aristotle's *Rhetoric*.

Until further work is done on the Arabic MS. in Paris, we must follow almost exclusively the Graeco-Roman route to trace the preservation of the *Rhetoric*. The earliest known Greek manuscript of the *Rhetoric* is a parchment housed in the *Bibliothèque Nationale* in Paris dating from the tenth century, while the oldest of the Latin translations from a lost Greek manuscript dates from the thirteenth century. How far removed are these copies from the manuscripts that Aristotle left to his successors at the peripatetic school in Athens? That is impossible to say. They could be anywhere from copies not far removed from the original to copies as remote as twenty times removed from the restored Roman version. The following discussion will present the highlights, as well as some of the lowlights, of the *Rhetoric* during the Medieval and Renaissance periods in an effort to clarify what we know about its method of survival.

THE NATURE OF THE LEADING GREEK MANUSCRIPTS

At the conclusion of *Der Text der Aristotelischen Rhetorik*, Kassel presented a schema showing what he considered to be the relationships among the Aristotelian manuscripts of the *Rhetoric*. (see Plate One) As the findings of our research invariably concurred with Kassel's asssumptions and as his research in this matter was more intensive in establishing the relationships among manuscripts than was the research done for this study, we have adopted the sequence and relationship of the manuscripts as proposed by Kassel.

Kassel concluded that there existed a lost archetype

PLATE ONE

an abridgement of Kassel's schema found at the conclusion of *Der Text Der Aristotelischen Rhetorik*

courtesy of Walter de Gruyter & Company

of the *Rhetoric* from which all of the extant Greek and Latin manuscripts have descended. Except for some minor contributions via the *scholia*, two lines of descent from the lost archetype account for all of what we know of the *Rhetoric*. The first direct descendant Kassel termed A, and it is extant in the *Bibliothèque Nationale* as Parisinus MS. Grec 1741 [known hereafter in this chapter as Grec 1741]. The second direct descendant termed by Kassel as β has been lost. Its three most immediate descendants Kassel termed γ, Δ and F. Although γ and Δ must be reconstructed from their descendants, F is Cantabrigiensis Ff.5.8, now extant in the main library at Cambridge University. Manuscripts A and F and all of the other important codexes that Kassel listed in his schema as well as a number of the minor manuscripts, unless otherwise noted, were examined for this study in their home depositories.

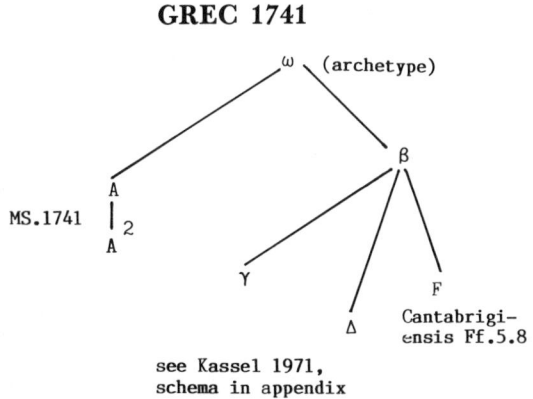

GREC 1741

see Kassel 1971, schema in appendix

The history of the nature of the leading Greek manuscript (see Plate Two) will assist us in understanding not only its own significance but also the role played by the numerous secondary Greek manuscripts. The origin of Grec 1741 and the manner in which it found its way into the national library in Paris are worth exploring.

How the MS. entered France from Italy is not clear. The catalogue of Greek manuscripts in the *Bibliothèque Nationale* lists Grec 1741 as having come from the library of Catherine de Medici (1519-1589). The evidence to support this assertion is provided by four inventories described in the "Mémoire Historique sur la Bibliothèque du Roy," the contents of which will be summarized below.[2]

The first of these inventories, B.N. Parisinus MS. Grec 3074, entitled "Index Librorum Nicolai Cardinalis Rudolphi," is a sixteenth century MS. that entered the library via Colbert's collection. (Omont, 1888, 104) Entries in Greek in the margin of the inventory, presumably added by a librarian at the *Bibliothèque Nationale*, identify two copies of Aristotle's *Rhetoric*: an entry on ff.28r-29v has been identified as Grec 1741 and a second entry on f.27v has been identified as MS.Grec 2038, a secondary manuscript to be discussed later. The descriptions of these entries in MS.Grec 3074 support the librarian's identifications, but there is no indisputable clue linking MSS.Grec 1741 and 2038 with these entries in the inventory of the collection of Nicolas Rudolphi.

The second inventory, B.N.MS. Latin 17917, formerly Fonds Bouhier 21, entitled "Index Librorum Bibliothecae Reginae Matris Catharinae de Medicis Graeco Latino et Italico Idiomate," has annotations on the title page commenting that the inventory came from the library of Nicolas Claude Fébry de Peiresc, a collector who had assembled a sizeable number of manuscripts at his home in Aix-en-Provence,[3] and further states that the inventory was made by one Jean Bouhier.[4] Each entry in this seventeenth century inventory is in Latin, bears a number, and the folios have individual numbers for their recto and verso sides. An inventory shows that the entry under #348 corresponds to Grec 1741 while the entry under #243 corresponds to MS.Grec 2038.

The third inventory, B.N.MS.Latin 14359, ff.462r-480r, was made in 1589 by the French government as an official list of Catherine's possessions. Folio 467v lists two entries that, although the descriptions are limited, appear to correspond to MSS.Grec 2038 and 1741 respectively.

The fourth inventory, B.N.MS.Français 5685, ff.1-57, was made six years later, in 1597, under the direction of François Pithou, to complete the delivery of Catherine's manuscripts to the *Bibliothèque Royale*, a task that Pièrre Pithou had begun in 1594. This MS. bears the title, "Inventaire des livres de la bibliothèque de la feu royne mère." Folio 16r lists two entries for Aristotle's *Rhetoric* that seem to correspond to MSS. Grec 2038 and 1741 respectively.

The consistency of the entries for Aristotle's *Rhetoric* in all four of these inventories only proves, however, that Catherine de Medici's collection did include two versions of the *Rhetoric*. There is still room for some small doubt as to whether these entries were actually entries for the MSS. that are known today as MSS.Grec 1741 and 2038.[5]

If we conclude from the preponderance of the circumstantial evidence that Grec 1741 and its lesser companion, MS. Grec 2038, did enter the *Bibliothèque Nationale* via the library of Catherine de Medici, how did they come to be a part of her estate? The lengthy "Mémoire Historique" cited above examined the several theories that could clarify how such manuscripts might have come into her possession. The investigation came to conclusions that Delisle[6] found sufficiently probative to quote in his *Le Cabinet des*

PLATE TWO

folio 120r of Parisinus Grec 1741

courtesy of the Bibliothèque Nationale, Paris

The Manuscript Period

Manuscrits. (1868, 1, 207-12) The author of the "Mémoire," Jean Boivin, discounted the theories that the manuscripts in Catherine's library resulted from conquest or from a family sharing of the Medici manuscripts. In the first place, Boivin reasoned, the library of the Medici did undergo some change of hands during the political upheavals in Italy. But it was restored to the Medici family. Therefore, these manuscripts must have arrived in France via another route. Boivin noted that the Cardinal Nicolas Rudolphi of Florence, nephew of Pope Leo X, amassed more than 800 Greek manuscripts.[7] In 1550 Pierre Strozzi, Maréchal of France, bought the collection, brought it to France, and looked after it carefully. Upon his death, Catherine, as one of his near relatives, decided that she wanted the collection, and, said Boivin, in order to make it look as if it rightfully belonged to her, she had the story spread that the collection was part of the once dissipated Medici library. In order to flatter the queen, it was also said that Catherine continued to add to the collection. But Boivin could find little evidence of anything that did not come from Strozzi. When Catherine died, her manuscripts came into the safekeeping of her confessor and librarian. There then developed efforts by the *Bibliothèque Royale* to acquire the holdings. Catherine had left so many debts that her creditors tried to stall the move to transfer any of her assets to the state. Finally, in 1594, a royal order was issued to incorporate the manuscripts into the royal library, but it took five more years before the creditors could be circumvented and the entry finally made.

If we assume that Grec 1741 came from the Strozzi collection as appropriated by Catherine de Medici, let us examine the appearance of the MS. itself and see what scholars have had to work with in establishing their collated Greek editions. During my early studies of Aristotle, my professors assumed that all of us students knew just what the Greek and Latin manuscripts looked like. But we did not. And we were often curious about their topography, more than what photographs could tell. Therefore this chapter includes, for those who do not already know, descriptions of what the manuscripts look like in their present depositories. Hopefully these descriptions will assist the readers in recapturing some of the excitement experienced by this researcher while he waited as one after the other of the frequently dusty manuscripts were carried in by guardians and even flopped onto the desks of foreign libraries, allowing the dust to fly up through the dim light to the high vaulted ceilings.

Grec 1741 is of parchment, approximately 17 centimeters by 22 centimeters, penned in varying shades of what is now brownish ink,[8] with emendations in at least two and possibly three hands. In the process of his monotonous work, the scribe made important, if not frequent errors, some of which he either took the pains to go back and correct or he was instructed to correct. But he tired of this labor or was diverted to other duties, for we agree with Ross[9] that, after f.131v in Book One, there are few if any corrections in the original hand.

The second set of corrections was done in a much more casual hand, almost a scrawl, with a wider quill, and appears to have been done impatiently and with vigor, as if the corrector was either exasperated with the work that had not been done properly by the original scribe or as if he were not dependent for his comprehension of the text on just this MS. so that he could afford to be even illegible in his corrections.

The third set of notes in Grec 1741 is, in our opinion, in the hand of Peter Victorius. We know that Victorius had access to MS.1741. We know that he was in the habit of making marginal comments. There was no such high value placed upon 1741 in Victorius' time that would have prevented him from writing his reactions on the MS. Not only are the handwritings identifiable, but the diagrams of Victorius edition of 1548 can, with some changes that he appears to have made before he published, be identified on ff.123r and 123v.[10] Although we have not found other researchers identifying the third hand as that of Victorius, this may well be due to the fact that they had not examined the materials in Munich as closely as we did. If the third set of notes is by someone other than Victorius, it had to be a person well acquainted with Victorius' work.

Since the leather-bound folio that contains Greek 1741 also includes other manuscripts, the text of the *Rhetoric* does not begin until f.120r. Book One includes ff.120r-143r; Book Two, ff.143r-167v; and Book Three, ff.167v-184r. The manuscript bears the title ἀριστοτέλους Τέχνης ῥητορικῆς[11] in the original hand. It is possible to distinguish without too much difficulty the divisions between the three books, which is not always the case with manuscripts of the *Rhetoric*. As is characteristic of all manuscripts examined, if there are what might be interpreted as paragraphs, they are few. No chapter divisions and no indications of line numbers appear. The folios consist of one solid page of Greek penned in a small but legible hand, with an equal number of lines on each folio which, for this MS., is generally forty-four lines to the folio.[12]

Now that we have a general idea of the topography of Grec 1741, let us examine a limited number of faults in the MS. so that the comments in the prefaces to the critical editions and in the extended notes that often accompany these editions can be more meaningfully understood. The discussion will be divided into three parts: (a) corrections that have been attributed to the original hand; (b) corrections that have been attributed to a second hand; and (c) the major lacuna in Book III.

Corrections to Grec 1741 in the first hand

The most important correction in the first hand occurs at f.123r, beginning with l.22 (1357a17)[13] where the scribe scratched off διο και with a sharp edge so that he could at least begin a lengthy omission lineally. The scribe then continued what he had omitted in the right-hand margin, continuing to write in the margin to the bottom of the folio. The lengthy insertion begins at 1357a17 with ἐὰν γὰρ ἦ τι τούτων γνώριμον and continues through γίνεται συλλογισμός (1357b6). It was an easy error for the scribe to make because he was deceived by the double appearance of συλλογισμός so that he omitted everything between the two appearances of the word, amounting to lines 1357a17 to 1357b6.[14] Either the scribe, in glancing up and down at his archetype, lost his place, or he was interrupted in his work at this point, and, upon returning, picked up his transcribing at the second appearance of συλλογισμός rather than at its first appearance. Or, if Grec 1741 was the product of the combined efforts of a dictator and a copyist, the dictator skipped the omitted passage so naturally the scribe omitted it as well. Following the Rhys Roberts translation, this omission begins on folio twenty-eight with the words: "For if any of these propositions is a familiar fact, there is no need even to mention it; the hearer adds it himself...." and concludes on folio twenty-nine, with the words; "By infallible signs I mean those of which syllogisms proper may be based..." This mistake was therefore an important omission, and its correction in the margin was a material addition.

Four other errors of omission attributable to the first hand will be sufficient to illustrate the sort of correction that the editors had to cope with. On f.128r32 (1362a37), the scribe had omitted the word ἅμα between the words κακόν and τῷ. The omission eliminated the word "simultaneously" from the following translation by Roberts (1954, 43): "...the latter entails freedom from the evil things simultaneously, while the former entails possession of the good things subsequently." Ross attributed this correction to the first hand, but it is doubtful, for the ink is darker and appears to fit another hand, more likely that of Victorius. The ἅμα that appears above the line resembles little the ἅμα appearing on f.128r26 (1362a31) which is certainly in the first hand.

As is often the case, once the scribe had made one mistake, he made others. On f.130r12 (1364a 11-13) two mistakes occurred, followed by a third three lines down. First the scribe omitted ἀρχῆς on 1364a 12 and had to write it above the line. The omission eliminated from the following translation by Buckley [1910 (1833), 47) the second appearance of the word "principle:" "And of good both proceeding from principles, that is the greater good which arises from the higher principle..." Thus the repetition of ἀρχή assisted in establishing the parallel structure of the sentence.[15]

Second the scribe was again fooled by two phrases beginning with the same words, this time καὶ δυοῖν so that he had to insert a notation on the line corresponding to the same mark in the margin and to add, in the right hand margin on f.130r12, καὶ δυοῖν αἰτίοιν τὸ ἀπὸ τοῦ μείζονος αἰτίου μεῖζον. Translating the insertion in a manner parallel to the literal Buckley translation in the error above, the correction supplied the following sentence: "And of good preceding from causes, that is the greater good that arises from the higher cause."

Third, the scribe omitted φαίνεσθαι on f.130r15 (1364a 16) and had to insert it in the left hand margin.[16] Without this insertion, the passage could be translated: "Therefore it is clear from what has been said that something may be greater in two ways..." [emphasis added]. With this insertion, the passage could be translated: "Therefore it is clear from what has been said that something may *appear* to be greater in two ways...." [emphasis added] The difference is a subtle one, but meaningful to the lawyer-rhetorician. When discussing the significance of the contribution of the Latin translations, such distinctions relate to the degree of proof that must be established. The difference in the revised translation does not really have to be greater; it only has to "appear" to be greater to one or more of the participants involved. In pleading self-defense, therefore, the lawyer would not have to show that the strength of the deceased was actually greater than that of the defendant, but only that it "appeared" to be greater to the defendant, causing the defendant to act in self-defense. It is often on such shades of meaning that trials turn.

Corrrections to MS. Grec in the second hand

We will now cite seven examples of corrections that can be attributed to the second hand. Folio 131v caused the first scribe considerable trouble for he had to scratch out several places with his sharp edge. One problem occured on f.131v13 (1365b15) in which the first scribe scratched out something and then erred by putting in τινι that had to be corrected by the second hand to read τείνει.[17] Since both words are pro-

The Manuscript Period

nounced the same, the scribe may have been saying the Greek to himself as he copied, and then falsely wrote τινι instead of τείνει, depending upon the guidance of his ear rather than watching the original from which he was copying. The sentence πρὸς ἀλήθειαν γὰρ τείνει ταῦτα needs a verb. An indefinite pronoun like τινι would not allow the passage to make sense. Once the τείνει was supplied by the second hand, the passage could be easily read as "for they are concerned with reality."

On f.135v20 (1369b21), the first scribe had swapped a kappa and a chi, producing οὐκ ἔχοντες which the second hand changed to read οὐχ ἑκόντες simply by scribbling a chi over the kappa and a kappa over the chi. Again the pronunciation of these two phrases is similar. Both are meaningful phrases in Greek. So the first scribe, in reading the phrase from the original copy, internalizing it, and then writing it in the new manuscript, made a very natural copying error and one which he would have been unlikely to have noticed in checking over his own work. The second hand apparently noted the error by observing the appearance of ἑκόντες [voluntarily] in the initial part of the sentence and by inferring that οὐχ ἑκόντες [involuntarily] would complete Aristotle's thought much more logically than οὐκ ἔχοντες [literally "not having"]. Note the revised Greek version below, followed by the Freese translation:

ἐπεὶ δ' ὅσα δι' αὑτούς, ἑκόντες
πράττουσιν, οὐχ ἑκόντες δὲ
ὅσα μὴ δι' αὑτούς...

...since men do voluntarily what they do of themselves, and involuntarily what they do not...

On f.158r14 (1393a4), the second hand falsely added an extra lambda to the word μελήσε [sic] and corrected the ending by adding an iota at the conclusion, making the text look something like this:

μελλήσει.[18]

Such an emendation by the second scribe was noted here because it shows how hastily the second hand made some of his changes. If the second hand had wished to change μελλήσει to μελήσει, and thus insert the future tense of μέλειν for the future tense of μέλλειν, he was in error because μέλω meaning "to care for" does not fit into the sentence. Furthermore, the sentence required a noun and not a verb at the point of the error. Therefore, although the second hand correctly amended the ending of the word, he modified falsely its internal structure. The restored passage should read as follows:

...[διὰ] ταῦτα καὶ [εἰ] ἐν ὁρμῇ τοῦ
ποιεῖν ἢ μελλήσει, ἔσται.

On this account, too, if persons be on the onset of doing something, it will likely be done.

On f.158r15 (1393a5), the first scribe had again allowed himself to be confused by the same word occurring close together and had omitted the word μέλλοντα. Roemer and Ross both proposed that the second hand added τὰ μέλλοντα but this is not exactly the case. What the second hand actually did was to take the word μᾶλλοντα, written by the first scribe, appropriate the first part of it for the word μᾶλλον, assign the τὰ at the end of the word to begin the phrase τὰ μέλλοντα, and then write μέλλοντα above the line. Thus the passage as written by the first scribe read:

ὡς γὰρ ἐπὶ τὸ πολὺ γίγνεται μᾶλλοντα ἢ τὰ μὴ μέλλοντα

whereas the second hand amended the passage to read:

ὡς γὰρ ἐπι τὸ πολὺ γίγνεται μᾶλλον τὰ μέλλοντα ἢ τὰ μὴ μέλλοντα

Without the correction, the passage would have been translated something like this: "For, as a rule, what is intended happens [more] than what is not [intended]." Two clues were available to the second hand to insert his correction: first, the appearance of "than" implied a comparison, and therefore the need for the word "more" was apparent: second, the appearance of "what is not intended to happen" in the second part of the passage needed a parallel phrase preceding it. Of course, the second hand could have had another copy of the *Rhetoric* available at the time he made the corrections, and so did not have to involve himself in reconstruction via logical inference. The phrase, properly restored, can best be translated as: "since generally speaking, if things that have happened naturally give rise to certain consequents, [those consequents are likely to have occurred.]"

On f.160r31 (1395b7), the first scribe had written τι whereas the second hand added lightly a sigma to make the Greek read τις. The corrected passage reads as follows:

οἷον εἴ τις γείτοσι τύχοι κεχρημένος ἢ
τέκνοις φαύλοις...

The error was easily observed, since it is more likely that Aristotle would have written "anyone who happens to have bad neighbors" rather than "anything who happens to have bad neighbors."

On f.160v31-32 (1396a12), the first scribe had written ἢ μὴ ἔχοιμεν that was corrected by the second scribe to read εἰ μὴ ἔχοιμεν. Here again the scribe was probably confused by the similarity in pronunciations, since ἤ and εἰ came to be pronounced the same. The reading with ἢ μὴ ἔχοιμεν [How could we praise them *or* we did not know of the naval engagement at Salamis....] reads more awkwardly than the reading with εἰ μή [How could we praise them, *if* we did not know of the naval engagement at Salamis....] [Underlining added]

The last example of a correction in the second hand involves f.160v33 (1396a14) in which the first scribe had mistakenly written λεχθέντα while the second hand corrected the text to read πραχθέντα by scribbling a pi, a rho, and possibly an alpha over the lamda and eta.[19] Spengel, Roemer, Kassel and Ross all honor this correction. The passage as originally written could be translated as "or what they said in behalf of the descendants of Hercules" whereas the revised version could be translated as "or what they did for the descendants of Hercules." Note the amended version below:

ἢ τὰ ὑπὲρ τῶν Ἡρακλει[ω]δῶν πραχθέντα.

The major lacuna

The third and last type of fault in Grec 1741 involves the major lacuna. On f.180v11 (1416b29), the archetype from which the copyist was transcribing apparently had had a lacuna repaired by the insertion of Aristotle's previous discusssion of "praise" from Book One (1367b26-1368a10). Therefore, Grec 1741 continues normally through the words οὐ γὰρ πολλοὶ ἴσασιν. Then the text begins ἔστιν δ' ἔπαινος λόγος ἐμφανίζων μέγεθος ἀρετῆς and continues through ὅταν τὸ μὲν κωλῦον τὸ δὲ μὴ κωλῦον μετατεθῇ. On f.180v28 (1416b30), MS. Grec 1741 picks up its new material with the words νῦν δὲ γελοίως....As a result, a fault in the text in Book Three has been patched up by reverting to Book One and substituting an earlier discussion for the missing section. [1367b26-1368a10]

This clumsy repetition had been honored in the printed editions until it was rejected by Victorius in 1548, and it has been rejected by scholars since. The lacuna is important because its consistent appearance in the Greek and Latin manuscripts[20] is a major indication that all versions go back to one archetype for which there may have been several copies. There is no clue as to why the manuscripts should be consistently faulty at this point. Speculation as to why the break occurs can range anywhere from carelessness on the part of the copyist to the existence of an archetype defective because of damage, loss, or illegibility. It could even be attributed to a misinterpretation of a note by Aristotle in his original manuscript which was meaningful to the philosopher himself but was distorted by later scribes. Or, if all of the surviving manuscripts are the descendents of one session in which one person dictated from the master manuscript while a series of copists each made a copy and that dictator erred in his reciting of Book Three, all of the surviving manuscripts would have the same error. The full implications of this lacuna will be discussed after the remaining leading Greek and Latin manuscripts have been surveyed.

The information lost by the appearance of this lacuna is impossible to reconstruct. The MS. breaks off with this comment: "But if you wish to praise Critias, narrative is necessary, for not many people know what he did...." (Freese, 445) The MS. picks up again with "but at the present day it is absurdly laid down that the narrative should be rapid...." (Freese, 445) The insertion from Book One is not altogether inappropriate at this point in Book Three, but its repetition serves no particular purpose.

The corrections to Grec 1741 are sufficiently similar to the corrections found in other Aristotelian Greek manuscripts of the *Rhetoric* to make unnecessary further examples of how other manuscripts were modified. Those who wish to become more acquainted with the variations of a particular manuscript can consult the work of Kassel. (1971) Later, in conjunction with a discussion of the contribution of Latin manuscripts, we will again pause to show the nature of other additions. But, the purpose of this discussion is not to detail each variation because that has been done by Kassel and Schneider, but to give sufficient information about the leading manuscripts and the nature of the corrections and lacunae so that we can grasp the degree to which the manuscripts have enabled us to approximate what Aristotle said in his lectures. Therefore, after surveying the manuscripts of the *Rhetoric*, we will discuss the problems that the editors of the *Rhetoric* faced in producing their definitive editions. For the present, we will continue our descriptions of the manuscripts, presenting them in a sequence appropriate to Kassel's schema.

Cantabrigiensis Ff.5.8

The second oldest of all the Greek manuscripts of

The Manuscript Period

Aristotle's *Rhetoric* is Cantabrigiensis Ff.5.8 [formerly Cantabrigiensis 1298] (see Plates Three A & B), consisting of 108 folios on vellum. As with Grec 1741, the specific date of the MS. is impossible to determine. The records in the University Library at Cambridge where the codex is housed suggest the thirteenth century. Kassel stated that the MS. dates from the twelfth to the thirteenth centuries. (Kassel, xviii) In his schema, Kassel assigned it chronologically near 1200, (Kassel, schema) and therefore more than two hundred years later than Grec 1741. The *Rhetoric* comprises ff. 3r-108v, and bears marginal comments by Demetrius Chalk(c)ondyles who, as Harlfinger pointed out, also made marginal notations in Laurentianus Conv. Soppr. 47. (Harlfinger, 229, n. 2 and 410) The *Rhetoric* comprises folios 1r-85v and the notations by Demetrius are infrequent). The chief corrections to Cantabrigiensis Ff.5.8 were made by a later hand, the author of which is unknown. Kassel detailed certain of these emendations. (Kassel, 1971, 25ff.) Although the significance of the errors and the manner in which they were corrected does not add significantly to our knowledge of the text, it is important to note that, regrettably, both Grec 1741 and Cantabrigiensis 1298 come from that same common archetype and therefore the differences between them are helpful only in making minor adjustments. Although Grec 1741 is a direct descendant from the archetype, whereas Cantabrigiensis Ff.5.8. is once removed from the archetype, what the two oldest of the manuscripts have in common is so much greater than the areas in which they differ that they fail to offer the contrasting texts that would have appeared had they come from two different archetypes.

THE DIRECT DESCENDANTS OF MS. GREC 1741

It was not until almost four hundred and fifty years after A was written that copies attributable exclusively to it are extant. Following the corrections in the first hand that were made relatively soon after the MS. was executed, the second set of corrections dates to the late fourteenth century. Furthermore, it was not until the middle of the fifteenth century that the MS. we now know as Dresdensis Da 4 was executed, copied from a model of Grec 1741 that has now been lost. This paper codex has the *Rhetoric* on ff.1-80, and was copied by Theodoros Gazes.[22] From the Dresden MS. there developed before the end of the fifteenth century Vaticanus Urbanus 47 and the Milan MS. Ambrosianus L 76 sup.21. Although our visas to East Germany

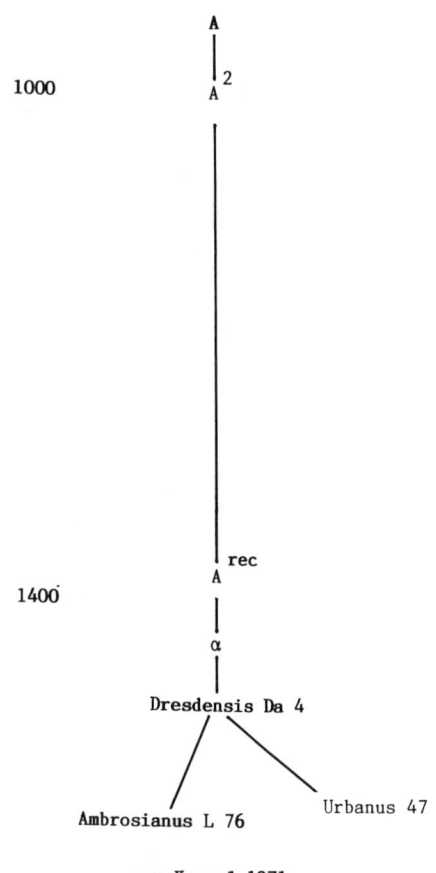

see Kassel 1971, schema in appendix

have not yet permitted us to examine personally Dresdensis Da 4, we have seen both of its descendants. Urbanus 47 is a neatly executed MS. of 120 ff, with red capital letters for the general title and for the first letter of each book. Book One consists of folios 1r-34v; Book Two of 37r-104v; Book Three of 105r-120r. Ambrosianus L 76 is an unexciting-looking parchment containing the *Rhetoric* and a fragment. The text begins on folio 1r and concludes on folio 67r, with the division between Books Two and Three not clearly marked.

It seems natural to ask why we have discovered so few direct descendants of Grec 1741 in comparison to what will be noted later as multiple descendants of the Cambridge manuscript, and why those descendants we do have were of such late execution. An obvious answer would be that the Cambridge MS. and its descendants were more easily available to copyists than was the Paris version. The history of Grec 1741 presented earlier established that it had remained for some time in private libraries and that it did not enter the royal library until 1594. Seemingly Grec 1741 was inaccessible. It was therefore not until the sixteenth century that scholars such as Victorius were able to

PLATE THREE A

folio 3r of Cambrigiensis Ff.5.8

courtesy of the Cambridge University Library

The Manuscript Period 19

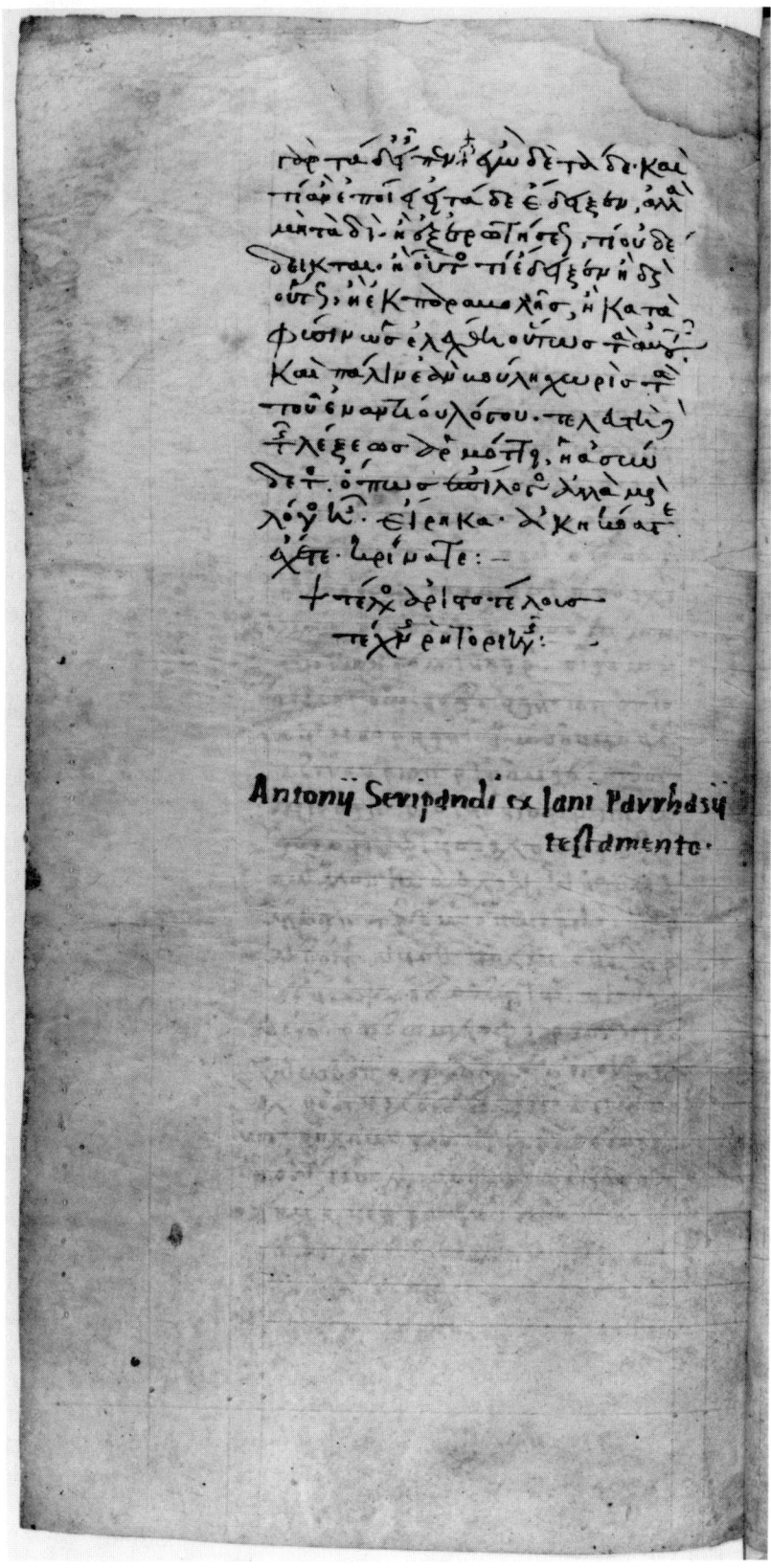

PLATE THREE B

folio 108v of Cambrigiensis Ff.5.8

courtesy of the Cambridge University Library

consult Grec 1741. Obviously Rudolphi had given Victorius access to Grec 1741 before it was bought by Strozzi and transported to France.

DESCENDANTS OF MS. GREC 1741 AND THE LOST β MANUSCRIPT[23]

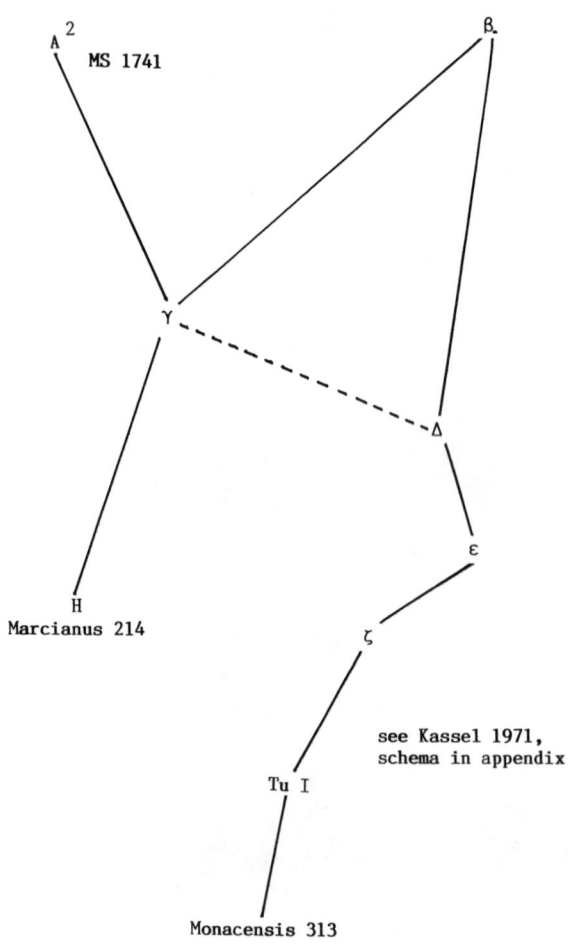

As will be pointed out later in this chapter, the Latin translations of the thirteenth century are important in establishing links between Grec 1741 or A and its lost contemporary, called by Kassel, β. Assuming that such links exist, let us look briefly at two Greek manuscripts that show indications of indebtedness to both A, which does exist, and β which is lost. Marcianus MS. Grec 214 and Monacensis Grec 313 are fragments that show indebtedness to A and its contemporary lost counterpart, beta.

The older of the two, Marcianus MS. Grec 214, ff.149v-150v (now renumbered 479, see Plate Four),[23] designated by Kassel as H, is a two-column codex dating from the earlier part of the fourteenth century. The three folios, bound with a number of other complete works of Aristotle, start at the beginning of the *Rhetoric* (1354a1) but break off abruptly just after Chapter 2 of Book One begins. (1356a2-3). It seems most likely that the entire work was copied from a connecting link between A and β, a link that Kassel termed γ, but that, for some reason, only three folios of the *Rhetoric* were bound with the other works of Aristotle included in H or Marcianus MS. Grec 214. There is the possibility that the scribe was instructed not to copy the *Rhetoric* but began on it by mistake and so broke off abruptly.

As the excerpt from Kassel's schemata indicates, there were a number of descendants from the lost manuscript, Δ, which has as its antecedents both A and β. Of these descendants, we will describe only one, dating from around the beginning of the sixteenth century. The incomplete Munich MS. 313 (see Plate Five), four-times removed from Δ, is composed of 105 folios, of which only five are devoted to the *Rhetoric*. Kassel identified the copyist as Adolf Okko. (Kassel, 9) Folio 32v, ll.1-11, begins the text of the *Rhetoric* (1354a1), but the MS. breaks off abruptly on f.32v11 with the word θεωρεῖν (1354a10). Someone, seemingly a second hand, added ἐνδέχεται to complete the thought. The scribe could have omitted the word ἐνδέχεται as not being absolutely essential to convey Aristotle's meaning. However, keeping in mind that the bracketed portion of the passage below could not be supplied if ἐνδέχεται had been omitted, it is evident that some liberal interpretation of the Greek would be necessary were ἐνδέχεται absent:

> ...for [it is possible] to examine the reason why some speakers succeed through extempore speaking and others through impromptu speaking...

The second fragment of Monacensis 313, which follows immediately after the first, picks up on f.32v12 (1359b17)[24] and continues through f.36v36 (1363b4), thus including most of what is now known as Book One, Chapter 4, and all of Book One, Chapters 5 and 6. It is difficult to say why these excerpts concerning the definition of rhetoric, the subjects on which people deliberate, and the amplification of happiness were of particular interest either to the person who commanded the manuscript, or to the scribe who transcribed them. The archetype from which these excerpts were taken was possibly fragmentary, or the scribe who executed the copy could not read Greek. Otherwise the first fragment might have been completed, and the second fragment would not have begun in the middle of a thought.

Monacensis 313 is quite small, written in an easily legible hand with some interlineal corrections by the

The Manuscript Period

PLATE FOUR

the beginning of the fragment, Marcianus Grec 214

courtesy of the Biblioteca Nazionale Marciana, Venice

22   A History of Aristotle's Rhetoric

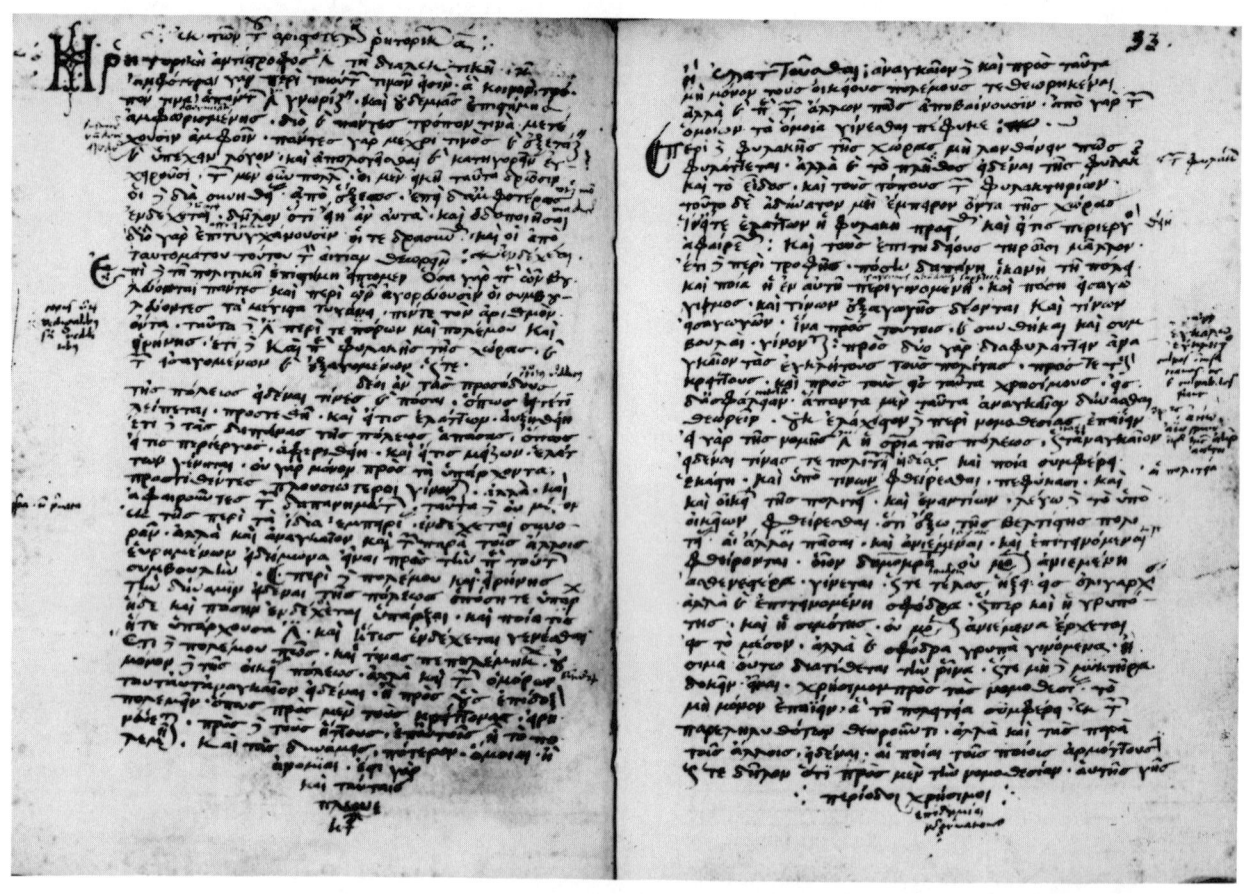

PLATE FIVE

the first excerpt from the *Rhetoric* (folio 32v,11.1-11) (1354a1-1354a10) and the beginning of the second excerpt from the *Rhetoric* (folio 32v,11.12-41) and continuing on folio 33r,11.1-17 (1359b17-1360a34) of Monacensis Graci 313

courtesy of the Bayerische Staatsbibliothek, Munich

The Manuscript Period

first hand. Roemer noted that the fragmentary manuscript was discovered by Wilhelm Meyer. Unfortunately Meyer's discovery did not add materially to our knowledge of the *Rhetoric,* but merely reinforced what had already been indicated by prior manuscripts. For example, Roemer does not footnote any variations from the first and shorter of the two fragments, and, although he does note variant readings from the second fragment as many as thirty-two times, the variations concern mainly the omission of an unimportant word in the fragment,[25] the addition of an unimportant word in the fragment,[26] the occasional joining of two words in the fragment,[27] or some similar minor deviation.[28]

The H manuscript (Marcianus 214) and Monacensis 313[29] are important to this discussion because they demonstrate that the editors of the critical editions did have available manuscripts that drew from both the extant A and the missing β. The fact that the editors had access to readings that reflected both of the direct descendants of the lost archetype tells us that the critics have been able to approximate sufficiently the text of the lost archetype to make us relatively confident of what must have been its contents.

DESCENDANTS OF THE UNREVISED VERSION OF THE CAMBRIDGE MS.

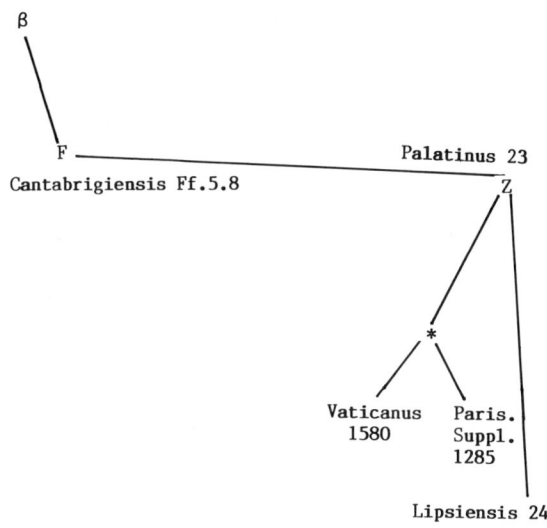

see Kassel 1971,
schema in appendix

A direct descendant of the Cambridge MS. is Palatinus MS. Grec 23, called by Kassel Z. Z and the other Greek manuscripts of the *Rhetoric* housed in the *Bibliotheca Apostolica Vaticana* are catalogued under three different codices because they entered the library from three different sources. Urbanus 47 is a direct descendant from A, and it will be important later when we discuss the descendants of the revised version of the Cambridge MS. Here, in connection with the descendants of the unrevised version, we are concerned with the Palatinus MSS. that were looted from the Palatinate when Tilly conquered Heidelberg during the Thirty Years War in 1622. Palatinus MS. Grec 23[30] was one of the some 3,500 manuscripts that formed a part of the library at Heidelberg.[31] A portion of those manuscripts that made a trek around Germany before they were presented to the Vatican in 1623 by Emperor Maxillian has been restored to Heidelberg.[32] The remaining Palatine MSS., including #23, have remained in the Vatican. The third codexes are labled simply Vaticanus.

Palatinus Grec 23 is a thirteenth century MS.,[33] written on paper in a black ink that changes to a brownish hue from time to time. As is true of several of the manuscripts examined for this study, the paper originally had a very thin gilded edge that is now indistinct. The handwriting is neat and precise. The MS. bears a simple heading and the advent of Book Two is clearly marked in red. However, the artist who was supposed to add a capital letter for the beginning of Book Three did not get around to the task, for there is a blank space in the middle of the line at f.11v11 where the capital letter ought to have been.

Probably because of the turmoils of the Thirty Years War, Palatinus MS. Grec 23 is in the worst condition of all of the Aristotelian manuscripts examined for this study. Some of the frequently appearing wormholes have been repaired but others have not. Folio 11 is severely torn. Some pages have been painstakingly remounted, while others have only been mended. It may be that the original title page was removed when the MS. was catalogued in the Vatican, perhaps because of the poor condition of the initial folio. However, the original index has been kept, but it has been so mounted on f.1v that it is impossible, without special detecting equipment, to see what may have been on the original f.1r. Some configurations appears to be at the bottom of f.1r, perhaps a large ink blot or an extended "doodle," for doodles appear in the margins of certain of the manuscripts. But the nature of these marks on f.1r is not clear. Book One of Palatinus MS. Grec 23 consists of ff.2r-11v; Book Two, of ff.11v-21v; Book Three of ff.21v-29r.

This Z manuscript had two lines of descent. The first, Lipsiensis 24, housed at the University of Leipsig, is penned in black ink on white paper. It was written at the turn of the 15th and 16th centuries (the paper watermark has been dated at 1490), with *marginalia* by Aristoboulus Apostolides and Manuel Gregoropoulos. Book One consists of folios 181r-193r; Book Two of 193v-201r; Book Three of 201r-235v. As it has no further descendants, it needs no further discussion here.

The second line of descent is represented by two manuscripts whose texts are sufficiently similar that they indicate a common source. Vaticanus 1580 is important because it served as one of the sources of the first printed edition of the *Rhetoric* by Aldus Manutius in 1508.

The second once-removed descendant of Z is Parisinus Supplementary Grec 1285, written on Italian paper made between the end of the fourteenth and the end of the fifteenth century. This fact, plus the knowledge that its first owner, Francesco Filelfo, died in 1481, not only dates the MS. in the fifteenth century but establishes that it was transcribed in Italy. The copyist is unknown. After passing through various private hands in Italy, the MS. was acquired in the eighteenth century by a convent in Venice. Following assignments to Rome in 1810 and to Florence in 1875, it was dispatched to Paris in 1898, presumably to be sold, for, in 1900, the *Bibliothèque Nationale* purchased it from a bookseller. The poorly written MS. is penned in brown ink on moderately sized paper 13 centimeters by 21 centimeters with the usual wide margins, the evenness of which was preserved in part by placing above the line the concluding letters or words that fell at the end of the line. The divisions into books are plainly marked by red headings. Some of the wormholes through the cover extend to the MS. itself, but the damage to readability is minimal. Book One consists of ff.1r-27r; Book Two of ff.27r-42r; Book Three of ff.42v-112v. Like the Leipsig MS, Parisinus 1285 had no further descendants. It is important to us because it illustrates the manner in which Vaticanus 1580, which was not examined for this study, is related to the Palatinus MS. Z.

DESCENDANTS OF THE REVISED VERSION OF THE CAMBRIDGE MS.

The descendants of the revised version of F follow a complex line of indebtedness. Perhaps the easiest way to clarify the complexity is by dividing the heirs into five parts.

The first group began with Vaticanus MS. Grec 1340.[34] This line is particularly important because, according to Kassel, Vaticanus MS. Grec 1340 was

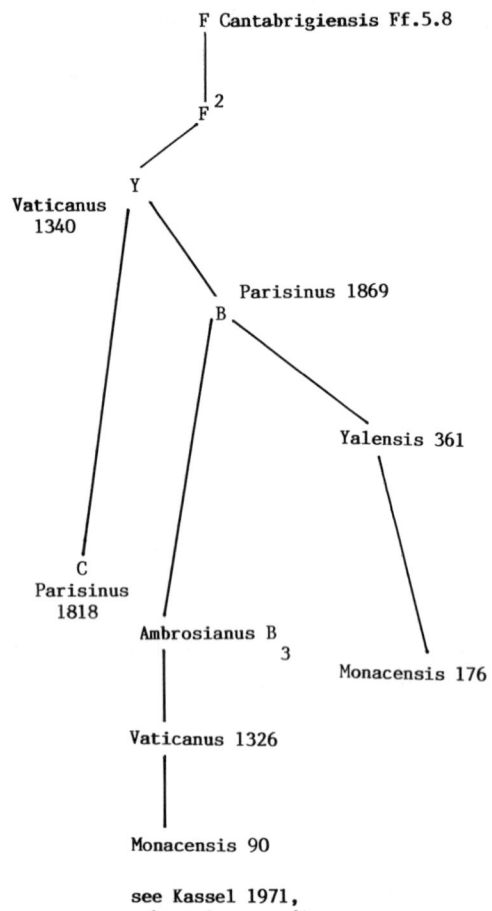

see Kassel 1971, schema in appendix

corrected by persons who were not only acquainted with A but β as well in addition to some of the *scholia* on the *Rhetoric*. It is important to us, therefore, because, like H, this MS. that Kassel designated as Y, provided the editors of the critical editions with a text of cross-fertilized indebtedness to both of the direct lines from the archetype. As far as its topography is concerned, Y, housed in the *Biblioteca Apostolica Vaticana*, is written on moderately thin paper of a size slightly smaller than Palatinus MS. Grec 23. The penmanship in brown ink begins in a legible manner, but a deterioration developed on f.22v where a change of scribes may have occurred. The second hand is more ornate, e.g., the betas and kappas are considerably more configured, but the total effect obscures legibility. There are further variations in handwriting that appear to represent changes in scribes, e.g., f.31r and, for a short period on f.41r. As with Palatinus MS. Grec 23, the divisions between Book One and Book Two are plainly marked, but there is only an incomplete line on f.33r14 to indicate a division between Books Two and Three. The MS. has many marginal annotations in another hand (or hands). Book One consists of ff.7r-19v; Book Two of ff.20r-33r; Book Three of ff.33r-42r.

Of some importance to the editors of the critical editions were two direct descendants of γ, Parisinus MS. Grec 1818 and Parisinus MS. Grec 1869. They demonstrate that a MS. such as Parisinus 1818 could reflect the *scholia*, whereas Parisinus 1869 or β simply produced a series of copies that, for the most part, were highly faithful to the prototype. We will therefore discuss briefly the nature of both of the Paris MSS. and two of the faithful descendants of β.

The more contemporary descendant of γ [Vaticanus 1340] is Parisinus 1869 dating from the fourteenth century. There appears to be no explanation as to how the MS. entered the *Bibliothèque Nationale*. This unimpressive MS. is written in black ink with red headings and occasional red capital letters on paper of a size somewhat larger than A. Despite the mediocre quality of the paper and some wormholes and torn places on ff.1 and 2, the MS. is in legible condition. It is bound in embossed leather over wood and formerly had metal clasps to insure closure. The embossing does not appear to indicate ownership. Book One of the *Rhetoric* consists of ff.1r-21r; Book Two of ff.21r-41r; Book Three of ff.41r-55r.

Of the eight copies of β or Parisinus 1869 that Kassel traced in his study, we will mention only Monacensis Graci Codex 90 (see Plate Six) and Monacensis Graci Codex 176 (see Plate Seven) because they were used by Victorius in the development of his printed edition. Both MSS. date from late in the fifteenth century and therefore were among the last of the manuscript copies made before the onset of the printing press. In order to illustrate more clearly the nature of the material available to Victorius, we will describe both MSS. briefly. Grec 176 is composed of 105 folios written with wide margins on thin paper in a moderately sized, elegant and very legible hand. The first folio has been mended so that the original title of the *Rhetoric*, written as is so often the case in red ink, is very difficult to read. There are the usual corrections in the first hand with a preference for interlineal notation rather than marginal notes. Some of the marginalia are by Victorius and others by Canbini. These notes begin in earnest in Book Two, with more frequent comments by Canbini than by Victorius. The catalogue in Munich dates the MS in the fifteenth century. Angelo Constantino of Hydrus is established as the scribe following an annotation in red given at the conclusion of the MS.[35] Monacensis 176 is another one of those manuscripts that failed to achieve the embellishments intended, for the copyist left room for an ornate "H" to begin Book One, f.1r1, and spaces for ornate "E's" to begin Book Two, f.40v8 and Book Three, f.80r5, but these were never supplied. There were headings for each of the three books supplied in red ink, but the ink has so faded that the most legible is on f.79r for Book III where there can be distinguished faintly the following title:
$\dot{α}ριστοτέλους\ τέχνης\ \dot{ρ}ητορικῆς\ βιβλίον\ τρίτον\ γ$[36]
Book One consists of ff.1r-40v5; Book Two of ff.40v8-79r9; and Book Three of ff.79r10-105v21.

Monacensis 90 is a fifteenth century paper codex composed of 187 folios. It has the typical embellishment across the top of the first folio of the *Rhetoric*. Except that it formed a part of Victorius' library, the MS. has no distinctive characteristics that deserve comment here.

The second of the two direct descendants of γ is Parisinus MS. Grec 1818 dating from the beginning of the sixteenth century. Kassel noted internal evidence showing that the MS. reflects the *scholia*.[37] The *Bibliothèque Nationale* acquired Parisinus 1818 from Mazarin's library and, as he lived from 1602 to 1661, Mazarin could have had Parisinus 1818 copied from Vaticanus 1340 or its equivalent expressly for him. *Bibliothèque Nationale MS. Nouvelle Acquisition Française 5763*, an inventory of Mazarin's library, listed on f.219r an entry #1589 for an Aristotle's *Rhetoric* in Greek that is presumably MS. 1818. The codex is written on paper in black ink of the same shade and color throughout. It has no main headings, but space was left to add ornate headings and capital letters that were never supplied. From the point of view of penmanship, it is the most poorly executed of all of the Aristotelian manuscripts of the *Rhetoric* examined for this study and the most casually assembled. Undoubtedly, by this point, the effect of the printing press had been felt sufficiently to make the work of a scribe less prestigious. The three books of the *Rhetoric*, labeled simply alpha, beta and gamma, are easily distinguishable, but the separation between books, unlike earlier manuscripts, is achieved with an economy of space and paper, as if the copyist were working on a limited budget. Book One consists of ff.83-107r; Book Two of ff.107r-133v; Book Three of ff.133v-152r.

Laurentianus 31.14 at the *Biblioteca Medicea Laurenziana* in Florence and Barocciunus 133 at the Bodleian Library in Oxford form the second and third lines of descent from the revised Cambridge MS. The former appeared toward the latter half of the fifteenth century, while the Oxford MS. dates much earlier, probably at the beginning of the fourteenth century. The Florence MS., a fifteenth century codex, bears the old iron chain by which it was affixed in place. It appears to be divided into four books, but Book One encompasses the first two divisions, ff.21r-40v and

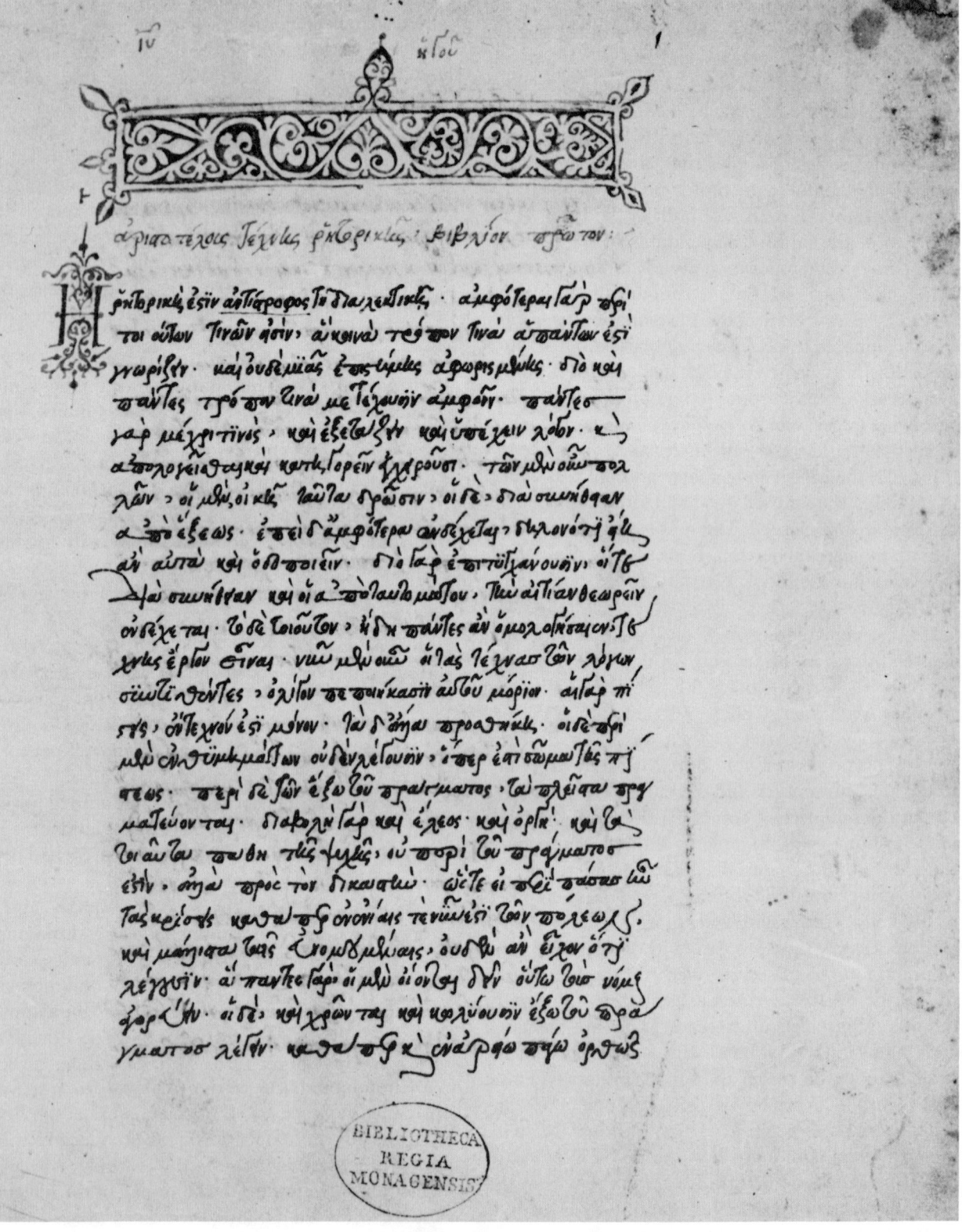

PLATE SIX

folio 1r of Monacensis Graci 90

courtesy of the Bayerische Staatsbibliothek, Munich

Rhetorica

ῥητορική ἐστιν ἀντίστροφος τῇ διαλεκτικῇ· ἀμφότεραι γὰρ περὶ τοιούτων τινῶν εἰσιν ἃ κοινά τρόπον τινα ἁπάντων ἐστὶ γνωρίζειν καὶ οὐδεμιᾶς ἐπιστήμης ἀφωρισμένης· διὸ καὶ πάντες τρόπον τινα μετέχουσιν ἀμφοῖν· πάντες γὰρ μέχρι τινὸς καὶ ἐξετάζειν καὶ ὑπέχειν λόγον καὶ ἀπολογεῖσθαι καὶ κατηγορεῖν ἐγχειροῦσι. τῶν μὲν οὖν πολλῶν οἱ μὲν ταῦτα δι' εἰωθυίας οἱ δὲ διὰ συνηθείας ἀπὸ ἕξεως ποιοῦσιν· ἐπεὶ δ' ἀμφοτέρως ἐνδέχεται, δῆλον ὅτι εἴη ἂν αὐτὰ καὶ ὁδῷ ποιεῖν· διὰ τί γὰρ ἐπιτυγχάνουσιν οἵ τε διὰ συνηθείας καὶ οἱ ἀπὸ τοῦ αὐτομάτου, τὴν αἰτίαν θεωρεῖν ἐνδέχεται· τὸ δὲ τοιοῦτον ἤδη πάντες ἂν ὁμολογήσαιεν τέχνης ἔργον εἶναι. νῦν μὲν οὖν οἱ τὰς τέχνας τῶν λόγων συντιθέντες οὐδὲν ὡς εἰπεῖν πεποιήκασιν αὐτοῦ μόριον· αἱ γὰρ πίστεις ἔντεχνόν ἐστι μόνον, τὰ δ' ἄλλα προσθῆκαι· οἱ δὲ περὶ μὲν ἐνθυμημάτων οὐδὲν λέγουσιν, ὅπερ ἐστὶ σῶμα τῆς πίστεως, περὶ δὲ τῶν ἔξω τοῦ πράγματος τὰ πολλὰ πραγματεύονται· διαβολὴ γὰρ καὶ ἔλεος καὶ ὀργὴ καὶ τὰ τοιαῦτα πάθη τῆς ψυχῆς οὐ περὶ τοῦ πράγματός ἐστιν, ἀλλὰ πρὸς τὸν δικαστὴν· ὥστ' εἰ περὶ πάσας ἦν τὰς κρίσεις καθάπερ ἐν ἐνίαις γε νῦν ἐστι τῶν πόλεων καὶ μάλιστα ταῖς εὐνομουμέναις, οὐδὲν ἂν εἶχον ὅ τι λέγουσιν· ἅπαντες

PLATE SEVEN

folio 1r of Monacensis Graci 176 with the capital letter not supplied

courtesy of the Bayerische Staatsbibliothek, Munich

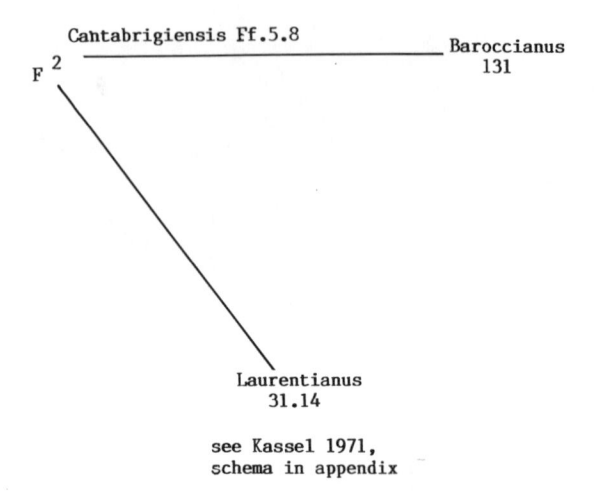

```
        Cantabrigiensis Ff.5.8
  F²  ─────────────────────── Baroccianus
                                  131
                        
                        
                        
                        
                   Laurentianus
                      31.14

         see Kassel 1971,
         schema in appendix
```

ff.40v-52r; Book Two, 52r-83v; and Book Three, 83v-105r. The manuscript even labels folios 83v-105r as Book Delta, but the labels were apparently made by someone unfamiliar with the *Rhetoric*.

The Oxford MS. is a fourteenth century fragment that begins on f.10r at Book Two, Chapter 23 (1398a32) and extends to f.20r in Book Three, Chapter 15 (1416a17). The codex starts off as if the copyist was not aware of what was being copied, and ends just as abruptly. Since, according to Kassel, neither of these MSS. had further descendants, and since neither had influence upon the early printed editions or contributed materially to the definitive Greek editions, we will not deal with them further.

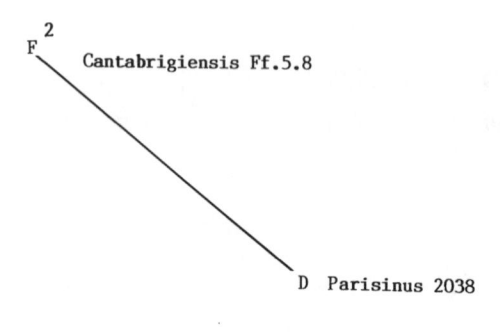

```
        ²
       F   Cantabrigiensis Ff.5.8
                    
                    
                    
                    
                D  Parisinus 2038

         see Kassel 1971,
         schema in appendix
```

The fourth line of descent from the revised Cambridge MS. began with Parisinus MS. Grec 2038, a fifteenth century MS. copied by Andronikos Kallistos. As was pointed out in the discussions of Grec 1741, there are entries in all four of the bibliographies of Catherine de Medici's library that most likely identify this MS. as a part of her collection. The paper is only slightly smaller than the parchment of MS. Grec 1741, and the handwriting in brown ink is small and rather difficult to follow. As is often true of Aristotelian manuscripts, it is not always possible to say whether some emendations were made by the original copyist as he went back over his work or whether they were made by subsequent users. The divisions between books are plainly marked, with the same basket weave or woven rope design in red and yellow as in Marcianus MS. Grec 200. (see the description of Grec 200 below) Book One consists of ff.1r-27v; Book Two of ff.27v-55r; and Book Three of ff.55r-75r.

Parisinus 2038, designated by Kassel as D, is important because it was one of the two MSS. upon which Aldus Manutius relied in 1508 in producing the first printed Greek edition of the *Rhetoric*. According to Kassel, Parisinus MS. Grec 2116 is a copy of the Aldine edition and therefore bears characteristics not only of D but also of Vaticanus 1580 discussed earlier. Although it may be common knowledge to some, it may surprise others that the prestige of a manuscript collection was still such in the sixteenth century, well after the advent of the printing press, that a copyist such as Ange Vergece[38] would reproduce manuscripts from printed books.[39] Not only did printers reproduce manuscripts, but scribes reproduced printed books. (Buhler, 1960, 16) But the diminished status of such a reproduction undoubtedly accounts for the radically different appearance and format of Parisinus 2116 from the other Parisian manuscripts of the *Rhetoric*. It is only 9.5 centimeters by 12.5 centimeters, approximating "book" size. The copyist used black ink on thin paper, with red capital letters. The work was probably done hastily for the hand is difficult to follow. A subsequent owner made frequent underlinings on almost every page with a red-orange pencil. The MS. bears on f.1r the number 6550 from Colbert's library.[40] The catalogue of Colbert's collection, B.N.MS. *Nouvelle Acquisition Latin* 1196, compiled by Colbert's librarian Baluze, includes, for entry number 6550, the three books of the *Rhetoric*. As Colbert lived from 1629 to 1683, the copy may have been made specifically for him. Book One of Parisinus 2116 consists of ff.1r-65r; Book Two of ff.65r-131v; and Book Three of ff.131v-178r.

The fifth branch of descendants from the revised Cambridge MS. stems from Matritensis 4684, a fourteenth century MS. housed in the *Biblioteca Nacional* in Madrid. The copyist, according to Harlfinger (1971, 416) was Georgios Schiolarios. Although the Madrid MS. had numerous descendants, now housed in such widely varying libraries as Alexandria, Florence, Cambridge, and Rome, it played only an indirect role in producing the printed editions of the sixteenth century, and was not of material assistance in developing the definitive Greek editions. Therefore, we will concern ourselves with only one of its descendants, Marcianus MS. Grec 200, because of four outstand-

The Manuscript Period

ing features "of that manuscript's topography."

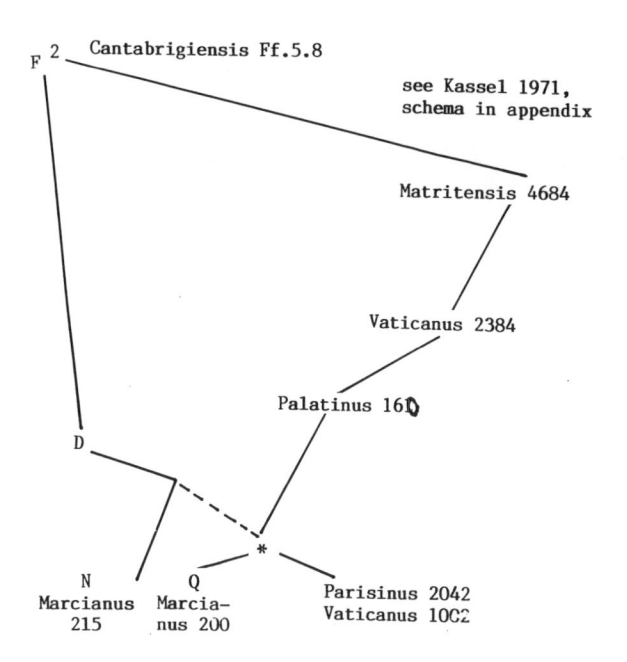

```
F 2   Cantabrigiensis Ff.5.8
                              see Kassel 1971,
                              schema in appendix

                 Matritensis 4684

              Vaticanus 2384

         Palatinus 160
    D
            *
    N     Q
 Marcianus Marcia-  Parisinus 2042
   215    nus 200   Vaticanus 1002
```

Marcianus 200 (see Plates Eight and Nine), a part of the collection in the *Biblioteca Nazionale* on St. Mark's Square in Venice, is a very well preserved parchment of the fifteenth century. It illustrates again that, even after the advent of the printing press, manuscripts produced early enough in the 1400's could receive considerable care in their execution. The printing press, therefore, did not replace the manuscript any faster than the automobile replaced the horse. Established customs give way slowly. Therefore this MS. is as elaborate as many of its predecessors produced before the printing press was ever an established fact.

The entire work, constituting a monumental task of 594 folios, is in the hand of John of Crete.[41] At the conclusion of the MS. on f.594r, the scribe (or possibly a second scribe because the concluding folio is written in very large letters filling a whole page in red and yellow ink) noted that the work was completed on the fifth of July, 1457, for the Cardinal Bessaroni [or Jean Bessarion (1389-1472)], Bishop of Tuscany. With the exception of the parts in red and yellow ink described above, the folios devoted to the *Rhetoric* itself are in black ink in a small, clear and very legible hand. The scribe worked diligently to keep his penmanship neat by scratching out his mistakes with a sharp edge, putting his corrections on the line.[42] But his system of copying was sufficiently perfected to keep these adjustments minimal. The initial folio of this volume of Aristotle's works, folio 4r, features a highly ornate, illuminated design in shades of blue, green and red interlaced with gold.[43] The remaining ornamentation that serves to introduce the several works of Aristotle, and, in the case of the *Rhetoric*, to introduce each of the three books, is not illuminated, but is still impressive. The design that introduces the *Rhetoric* is 1 centimeter by 18 centimeters, extending along the inner margin of the page, consisting of a basket weave or woven-chain embellishment in red and yellow, topped by capital letters about 9 centimeters by 7 centimeters.

The care in the execution of such a manuscript never ceases to be of interest. This particular MS. has four features that distinguish it from the other manuscripts examined. First, its folios are the largest we examined measuring 26.5 centimeters by 42.5 centimeters. Second, it is impressively ornate. Third, there are running heads in red ink at the top of each page which, for the *Rhetoric*, feature ἀριστοτέλους [sic] on the verso headings and περὶ ῥHτορἰKHς [sic] on the recto headings.[44] Fourth, Marcianus 200 is in the best state of preservation of any of the MSS. examined, with a minimal amount of scribbled *marginalia*. But, because of its relatively recent date of execution, it contributed little to assisting scholars in establishing the lines of descent of the manuscripts.[45] Book One consists of ff.543r-553v; Book Two of ff.553v-564v; and Book Three of ff.564v-572r.

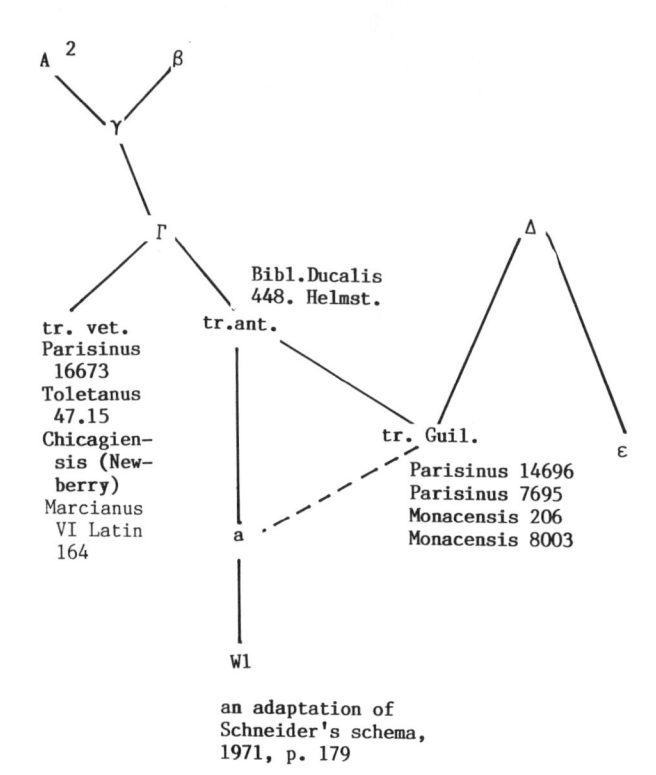

```
     A 2     β
       \   /
        γ
        |
        Γ                        Δ
       / \      Bibl.Ducalis    / \
      /   \    448. Helmst.    /   \
 tr. vet.  tr.ant.            /     \
 Parisinus   |          tr. Guil.    ε
 16673       |          Parisinus 14696
 Toletanus   |          Parisinus 7695
 47.15       |          Monacensis 206
 Chicagien-  |          Monacensis 8003
 sis (New-   |
 berry)      a
 Marcianus   |
 VI Latin    |
 164         |
             W1
```

an adaptation of
Schneider's schema,
1971, p. 179

29

PLATE EIGHT

folio 4r (the beginning of the *Physica*) of Marcianus MS. Grec 200 showing the illuminated decorations that begin the lengthy manuscript

courtesy of the Biblioteca Nazionale Marciana, Venice

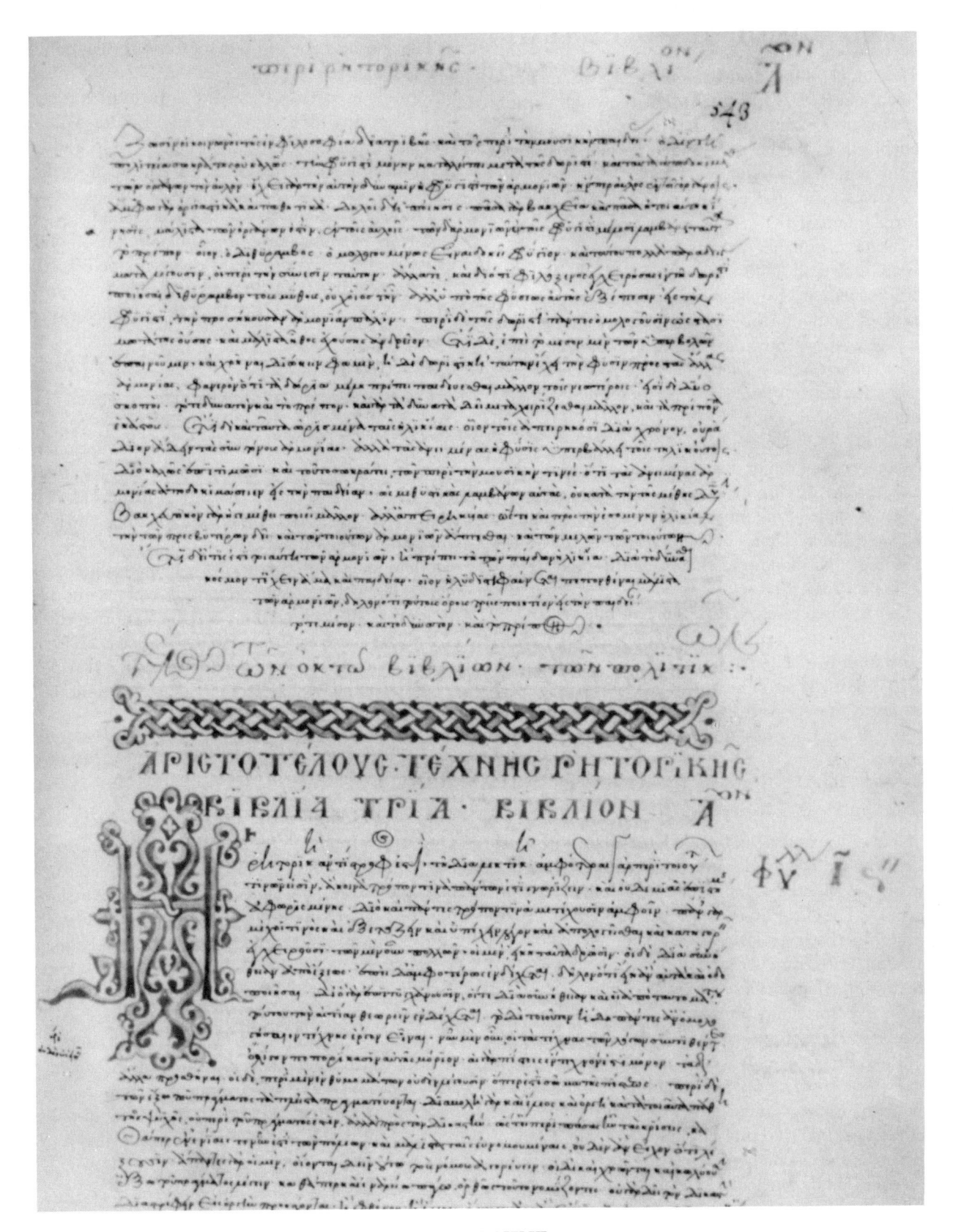

PLATE NINE

folio 154r (the beginning of the *Rhetoric*) of Marcianus Grec 200

courtesy of the Biblioteca Nazionale Marciana, Venice

THE NATURE OF THREE MANUSCRIPT VERSIONS OF THE RHETORIC IN LATIN

For much of this dicussison below, we are indebted to Schneider (1971 and 1978). His thorough work in the area of the Latin MSS. has made an outstanding contribution. We have footnoted specific references in the material below.

As was intimated earlier, not only were various Greek manuscripts helpful in developing a collated Greek text, but the Latin translations executed between 1250 and 1300 were also useful in filling in certain lacunae, in clarifying selected controversial passages, and in confirming opinions about other passages. Apparently, the Latin translators had available to them Greek versions that have now been lost,[46] for the Latin translations are at times more complete and/or at variation with the Greek versions. Although the additions that have been supplied by the Latin versions are not major, the clarifications they provide have been gratifying to scholars in their attempts to interpret some of the more problematic points of the text, and the subtleties of readings they provide are meaningful to the lawyer-rhetorician in interpreting Aristotle's advice to attorneys.

Our research revealed two Latin versions whose text contributed to clarifying the Greek text. A third translation was called to our attention by Schneider. (1970, 165ff.) We will begin by describing several of the Latin manuscripts examined for this study, and then indicate how these Latin translations have been useful.

The William of Moerbeck Latin Translation

George Lacombe (1955, II, 1348) in his *Aristoteles Latinus* acknowledged ninety-eight manuscripts following the Moerbeck translation, and Schneider concurred.[47] The *Bibliothèque Nationale* houses eleven copies of the Moerbeck version, two of which were examined in detail, one dating from the thirteenth century and one from the fourteenth century. Parisinus MS. Latin 14696 is a thirteenth century parchment of unusual beauty and is even more ornate than Marcianus 200. The parchment is cut so thin that it resembles rice paper. The copyist used a monotonous hand in black ink with ornate capital letters. The original scribe sometimes corrected himself, either in the margin or above the line, and there are *marginalia* in Greek by a second hand, particularly at the beginning of the MS. There appear to have been dates written at the bottom of several folios, but, after the MS. had its pages clipped, only the date 1281 is clearly legible on f.96r. Book One includes ff.88r-108v; Book Two ff.108v-129r; and Book Three ff.129r-143r.

The second copy of the Moerbeck translation examined in detail was Parisinus MS Latin 7695, a beautifully executed parchment of the fourteenth century. The copyist's hand is very legible and so are the *marginalia*, both in the original hand and in a second hand using a second shade of ink. Events have damaged the MS. First, its pages were trimmed, perhaps to reduce frayed edges that had developed from wear and tear. Second, there are sufficient wormholes to cause some MS. distortion. Book One includes ff.1r-10r; Book Two 97ff.10r-19r; and Book Three, ff.19r-24v. On f.24v, the scribe wrote: "Explicit liber rhetoricorum Aristotelis secundum translationem. Guilielmi. Deo Gratias. Amen. Amen. Amen."[48]

The *Handschriften und Inkanabelabteilung* section of the *Bayerische Staatsbibliothek* in Munich has two copies of the Moerbeck translation that are of particular interest because the first was formerly in the library of Victorius and the second was used by Dittmeyer in 1882 to complete his work comparing the Greek and Latin translations.[49] Monacensis Latin Codex 206, a thirteenth to fourteenth century MS., contains the *Rhetoric* on ff.171r-227r. It was used by both Spengel and Dittmeyer in their documentation of the Victorius edition of 1548. Monacensis Latin Codex 8003, ca. 1300, that includes the *Rhetoric* on ff.65r-100v, enabled Dittmeyer to complete the work begun by Spengel in annotating the William of Moerbeck version.

The Antiqua Translation

In examining Guelferbytanus, Bibl. Ducalis 448. Helmst., composed of four parts that appear to have been the work of different copyists, Schneider noted that the fourth part presented a Latin version of the *Rhetoric* so different from the others that it must have come from a source not previously recognized. Schneider concluded that, from the lost Greek manuscript that he and Kassel designated as Γ, there developed at first two Latin translations, one the Translatio Vetus that we will discuss next, and, contemporary to it, the Translatio Antiqua. From the Antiqua came the Guelferbytanus, and also the Moerbeck, which in turn also drew from another lost Greek manuscript that Schneider and Kassel called Δ. The diagram above, derived from Schneider (1970, 179), demonstrates these relationships.

The variations of the Antiqua translation are of such relatively minor importance in clarifying the Greek text that they need not detain us here. However, it is important to remember that, during the thirteenth

The Manuscript Period

century, there was sufficient interest in the *Rhetoric* that at least three different translations appeared.

The Vetusta Translation

The third Latin version of Aristotle's *Rhetoric* is by an unknown translator and therefore is commonly referred to as the Vetusta or "old" translation. (Hall, 1913, 147-8) However, the term, "Vetusta translation," is sometimes loosely applied and has been used by scholars like Spengel to refer to the Moerbeck version as well as to the anonymous translation. Such confusion is largely absent from the works of twentieth century scholars. Schneider refers to the work as the Vetus translation.

Amable Jourdain first called attention to this third Latin version. (1960, 444 & 182) Both Lacombe and Schneider acknowledge only four manuscripts of the Vetusta, two of which are complete:

13th century. . Parisinus MS. Latin 16673 (Paris)

13th century. . Toletani MS. Latin 47.15.20
(*Bibilioteca del Cabildo de la Santisma Iglesia*, Toledo)

13th/14th . . . . . Chicagiensis, no number
centuries (Newberry centuries Library, fragment on f.104r-113r)

14th/15th . . . . . Marcianus MS. Latin. VI, 164
centuries (*Bibilioteca Marciana*, Venice, fragment on ff. 40r-42r)

We will limit our discussion to the two complete manuscripts.

Parisinus 16673 is less ornate than the Moerbeck Parisinus MS. Latin 14696 discussed previously, but bears a similar monotonous penmanship. Whereas MS. Latin 7695 concludes with "Deo Gratias. Amen. Amen. Amen.," MS. Latin 16673 concludes simply with "Completus est. Deo gratias." Parisinus 16673 bears the usual corrections both above the line and in the margins. Book One includes 86ff.1r-24v; Book Two ff.25r-48r; Book Three ff.48r-61r.

The second complete copy of the Vetusta translation, Toletanus MS. Latin 47.15, housed in the unpretentious cathedral library high above the cloisters in Toledo, is an extra large sized parchment, with three columns to a folio, written in an even and very legible hand. A semi-circular area at the top of the folios has suffered badly from what appears to be water damage. But the text is sufficiently legible so that scholars have been able to collate the two complete Vetusta MSS. without difficulty. Book One includes f.25r, col.2, lines 1 to f.29r, col.2, line 14; Book Two, f.29r, col.2, line 15 to f.33r, col.2, line 89; Book Three, 53f.33r, col.3, line 1 to f.35v, col.3, end of folio.

Parisinus 16673 and Toletanus 47.15 have in common not only that they contain the Vetusta version of the *Rhetoric*, but also that they include the commentary on Aristotle's *Rhetoric* by Averröes in a Latin translation from the Arabic.[50]

CONTRIBUTIONS OF THE LATIN MANUSCRIPTS TO THE GREEK DEFINITIVE EDITIONS

In 1971, Bernd Schneider presented in detail the variant readings of the Moerbeck, Vetusta, and Antiqua versions, and, in 1978 he edited the texts of the Moerbeck and Antiqua translations. It is not necessary to duplicate his work here, and it will be discussed further in Chapter Four. But, in order that we may understand the degree to which the Latin versions augmented our knowledge of the Greek text, we will cite here two instances called to our attention by Ross. (1959, vii) As the Moerbeck version has perhaps been the most influential of the three Latin translations, both of the illustrations given here are taken from it.

First, on f.8v, col.2, line 15 (1374a16) of Parisinus 7695, William of Moerbeck had translated the Greek to read *"eius, a quo accepit,"* whereas Grec 1741 on f.140r6 had only the reading ἔκλεψεν. After consulting Moerbeck, certain editors amended their Greek text to read as Moerbeck had indicated. The two Greek versions are given below:

original version without Moerbeck

οὐδὲ πάντως, εἰ λάθρα ἔλαβεν, ἔκλεψεν, ἀλλ' εἰ ἐπὶ βλάβῃ ἐκλεψεν καὶ σφετερισμῷ ἑαυτοῦ.

Nor is it altogether true that because a man takes something by stealth, that he has committed a theft, unless he stole it for injury, or to get something for himself.

revised version after collation with Moerbeck

οὐδὲ πάντως, εἰ λάθρα ἔλαβεν, ἔκλεψεν, ἀλλ' εἰ ἐπὶ βλάβῃ τούτου ἀφ' οὗ ἔλαβε καὶ σφετερισμῷ ἑαυτοῦ

Nor is it altogether true, that, because a man takes something by stealth, that he has committed a theft, unless he stole it to injure the party from whom he took it, or to get something for himself.

The distinction between the two passages is subtle, but, as the clarification of "intent" or *mens rea* remains for lawyers one of the two principal factors that must be proved to establish a tort, the distinction is significant. Establishing the legal intent of those accused remains a difficult problem in the courtroom and must largely be achieved by circumstantial evidence. Unless the accused tell us what their states of mind were at the time of the event and we believe what the accused say, lawyers must establish intent by inference. Therefore, any precepts widely accepted by the court that designate the degree of proof that the plaintiff must establish to convince the court that a tort has been committed, are important to lawyers. The Moerbeck reading shifts more of the burden of proof onto the plaintiff than did the original reading. The Latin makes it clear that, if the plaintiff wishes to establish the defendant as a thief, the plaintiff must prove (a) that the defendant intended to injure the persons from whom he took the item or (b) that the defendant intended to profit himself. Therefore borrowing the item with the intent to return it would not be sufficient intent. The burden that the plaintiff carries to prove guilt is important in law, and many contemporary decisions turn on distinctions of wording as subtle as the variant reading from Moerbeck.

It is interesting to explore why such a difference occurs. What caused the Moerbeck Latin version to have a fuller meaning than the Greek manuscripts? There can, of course, be no definite answer to such a question. One reasonable explanation is that a copyist of the Greek, who knew something of law or who was interested in preserving subtleties, carefully retained the additional verbage in the Greek text from which Moerbeck did his translating. That the work of the copyists of Kassel's and Schneider's MSS. Γ and Δ has been lost prevents us from reasoning further along this line. Another possibility was offered by Jebb who, in his English translation, suggested that the clause supplied by Moerbeck "must have dropped out owing to the similarity between βλάβη and ἔλαβε, and, once the clause had been omitted, its place was wrongly supplied by the insertion of ἔκλεψε." (Jebb, 58, n.1) Perhaps a combination of the legal and linguistic reasons could best account for the discrepancies between the Greek and the Latin.

The second variant reading from the Moerbeck translation that we will examine here is found in Parisinus 7695 on f.10v, col.1, ll.29-30 (1379a21) [144v24 of MS. Grec 1741] where the Moerbeck reads "si autem non, et quodcunque aliud parvipendat quis," causing some editors of critical editions to add the words εἰ δὲ μή, κἂν ὁτιοῦν ἄλλο ὀλιγωρῇ τις. Aristotle had been speaking of those who are prone to anger, saying that slights against one's adversities cause particular anger, e.g., the sick get angry if their ailments are made light of, the poor if their poverty is slighted, those at war by indifferences to the problems caused by fighting, the lover if his affection is not taken seriously, and so on. The Moerbeck phrase permits a completion of Aristotle's line of reasoning by offering what the lawyer may seek in order to establish slight in general, in contrast to the things that cause anger in particular. The Moerbeck variant reading allows the addition of the second phrase in brackets:

> If special slights [of the sort I have given above] are lacking, then any other sort of slight [will serve to provoke anger].

In the revised Greek version given below, therefore, the phrase εἰ δὲ μή responds to the words μάλιστα μέν that Aristotle had used earlier: (Roemer, 1897, n. for line 21)

διὸ κάμνοντες, πενόμενοι, [πολεμοῦντες], ἐρῶντες, διψῶτες, ὅλως ἐπιθυμοῦντες τι καὶ μὴ κατορθοῦντες ὀργίλοι εἰσὶ καὶ εὐπαρόρμητοι μάλιστα [μὲν] πρὸς τοὺς τοῦ παρόντος ὀλιγωροῦντας οἷον κάμνων μὲν τοῖς πρὸς τὴν νόσον πενόμενος δὲ τοῖς πρὸς τὴν πενίαν πολεμῶν δὲ τοῖς πρὸς τὸν πόλεμον, ἐρῶν δὲ τοῖς πρὸς τὸν ἔρωτα, ὁμοίως δὲ καὶ τοῖς ἄλλοις εἰ δὲ μή, κἂν ὁτιοῦν ἄλλο ὀλιγωρῇ τις

si autem non, et quodcunque aliud parvipendat quis.

Again we should ask what the significance of such an addition could be and why it may have occurred. The element of provocation is important to the lawyer, particularly if the law allows distinctions between what reasonable men in general might do and what would be considered reasonable for a particular man to do. If slight can be established, then provocation can be established, and then perhaps self-defense can be used as an affirmative defense to acts of violence. If, as Aristotle implied from his discussion, the slights that would arouse the anger of a particular man [because he was ill, or poor, or at war, or in love] can be used to establish provocation, then the lawyer has an easier task than if it is necessary to prove that the hypothetical reasonable man would have been angered, and therefore acted without malice to commit a crime in self-defense. Aristotle is opening the door for what some current jurisdictions call the "imperfect right of self-defense," i.e., it is imperfect in that a reasonable man might not have used self-defense under those circumstances, but it is allowable because this particular man, having been slighted in a way particularly grievous to him, would consider it reasonable to use self-defense. The additional phrase from Moerbeck emphasizes to the lawyer to seek out any and all justifications for slight, whether special or general, to establish why a particular man, in contrast to the hypothetical reasonable man, might have become angry and therefore, without malice, have committed a crime. Such subtleties are as important to lawyers now[51] as they were to lawyers in Aristotle's time.

Why did such a variant reading come into being? Of course Moerbeck or the scribes of the Greek manuscripts from which Moerbeck worked could have added the phrase to complete Aristotle's thought. But a more likely explanation is that the feeling in the Greek language for balance provoked the completion of "in particular" with "in general." Certainly Aristotle had this feeling of balance about language throughout his discourse so the phrase could well have come directly from him and been left out of some manuscripts because the scribes did not understand enough about law to include it.

These two examples are sufficient to illustrate the nature of the variant readings supplied by the Latin translations and will clarify the sort of contribution they made to the development of a definitive edition in Greek.

THE PROBLEMS THAT THE GREEK AND LATIN MANUSCRIPTS POSED TO EDITORS OF THE CRITICAL EDITIONS

Now that we have a general comprehension of what manuscripts the editors of the critical editions had at their disposal[52] and some indication of how the nature and extent of the variant readings of the Latin versions contributed to establishing the Greek text, we are ready to consider our final inquiry in this chapter, i.e., what problems were posed to the editors of the critical editions by the manuscripts and how in general the editors went about solving these problems.

A single or a multiple source

First, did the editors confront manuscripts descending from single or multiple sources? The examples previously cited are illustrative of the relatively minor differences among the Greek manuscripts of the *Rhetoric* and between the Greek and Latin manuscripts of the *Rhetoric*. Therefore Kassel found it possible to construct a schema in which he could place all of the known Greek and Latin manuscripts of the *Rhetoric* as derived from a single lost archetype. Kassel's only exceptions are some *scholia* entered at the time that the first revision of A was made, readings in Grec 1741 that could have come via the Syrian and Arabic scholars. Perhaps the Arabic manuscript, Parisinus 2346, can add in either a major or minor way to our knowledge of the text of the *Rhetoric*.

The fact that the Greek and Latin manuscripts of the *Rhetoric* have descended from a common archetype has made the development of a critical edition a relatively simpler task in comparison to the development of critical editions of other of Aristotle's works where existing manuscripts can be traced to widely varying archetypes. During the nineteenth and twentieth centuries, as knowledge of the number of manuscript copies of the *Rhetoric* began to increase,[53] undoubtedly scholars continued to hope to uncover a Greek or Latin manuscript that would provide sufficient contrast to Grec 1741 to permit a major enrichment of our knowledge of the *Rhetoric*. Certainly scholars hoped to find a manuscript that would complete the major lacuna in Book Three. But no such discovery was made, and, unless the Parisian manuscript in Arabic proves helpful, such a discovery now seems unlikely. Therefore, although such relative consistency among the manuscripts made the tasks of the collator easier in one respect, such consistency made the editors' tasks more difficult in that, where clarification was needed, there were only limited resources available.

How were the critical editions produced?

With the reassurance (and disappointment) that the editors of the critical editions were working from one archetype, how did the craftsmen of the critical editions proceed? It seems possible to assume that all of the editors produced a working copy similar to that developed by Victorius. Therefore, the editors may have begun with one trustworthy copy mounted in the middle of large sheets of paper to which variations could be noted in the margins. If the editor intended to produce a commentary, as did Victorius and Cope, there could be separate pages on which ideas could be noted as the editor proceeded through the text.

In developing his edition, Victorius had one advantage that later editors have not had. He was able to assemble in one place, at one time, a number of manuscripts plus the printed editions that had been issued up to that time.[54] Victorius could put them side by side and observe the differences. Other editors had to take their working copy from place to place, entering notes as they went, making the circuit of the several manuscript collections. Undoubtedly they had to retrace their steps because they forgot to make such and such a notation or they failed to enter a required detail. Occasionally one scholar has relied upon the authority of a previous scholar and therefore, instead of correcting the errors of those who came before him, he has perpetuated them. Contemporary scholars such as Kassel[55] not only can take advantage of the increased ease of transportation to visit the libraries themselves but also can employ microfilm that may eliminate the time and expense of travel. However, microfilm presents the mechanical problems of trying to set up a number of texts side by side for comparison. But at least the holders of the microfilm do not have to become exasperated because they failed to note a particular variation, for they have the raw material available for re-examination. And, of course, they can have photographic reproductions made from the microfilm that will permit a direct comparison of versions without the use of machines. Additional comments will be made about the development of the definitive editions of the text in Chapter Four.

How were the decisions about collation made?

Assuming that editors of the critical editions have before them a basic working copy of the *Rhetoric*, possibly Grec 1741 or a printed version with which they are already highly familiar such as the Bekker, and have noted variations from other manuscripts, how then do they proceed? What changes do they accept? What variations do they reject? Should they allow for multiple readings, or should they establish one Greek text, perhaps with the sources for their decisions entered as footnotes? Should they develop not only a critical edition but a commentary that attempts to interpret what Aristotle meant by controversial or critical passages? These are the main questions that editors have had to answer for themselves, and we should not expect them to agree. After working with the text over a period of time, editors get a feel for their material. In instances where the problem must be decided subjectively, e.g., where it is not a matter of perfecting an obviously faulty reading but rather where a decision must be made between two plausible variant readings, editors must rely upon their intuitive judgment. Further discussion of this question will be found in Chapter Four.

Yet one final comment needs to be made here concerning methodologies used by the editors. Scholars should not expect editors to be consistent within their own system. Editors who appear to note carefully readings that differ from their own in one instance may elect to omit a variation in another instance, and there does not always appear to be a reasonable explanation for the omission. Therefore, it is again preferable to have available the works of Victorius, Spengel and Cope together with the texts of Bekker, Roemer, Dufour, Tovar, Ross, and Kassel.[56]

WHAT SHOULD THE ATTITUDE OF CONTEMPORARY SCHOLARS BE TOWARD THE CRITICAL EDITIONS OF THE RHETORIC

We now come to our final inquiry of Chapter Two. What should be the attitude of contemporary students of the *Rhetoric* toward the critical Greek editions? First, modern scholars can feel secure that, if they follow the critical editions of Gaisford, Cope, Bekker, Roemer, Dufour, Tovar, Ross or Kassel plus the critical editions and commentaries by Victorius, Spengel and Cope, they will have available to them what can be known about the Greek text of the *Rhetoric*. With these resources at their disposal, contemporary scholars have the raw material from which they can draw their own conclusions about what Aristotle had in mind when he "wrote" the *Rhetoric*. If scholars wish to consult the manuscripts themselves, the critical editions in Greek will guide them to the particular manuscripts that are relevant to the passages concerned.

Second, contemporary students cannot feel secure in their knowledge of the *Rhetoric* if they have only consulted translations. There are two aspects of the translations that pose difficulties for the rhetorician, and these will be enlarged in the final chapter. If we assume that those who translated the Greek were as proficient in Greek as was Aristotle and therefore met Aristotle's first proficiency, are the translators able to meet the second two proficiencies of Aristotle, a proficiency in rhetoric and a proficiency in law? When comparing the Greek version with the translation, rhetoricians may be particularly disturbed that translators not acquainted with rhetoric render terms that have specific meanings in rhetoric in varying ways, seemingly in order that the rhythm of the sentence can suit the translator or that there can be what the translator may consider variety in style. Furthermore, modern rhetoricians who are acquainted with law can be doubly exasperated because the translator did not realize the degree to which Aristotle was addressing "lawyers." As will be pointed out in the final chapter, words and phrases in law have distinctions that do not exist elsewhere. Modern translations often fail to reflect the legal implications of the treatise.

Third, scholars should realize that, because of the rather consistent nature of the manuscripts from which the editors have had to work, students have available to them either a very faithful text or a relatively poor text. If the agreement of the manuscripts is interpreted to mean that they stem from one archetype that was itself a rather close approximation to Aristotle's notes, then students should conclude that they have a very faithful Greek text from which to work. But, if the agreement of the texts is interpreted to mean that only one major variation of Aristotle's *Rhetoric* has been preserved and that other versions that were considerably different have been lost, and that their loss makes any realistic collation of substantially varying texts impossible, then scholars must conclude that they have a poor text that is prejudiced by whatever bent or circumstances surround the production of the archetype from which the extant manuscripts stem.

Fourth, scholars should feel that, even though the variations in the manuscripts of the *Rhetoric* are comparatively minor, they indicate that the *Rhetoric* should be interpreted as a result of its total impact and not from the manner in which a given phrase is worded or a particular attitude is expressed. We are not that close to Aristotle's teachings. Too many factors have intervened. Scholars would do better to absorb the *Rhetoric* for its overall effects, hoping that they can draw from its totality what may be obscured by the likelihood that its details have been poorly transmitted.

Fifth, we may hazard the guess that the working copy of Aristotle's notes left behind him was more fully developed at its beginning than at its end, i.e., Aristotle had more assiduously perfected the earlier part of his treatise than he had the concluding portions. However, in this very perfecting, the initial sections of Aristotle's notes were probably more confusing to subsequent interpreters than were his concluding remarks. If Aristotle annotated and amended carefully the opening of his treatise, as we think he did, then those who were left behind to interpret his notes may well have been perplexed by the confusion of ideas. Such confusion resulted in some non-sequiturs that have remained until today. Furthermore we must remember that Aristotle himself did not divide his notes into chapters. Such divisions were a later innovation. The fact that a number of the manuscripts of the *Rhetoric* do not make a clear distinction between Book Two and Book Three and that the major lacuna in the manuscript falls in Book Three are only two obvious pieces of evidence to support the supposition that the initial stages of the treatise were more fully developed than were the concluding remarks. Aristotle may have made only a casual indication of where Book Two ended and Book Three began, knowing full well himself where he made the distinction and intending at some time to go back over his notes and clear them up. Furthermore, Aristotle may have made some hasty reference to Book One where the lacuna in Book Three occurs, a reference that was meaningful to him but that was obscure to those who followed. What modern professor's lecture notes do not have similar notations? Aristotle's remarks to himself in the neighborhood of the lacuna in Book Three, assuming that they existed in Aristotle's notes, may have referred in some manner to his previous comments on the same subject in another one of his treatises or on the same subject in Book One, causing some editor, possibly Tyrannion, to substitute a portion of Book One for the reference in Book Three. Aristotle's notes may have been more and more sketchy as the treatise progressed, until they became no more than indications of what he intended to say, resulting in the opinion held for some time that Book Three was spurious, an opinion that has now been largely rejected but that could have been provoked by the degree to which the concluding portion of the text had to be interpreted and edited by those to whom we are indebted for the preservation of the *Rhetoric*.

SUMMARY

This chapter has shown how the *Rhetoric* emerged in manuscript form after the fall of Rome had relegated it to obscurity. All of the Greek and Latin copies that have been found stem from one archetype, and a comparison of the Greek and Latin versions of the descendants of this archetype has permitted scholars to make minor adjustments in the Greek text, but has not permitted major revelations that could be getting us closer to what Aristotle may have said as a teacher in Athens. We must be content with either a relatively accurate version of his notes or a rather poor version, and there appears to be no way of knowing whether what we have is highly accurate or discouragingly distorted.

The significance of this discussion of the transition from the Roman period through the manuscript period gives rise to five observations that should be kept in mind in working with the *Rhetoric*. First, the critical editions produced in the nineteenth and twentieth centuries, can be relied upon to tell us what it is possible to know about the Greek text. Second, the Greek must be consulted because translations may not reflect Aristotle's knowledge of rhetoric and law. Third, the Greek text that we have is either very faithful or very unfaithful to Aristotle's teachings. Fourth, the variations we have, even though they are minor, should warn us not to draw conclusions from any particular passage in the *Rhetoric*, but rather to look at its general impact. Fifth, if, as we believe, Aristotle amended and revised and made notations in the earlier parts of the *Rhetoric* to a greater extent than in the latter part, we should be prepared for nonsequiturs and confusion in Book One and much of Book Two, confusions that Aristotle himself could have easily clarified by explaining the meaning of his notes, but confusions which are now troublesome because we have only conjecture on what may have been Aristotle's plan.

NOTES

1. Boggess, in following the Parisinus MS. Lat. 16673 of the *Poetics* that was published in 1481, but which Boggess stated was translated from Arabic and written into manuscript form in 1256, traced the *Poetics* back to its Greek origin via several languages other than Greek. Boggess proposed that one Greek text of the *Poetics* was translated into Syriac in the fifth or sixth century. From thence, it was translated into Arabic, one copy of which is dated from the tenth century. Hermannus Alemannus then translated the Arabic version of the *Poetics* by Averröes into Latin, providing a source for the *Poetics* by a route other than through Greece and Rome. Furthermore, Boggess proposed that still other versions of Averröes' Arabic version of the *Poetics* went from Arabic into Hebrew, and thence into Latin. (Boggess, 1965).

2. For descriptions of these inventories, see xvii-xxi of *Mémoire Historique sur la Bibliothèque du Roy* by l'Abbé Jourdain (first name seemingly unknown) that forms the preface to volume one of the series "Théologie" in the set, *Catalogue des Livres Imprimez de la Bibliothèque du Roy* (Paris, 1739). Note that the copy of the set in the catalogue room of the *Bibliothèque Nationale* lacks this preface so that it is necessary to consult the copy in the stacks under the call number Q.351. Parts of this preface were reprinted by Delisle (1868, 1, 207-212). It would appear that l'Abbé Jourdain drew much of his material from two MSS. in the B.N.: Parisinus MS. *Nouvelle Acquisition Française* 1328 and a copy of the aforesaid, Parisinus MS. Français 22571. These MSS. contain a work by Jean Boivin entitled *Mémoire pour l'Histoire de la Bibliothèque du Roy*. Folios 365r-390v of MS. Fr. 22571 are entitled *Comment la Reyne Catherine Requit sa Bibliothèque et d'Où Elle lui Estoit Venue*. See also Leroux de Lincy (1858). "Notice sur la Bibliothèque de Catherine de Medicis," *Bulletin du Bibliophile*, 13e series, 915-941.

3. This MS. was one that escaped destruction during the period when the grand niece of Pieresc, after the death of her great uncle, acquired the habit of lighting fires with folios from the manuscript collection. (Delisle, 1868, 1, 283)

4. Apparently the Jean Bouhier (1673-1746) who left his manuscript collection to the *Bibliothèque Nationale*, although he would have had to complete the work as a very young man.

5. These two MSS. are bound in the coat of arms of Henry IV. If Catherine had taken care to bind more of her manuscripts in her own coat of arms, the identification would have been more complete.

6. Delisle was, from 1871 to 1874, head librarian of the manuscript collection at the *Bibliothèque Nationale*, and, from 1874 to 1905, its *administrateur général*.

7. It was through the courtesy of the Cardinal that Peter Victorius had access to what is now Grec 1741.

8. Roemer (1898, vi) noted that the darker ink of the first scribe appeared to have begun on f. 135r24 (1369a23) with the words τῷ δ' ἀκολάστῳ, but the division is not so clear cut. It appears more likely that, at this point, the scribe took up a new pen and was having trouble with it, for the ink here varies from light to dark for about eight words before the darker pen carries on.

9. Ross (1959,v) concurs with Roemer.

10. Compare the sketches in the margins of ff.122v and 123v with the diagrams of Victorius (1548,49-51).

11. The mixed capital and lower case letters of the title as written on the MS. have been preserved here.

12. The scribe for MS. Grec 1741 used a common device for keeping his lines straight, so that the parchment at the exterior ends of each line has small holes in it, and there are traces of faint lines, stemming from these holes. Van Groningen (1967, 22) described the technique as follows: "On parchment the scribes often marked the horizontal lines as well as the vertical margins with a sharp stylus, since the XIth cent. with a small leaden wheel. It was sufficient to draw the lines on one side of the leaf, since they were at the same time visible on the other side...."

13. Hereafter the numbers in parentheses will refer to the Bekker edition (1831-1870).

14. The διὸ καὶ belongs on Bekker's 1357b6, and, once removed by the scribe from f.123r22, it had to be inserted by the first scribe in the left hand margin on f.123r23, to introduce the words τεκμήριον τὸ τοιοῦτον τῶν σημείων ἐστίν. The notations of Victorius and the marginal insertions by the scribe make the MS. very confusing at this point.

15. Spengel (1867,23) did not honor this correction.

16. Bekker and Spengel did not honor this correction by the first scribe, but Roemer, Ross and Kassel did.

17. Both Roemer and Ross propose that the second hand amended the τινι to make it read τείνει but the MS. shows that the correction was made only by scribbling ∂ (the scribe's abbreviation for ει) above the first iota, undoubtedly intending this correction to substitute for both the medial and terminal errors. Also the MS. has been tampered with at this point, for there is something scratched out where the second iota for the original τινι has been written.

18. One need only compare the handwriting of the first scribe on f.158r15 (1393a5) for an examination of the words μᾶλλον τὰ to identify the manner in which the first scribe wrote the letters λλ, and his handwriting

The Manuscript Period

on f.158r5 (1392b27) for the word ἐπείρασε, to identify the manner in which the scribe wrote the ending letters, σε, to establish what the first scribe had written on f.158a14 (1393a4).

19. On the same line, f.160v33 (1396a14), the second hand struck out an extraneous ω that the first scribe had mistakenly put in Ἡρακλει[ω]δῶν. The phrase, ὑπὲρ τῶν Ἡρακλειδῶν, is translated as "for the descendants of Hercules."

20. For example, nine of the other Greek manuscripts of the *Rhetoric* examined for this study observe the lacuna on the following folios: Parisinus MS.Grec 1869, lacuna begins on f.52r24, ends on f.52v4; Parisinus Supplementary MS.Grec 1285, lacuna begins on f.107r15, ends on f.105v11; Parisinus MS.Grec 2038, lacuna begins on f.70v17, ends on f.71r5; Parisinus MS.Grec 2116, lacuna begins on f.168r6, ends on f.168v18; Parisinus MS.Grec 1818, lacuna begins on f.148r6, ends on f.148r21; Palatinus MS.Grec 23, lacuna begins on f.27r29, ends on f.27v5; Vaticanus MS.Grec 1340, lacuna begins on f.40r15, ends on f.40r26; Marcianus MS.Grec 200, lacuna begins on f.560v39, ends on f.571v1; Monacensis MS. Grec 176, lacuna begins on f. 100r14, ends on f.100v10.

21. Kassel termed the lost parent of Dresdensis Da 4, α.

22. Dresdensis Da 4 was not examined for this study. For its description, see Moraux, 1976, I, 125-126.

23. In his schemata, Kassel assigned Roman letters to known manuscripts and Greek letters to lost manuscripts.

24. A typographical error in Ross made this read 1359a17. Roemer observed the variation in wording from MS. Grec 1741 with which Monacensis 313 begins. (1897, xx)

25. For example, on f.34v21-22 (1361b7), Monacensis 313 omits οὖν and adds ίσκου to generate νεανίσκου. The two versions are given below:

Parisinus MS. Grec 1741	Monacensis Graci Codex 313
νέου μὲν οὖν κάλλος τὸ πρὸς τοὺς πόνους χρήσιμον ἔχειν τὸ σῶμα τούς τε πρὸς δρόμον καὶ πρὸς βίαν	νεανίσκου μὲν κάλλος τὸ πρὸς τοὺς πόνους χρήσιμον ἔχειν τὸ σῶμα τούς τε πρὸς δρόμον καὶ πρὸς βίαν.

The Monacensis version uses the less common term νεανίσκος rather than the more common νέος. The omission of the οὖν in the Munich MS. eliminated only a "therefore." Both versions are faithfully translated by Roberts: "In a young man beauty is the possessions of a body fit to endure the exertion of running and of contests of strength." (1984,40)

26. For example, on f.32c16 (1359b22), καί is added.

27. For example, on f.35r26 (1362a7), the words παρά and λόγον are joined, resulting in παράλογον. This juncture does change the meaning and probably occurred because, as in Parisinus MS. Grec 1741, f.128r5-6, παρά appears at the end of one line while λόγον begins a new line. A translation of the phrase in which these variations appear should read: "Luck is also the cause of happy turns of events that exceed expectation."

28. The closest to a substantial variation in Monacensis 313 is on f. 36v31-32 (1363a38-1363b1) in which the words χαίρουσιν ἐπιθυμοῦντες were added after μάλιστα by a second hand as a correction to the MS. The two versions are given below:

Monacensis Graci Codex 313	καὶ μάλιστα χαίρουσιν, ἐπιθυμοῦντες ἕκαστοι πρὸς ἃ τοιοῦτοι
MS.Grec 1741 129v1-2	καὶ μάλιστα ἕκαστοι πρὸς ἃ τοιοῦτοι

29. Kassel did not assign Roman letters to a number of the manuscripts in his schema, particularly the later codexes.

30. Both Roemer (1897,xvii) and Ross (1959, xiii) refer to this MS. as Vaticanus Grec 23, which was the name of the manuscript before it was changed to Palatinus Grec 23.

31. The Palatine Library at Heidelberg had been founded by the Elector Philip during the close of the fifteenth century. Important additions were made by Rudolph Agricola, Johann Dalberg, and Ulrich Fugger.

32. In 1797 thirty-eight of the manuscripts were dispatched by Napoleon to Paris. These were restored to Heidelberg on Jan. 14, 1816, by the Congress of Vienna. On July 8, 1816, 852 additional manuscripts, mostly in Old German, were sent from Rome to Heidelberg.

33. See *Codices Manuscripti Palatini Graeci Bibliothecae...* Henry Stevenson, ed. (Rome, 1855), 12. Stevenson, xix ff., also included a discussion of the history of the Heidelberg MSS. There is some doubt that all of the Palatine MSS. were ever sent to Rome. See Friedrich Wilfen, *Geschichte der Bildung, Beraubung und Bernichtung der Alten Heidelbergischen Büchersammlungen* (Heidelberg, 1817), 1-3. For a summary of the history of this and other Heidelberg manuscripts see 190ff. for a more detailed account.

34. The printed catalogue that will include this number has not yet been issued by the Vatican. At present there is a catalogue in longhand available to readers in the *Biblioteca Apostolica Vaticana*.

35. See *Catalogus Codicum Manuscriptorum Bibliotecae Regiae Bavaricae*, ed. Maximilian Joseph with notes by I.C. de Arentin (Munich, 1806), I, part two, 210. Volume One of this series was edited by Ignatius Hart. For a brief citation to the limited work of Angelo Constantino, see Vogel and Gardthausen (1966, 6). The only date listed is circa 1523.

36. Cf. f.79r13 for the scribe's handwriting for τρίτον.

37. Kassel (1970), schema.

38. Andre Vergece was a Cretan who came from Venice to Paris where he was employed by Francis I and three succeeding French kings. He died during the reign of Charles IX. Vergece worked from 1535-1566, copying many Greek manuscripts. See Bradley (1889, III, 373).

39. Kassel noted in his schema that Parisinus 2116 also had associations with the 1536 printed edition of Trincavelli.

40. The Colbert collection was a valuable addition for, at his death, Colbert had assembled 41,844 books and 13,014 manuscripts (Delisle, 1868, I, 477). Some of Colbert's Greek manuscripts had been bought in the Levant. The collection continued to grow after Colbert's death until about 1700 (Delisle, 1868, I, 82) when, for some unknown reason, the librarian who had assembled the collection retired. When subsequent heirs were not as interested in a library as their illustrious forefather and began to disperse the collection, the king purchased it in 1732.

41. John of Crete (or Rhodes) appears as a coypist in Vogel and Gardthausen (1966, 187-193) as having supplied numerous manuscripts between 1447 and 1497, including Marcianus MS. Grec 200. For information on miniaturists, see Bradley, previously cited, or Umberto Gnoll, *Pittori e Miniatori Nell-Umbria (Spoleto, 1923)*, or Erhard Aeschlimann, *Dictionnaire des Miniaturists du Moyan Age et de la Renaissance dans les Differentes Contrees de la Europe* (Milan, 1940), or the revised Aeschlimann published with Paola d'Ancona (Milan, 1949).

42. See f.544v14; f.550v34; and f.551r23.

43. The Marcianus catalogue, *Graeca d. Marci Bibliotheca Codicum Manuscriptorum per Titulos Digesta*, Laurentio Theupola, ed. (Venice, 1740), 100-11, pointed out that the works on logic are missing from this MS. of Aristotle's works.

44. Again the stylistic dotting of the iotas plus the mixture of capital and small letters has been retained. The contemporary form would be Ἀριστοτέλους and περὶ ῥητορικῆς.

45. The library in Venice has preserved a list of the scholars who have consulted their MSS. since 1906. If the list is accurate, of the twenty-eight scholars who have used MS. 200 between 1906 and 1969, not one appears to have been English or American. The list does include the names of Jaeger of Berlin University in 1925 and Kassel of Berlin in 1967 and 1968.

46. According to the Kassel schema, Δ, Γ, and γ.

47. William of Moerbeck was a Dominican, born in Moerbeck, Flanders, in the thirteenth century. Known also as William of Brabant, William of Flanders, and William of Corinth, his name is spelled in a variety of ways. After serving the Pope in a number of capacities, William was appointed Archbishop of Corinth in 1277. Moerbeck died around 1281.

48. In this citation, those words that were abbreviated in the MS. have been spelled out.

49. The catalogue of the Latin manuscripts in Munich that was completed in 1806 does not include Monacensis Latin Codex 8003 as coming from Victorius' library.

50. The significance of this commentary will be explained in Chapter Three.

51. See *Bedder v. Director of Public Prosecutions*, House of Lords, 1954, 2 All. E.R.

52. A partial compilation of the Greek and Latin manuscripts of Aristotle's *Rhetoric* can be obtained from two sources: Wartelle (1963) and Lacombe (1939 and 1955). Kassel (1970, 2) noted several corrections in Wartelle, and then (Kassel, 1970, 2-18) gave important details on selected Greek manuscripts of the *Rhetoric*.

53. Scholars became more and more knowledgeable about the available manuscripts for three reasons: first, the British and German scholars began to publish their critical editions in which they footnoted references to manuscripts and one critical edition built on the next; second, libraries with manuscript collections began to publish catalogues of their holdings; and third, each researcher, encouraged by the findings of his predecessors, pressed on to extend and improve on what had been done before.

54. In addition to the MS. 1741, Victorius had available to him three MSS. that have remained in Florence: Laurentianus MS. Pl. 86, Codex 19; Laurentianus MS. Pl. 31, Codex 14; and Laurentianus MS. Pl. 60, Codexes 10 and 18. (Niccolai, 1914, 229). The *Rhetoric* comprises folios 111r-168r of MS. Pl. , Codex 19 which has some *marginalia* that could be by Victorius. The books for MS. Pl. 31.14 are given in the text. MS. Pl. 60, Codex 10 dating from the fifteenth century, was copied in Florence by Markos Ioannu, and comprises folios 1r-58v. There are some *marginalia* that could be by Victorius. MS. Pl. 60, Codex 18 was copied by Georgios Chrysokokkes and comprises ff. 1r-109v of the manuscript dated May, 1427. MS. Pl. 86., Codex 19 and MS. Pl. 60, Codexes 10 and 18 still have attached to them the large chains with which they were formerly affixed to prevent removal. The books for the above named Laurentianus MSS are as follows:

	Bk One	Bk Two	Bk Three
Pl.86,19	111r–124v	124v-132v	132v-158r
Pl.31,14	1r-40v	40v-52r	81v-105r
Pl.60,10	1r-22v	23r-43v	44r-58v
Pl.60,18.	1r-25r	25r-40r	40r-109v20

From the Munich collection, Victorius had available Monascensis Codexes Grec 90, 175, 176, 234 and Codexes Latin 206 and 8003. Victorius also had the Latin MS. Harvardiana Latin 39, which includes the *Politics*, the *Rhetoric* and the *Magna Moralis*. There are a few notes by Victorius on folios 2v and 93r. A note in the fly leaf says that the MS. was used by Victorius. This Moerbeck version had at one time been owned by the Convent of Santa Maria Novella at Florence. Book One comprises ff.92v-113v; Book Two, 113v-135r; Book Three, 135r-150.

55. European libraries often request users to sign for materials on a form that reveals previous users. Kassel's name appears frequently. In his discussion of the text, Kassel is careful to note the instances in which he used microfilm and in which he used the original. The names of certain editors, who worked before microfilm was available, had not signed to use the originals and yet some of these editors referred to those manuscripts in a manner that would indicate personal association with the material. Library regulations are frequently subject to change.

56. Some published indexes and card catalogues confuse the researcher because they list critical editions that

are accompanied by a commentary as only an "edition" or as only a "commentary," rather than indexing them under both. Other bibliographies do not include commentaries under the heading of "Aristotle," even though the commentary may be accompanied by a critical edition. Cope's work illustrates how the confusion arises, because he published his commentary in 1867 in one volume, whereas his three volume critical edition plus additional commentary was issued posthumously in 1877.

BIBLIOGRAPHY

Badawi, A. (1959). *Arisṭūṭalis: al-Kitābah al-Tarjamah al-'Arabīyah al-Quadīmah*, Cairo.

Bekker, I., ed. (1831-1810). *Aristotelis Opera*, Edidit Academia Regia Borussica, Berlin.

Boggess, W.F. (1965). Averroës Cordubensis Commentarium Medium in Aristotelis Poetriam, unpubl.diss. University of North Carolina.

Boggess, W.F. (1968). "Hermannus Alemannus's Rhetorical Translations." *Viator: Medieval & Renaissance Studies* 2, 227-350.

Bradley, J., ed. (1887-1889). *A Dictionary of Miniaturists*, 3 vols, London.

Buckley, Theodore. [1910 (1833)]. *Aristotle's Treatise on Rhetoric*, London.

Buhler, Curt. (1960). *The Fifteenth Century Book, the Scribes, the Printers, the Decorators*, Philadelphia.

Christopher, H.G.T. (1938). *Palaeography and Archives*, London.

Cope, E.M. (1867). *An Introduction to Aristotle's Rhetoric*, Cambridge, England.

Cope, E.M. (1877). *The Rhetoric of Aristotle*. ed. J.E. Sandys, 3 vols, Cambridge, England.

Delisle, L. (1868-1881). *Le Cabinet des Manuscrits de la Bibliothèque Imperiale*, 4 vols, Paris.

Dittmeyer, L. (1883). Quae Ratio inter Vetustam Aristotelis Rhetoricorum Translationem et Graecos Codices Intercedat, unpubl. diss. University of Wittenburg, Munich.

Eisenstein, Elizabeth. (1979). *The Printing Press as an Agent of Change*, Cambridge, England.

Freese, J.H. (1926). *The "Art" of Rhetoric*, London.

Gaisford, T. (1820). *Aristotelis de Rhetorica Libri Tres*, Oxford.

Hall, F.W. (1913). *A Companion to Classical Texts*, Oxford.

Harlfinger, D. (1971). *Die Textgeschichte der Pseudo-Aristotelischen Schrift*, Amsterdam.

Jebb, R.C. (1909). *The Rhetoric of Aristotle*, Cambridge, England.

Jourdain, A. (1960). *Récherches Critiques sur l'Age et l'Origine des Traductions Latines d'Aristote...*, New York. A reprint of the 1843 Paris edition by Burt Franklin of New York.

Kassel, R. (1971). *Der Text der Aristotelischen Rhetorik*, Berlin.

Kassel, R. (1974). *Aristotelis Ars Rhetorica*, Berlin.

Lacombe, G. (1939). *Aristoteles Latinus, pars prior*, Rome.

Lacombe, G. (1955). *Aristoteles Latinus, pars posterior*, Cambridge, England.

Margoliouth, D.C. (1897). "On the Arabic Versison of Aristotle's Rhetoric," in *Semetic Studies in Memory of Rev. Dr. Alexander Kohut*, ed. G.A.Kohut, Berlin, 376-387.

Moraux, P. (1976). *Aristoteles Graecus*, New York.

Niccolai, F.N. (1914). *Pier Vettori (1499-1585)*, Florence.

Omont, H. (1888). *Inventaire Sommaire des Manuscsrits Grecs de la Bibliothèque Nationale*, Paris.

Roberts, W.R. (1924). "Rhetorica," in J.Smith and W. Ross, eds., *The Works of Aristotle* (1908-1931), 11 vols, Oxford.

Roemer, A. [1898 (1885)]. *Aristotelis Ars Rhetorica*, Leipsig.

Ross, W.D. (1959). *Aristotelis Ars Rhetorica*, Oxford.

Schneider, B. (1971). *Die Mittelalterlichen Griechisch-lateinischen Ubersetzungen der Aristotelischen Rhetorik*, Berlin.

Schneider, B. (1978). *Aristoteles Latinus*, Leiden.

Spengel, L. (1867). *Aristotelis Ars Rhetorica*, 2 vols, Leipzig.

Stern, S.M. (1956). "Ibn al-Samh," *Journal of the Royal Asiatic Society*, 31-44.

Tkatsch, Jaroslaus. (1928). *Die Arabische Ubersetzung der Poetik des Aristoteles und die Grundlagbe der Kritik des Griechischen Textes*, 2 vols., Akademie der Wissenschaften in Wien, Vienna and Leipzig.

Van Groningen, B.A. (1967). *Short Manual of Greek Palaeography*, Leyden.

Victorius, P. (1548). *Petri Victorii Comentarij in Tres Libros Aristotelis de Arte Dicendi*, Florence.

Vogel, M. & V. Gardthausen. (1966). *Die Griechischen Schreiber des Mittelalters und der Renaissance*, Hildesheim.

Wartelle, A. (1963). *Inventaire des Manuscrits Grecs d'Aristote et ses Commentateurs*, Paris.

CHAPTER THREE

THE FIFTEENTH AND SIXTEENTH CENTURY GREEK AND LATIN PRINTINGS OF ARISTOTLE'S RHETORIC

The purpose of this chapter is to indicate in what manner and to what degree the printings of Aristotle's *Rhetoric* in Greek and Latin became available in the fifteenth and sixteenth centuries. Since the printings rather than the manuscripts on which they were based served as the impetus for the renaissance in the study of the *Rhetoric*, an exposition of their contribution is long overdue.

Once the printing press had been invented, the "publication" of books turned from a personalized, often non-profitable copying of manuscripts by scribes for their patrons, to the business of printing copies of manuscripts for public sale. Not only were printing presses expensive, but the personnel to run them cost more than the services of one scribe. Eisenstein (1983, 26) pointed out that the master printer was an entrepreneur who had to obtain capital, supplies, and labor "while developing complex production schedules, coping with strikes, trying to estimate book markets and lining up learned assistants." He had to cater to the officials for protection, said Eisenstein, and to cultivate artists and authors who would bring prestige to his establishment. In short, he became more than a printer. He became an editor, and, in some instances, by collating and correcting manuscripts, an "indexer-abridger-lexicographer-chronicler." (Eisenstein, 1979, I, 87)

Such master printers began to search for manuscripts to produce saleable copy. Unfortunately the successful printing and sale of books often resulted in the demise of established vendors dealing exclusively in manuscripts. (Eisenstein, 1979, I, 49) But printing was the wave of the future, and those long-established sellers of manuscripts who did not join in the printed book market risked failure.

Certain of the printers chose to issue editions of the *Rhetoric*. The number of editions that appeared between 1475 and 1599 indicates that there was a steady European market for the *Rhetoric*.

METHODLOGY

In order to determine what printings of the *Rhetoric* occurred between 1477 and 1599, pertinent bibliographies and library catalogues were used to develop a chronological list of editions.[1] The location (and call numbers, when available) were recorded. Equipped with this list, the researcher visited eighty-three libraries where holdings had been listed or were likely to be found.[2] At the same time, libraries noted in the Primo Catalogo (1962-), the Index Aureliensis (1962-), the Gesamtkatalog der Wiegendrucke (1925-1940), the Gesamtkatalog der Preussischen Bibliotheken (1931-1939), and the National Union Catalogue: Pre-1956 Imprints (1968-1980), that could not be visited because of time and financial restraints,[3] were mailed forms seeking verification of their holdings.[4] Information collected from on-site visits and mailings was catalogued. (see Table Three)

These findings furnished the data for the following report on the availability of printed editions of the *Rhetoric* during the late fifteenth and sixteenth centuries.

THE INCUNABULA AND EARLY 16TH CENTURY EDITIONS

The incunabula were all in Latin. Two of the three lack title pages because the early printers imitated the manuscripts from which they took their copy, and since the scribes signed and dated their work at the end (if they signed and dated it at all), the early printed books followed the same custom and put their details about publication on the colophon. Although before 1500, printers had begun to experiment with title pages and indexes (Eisenstein, 1983, 52), these innovations did not show up on two of the three early editions of the *Rhetoric*.

The earliest printed edition is variously dated from 1475 to 1477. (see Table Three) As no identification marks appear in the volume, details must be inferred from printer's marks. The *Bibliothèque Nationale* that holds two of the four known copies of this work[5] attributes the edition to Paris printers Jean Stall and Pierre César and proposes a publication date of c.1477. The volume reproduced the Latin translation of the *Rhetoric* by George of Trebizond.[6] Vaticanus Latin

4564 preserves the working copy of Trapezuntius' translation (see Plate Ten) that was begun as early as 1442 (1976, 57, n.131) and was probably completed between 1443 and 1446 (1976, 55). It is easy to see from the MS. of his working copy how Trapezuntius went back over his notes and rethought his translation. The fifty-six folios of Trapezuntius' draft are written in several shades of ink. As is often true of writers, the first several pages of the manuscript, and particularly the first few sentences, were given vigorous revision. There are chapter divisons in the working copy, and the following manuscripts of Trapezuntius' translation were divided into chapters:

Berolinensus Borussica Publica Hamil 43

Parisinus MS. Latin 1735

Therefore, it was Trapezuntius himself, as Monfasani verified for us by looking at his microfilm of the working copy from the Vatican, who introduced the chapter headings. By the time of the first printed edition, the customary chapter headings in the Trapezuntius translation were firmly established. Table Two of Chapter Four shows that, although many authors followed the divisions that Trapezuntius established, the custom of dividing the *Rhetoric* into chapters preceded Trapezuntius and has persisted until the most recent Greek editions, commentaries, and English translations of the *Rhetoric*.

Judging from the twenty-three manuscripts of the Trapezuntius translation that have survived (Monfasani, 1984, 699-700), the Trapezuntius translation was a likely choice for the printer because he would not have had much difficulty in obtaining copy. Following the 1475-1477 edition, the Trapezuntius version was reprinted in 1504 in Venice, and in 1515 in Paris. Its numerous appearances later in the 16th century will be detailed below.

Another Latin translation used by early printers was the version by William of Moerbeck.[7] Moerbeck's knowledge of Arabic and Greek plus his strategic location as Bishop of Corinth provided him access to manuscripts now seemingly lost. Therefore, his Latin version, completed by 1273, is somewhat at variance with leading Greek manuscripts. Again, it can be inferred from the existing number of manuscripts of the Moerbeck translation[8] that it was not difficult for a printer to obtain copy.

The confusion that has developed in cataloguing the first printing of the Moerbeck version of 1481 demonstrates the manner in which printers may have worked from manuscripts. It may be that the publisher had three versions to work from, perhaps the following MSS. now housed in the *Bibliothèque Nationale* in Paris:

Latin 16673	Latin 16097*	Latin 7695
1. Hermannus' tr of an Arabic version of A's R, with only four omissions but Hermannus added from Averroës and Avicenna to amplify the text**	a work divided into two parts: a. Alfarabi's introduction to A's R in general + a review of major and minor aspects of A's R***	the Moerbeck tr of A's R
2. the Vetus tr of A's R 3. Hermannus' tr of the Poetics	b. a second part, a short excerpt from Alfarabi's commentary on Aristotle's Rhetoric, using A's Rhetoric to support the interpretations of Alfarabi****	

*as would be natural, Hermannus made his own short "introduction" to Alfarabi's introduction. Boggess termed Hermannus' own work as the "prologue of the 'gloss'" (249)

**Hermannus again added his own introduction to the text of the Rhetoric. (Boggess, 249)

***Alfarabi's introduction to the Rhetoric, later known as a "gloss" or "didascalion" (Boggess, 245)

****"a series of quotations from the Rhetoric alternating with Alfarabi's own expositions" (9, 245). Not only did Alfarabi not extend his work to the conclusion of the Rhetoric, but Hermannus did not translate all of what he had before him that Alfarabi had done (Boggess, 245)

What should the printer select? Assuming his purpose was to publish the *Rhetoric* and the *Poetics*, he rejected Hermannus' piecemeal translation of the *Rhetoric* in MS. 16673. For an introduction to the *Rhetoric*, he choose Alfarabi's Declaratio from MS. 16097, altering it for his own purposes. After seemingly comparing (a) the Hermannus translation of the *Rhetoric* from an unknown source, (b) the Vetus and (c) the Moerbeck translations, the printer chose the Moerbeck from a source such as MS. 7695 and then selected Hermannus' translation of Aristotle's *Poetics*. Hermannus

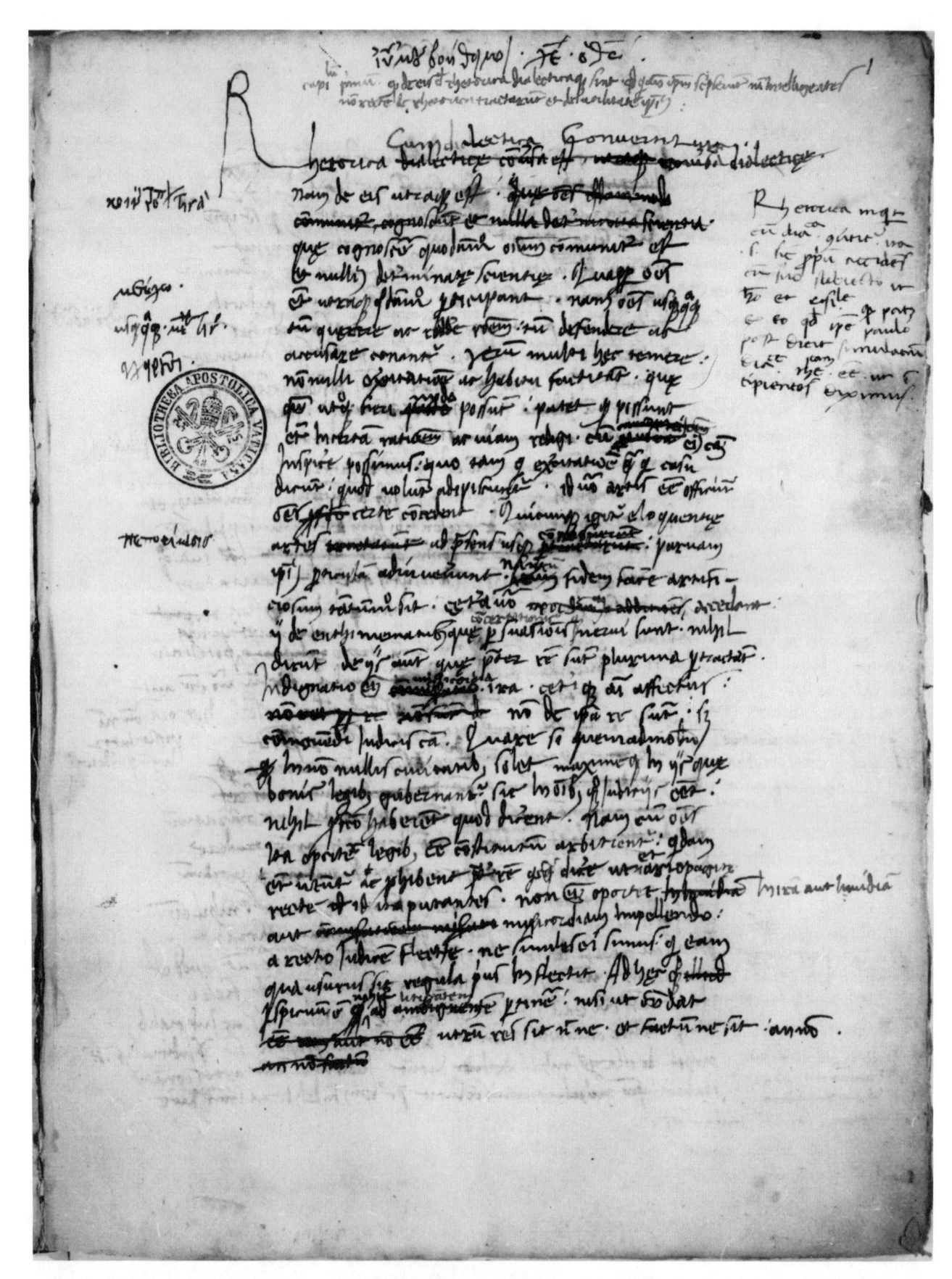

PLATE TEN

Vaticanus 4564, the first folio of the working draft of Trapezuntius' translation of Aristotle's *Rhetoric* courtesy of the Biblioteca Apostolica, the Vatican

Early Printings

became involved only because he translated into Latin from the Arabic the first and third parts of the 1481 edition. (Boggess, 1971)

Therefore the work is sometimes attributed to "Farabi, Mohammad Abu-Nasr al-" and occasionally referenced to Hermannus Alemannus, e.g., the catalogues of the *Bibliothèque Nationale* and the British Library. Such errors may have resulted from the French bibliographers examining only the first work by Alfarabi as translated by Hermannus Alemannus, and so listing the work under Alfarabi, without detecting that the major part of the work was the Moerbeck *Rhetoric* and Averroës' commentary on the *Poetics*. The British bibliographers appear to have copied the French entry.[10]

The Moerbeck version was reprinted in Leipsig in 1499 and again in Venice in 1515. (see Table Three) The Leipsig edition is notable for being the first issue of the *Rhetoric* from Eastern Europe. The third printing of 1515 closely followed B.N. MS. N.A. Latin 1876, a fourteenth century manuscript from the Phillips' collection that included a commentary by Egidio Colonna.[11] For the manner in which the printer varied the format of the printed edition from the manuscript version, see Plates Eleven, Twelve, Thirteen, Fourteen, Fifteen and Sixteen). The Moerbeck version appeared again in Venice in 1537 and in 1540 in Bologna, both with some editing. It was reissued in Frankfurt in 1968.[12]

THE FIRST PRINTED EDITION IN GREEK (1508)

There are three reasons why no Greek edition of the *Rhetoric* was printed in the fifteenth century. First, there were more people who could read Latin than Greek. Early publishers were working on limited capital, and their choices had to reflect what the expanding but yet small public would buy. Second, Greek manuscripts of the *Rhetoric* were not so easy to come by as were the more widely circulated Latin manuscripts. Third, there were fewer printers with Greek type than with Latin type. Lowry (1979, 80) estimated that "only a dozen or so books had been printed entirely in Greek before 1494," of which there had been issued twenty-seven separate editions. Therefore it was going to take a printer of some substance to publish the first complete Greek edition of Aristotle.

Aldus Manutius of Venice was such a publisher. Lowry (1979, 94) said that, as far as he could reconstruct Aldus' business conditions, i.e., the household in Venice, which contained some thirty members, was an "almost incredible mixture of the sweat-shop, the boarding house and the research institute." Aldus had therefore become an entrepreneur of some stature, with considerable investments and resources.

When Aldus exhibited his strength and issued between 1495 and 1498 the first collected works of Aristotle in Greek, he did not include the *Rhetoric* or the *Poetics*, either because he could not locate suitable manuscripts or because he was saving them for a later publication that might be more profitable, or for some other reason that we do not know. It was not until 1508 that Aldus included the Greek text of the *Rhetoric* and the *Poetics* in a collection of works entitled *Rhetores in hoc volumine habentur hi*. According to Kassel (1971, 61-2), Aldus Manutius used for his text what are now Parisinus 2038 and Vaticanus 1580. The reasons why these particular MSS. were available to Aldus are unknown. Printers of that period sought far and wide for suitable manuscript copy and profited from whatever leads or connections they might have. Lowry (1979, 257) commented that it was not possible "to make an exact calculation of the number of copies that Aldus distributed through Europe..." Lowry said that most authorities accept 1,000 copies as the average run, but we can speculate that, for a book of rhetorics, the number may have been smaller. Whatever the number, the edition appears to have sold. The 1508 venture was seemingly successful enough for Aldus to issue his *Rhetorum Graecorum Orationes* in 1515.

Aldus was still under the influence of the manuscript-to-printed book methodology so "he turned to the cursive hand" (Lehmann-Haupt, 1978, 204) as a model for his style of Greek type, in imitation of the Greek scholars who left Constantinople in 1453 after it fell to the Turks. (Lehmann-Haupt, 1978, 204) (see Plates Seventeen, Eighteen, Nineteen, Twenty, and Twenty-One). The writing of the scholarly calligraphers was refined and functional to scholars, but unfortunately was not particularly readable to a wider public. Lowry (1979, 131) stated that Aldus' Greek fonts "strove to reproduce the most fashionable manuscript-styles and so make good a repeated claim that his letters were 'as good, if not better, than any written with a pen.'" Lowry (1979, 131) described Aldus' Greek letters as "a fussy, flamboyant cursive, full of ligatures and ornamental flourishes..." The imitation of Aldus' type style by subsequent printers unfortunately made the text of the *Rhetoric* more difficult to read than was desirable.

PRINTINGS OF THE TRAPEZUNTIUS TRANSLATION AFTER 1515

It was a relatively easy task for sixteenth century

PLATE ELEVEN

The beginning of Parisinus Nouvelle Acquisition Latin 1876 (folio 1r) showing the topography of the commentary
courtesy of the Bibliothèque Nationale, Paris

PLATE TWELVE

Folio 1v of the commentary in Parisinus N. A. Latin 1876 showing that the text of the *Rhetoric* had not yet been presented

courtesy of the Bibliothèque Nationale, Paris

PLATE THIRTEEN

Folio 2r of Parisinus N.A. Latin 1876 illustrating how, in this MS., Aristotle's text was placed in the middle, surrounded by commentary (note the indication of the number of the MS. in the Phillipps' collection)

courtesy of the Bibliothèque Nationale, Paris

PLATE FOURTEEN

The initial folio (a) of the printed edition of 1515, showing how the printer elected to intersperse the text of the *Rhetoric* with the beginning of the commentary and placed both text and commentary in two columns

courtesy of Minerva G.M.B.H., Frankfurt

PLATE FIFTEEN

Folio 2v of Parisinus N.A. Latin 1876 showing how the MS. copy continued placing the text in the center of the page with surrounding commentary

courtesy of the Bibliothèque Nationale, Paris

PLATE SIXTEEN

The second folio (az) of the printed edition of 1515, showing how the printer continued two columns, with the text of the *Rhetoric* interspersed

courtesy of Minerva G.M.B.H., Frankfurt

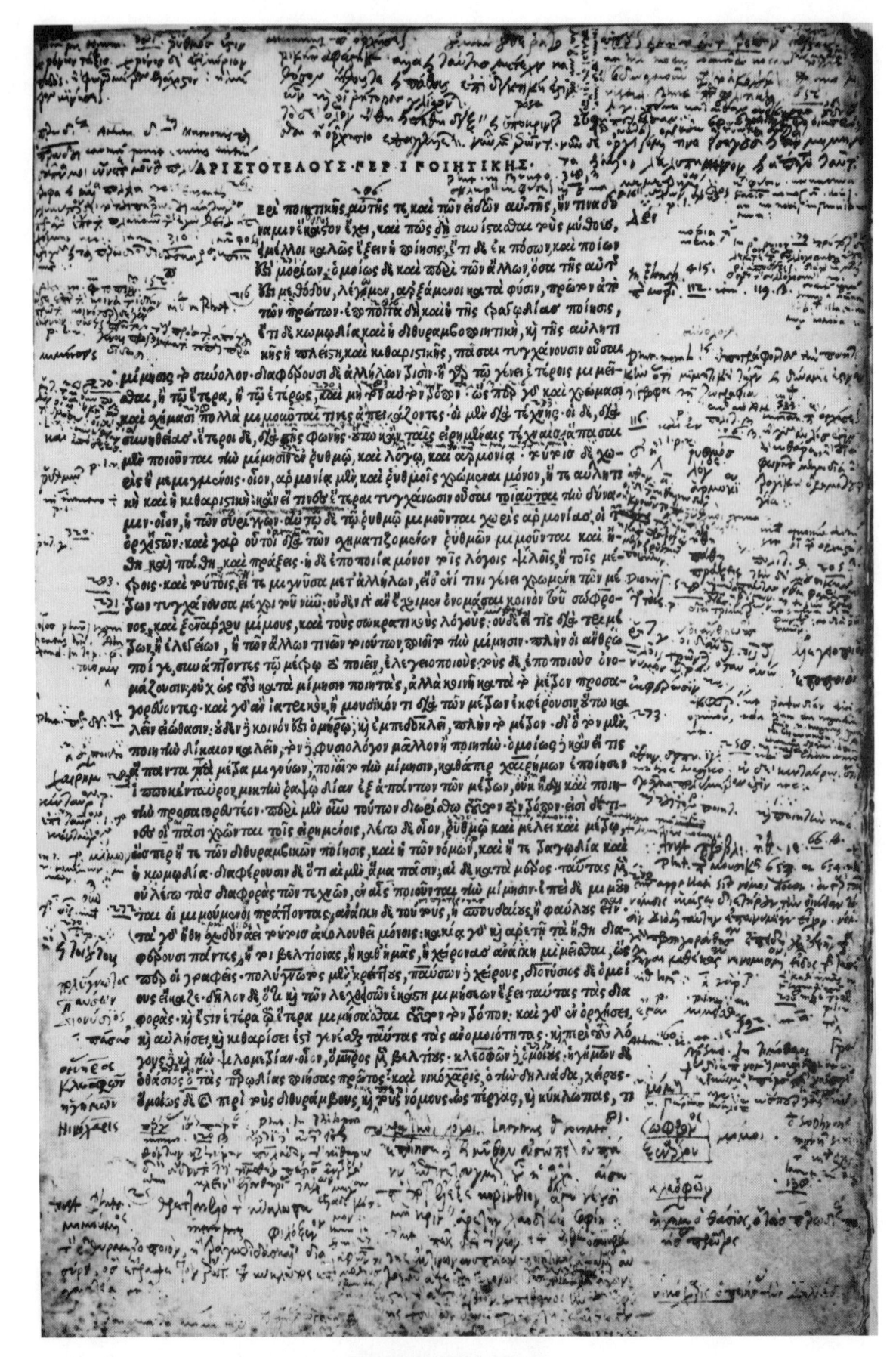

PLATE SEVENTEEN

L.impr.c.n.mss. 81/1b, folio 269, first folio of Victorius' annotations of the 1508 Aldine edition of the *Poetics* courtesy of the Bayerische Staatsbibliothek, Munich

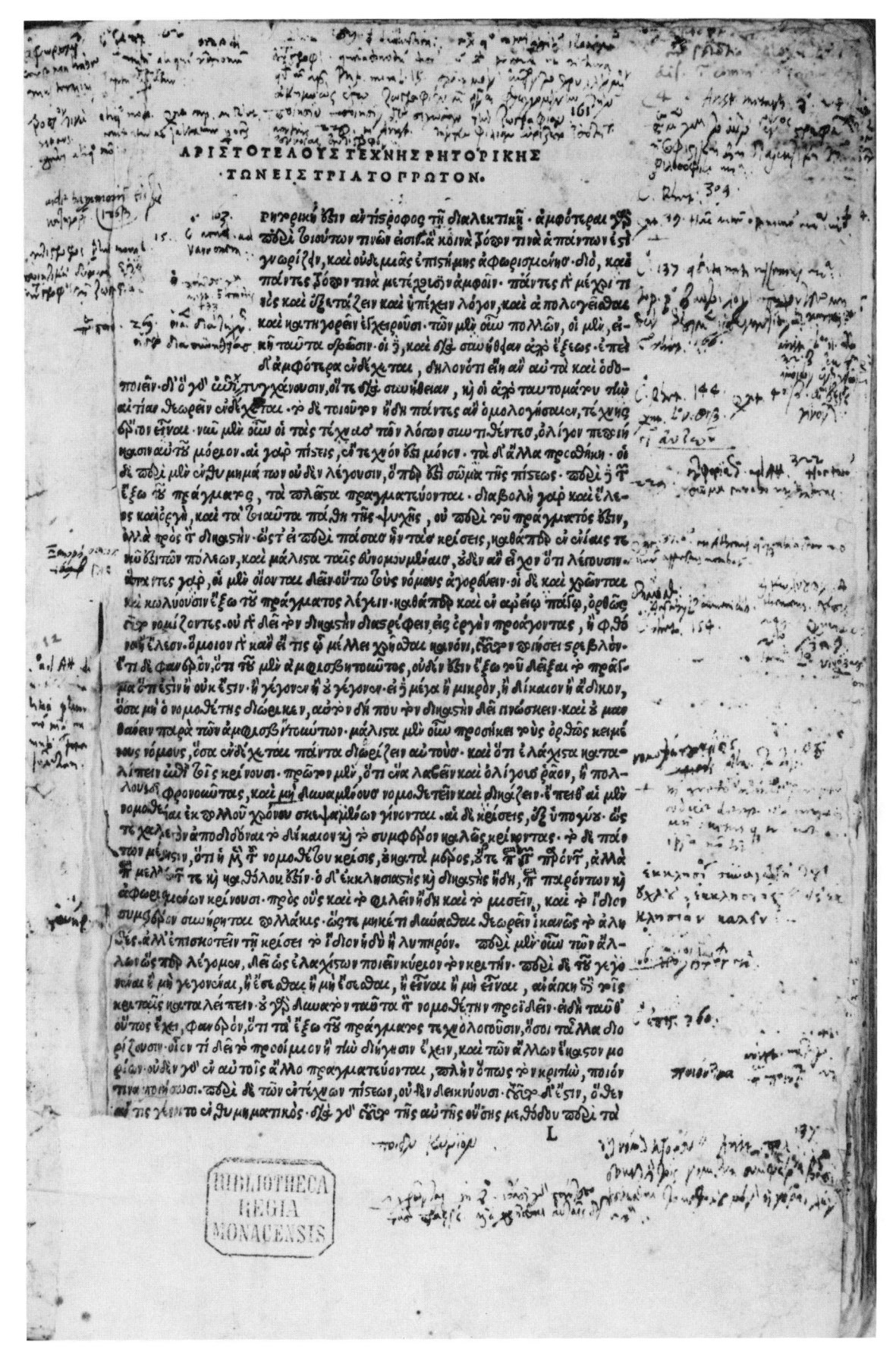

PLATE EIGHTEEN

L.impr.c.n.mss.81/1b, folio 161, showing the first folio of the 1508 Aldine edition of the *Rhetoric*, annotated by Victorius

courtesy of the Bayerische Staatsbibliothek, Munich

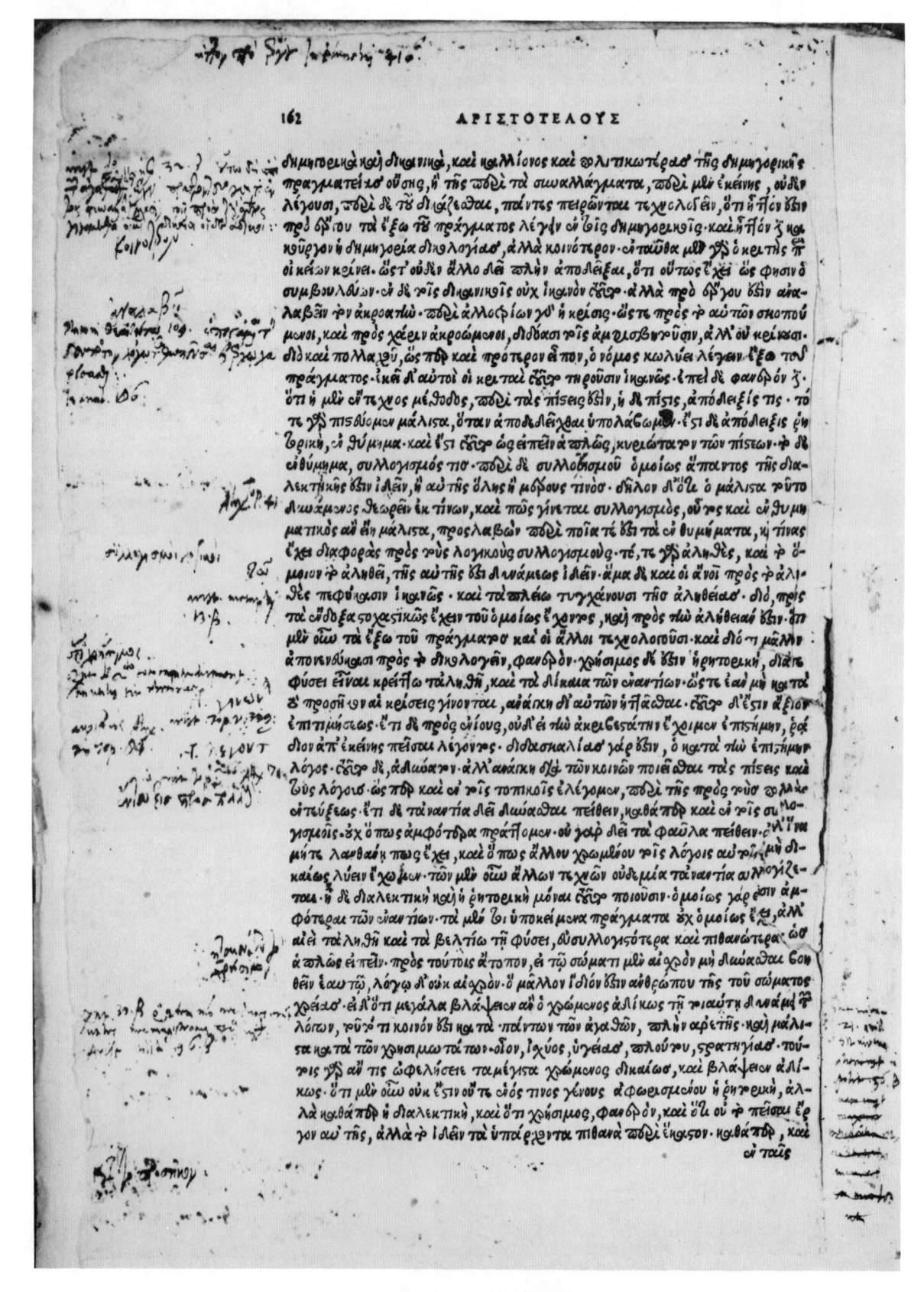

PLATE NINETEEN

L.impr.c.n.mss.81/1b, folio 162, showing the second folio of the 1508 Aldine edition of the *Rhetoric*, annotated by Victorius

courtesy of the Bayerische Staatsbibliothek, Munich

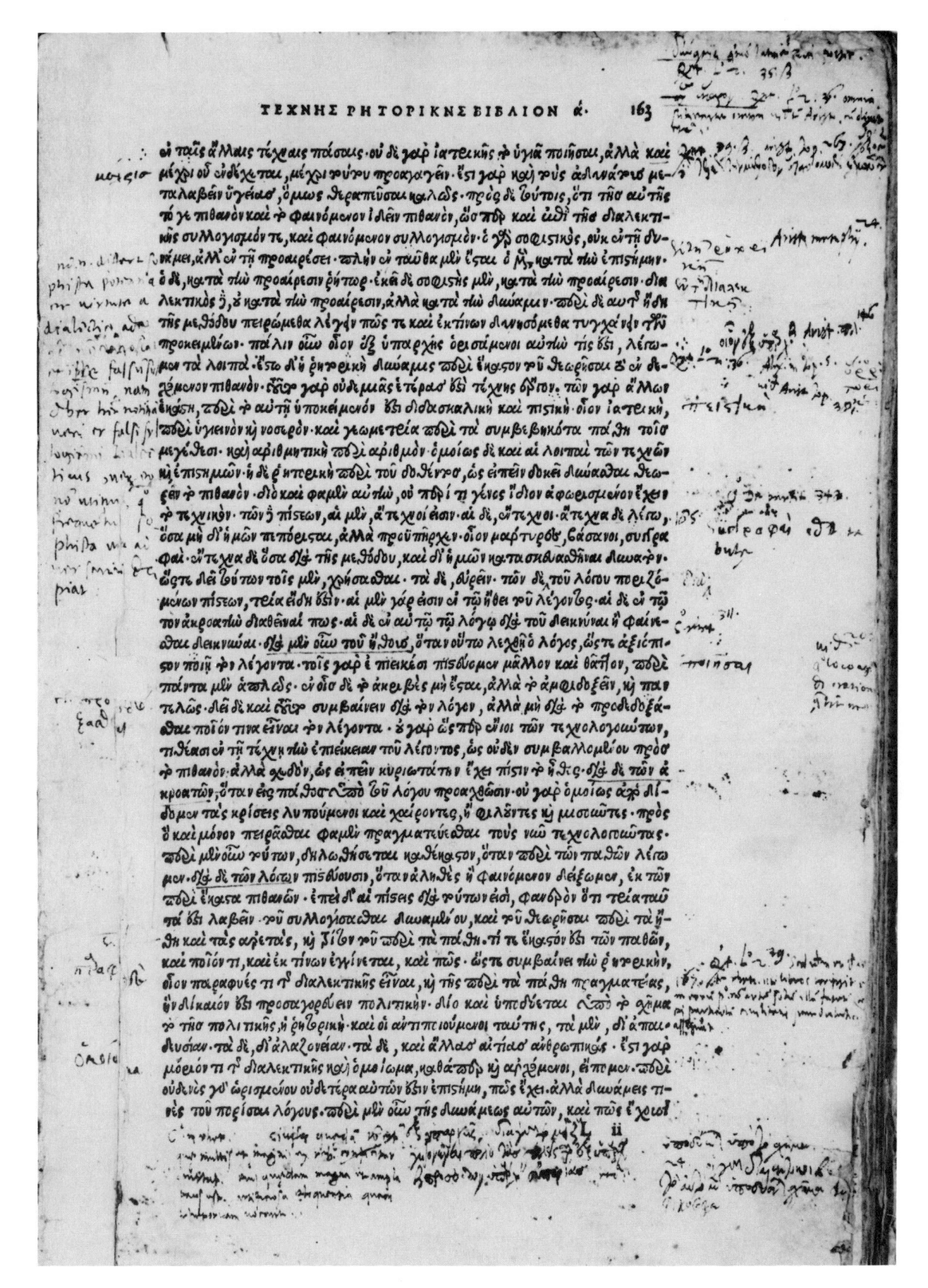

PLATE TWENTY

L.impr.c.n.mss 81/1b, folio 163, showing the third folio of the 1508 Aldine edition of the *Rhetoric*,

annotated by Victorius

courtesy of the Bayerische Staatsbibliothek, Munich

PLATE TWENTY-ONE

L.impr.c.n.mss. 81/1b, folio 164, showing the fourth folio of the 1508 Aldine edition of the *Rhetoric*, annotated by Victorius

courtesy of the Bayerische Staatsbibliothek, Munich

printers to reissue the Trapezuntius edition. Evidently a combination of a literary revival plus the desire of the wealthy to develop home libraries made sales profitable. Table Two points out that at least twenty-two printings of the Trapezuntius were issued between 1530 and 1581.[13] As the century progressed, new translations of the *Rhetoric* appeared, causing publishers to shift from Trapezuntius to one of the more recent humanists who could boast he had consulted with the amended revised Greek texts. As Schmitt (1983, 64) observed, "since Aristotle remained the core of instruction in the arts, it was obviously quite important to read him in an accurate, as well as stylish, Latin version." But it was the Trapezuntius edition that introduced much of the early Latin-reading public to Aristotle's *Rhetoric* and demonstrated that the *Rhetoric* would be a successful venture for printers.

GREEK EDITIONS PRECEDING 1548

While the printers kept the public supplied with a steady sequence of Latin translations by Trapezuntius and others, Greek editions were being issued steadily but more cautiously. The first Greek edition printed after the 1508 Aldine was issued at Basel in 1529, followed by eight other printings before Victorius issued his edition of 1548. (See Table One) Of these ten Greek editions, two deserve comment because of their individuality.

First, the two volume set of Aristotle's works, released in Basel in 1531 and again in 1539, undoubtedly owed its widespread sale to the fame of its editors, Desiderius Erasmus (see Plate Twenty-Two) and Simon Grynaeus. The data for this study demonstrated what would be expected, that more copies of the late sixteenth century editions are now housed in libraries than are copies of the fifteenth and early sixteenth century editions. The Basel Greek edition is an exception to this trend. Of the 1531 edition, forty-three were located, not including those identified by previous researchers at Kiel, Bonn and Berlin and reported by those libraries as destroyed. Forty-one copies of the 1539 reissue were located, with Kiel reporting that its copy was lost in World War II, and Griefswald and Würzburg certifying that their collections had had copies that are now missing.[14] The relatively large number of copies of the 1531 and 1539 printings still in existence demonstrate that the Erasmus-Grynaeus version was widely disseminated.

The second Greek edition making a special contribution appeared in 1536 under the editorship of Joannis Francisco Trincavelli and was a crude first attempt to establish a Greek text superior to that of the 1508 Aldine edition. (see Plates Twenty-Three, Twenty-Four and Twenty-Five) Trincavelli, who according to Kassel (1971, 99) consulted Parisinus 1869 or one of its descendents, reprinted the 1508 Aldine edition, noting variations in the margins. However, because of his inferior sources, Trincavelli's work fostered additional errors. But he did challenge the Aldine version and was therefore a forerunner to Victorius. The library in Munich has a copy of the Trincavelli, heavily annotated by Victorius.[15]

As Kassel pointed out (1971, p.98, n.2) Victorius referred to the Trincavelli as *"Venetiis hoc volumen excuserunt,"* while Buhle cited it as "Veneta." This can result in some confusion since Spengel in his 1867 edition referred to the 1546 Gryphius edition as "Veneta" because, as Kassel explained, Spengel did not have available to him the 1536 Trincavelli, and Roemer followed Spengel's lead. Kassel, on the other hand, for purposes of clarification, called the Trincavelli *"die ältere Ausgabe."* (1971, 98, n.2)

Kassel's collations led him to conclude that the 1546 edition was directly dependent upon the 1536 Trincavelli, including a similarity of the marginal variants. (1971, 98, n.2) (see Plates Twenty-Six, Twenty-Seven and Twenty-Eight)

A COLLATED GREEK TEXT: VICTORIUS' THREE EDITIONS OF 1548, 1549 AND 1579

(see Plates Twenty-Nine, Thirty and Thirty-One)

Victorius, for almost fifty years professor of rhetoric at Florence,[16] had been contemplating an edition of the *Rhetoric* since April of 1542. To prepare himself, he had been studying the *Ethics* and the *Poetics* (Niccolai, 1914, 227-8). As Niccolai (1914, 227) pointed out, Barbaro's Latin translation, published posthumously in Venice in 1544, did not supply the need for a definitive text. (see Plate Thirty-Two) Barbaro did not produce as definitive a text as was possible from the resources available at that time. Therefore, when, in his workroom in Florence, Victorius assembled a number of manuscripts and printed editions of the *Rhetoric* and began his restoration of the Greek text, he was to produce a restored Greek text that exerted wide influence in the classical world.[17]

Eisenstein (1979, I, 199) reminded us that sixteenth century scholars worked under disadvantageous conditions. "They did not have access to well-ordered collections of printed books.... Most of the texts that they handled were of uncertain origin," said Eisenstein, "and labeled with titles only recently assigned them." But, although these limitations do apply to Victorius, he was more fortunate than others. Victorius had

PLATE TWENTY-TWO

Erasmus of Rotterdam from Jean Jacques Boissard, *Icones uinquaginta vivorum illustrium* (Frankfurt, M. Becker, 1597-99), vol. 1, p. 220.

courtesy of the Folger Shakespeare Library, Washington, D.C.

Early Printings

PLATE TWENTY-THREE

The conclusion of Book One and the beginning of Book Two of the 1536 Trincavelli edition showing alternative readings in the margins

courtesy of the library of the University of Illinois at Champaign-Urbana

PLATE TWENTY-FOUR

The continuation of Book Two of the 1536 Trincavelli edition, showing a continuation of the alternative readings in the margins

Early Printings

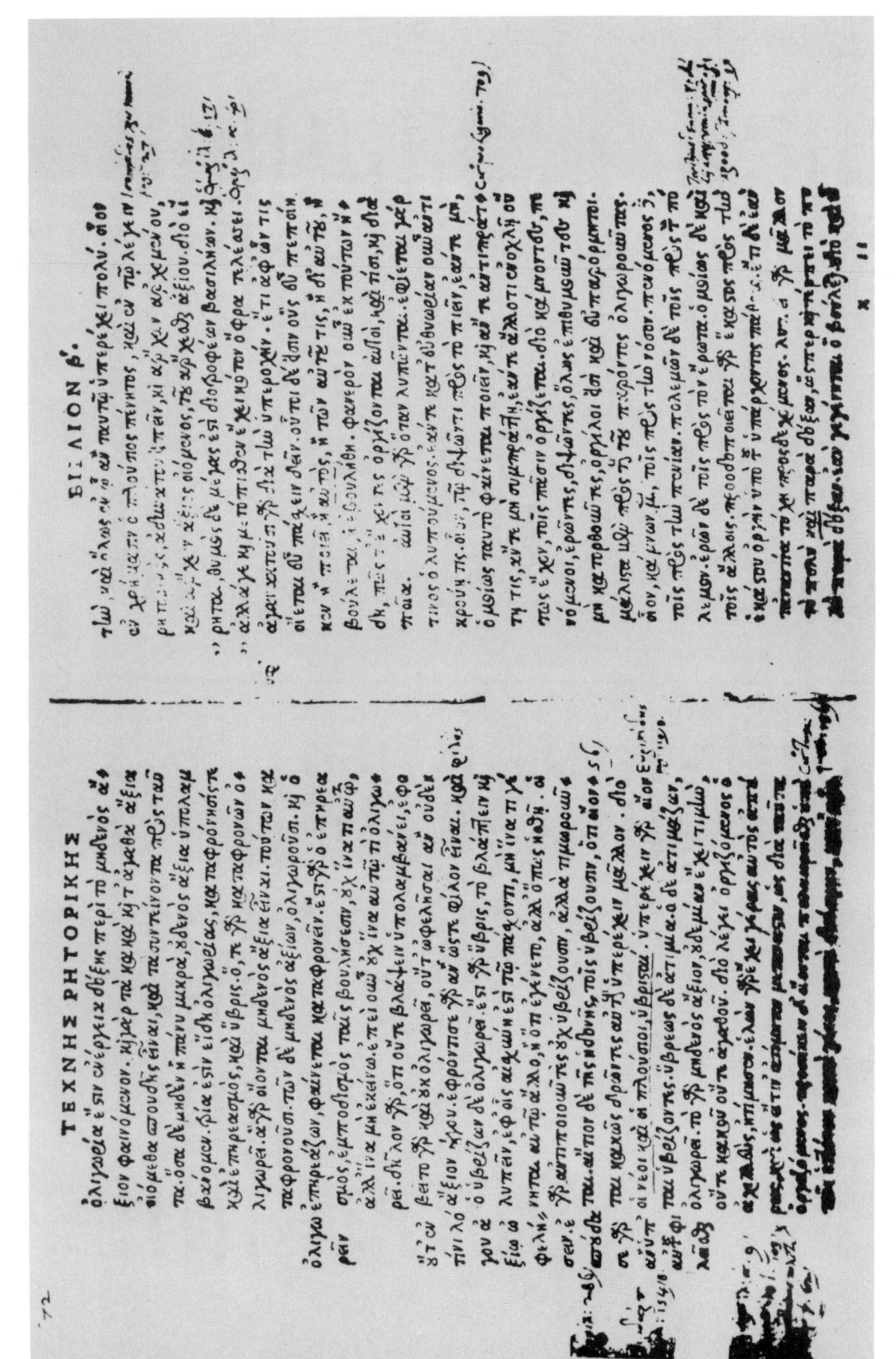

PLATE TWENTY-FIVE

The continuation of Book Two of the 1536 Trincavelli edition, showing again the alternative readings in the margins

courtesy of the library of the University of Illinois at Champaign-Urbana

PLATE TWENTY-SIX

The same conclusion of Book One and the beginning of Book Two of the 1546 edition, illustrating the similarity of the 1536 and 1546 editions

courtesy of the library of the University of Illinois at Champaign-Urbana

Early Printings

PLATE TWENTY-SEVEN

The continuation of Book Two of the 1546 edition, showing the similarity of the alternative readings to the 1536 edition

courtesy of the library of the University of Illinois at Champaign-Urbana

PLATE TWENTY-EIGHT

The further continuation of Book Two of the 1546 edition, showing how the similarity of the alternative readings to the 1536 edition continues

PETRI VICTORII
COMMENTARII
IN TRES LIBROS
ARISTOTELIS
DE ARTE DICENDI.

POSITIS ANTE SIN
GVLAS DECLARA=
TIONES GRÆCIS VER
BIS AVCTORIS.

FLORENTIÆ
In officina Bernardi Iunctæ.
M. D. XLVIII.

PLATE TWENTY-NINE
title page of the Victorius Florence edition of 1548
courtesy of the Library of the University of Illinois at Champaign-Urbana

PETRI VICTORII
Commentarij longe doctissimi, in tres libros Aristotelis de Arte dicendi, nunc primum in Germania editi.

Cum locuplete rerum & uerborum in ijsdem memorabilium Indice.

BASILEAE.

PLATE THIRTY
title page of the Victorius Basel edition of 1549
courtesy of the Library of the University of Illinois at Champaign-Urbana

PETRI VICTORII
COMMENTARII
In tres libros Aristotelis de arte dicendi.

Positis ante singulas declarationes, valde studio & noua cura ipsius auctas, Graecis verbis auctoris, iisque fideliter Latine expressis.

Cum vetere exquisito indice, cui multa addita sunt, modo animaduersa.

FLORENTIAE.
Ex officina Iunctarum. An. CIƆ IƆ LXXIX.

Cum licentia & priuilegio.

PLATE THIRTY-ONE

title page of the Victorius Florence edition of 1579

courtesy of the library of the University of Illinois at Champaign-Urbana

RHETORICORVM
ARISTOTELIS, LIBRI TRES,
INTERPRETE HERMOLAO
BARBARO P. V.
COMMENTARIA IN EOSDEM
DANIELIS BARBARI.

PAVLI GERARDI OPERA,
CAVTVM EST SENATVS VENETI.
Et Pauli. III. Pont. Max. necnon Cæsaris Decreto, ne quis alius per
Decennium hos Libros imprimat, aut impressos vendat.
M. D. XXXXIIII.

PLATE THIRTY-TWO
title page of the 1544 Venice Barbaro edition
courtesy of the Library of the University of Illinois at Champaign-Urbana

Early Printings

powerful friends to help him. Francesco Pucci and Cardinal Nicolas Rudolfi assisted him in locating manuscripts. (Kassel, 1971, 100) Francesco Medici advised him on the interpretation of selected passages.[18] Victorius' most important find was what is now known as Parisinus Grec MS. 1741 which, as Kassel pointed out, was in itself sufficient for Victorius to straighten out most of the corruptions that had entered the Greek text.[19] Victorius had other manuscripts available to him as well, including the Latin version of Moerbeck. He also used three MSS. now housed in the *Bayerische Staatsbibliothek* in Munich, bearing *marginalia* in his hand.[20] A note in Munich's L.impr.c.n.mass. 81/1a, Victorius' working copy of the 1508 Aldine edition, states that Victorius must also have had Vaticanus 2228 available to him.

Victorius' methodology was what one would expect. He began by making notations in the margin of his copy of the 1508 edition. When this procedure became too confining, he clipped ff.161-234 from the Aldine edition and mounted them in the middle of blank pages so that he could write his emendations in the margins. The annotated versions of the 1508 edition for both the *Rhetoric* and the *Poetics*, bearing Victorius' bookmark, are extant in Munich under L.impr.c.n.mass. 81/1b. (see Plates Thirty-Three, Thirty-Four, Thirty-Five, and Thirty-Six) The pages clipped from the original edition had to be pasted onto small pieces of paper sticking out of the binding of 81/1b. (see Plate Thirty-Three)

The notes Victorius made in the margins from both manuscripts and printed editions[21] are copious.[22] Although Victorius was a careful scholar, he was not a neat one. Furthermore, he saw no need to acknowledge from what sources he eventually took a particular reading. The scholarship of his time did not require such referencing. Therefore the notes he put in the margins of the 1508 edition are a hodge-podge, meaningful to himself but difficult for anyone else to follow. Undoubtedly, from these notes, Victorius prepared a copy for his publisher. That copy has not been preserved. It could have been discarded by the printer, presumably when Victorius returned it with the proofs to be corrected. Or Victorius himself could have discarded it. It may surface—in Mannheim, in Munich, or in Florence. What an interesting document that would be to see!

A number of Victorius' sources were corrupt. Kassel's careful collations led him to conclude that the Aldine text was based upon two corrupt manuscripts. The Trincavelli edition, concluded Kassel (1971, 98-99), also bore errors. Victorius himself realized that two of the Monacensis MSS. contained faults, and that Monacensis 175 (see Plates Thirty-Four, Thirty-Five and Thirty-Six) was based upon Trincavelli. If we keep in mind that Victorius did not realize the dominant position that Parisinus Grec 1741[23] should have assumed in his collations, we can comprehend better Victorius' puzzlement until it became clear to him that some of his sources were more authentic than others. As was stated above, Victorius was meticulous.[24] He knew he was breaking new ground. He deplored the errors of previous scribes and editors and did not wish to add to the confusion. Kassel concluded that Victorius proceeded with *"übergrossen, oft in Anstglichkeit ausartenden Vorsicht,"*[25] avoiding conjecture and questioning each point carefully.

Even with its limitations, Victorius' critical edition of 1548 made changes in the Greek text that were to be honored repeatedly during the remainder of the sixteenth century and during the centuries to follow. Editors customarily referenced their Greek and Latin editions to Victorius' readings. His interest in the *Rhetoric* continued, for not only did a second printing of the 1548 Florence edition appear in Basel in 1549, but Victorius issued a new edition in Florence in 1579, accompanied for the first time by Victorius' own Latin translation.

LATIN TRANSLATIONS OF THE SECOND HALF OF THE SIXTEENTH CENTURY

Although we can look to the Greek editions for progress in establishing a definitive text, we need to consider the degree of circulation of the Latin translations to measure the revival of the *Rhetoric* in the latter part of the sixteenth century. We can capture a part of the thrill that some students and scholars must have experienced by comparing the discovery of the Greek texts with what would happen today if an archeologist were to announce that the library at Alexandria had been discovered in some secluded caves. Certainly there would be an immediate market for those long-lost works, just as there developed, more slowly to be sure but still steadily, a market for the rediscoveries and reinterpretations of the manuscript finds of the fifteenth and sixteenth centuries. Without doubt the *Rhetoric* became available to play its part in the Renaissance.

Who were the translators who began to replace Trapezuntius as the sixteenth century progressed? In contrast to the trend reported by Schmitt (1983, 70) who found that, during the sixteenth century, many more translations were produced in the North than in Italy, the translators of the *Rhetoric* were largely Italians. The influence of Victorius we have already

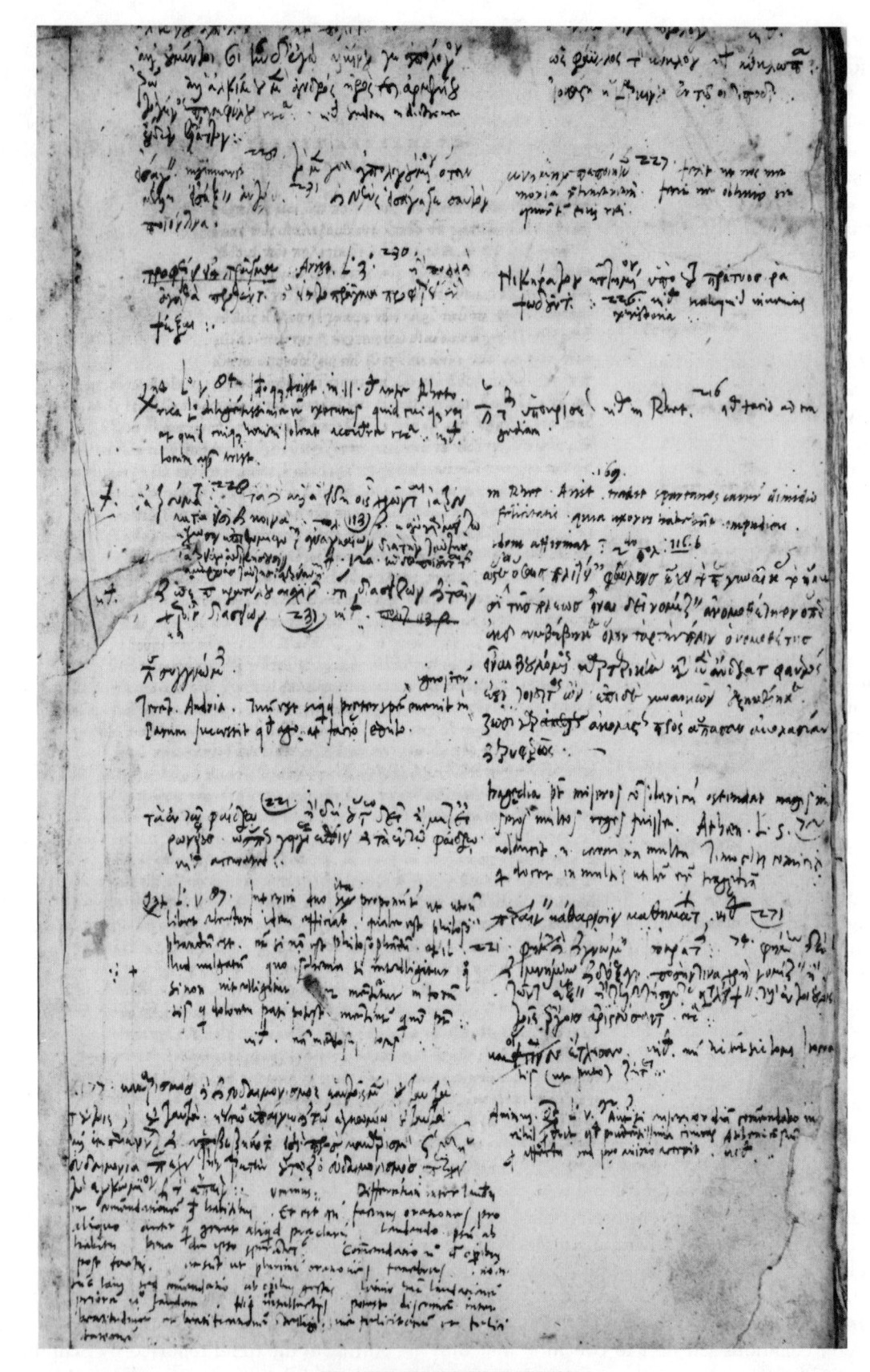

PLATE THIRTY-THREE

L.impr.c.n.mss.81/1a, showing where the pages of the *Rhetoric* of the 1508 Aldine edition were clipped from the book to be mounted separately, apparently so that Victorius could make his comments more easily, although there is always the possibility that the dismantling of the 1508 edition was done after Victorius' death. The last page of Victorius' comments remained within the original edition and is reproduced here

courtesy of the Bayerische Staatsbibliothek, Munich

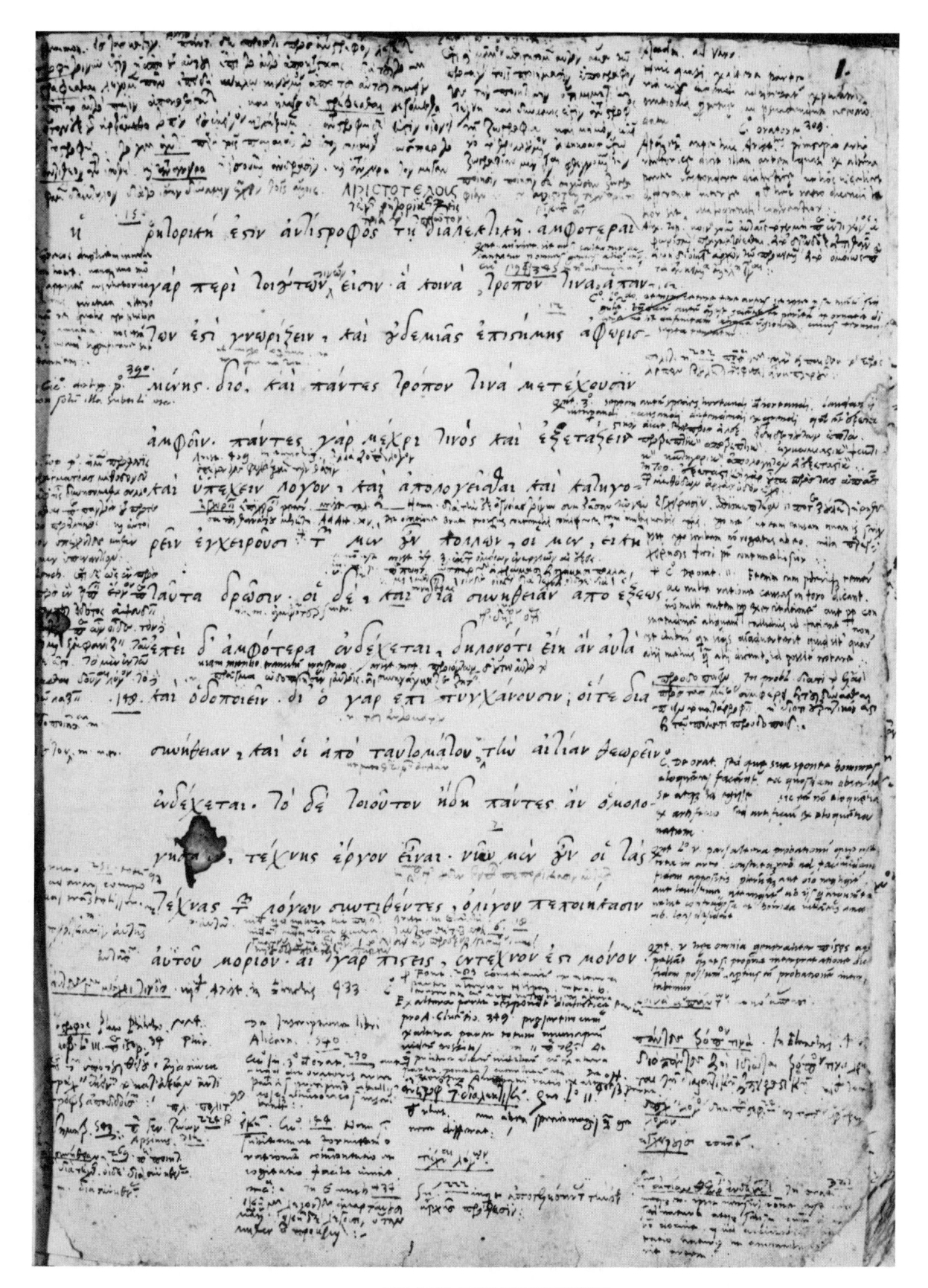

PLATE THIRTY-FOUR

folio 1r of Monacensis Graec 175, showing annotations by Victorius

courtesy of the Bayerische Staatsbibliothek, Munich

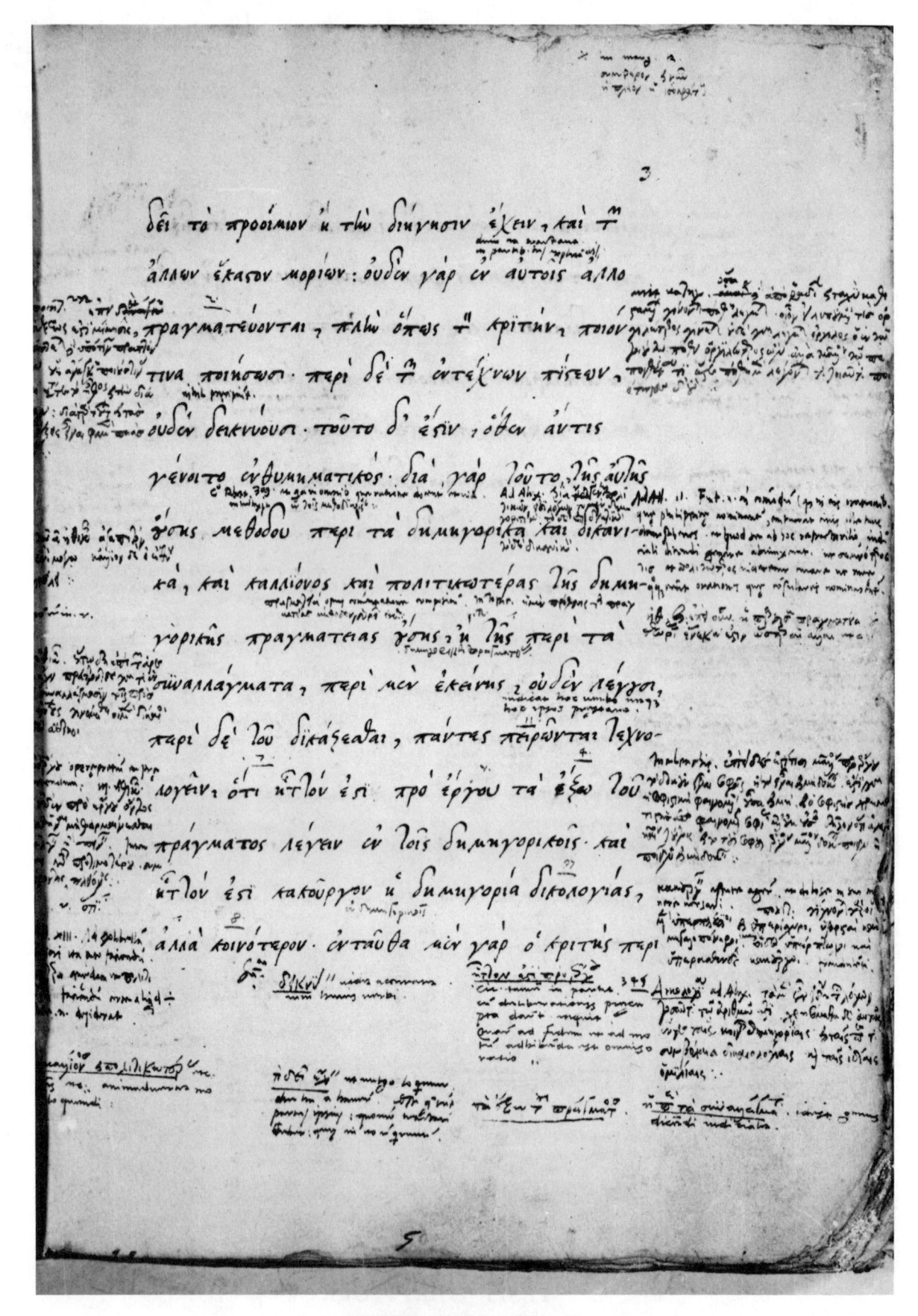

PLATE THIRTY-FIVE

folio 3r of Monacensis Graec 175, showing continued annotations by Victorius

courtesy of the Bayerische Staatsbibliothek, Munich

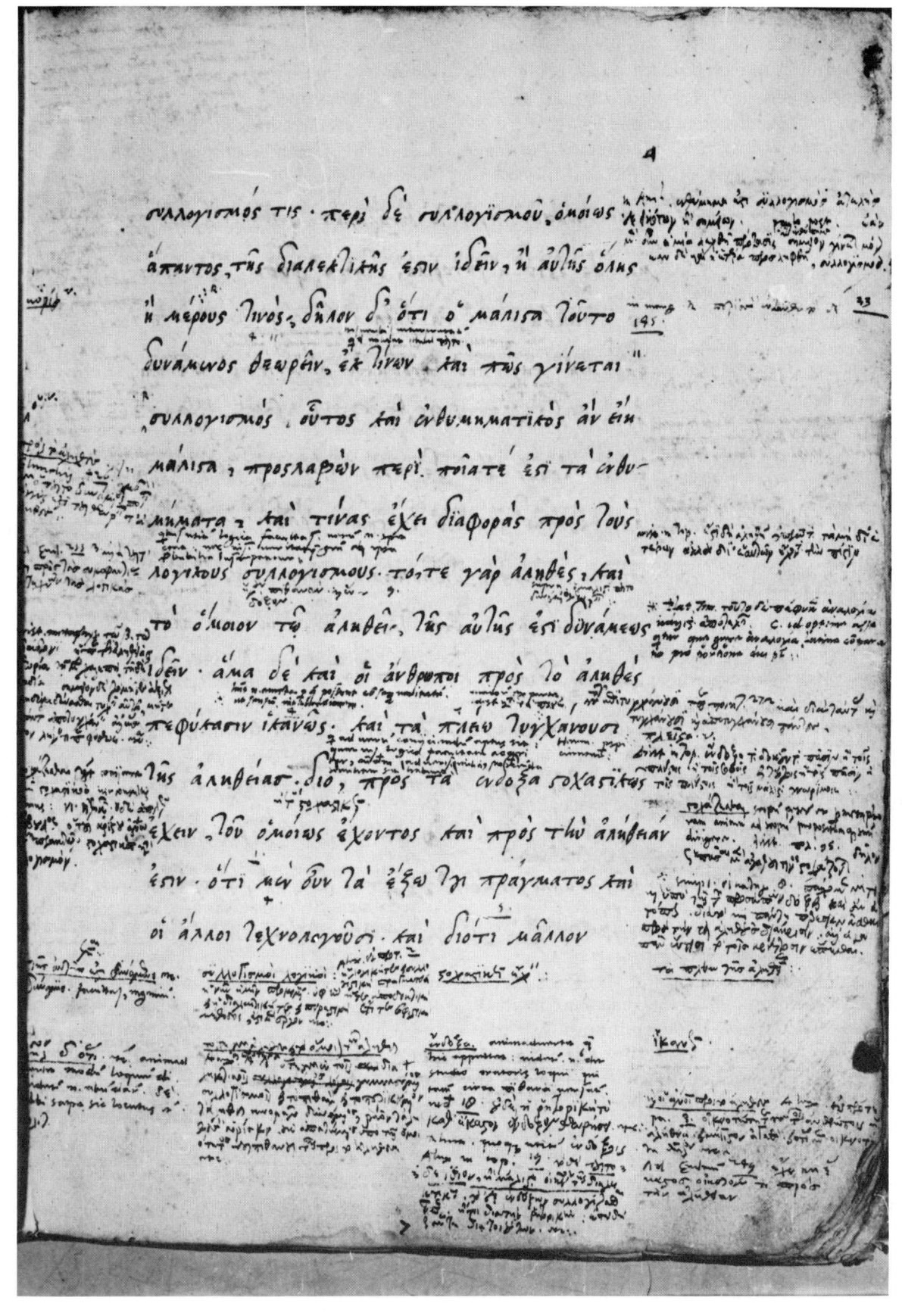

PLATE THIRTY-SIX

folio 4r of Monacensis Graec 175, showing further annotations by Victorius

courtesy of the Bayerische Staatsbibliothek, Munich

discussed. Although Victorius was the holder of the chair of eloquence at Florence, he was also something of a politician and statesperson. (see Plates Thirty-Seven A and B) The five other humanists whose translations appeared between 1544 and 1599 did play minor roles in the politics of the day, but they were largely professors who found in the *Rhetoric* a valuable instrument for their teaching. Four of the five were native Italians, namely, Hermolao Barbaro (1454-1493) of Venice and Rome;[26] Antonio Maioragio (1514-?) of Milan[27] (see Plate Thirty-Eight); Carlo Sigonio (1524-1584) of Modena (see Plate Thirty-Nine), Venice and Padua;[28] and Antonio Riccobono (1541-1599) of Padua.[29] The fifth, Huguenot Marc Antoine Muret (1526-1585), who translated only the first two books of the *Rhetoric*, fled Paris to establish himself in Rome.[30] All five of these humanists had their versions printed three or more times[31] and accumulated a total of thirty-seven printings of the *Rhetoric*, largely published in Venice, Lyon, Paris and Basel. (See Table Two) There were additional single issue translations in 1570 by the Calvinist John Sturm (1507-1589), principal of a preparatory school in Strasbourg, and in 1598 by Emilio Porto (c.1550-1610) of the University of Lausanne.[32] As Kristeller (1955, 50) noted, "Aristotle's *Rhetoric*, which in the Middle Ages had been neglected by the professional rhetoricians and treated by the scholastic philosophers as an appendix to the *Ethics* and *Politics*, became during the sixteenth century an important text for the humanist rhetoricians." Victorius, Barbaro, Maioragio, Sigonio, Riccobono and Muret were prominent among those humanist professors who provided themselves and others with the *Rhetoric* as a viable text.

GREEK EDITIONS BETWEEN 1549 AND 1599

The 1548 Victorius collation of the manuscripts had an immediate influence on later printings. As early as 1549, a Greek edition issued in Paris acknowledged that its text reflected Victorius' readings, and the 1550 reissue of the Erasmus-Grynaeus edition acknowledged its indebtedness to Victorius. Nineteen printings of various Greek editions appeared during this latter half of the sixteenth century. (See Table One) Although this number does not match the flow of Latin translations discussed above, it demonstrates that there was a market for the Greek text. Early publishers were no different from their contemporaries. Again, what was printed had to be profitable. Even the well-established publishers had not the reserve resources to take many risks. Nineteen printings by a variety of publishers is an indication that the *Rhetoric* in Greek remained available to scholars of the Renaissance.

Two Greek editions published during the second half of the sixteenth century deserve discussion. As was stated earlier, the preservation of sizeable numbers of an edition in contemporary libraries can be interpreted as some evidence that the edition was in wide use at the time. This researcher was impressed not only with the some seventy-five copies of the *Rhetoric* that have survived of the ten volume Frankfurt edition of 1584-1596,[33] but also with the number of these editions that were well annotated in Greek and Latin, and showed signs of use.[34]

The massive Greek 1590 edition of Aristotle's works in two volumes has caused bibliographers confusion because volume one is sometimes credited to the publisher Jacobus Bubonius and sometimes to the publisher Guillelmus Laemarius. The library at Halle has two volumes one's with the varying credits. The situation gets even more complex with the knowledge that Laemarius was a Geneva publisher named Leymarie who only attributed his printings to Lyon, so they would not offend the censors in the Roman Catholic countries. The *Rhetoric* however, located in volume two, is consistently credited to Bubonius. The copies of the 1590 edition at Braunsberg, Bonn and Kiel were destroyed in World War II, but the Berlin copy survived, making a total of forty-six extant copies identified for this study.

SUMMARY

It can be concluded that numerous fifteenth and sixteenth century Greek and Latin printings of Aristotle's *Rhetoric* were available to facilitate scholarship. The advent of the printing press, therefore, greatly increased the potential use of the *Rhetoric* during the Renaissance. Recorded for this study were seventy-two printings in Latin, nineteen in Greek, and eleven in Greek and Latin, totaling one hundred and two printings between the years 1477 and 1599.[35]

Furthermore, the continuing interest of printers in the *Rhetoric* suggests not only that there were copies available, but that printers could make a profit from their ventures. The repeated printings of the Latin translations of Trapezuntius, Barbaro, Maioragio, Sigonio, Riccobono and Muret would indicate a growing demand for the *Rhetoric* that encouraged early printers to keep the treatise in press.

Third, the early printings illustrate what should be obvious but not always is, that printers secured manuscripts to furnish them copy. Sometimes the printers

Early Printings 75

PLATE THIRTY-SEVEN A

Victorius' bookplate

courtesy of the Bayerische Staatsbibliothek, Munich

PLATE THIRTY-SEVEN B

Medallions struck in honor of Victorius

courtesy of the Bayerische Staatsbibliothek, Munich

Early Printings

M. ANTONII MAIORAGII
Sepulchrum Mediolani in porticu, addita dextro ædis diui Ambrosij lateri, cum hac inscriptione conspicitur.

M. ANTONIO
MAIORAGIO
DICENDI MAGISTRO
SINGVLARI,
LATINIS GRAECISQ. LITERIS
PERPOLITO,
ET LIBRIS EDITIS ILLVSTRI,
QVI PVBLICE DOCVIT ANN. XIIII.
VIXIT XLI.
BARTHOLOMAEVS COMES
VXORIS FRATRI
B. M. POSVIT.

C. PETRONII VENETI.

MAIORAGIVS LOQVITVR.

Ediderdm iam multa tibi, cordata iuuentus;
   Quæ legis, in studijs ocia grata terens:
Et multò lætus mox edere plura parabam,
   Condita tunc fuerant quæ mihi scripta domi.
Plurima quin etiam meditabar scribere, solers
   Dum cupio studijs inuigilare tuis.
Approperata nimis, mors importuna, sed omnes
   Lusit conatus, destituitq; meos:
Nec malè tornatos incudi sæua libellos

Reddere me siuit, nec reuocare rudes:
Nec iam finitos permisit promere capsis,
   Nec passa extremam est his adhibere manum.
Rursus inexpletos imperfectosq; reliqui,
   Quos aggressus eram scribere nuper ego.
At tu, cui uiuus semper prodesse cupiui;
   Ossibus, & cineri fausta precare meo:
Et, si quid uitij rude sæpe uolumen habebit,
   Emenda; idq; mihi non licuisse, puta.

✳ 2   M. ANTONII

PLATE THIRTY-EIGHT

a medallion-like etching of Maioragius from the title page of the 1563 Basel Latin edition

courtesy of the Bayerische Staatsbibliothek, Munich

PLATE THIRTY-NINE

title page of the Sigonio 1577 Rostock edition; the representation of Aristotle could possibly have been used to depict a number of authors or translators, because in the sixteenth century one sketch was attributed to several persons.

Early Printings

followed rather literally the format of the manuscript, whereas in other instances they not only changed the topography but felt free to make content changes.

Fourth, scholars had access to Victorius' contribution toward reconstructing an authentic Greek text. Although Victorius had sources that would have permitted establishing a better restoration than he achieved, his pioneer efforts at collation were a decided improvement over the Aldine text of 1508 and had a strong influence on subsequent issues of the *Rhetoric*, both in Greek and Latin. Only in the nineteenth and twentieth centuries was Victorius' work superceded by the more definitive editions appearing in England and Germany.

The somewhat restricted areas where the *Rhetoric* was repeatedly published indicate that its dissemination depended upon its purchase by private scholars and collectors. Venice, Basel, Lyon,[36] Paris[37] and Frankfurt were locations where the climate of the times and the development of trade centers encouraged printers to work. The middlemen, i.e., "the translators, the printers, the travellers, the foreigners who visited Italy. . ." (Burke, 119 ff.) became the distributors of the rediscovered ideas from the ancient world. However, even assuming wide dissemination, the extent of the influence of the *Rhetoric* on instruction and scholarly thought during the fifteenth and sixteenth centuries is an area of research that has only "been provisionally covered."[38]

LaRusso (1983, 54) made the discouraging comment that, during the Italian Renaissance, if contributions by rhetorical scholars appeared at all, they "bear the unmistakable stain of toasts offered by arriving relatives come late to the banquet." However, there were the five humanist professors plus Victorius whose Greek and Latin versions of the *Rhetoric* were repeatedly published in Italy during the Renaissance. And there were the two printings of the Victorious Latin translation, and the one-time issuance of the Sturm and Porto versions. At least the quest for the contribution of the *Rhetoric* to sixteenth century thought would be worth more effort than has been made so far.

For inspiration, researchers can look to Artz' short essay, "The Significance of Renaissance Humanism." (1978, 310-313). We have touched here on one of the contributions that Artz claimed for the humanists, i.e., "the collecting, copying, and diffusion of manuscripts" (1978, 310). "In the end," said Artz, "the Humanists restored the whole surviving heritage of Greek and Latin Literature, edited all of it, and later, brought out printed editions of the whole." (1978, 310) After pointing out the several areas to which the humanists made contributions, Artz ended by saying that "humanism was one of the currents, though not the deepest one, out of which came the Protestant Reformation." (1978, 313) Our research was able only to touch briefly upon this area, e.g., in investigating the use of the Alphabet of the Dead in certain of the editions of the *Rhetoric*. A whole area of research could be developed in what may have been the contribution of the printing of the *Rhetoric* to the Protestant Reformation and the Catholic Counter-Reformation, including the displacement of manuscripts of the *Rhetoric* caused by the European wars.

Artz (1978, 313) concluded his essay with this explanation of why scholars have not paid more attention to the humanists:

> The reason the Humanists, so much esteemed in their own day, were neglected by later generations is that what they found in the classics and strove to disseminate was then new, and later became, thanks to their efforts an integral part of Western civilization, and as such seemed commonplace. Thus, one of the proofs of the success of the Humanists lies in the fact that they are largely forgotten today.

NOTES

1. The bibliographies and catalogues consulted are given here for the most part by short title or by name of author for the incunabula:

    Catalogue Général Bibliothèque Nationale; A Catalogue of Incunbula in All the Libraries of Oxford University Outside the Bodleian; General Catalogue Printed Books, British Library; Brunet; Coppinger; *Gesamtkatalog der Wiegendrucke*; Goff; Hain; *Indici/e Cataloghi*; Johnson & Scholderer; Mitarelli; National Union Catalogue Pre-1956; Pellechet; Pollard & Scholderer; Proctor; Renouard; and Schwab. For the sixteenth century editions, in addition to those above when applicable: Adams; Chaix; Chevalier; Cranz; Delisle; Englemann; Erickson (1975); Fabricci; *Gesamtkatalog der Preussischen Bibliotheken*; Hoffman; *Index Aureliensis*; Marshall; Murphey (1971); Oxford Libraries Outside the Bodleian; *Primo Catalogo*; Schweiger; and *Verzeichnis der im Deutschen Sprachbereich Erschienenen Drucke des XVI Jahrhunderts* (VD16) (Stuttgart, Anton Hiersemann, 1983).

2. In Great Britain: the Bodleian and the college libraries of All Souls, Christ Church, Pembroke, and Queens; British Library; Cambridge University Library and all college libraries, including access to Adams' notes in Trinity College Library; National Library of Scotland; on the continent, West Zone: in Greece, Gennadius, Athens; in Switzerland: *Université de Basel*; in France: *Bibliothèque Nationale; Bibliothèque Mazarine; Bibliothèque Municipale*, Lyon; *Bibliothèque Sainte-Genviève; Bibliothèque Universitaire*, Lyon; in West Germany: *Deutsche Staatsbibliothek*, West Berlin; *Universitäts Bibliothek*, Göttingen; *Staatsbibliotek*, Bamburg; *Universitäts Bibliothek*, Erlangen; *Universitäts Bibliothek*, Heidelberg; *Universitäts Bibliothek*, Tübingen; *Bayerische Staatsbibliothek*, Munich; in Austria:

Vienna Staatsbibliothek; in the Netherlands, *Universiteitsbibliotheek,* Leiden; *Universiteitsbibliotheek,* Amsterdam; in Italy, *Biblioteca Vallicelliana,* Rome; *Biblioteca Angelica,* Rome; *Biblioteca Nazionale Centrale,* Rome; *Biblioteca Vaticana,* Rome; *Biblioteca Allesandra,* Rome; *Biblioteca Casanatense,* Rome; *Biblioteca Nazionale Braidense,* Milan; *Biblioteca Laurenciana,* Milan; *Biblioteca Nazionale,* Naples; *Biblioteca Nazionale Centrale,* Florence; *Biblioteca Marciana,* Venice; on the continent, East Zone: in East Germany, *Deutsche Staatsbibliothek,* East Berlin; *Universitäts-Bibliothek Humbolt,* East Berlin; *Universitäts Bibliothek,* Leipzig; *Martin Luther Universitäts Bibliothek,* Halle; in Hungary, *Egyetemi Könyvtár; Magyar Tudományos Akadémia Könyvtár; Országos Széchényi Könyvtár;* and *Ráday Gyüjtémenye,* all in Budapest; in Poland, *Biblioteka Jagiellónska,* Krakow; in Czechoslsovakia, *Státní Vedecká Knihovna,* Olomouc; *Státní Knihovna,* Prague; in the Netherlands: *Universiteitsbibliotheek van Amsterdam; Bibliotheek der Rijksuniversiteit Leiden;* in the United States: Boston Public; U.C.L.A.; University of California at Berkeley; Catholic University; University of Chicago; Columbia University; Duke University; Folger Library; Harvard University; University of Illinois; Indiana University; Library of Congress; University of Michigan; University of North Carolina; Northwestern University; Ohio State University; University of Pennsylvania; Princeton University; University of Virginia; and Yale University.

3. Research in countries under domination by the U.S.S.R is usually not impossible, but poses visa and permit problems that make travel difficult, e.g., the researcher had planned to visit both of the major libraries in Wroclaw, Poland (formerly Breslau) (see footnote 4) while in Krakow, but although the distances were short, the tourist bureau was unable to arrange train transportation, and flights between minor cities are non-existant. A subsequent application to visit Wroclaw and Warsaw to examine collections in Poland received no response. The Lenin State Library of the U.S.S.R.in Moscow was willing to search its union catalogue of foreign books housed in the Soviet Union to see if the books formerly at Königsberg were among its listing of consolidated libraries in the Soviet Union, but a general search of U.S.S.R. holdings has not been possible.

4. The letters sent to the libraries were accompanied by duplicates of the bibliographical entries as previously developed by the researcher. Replies to the mailing have been more than generous, and there have been one or two follow-up inquiries to many libraries. The rare book librarians who responded were meticulous in their comments, amendations or corrections. Unfortunately a number of libraries had their copies destroyed or lost in World War II. This was particularly discouraging in Berlin, Bonn, Wroclaw, Kiel, Louvain-la-Neuve, and Braunsberg. A fire in Tours in 1940 appears to have seriously damaged its collection. Berlin, which had been a major Aristotelian repository, lost what was perhaps one fourth of its holdings of the *Rhetoric.* The researcher noted each edition that the *Gesamtkatalog* listed as being held in Berlin and personally searched the collection. For those issues that appeared to have been destroyed, the researcher had the library make a special search and an official report in writing from Berlin was received, confirming the losses. The East Berlin library suggested that the missing copies might be located in West Berlin, but a personal search of the *Deutsche Staatsbibliothek* in West Berlin located only one of the missing copies.

Special mailings continue the search for rare editions and for copies of editions referred to in the catalogues or bibliographies but for which no locations can be found. An attempt to clarify the holdings in the university library at Wroclaw was finally successful, thanks to the cooperation of the Polish Cultural Attaché in Washington. The holdings of the *Biblioteka Uniwersytecka* and the *Polska Akademia Nauk, Zaklad Narodowy im Ossolińskich* in Wroclaw, both of which have major Aristotelian holdings, now appear to be clarified. Unfortunately, again, the holdings of the university library were in part destroyed in WWII.

5. *Bibliothèque Nationale,* Rés.X.269 and Rés.X.637; Basel F.I.12; Bourges Incunable 179.

6. George of Trebizond (1395-c.1473) was of a Greek family that left the island of Trebizond to settle in Crete. Therefore George signed his names Georgius Trapezuntius Cretensis. He spent most of his life in Italy as teacher and writer. Probably while he was in Venice between 1433-34, he wrote his own *Rhetoricorum libri V* of which there are manuscript copies in Vienna (MS. Wien Lat. 2329), in Bologna (MS. Bologna UB 2400), in Chicago (MS. U. of Chicago 851), in the Vatican (Palatinus lat. 1591 and Vaticanus lat. 1958), as well as numerous other libraries. (Monfasani, 1984, 459) The Vienna MS.is dated Sept. 23, 1434. Trapezuntius' own rhetoric was issued in several printed editions, e.g., in Venice in 1472, in Milan in 1493, and by Aldus Manutius in 1523. It is likely that Trapezuntius began his translation of Aristotle's *Rhetoric* as early as 1442, as part of a plan to translate Aristotle's *libri naturales.* The version was probably completed c. 1441-1446 and is the only one of Trapezuntius' Aristotelian translations to be published. Trapezuntius himself in his *scholia* (Monfasani, 1984, 466, 1.1366b1-3) said that the translation was based on a single Greek manuscript. Kassel (1971, 102, n.13) concluded from his collations that this single Greek text referred to by Trapezuntius in his *marginalia* was a descendant of the Cambridge Ff.5.8. For much of this discussion the author is indebted to Monfasani (1976) and Monfasani (1984). Lacombe (1939, pp. 838; 925) referred to two existing MSS. of Trapezuntius' translation whereas Monfasani (1984, pp. 699-700) identified twenty-three.

7. The Belgian Dominican, William of Moerbeck, was born in the town from which he took his name. Not much is known of his life. He was educated at Louvain and may have been sent from Flanders to Greece to learn Greek. He held the post for granting special

Early Printings

dispensations at the courts of Popes Clement IV and Gregory X. He assisted in the Council of Lyon in 1274 and in 1277 was named Archbishop of Corinth. He died sometime between 1281 and 1300. His command of both Arabic and Greek gave him access to the two main sources of classical thought. The nature of his position undoubtedly made available to him versions of the *Rhetoric* that are no longer extant. His Latin translation of 1273 is sufficiently literal and at variance with the leading Greek manuscripts, as was indicated in Chapter Two, that his translation has been able to clarify certain passages for the nineteenth century collators.

8. Lacombe (1956,1348) acknowledged ninety-four extant manuscript copies.
9. See Boggess (1971, 236-245).
10. It is necessary to have some knowledge of three Medieval figures in order to understand the significance of the 1481 edition. First, the translator of the initial part of Alfarabi's commentary on the *Rhetoric*, Hermannus Alemannus, was born during the early part of the thirteenth century. He is known to have been at Toledo in 1240 where, with the assistance of Sarasens and not Jews, he translated several of Aristotle's works, including the *Ethics* (M.S.Laur.lxxix 18), the *Politics*, the *Rhetoric*, and the *Poetics*. As is pointed out in the outline of the contents of the three manuscripts *supra*, the 1481 edition contains only the translation of the commentary of Alfarabi, and did not reproduce the translation that Hermannus made of the *Rhetoric* itself. Although the Latin MSS. of the *Rhetoric* and the *Poetics* are not dated, Boggess concluded from internal evidence in the prologues that the commentary by Alfarabi, the translation of the *Rhetoric*, and Hermannus' translation of the *Poetics* were all completed by 1256. (Boggess, 1971, 249)

The second scholar featured in the 1481 edition, Alfarabi (c.870-950), was born in the district of Farab in Turkish Traxoxiana in Central Asia. After having lived in Bagdad for a considerable time, he went to Alepo. He died in Damascus while on a journey. Taught by Christian philosophers at Bagdad and knowledgeable in many languages, including Arabic, Alfarabi became an interpreter of the works of Aristotle, paraphrasing and writing commentaries on many of his works. As the materials from which Alfarabi worked may well now have been lost, it is regrettable that we do not possess his complete translation of the *Rhetoric*, if, indeed, he made one.

Averroës (1126-1198), the third scholar from the Medieval period featured in the 1481 edition, worked much later than Alfarabi. Born in Cordova in a period when the Muslims were in control of that area, he found his ideas tightly monitored by the controlling factions of the time. Around 1195 he was dishonored and banished. Averroës was later recalled and restored, but only a few years before his death. He published works in law, grammar, astronomy, medicine and philosophy, and produced major commentaries on the *Posterior Analytics*, the *Physica*, *De Caelo*, *De Anima*, and the *Metaphysics*. De Boer (1967, 188) noted that "writings of the Greeks, which are now lost either entirely or in part, were still known to Ibn Roshd [Averroës] in translated form... He paraphrases Aristotle and he interprets him, now with comparative brevity, and anon in greater detail, both in moderate-sized and in bulky commentaries." It was Averroës' version of the *Poetics* that was translated from the Arabic into Latin by Hermannus and that appears as the last work in the 1481 edition.

In summary, Herrick (1926, 244) was correct in saying that Hermannus translated the entire *Rhetoric*, but that translation does not appear in the 1481 edition.

11. See Murphy (1971, 33) and Murphy (1969). Aegidio Colonna (?-1316) was born in Rome and died in Avignon. The Latin version of his name was Aegidius Romanus, and the French version was Gille de Rome. Leaving his native land and his illustrious family in Naples, he came at an early age to the French capital where he became a pupil of St. Thomas Aquinus. He introduced Thomism into the schools of the Augustinians, and the scholastic effects of his teachings were felt in Italy. Aegidio served as tutor for Prince Philippe and established himself at Bourges where he wrote most of his works, among which were commentaries on Aristotle's *Physica*, *De Anima*, the *Prior Analytics*, and the *Rhetoric*.
12. Aegidius Romanus (Aegidio Colonna). (1515). *Commentaria in Rhetoricam Aristotelis*. Venice. Republished (1968). Frankfurt. Minerva GMBH.
13. This research and Monfasani's findings (1984, 700-701), done independently of each other, concur. The methodology for this study lists independently the two printings of 1561, sometimes attributed to the printer Frellonius and sometimes to the printer Vincentius, as well as the two printings of 1581, sometimes attributed to the publisher Michaelis and sometimes to the publisher Honoratus, making the total twenty-two instead of the twenty listed by Monfasani.
14. The Würzburg copy L.gr.f.108 has been missing since 1963, while the Griefswald copy is simply reported as being lost, presumably not in World War II but from other causes.
15. *Bayerische Staatsbibliothek*: A.gr.b.626 (defective).
16. Peter Victorius (1499-1585) came from an aristocratic family of Florence. He studied law at nearby Pisa where he married Madeleine Medici. In 1522 he accompanied one of his relatives on a papal expedition to Spain where he developed an interest in antiquities. Like all Italian humanists, he became embroiled in the turmoil of sixteenth century Italy, supporting the faction opposed to the Medicis. He spent 1537 in Rome, but was recalled in 1538 by Cosmo de Medici to hold the chair of eloquence at Florence, a post that he retained for almost fifty years. Medallions were struck in his honor, and he was appointed by Cosmo to the rank of Senator. Not only did he publish a commen-

tary on the *Rhetoric*, but he issued similar volumes on the *Poetics* and the *Politics*. His other publications were numerous. He died at age 87, well respected in Florence not only for his scholarship but also for his character.

17. The *Bayerische Staatsbibliothek* in Munich has two inventories of the works from Victorius' library in its collection:

    Cbm. Cat 85d...a catalog compiled by Wilhelm Meyer circa 1880

    Cbm. Cat 209.A. probably made by the librarian Maillot de la Treille on March 27, 1780

    Unfortunately neither of these sources gives a complete list of the works of Victorius in the Munich library. Dr. E. Hartrich of the manuscript room of the *Bayerische Staatsbibliothek* wrote this researcher on June 30, 1983, that other items from Victorius' collection not mentioned in these sources were housed in various subject areas of the Munich library.

    From our research, the following printed books, some marked with Victorius' bookmark, are in the Munich library and appear to have served Victorius in the preparation of his editions:

    the 1508 Aldine
    the 1534 Basel Frobenius
    the 1536 Venice Trincavelli
    the 1546 Gryphius
    the 1548 Florence (2oA.gr.b.168 and A.gr.b.169)
    the 1549 Basel

    Meyer listed the following in his inventory of Victorius' library:

    1508   Venice............A.gr.coll.L.impr. impr.c.n.mn.81
    1544   Paris Barbaro.......A.gr.b.241
    1546   Venice............A.gr.b.625 & 626
    1548   Florence..........A.gr.b.169 & 168
    1549   Paris.............A.gr.b.628
    1562   Paris.............A.gr.b.235m
    1571   Venice Maioragius..A.gr.b.240
    1587   Frankfort.........A.gr.b.165

    De la Treille listed the following. There may be others, but the bibliography is very difficult to follow and the information on some entries is too limited to make a positive identification.

    MSS.Greek (*Rhetoric* & *Poetics*).
    *(1549) Paris.............8oA.gr.b.628
    *1508   Venice............(not given)
    1538   Paris.............(not given)
    *1546   Venice............8oA.gr.b.625
    1562   Paris.............4o A.gr.b.235m
    **1544 Venice............4oA.gr.b.241
    1584   Frankfort.........4o A.gr.b.165
    1585   Venice............(not given)

    *bibliography notes *marginalia* by Victorius
    **wrongly listed as 1554

    According to de la Treille, about 250 volumes that included the Victorius collection came from Rome to Mannheim in November, 1779, and from Mannheim to Munich in 1783. The line of Bavarian kings in Munich had died out, so that an allied line presiding in Mannheim was called to Bavaria, bringing the Victorius collection from Mannheim to Munich. At the heading of Meyer's bibliography, in what appears to be another hand, are notes that indicate that the collection went from Rome to Mannheim in 1780, and from Mannheim to Munich in 1783.

18. "Finally, for completeness sake, it should be added that Victorius sought Francesco Medici's advice to correct various passages; to resolve doubts about the authenticity of certain parts; and to clarify obscure concepts and sentences." (Niccolai, 230)

19. "Mit dem Parisinus aber hatte der Editor das Instrument zur Hand, die aristotelische Schrift von zahllosen Verfälschungen zu befreiden..." (Kassel, 1971,100). "But, with the Paris manuscript, the editor had the instrument at hand to rescue Aristotle's text from its numerous errors."

20. Monacensis 90; Monacensis 175; Monacensis 176.

21. Niccolai (1912,230) cited only the 1546 and 1549 editions as being in Victorius' library possibly because Niccolai was relying on Ruediger (1896) as his source and had not visited the Munich library himself.

22. The copy at Munich with the pages removed is catalogued as 2o L. impr. c.n.mass.81/1a. Although the pages have been cut out, what remains of the annotations are still visible in the parts of the pages close to the binding that could not be clipped out. There also remain in this copy the last page of the notes, as well as some notes on the verso side of the beginning page, a page that was added to the volume and does not exist in the original 1508 printing.

23. Although Grec 1741 undoubtedly came from the collection of Rudolphi, there was nothing about it to signal its importance. Rudolphi and others made available to Victorius many manuscripts, so it was only by painstaking collation that Victorius realized to some extent the dominant position of Greece 1741.

24. For example, Niccolai (1912, 228) pointed out: "...in order to understand better and therefore, when necessary, to correct and illustrate the passages of the orators and of the ancient poets quoted as evidence by Aristotle, Victorius read a great many of them (Vict. Epp. IX.12)."

25. Kassel (1971, 101): "But in the preparation of the text, however, Victorius had also left a lot undone that, with his resources, could easily have been set right. The basis for this failure lies in his enormous, frequently even debilitating care in being scrupulous that made him suspicious, not only in protecting himself against ticklish and unusual conjecture, but actually inclined him to set himself in general against major changes, even if they could be resolved by manuscript authority." As will be detailed in Chapter Four, Kassel (1976) published his own edition of the Greek text in 1976.

26. Hermolao Barbaro (1454-1493) experienced in the short forty-nine years of his life the turmoil that was cus-

tomary in plague-infested and war-torn fifteenth century Italy. His life was also subject to the religious disputes that often absorbed too much time of Renaissance scholars. A native of Venice, Barbaro took a degree at Padua and was appointed to a chair of philosophy in that city in 1477. He performed missions for a number of important people, including Pope Innocent VIII, who nominated him to a prestigious post which his native city of Venice refused to ratify, because Barbaro had accepted the position without getting Venice's permission. Banished, Barbaro went to Rome where he lived in comparative povery until his death. He translated a number of Aristotle's works other than the *Rhetoric*.

27. Antonius Maioragius (1514-?) was born at Majoragio, a small town not far from Milan. After completing his education with difficulty because of the Italian wars that ruined his families' finances, he went to Milan to continue his interest in the classics. In 1541 he was named to the chair of eloquence at the college at Milan. Except for interruptions caused by the war, he remained there, teaching eloquence until his death. He published a series of classical treatises and translations.

28. Carlo Sigonio (1524-1584) was born in Modena, studied Greek under Portus of Candia and attended the philosophical schools of Bologna and Pavia. In 1545 he was chosen professor of Greek in Modena to replace his master Portus. He subsequently held professorships in Venice and Padua. He died in his country house near Modena. Sigonio authored a number of translations and essays on classical subjects.

29. Antonio Riccobono (1541-1599) was born in Rovigo, Italy, and attended schools in Venice and Padua where he studied under Sigonio and Muret. At an early age he was chosen teacher at Rovigo. In 1571, Riccobono received his diploma in jurisprudence, as he thought law was the best way to support himself. But his friends persuaded him to take the chair of rhetoric at Padua which he held until his death. He published a number of classical works, including translations of Aristotle's *Rhetoric*, *Poetics* and *Ethics*. His translations have been criticized as not being sufficiently faithful to the text.

30. Marc Antoine Muret (Muretus) (1526-1585) was a French scholar born at Muret near Limoges. After Muret had gained some prestige as a scholar, including delivering a series of lectures in Paris attended by Henry II, Muret was thrown into prison by his enemies, from which his friends secured his release. He had to flee from France as a Huguenot, going to Italy where he settled in Rome in 1559. Because of his fame as a lecturer, the King of Poland invited him to teach jurisprudence at Krakow, but Gregory XII persuaded Muret to remain in Rome where in 1576 he had taken holy orders. Muret edited and translated a number of classical works.

31. Counting the slightly revised Victorius Latin translation appearing in Bardi in 1592, there were two editions of the 1579 edition published in the period examined; counting the slightly revised Moerbeck Latin translations appearing in 1537 in Venice and in 1540 in Bologna, there were five printings of the Moerbeck version published during the period examined.

32. Although the 1570 Sturmio translation had only one printing, the Porto 1598 translation proved to be rather popular during the seventeenth century.

33. In addition to the more than seventy-five sets of this work that contain the *Rhetoric*, there were found a number of other incomplete sets which did not contain the *Rhetoric* at such locations as the University of Virginia, Boston Public, *Universitäts Bibliothek* Göttingen, and *Universitäts Bibliothek* Heidelberg.

34. The editor of the 1584 edition, Frederick Sylburg, did not number his volumes but was content to list what he considered to be their order in the preface to volume one that appeared in 1587, three years after the first volume containing the *Rhetoric* had been issued. He therefore opened the door for librarians to establish their own order for his ten volumes, causing problems in identifying the 1584 *Rhetoric* in a collection that does not index the holdings by volume, or that may not have identified the *Rhetoric* as belonging to the ten volume series. Libraries with the set generally classify the *Rhetoric* as volume two to conform to the 1587 preface, but the *Bibliothèque Nationale* has the *Rhetoric* as volume nine, the Cambridge University Library as volume eight, Emmanuel College Library at Cambridge as volume five, and Northwestern University Library as volume one.

35. Cranz (1971, viii) provided a table showing, in five year periods, the frequency of all Aristotelian publications between 1466 and 1600. The printings of the *Rhetoric* do not conform to the pattern of the Aristotle editions in general. The *Rhetoric* appeared in a much steadier stream than did Aristotle's overall publications and does not show the skewing toward the middle of the sixteenth century.

36. The rise of Lyon as a center of printing was due, not to any base of scholarly activity (Martin & Chartier, 1982, I, 165), but because Lyon was the trade center between the cities to the north and Italy and Venice to the south. (Hours, 1972, 106) It was not necessary to cross the Alps if routes ran via the Rhone River. (see Hours, 1972, map, 73) Therefore, Lyon grew as a trade center. There were more difficulties with censors than at Venice, but business was possible, until events in France caused a general exodus of printers from Lyon to Geneva. For some time, there had been an interchange between the two cities, but, during the second half of the sixteenth century, the movement began all one way. (Eisenstein, 1983, 169) What remained in Lyon were largely packing and distributing centers for books. A book with Calvinistic taint could be shipped to Lyon, disguised with a Lyon title page, and sold freely in areas where Calvinist thought was prohibited. This is undoubtedly what occurred with the 1590 quarto Lyon edition. A letter from the *Biblio-*

thèque Municipale of Lyon attested that Laemarius never had a printing house in Lyon. Undoubtedly, the printer, Lemarie of Geneva, shipped his books to Lyon, had the false title page inserted, and then distributed them without fear of loss of sales. The emigration from France was not confined to Lyon. "Throughout the Continent," said Eisenstein (1983,168), "the movement of printers toward Protestant centers and the tendency for markets to expand and diversify more rapidly under Protestant than Catholic rule. . ." caused a general shift of emphasis to more Northern Europe.

37. Paris, and the Sorbonne itself, established itself early as a source of printed books, but theological censors delayed publication, causing Paris to become less and less hospitable to printers. (Eisenstein, 1979, 399)

38. Among those who have made contributions toward the exploration of the use to which the Rhetoric was put during the Renaissance are Herrick (1926), Hultzen (1932), Murphy (1960), Weiss (1967), Curtis (1959, 87 and 106), C.H. Haskins (1924), and Rashdall (1936). Murphy (1960, 346) established that the Rhetoric was in use at Oxford as early as the first half of the fifteenth century. If the Rhetoric was evident at the advent of the printing press and during the time of the Petrarchian Renaissance, there should be records available to trace its use in more detail than has now been established. If, as Eisenstein (1983, 119-20) suggested, the new view of antiquity did not begin until the advent of printing, and if it took some fifty to one hundred years for the printed book to make its full impact on society (Eisenstein, 1979, 33), the search could well be centered between 1550 and 1650.

BIBLIOGRAPHY

American Library Association, Resources & Technical Services Division, Resources Section, Subcommittee on the National Union Catalogue. (1968-1980). *The National Union Catalogue: Pre-1956 Imprints*, London.

Artz, F.B. (1978). "The Significance of Renaissance Humanism," in *Reader in the History of Books and Printing*, ed. P. Winckler, 310-313, Englewood, Colorado.

Boggess, W.F. (1971). "Hermannus Alemannus' Rhetorical Translations," *Viator: Medieval and Renaissance Studies* 2, 227-250.

Brandes, Paul. (1985). "Printing of Aristotle's Rhetoric during the Fifteenth and Sixteenth Centuries," *Communication Monographs* 52, 368-376.

Burke, P. (1964). "The Renaissance," in *Problems and Perspectives in History*, ed. H.F.Kearney, London.

Capelli, Adriano. (1954). *Lexicon Abbreviaturam Dizionario di Abbreviature Latine ed Italiane*, Milan.

Centro Nazionale per il Catalogo Unico della Bibliotheche Italiane e per le Informazioni Bibliografiche. (1962-). *Primo Catalogo Collettivo delle Biblioteche Italiane*, in Rome.

Cooper, L. (1932). *The Rhetoric of Aristotle*, New York.

Curtis, Mark H. (1959). *Oxford and Cambridge in Transition: 1558-1642*, Oxford.

De Boer, T.J. (1967). *The History of Philosophy in Islam*, New York.

Eisenstein, Elizabeth L. (1979). *The Printing Press as an Agent of Change*, Cambridge, England.

Eisenstein, Elizabeth L. (1983). *The Printing Revolution in Early Modern Europe*, Cambridge, England.

Erickson, K.V. (1975). *Aristotle's Rhetoric: Five Centuries of Philological Research*, Metuchen, N.J.

Grimaldi, W.M.A. (1980). *Aristotle, Rhetoric I: a Commentary*, New York.

Haskins, C.H. (1924). *The Renaissance of the Twelfth Century*, Cambridge, Massachusetts.

Herrick, M. (1926). "The Early History of Aristotle's Rhetoric in England," *Philological Quarterly* 5, 242-257.

Hours, Henri et al. (1972). *Le Siècle d'Or de l'Imprimerie Lyonnaise*, Paris.

Hultzen, L. (1932). Aristotle's *Rhetoric* in England to 1600, unpubl. diss. Cornell.

Index Aureliensis Catalogus Librorum Sedecimo Saecul Impressorum. (1962-), Geneva.

Jourdain, A. (1960). *Récherches Critiques sur l'Age et l'Origine des Traductions Latines d'Aristote*, New York, new ed. by C. Jourdain.

Kassel, R., ed. (1976). *Aristotelis Ars Rhetorica*, Berlin.

Kassel, R. (1971). *Der Text der Aristotelischen Rhetorik*, Berlin.

Kristeller, P.O. (1961). *Renaissance Thought*, New York.

Lacombe, G. (1939). *Aristoteles Latinus, Pars Prior*, Rome.

Lacombe, G. (1955). *Aristoteles Latinus, Pars Posterior*, Cambridge.

LaRusso, Dominic A. (1983). "Rhetoric in the Italian Renaissance," in *Renaissance Eloquence*, ed. J. Murphy, Berkeley 37-55.

Lehmann-Haupt, Hellmut. (1978). "The Heritage of the Manuscript," in *Reader in the History of Books and Printing*, ed. P. Winckler, 179-229, Englewood, Colorado.

Lowry, Martin. (1979). *The World of Aldus Manutius*, Ithaca, N.Y.

Martin, Henri-Jean & Robert Chartier. (1982). *Histoire de l'Edition Française*, 2 vols, Paris.

Monfasani, J. (1976). *George of Trebizond*. Leiden.

Monfasani, J.,ed. (1984). *Collectanea Trapezuntiana: Texts, Documents, and Bibliographies of George of Trebizond*, Binghamton, New York.

Morgan, Paul, ed. (1980). *Oxford Libraries Outside the Bodleian: A Guide*, Oxford.

Murphy, J.J. (1960). "The Earliest Teaching of Rhetoric at Oxford," *Speech Monographs* 27, 345-7.

Murphy, J.J. (1969). "The Scholastic Condemnation of Rhetoric in the Commentary of Giles of Rome on the Rhetoric of Aristotle," in *Arts Liberaux et Philosophie au Môyen Age* (Acts du Quatrième Congres International de Philosophie Médiévale) 833-841, Montreal.

Murphy, J.J. (1971). *Medieval Rhetoric: a Select Bibliography*, Toronto.

Niccolai, F. (1912). *Pier Vettori (1499-1589)*, Florence.

Early Printings

Prussian Board of Education. (1931-1939). *Gesamtkatalog der Preussischen Bibliotheken mit Nachweis des Identischen Besitzes der Bayerischen Staatsbibliothek in München und der Nationalbibliothek in Wien.* Berlin. 14 vols. Interrupted by World War II. Manuscript destroyed in WW II, and, according to a letter dated Nov. 18, 1985 from the *Deutsche Staatsbibliothek*, the work has not been recommenced.

Prussian Board of Education. (1925-1940). *Gesamtkatalog der Wiegendrucke Herausgeben von der Kommission für den Gesamtkatalog der Wiegendrucke,* Leipsig. 8 vols. Interrupted by World War II.

Rashdall, Hastings. (1936). *Universities of Europe in the Middle Ages,* Oxford University Press, Oxford.

Rhodes, Dennis E. (1982). *A Catalogue of Incunabula in All the Libraries of Oxford University Outside the Bodleian,* Oxford.

Ruediger, W. (1896). *Petrus Victorius aus Florenz; Studien zu einem Lebensbilde,* Halle.

Schmitt, C.B. (1983). *Aristotle and the Renaissance,* Cambridge, Mass.

Schneider, B. (1971). *Die Mittelalterlichen Griechisch-lateinischen Ubersetzungen der Aristotelischen Rhetorik,* Berlin.

Wartelle, A. (1963). *Inventaire des Manuscrits Grecs d'Aristote et de ses Commentateurs,* Paris.

TABLE 1

GREEK PRINTINGS OF THE RHETORIC BETWEEN 1508 AND 1599

DATE	PLACE	PUBLISHER	ANNOTATIONS
1508	Venice	Aldus Manutius	appeared in Rhetores in hoc volumine habentur hi.
1529	Basel	Hieronymius Froben & John Herwagen	Fabricii links to 1508 edition
1530	Paris	ex officina Gerhardi Morrhii [Gerard Morrhy] Campensis apud collegium Sorbonae	linked to 1529 edition
1531	Basel	John Bebel	eds. Desiderius Erasmus & Simon Grynaeus
1536	Venice	Barthomew Zanetti	ed. Joannis Francisco Trincavelli who made first attempt at correcting the Aldus text
1538	Paris	Chrestien Wechel [sic]	title in both Greek & Latin
1539	Basel	John Bebel & Michael Isingrinius	linked to the 1531 edition
1546	Basel	Michael Isingrinius	linked to 1539 edition
1546	Venice	John Gryphius	linked to 1536 edition
1547	Strasbourg	W. Rihelius	only one copy located
1548	Florence	Bernardus Junta	Victorius' collation of Greek manuscripts
1549	Basel	J. Oporinus	the 1548 edition published under a slightly different format
1549*	Paris	apud Vascosanum	Greek with Barbaro's Latin acknowledges Victorius
1550	Basel	John Bebelius & Michael Isingrinius	two vols. in one reissue of the Erasmus edition of 1531/1539 acknowledges Victorius
1551*	Basel	ex officina Iacobi Parci, Impensis John Oporinus	Greek with Barbaro's Latin
1551	Venice	apud Aldi Filios	linked to the 1536 and 1546 editions ed. J.B.Camotius
1559*	Paris	Guil. Morelius	some copies accompanied Barbaro's Latin
1562*	Paris	Guil. Morelius	reprint of 1559 edition some copies issued with Barbaro's Latin
1564	Wittenberg	not identified (no copies located; 3 identified all lost in WWII)	presumably the first edition of what John Caselly reissued in 1577
1570*	Strasbourg	Theodosius Rihelius	Greek and Latin with commentary by Johannes Sturmius
1573	Florence	in officina Iunctarum	rare:Florence & Pisa

Table One (conluded)

1575	Paris	apud Ioannem Benenatum	reprint of 1559 edition
1577	Rostock	ex officina Iacobi	edited by John Caselly
1579*	Florence	ex officina Iunctarium	new edition by Victorius with his Latin version
1582	Paris	Steph. Preuosteau, heirs of Guil. Morelius	reprint of 1559 version
1584	Frankfurt	Andreas Wechelius, Claudius Marnius, & Joannes Aubrius	popular edition ed. Frederick Sylburg 10 vol. set of works
1588*	Frankfurt	apud heredes Andrea Wecheli, Claudius Marnius, & Joannes Aubrius	Greek with Riccobono's Latin acknowledges Victorius
1590*	Lyon (Geneva)	apud Iacobus Bubonium	Greek with Riccobono's Latin complete works in 2 vols
1591*	Venice	apud Franciscum de Franciscis Senensem	Greek with Maioragius' Latin acknowledges Victorius
1597*	Lyon (Geneva)	Guil. de Leymarie	Greek with Riccobono's Latin 2 vol set of works
1598*	Bern	apud Bernardum Albinum [Bernard Albinum]	Greek with Aemilio Porto's Latin

*contains both Greek and Latin texts

TABLE 2

LATIN PRINTINGS OF ARISTOTLE'S RHETORIC BETWEEN 1475 AND 1599

DATE	TRAPE-ZUNTIUS	BARBARO	MAIOR-AGIUS	SIGONIO	MURETO	RICCO-BONO	OTHER
1475-1477	Paris						
1481							Venice – Moerbeck
1499							Leipsig– Moerbeck
1504	Venice						
1515							Venice – Moerbeck
1515	Paris						
1523	Venice						
1530	Paris						
1534	Basel						
1537							Venice – Moerbeck with some editing
1538	Basel						
1540	Paris						
1540							Bologna– Moerbeck with some editing
1541	Lyon						
1542	Basel						
1544		Venice Lyon					
1545	Lyon	Basel					
1548	Basel	Lyon					
1549	Lyon	Paris					
1550	Venice		Milan				
1551		Basel					
1552			Venice				
1558	Paris	Lyon					
1559		Paris					
1560	Venice						
1561	Lyon* Lyon* Lyon						
1562			Venice				
1563	Lyon		Basel				
1565				Bologna Venice			

Table Two (concluded)

DATE	TRAPE-ZUNTIUS	BARBARO	MAIOR-AGIUS	SIGONIO	MURETO	RICCO-BONO	OTHER
1566				Venice			
1570							Strasbourg, tr.Johannes Sturmio
1571			Venice				
1572			Venice	Venice			
1574				Venice			
1575			Venice Venice				
1576	Venice						
1577				Krakow Rostock	Rome	Padua	
1578	Lyon						
1579	Lyon					Venice	Florence tr.Victorius
1580	Lyon						
1581	Lyon**						
1584			Venice	Brescia			
1585					Rome		
1588						Frankfurt	
1590						Lyon	
1591			Venice				
1592							Bardi,Pomerania Victorius with some editing
1593						Frankfurt	
1594			Cologne. <3rd bk only>		Cologne <1st 2 bks only>	Vicenza	
1597						Lyon	
1598							Bern,tr.Emilio Porto
1599					Avignon		

* Apparently there were three printings of the Trapezuntius edition in Lyon in 1561. One edition is sometimes attributed to the publisher Ioannes Frellonius and sometimes to Antonius Vincentius. Both appear to have been printed by Symphorianus Barbierus for Frellionius and Vincentius. The third is consistently attributed to the heirs of Iacobus Iunta.

** The 1581 Trapezuntius edition is sometimes attributed to the publisher Stephanus Michaelis (copies in St. Johns,Cambridge; Halle; Marburg, Rome BNC, and possibly Wroclaw and Kalingrad) and sometimes to Honoratus (copies in the British Library, Illinois, Gotha, Prague, Kenyon, and Northwestern)

TABLE THREE

ANNOTATED BIBLIOGRAPHY OF THE PRINTINGS OF ARISTOTLE'S RHETORIC BETWEEN 1477 AND 1599

DATE	LOCATIONS	TITLES	ANNOTATIONS	SOURCE
circa 1477	Basel:F.I.12 BN:Res.X.269; Res.X.637 Bourges:Inc. 179	TITLE PAGE: none page 1: Ad reverendum in christo patrem ac dominum dominum F. de padua [sic] domini notri pape [sic] [nostri papae] thesaurium georgii trapezoncii in libros rhetoricorum aristotelis traductionis Prefacio. [Paris]:[Jean Stoll & Pierre Cesar], n.d. No date, publisher, or or place is given in the work.	in 4° chaps:a-15;b-26;g-19 Bks:One=2-47;Two=47-93;Three=93-=124 (pages unnumbered by publisher, done in Paris copies by BN) This translation by Trapezuntius should not be confused with Trapezuntius' own 5 bk. rhetoric that received a number of printings, including a Venice edition of 1472 and a Milan edition of 1493. See Monfasani, George of Trebizond, 27 & 30, and Monfasani, Collectanea Trapezuntiana. A MS. of Trapezuntius' own rhetoric dated 1433-4 is in Vienna (MS Wien, Bn.Lat. 2329). Copies of the 1472 edition are at the BN (Res.X.636);s at the BM(167. i.3); at the LC(Inc.X.G.75) and elsewhere. The 1493 edition is at Cambridge (Trinity 6.15.54). Other editions appeared in 1525 and 1522. See Hain 7609 and Proctor 5994. The Basel copy of the 1477 tr. is bound with other MSS. and printed matter. Its pages have been numbered as 268-330. The Basel copy has some blue and red capital letters for chapter headings with first words of the sentences in gold. The Louvain-la-Neuve copy was burnt in WWII. The Bourges copy has no title page.	Pellechet 1189 Gesamt der Wiegendrucke II,2480 Hain 1680 Legrand III 93
1481	Aarau:Inc.F.87(a) Augsburg:2°Inc.486 Basel:ke I 15 no.2 Berlin:ooBl.i.Inc. 3733 (old Vu 7873) BM:G.7999 BN:Res.X.270 Bodleian:Auct.2.Q. 2.15 Camb:Emmanuel MSS 5.2.13(3) Erl:Inc.44/2 Got:4°A.gr.IV.590 Inc. Harv:Film W583(Mas. 503 renumbered w583;this film from BN lacks title page) Ind:PA3892.R3 1481 VAULT Krakow:Inc.643 Madrid:Inc.598 Mainz:Ink 1024	TITLE PAGE: none page A z: Declaratio cō[m]pendiosa per uiā[m] diuisionis alfarabii super libris rethorico &[rum] Aristotelis ad formā[m] tñ[tamen] clariotē[m] et tabule[a] reducta ꝑ[per] ī[n]frascriptū[m], d. correctorē[m]. Venice:Philipum Venetum,1481. (specific date of June 22, 1481, on colophon)	in 4° chaps:a=7;b=6;g=6 Bks:One=10r-24r;Two=24r-39r;Three=39r-49r. The edition contains an uninterrupted text, with nothing to mark the divisions between books. Book One begins: [R]ethorica [sic] assecutiva dialectice est; ambe enim de talibus quibusdam sunt que communiter quodammodo omnium est cognoscere et nullius scientie determinate; proter quod et omnes modo quodam participant ambadus; omnes enim usque ad aliquid et exquierere et substinere sermonem et defendere et accusare conantur. (These opening words on folio 1r,col.1 show plainly that the edition contains the Moerbeck translation.) Listed in BN catalogue under FARABI, ABOU NASR MOHAMMAD, with date inverted from 1481 to 1841. Error later noted, so under sub-heading "Rhetoric & Poetics," it is listed accurately. BM not only gives date incorrectly but attributes Latin tr. of R. to Hermann	NUC 21,18; 0403877 Goff 56,A-1046 Pellechet 512 Gesamt 6, 6367 Gesamt der Wiegendrucke 2,2478 Schwab 2955 Indice Generele delgi Incunaboli I,852 Fabricci III 335

Hoffman, 336, listed under Aristotle's works a 1478 "Aristotelis Rhetoricorum Libri quinque ex interpretione Georgii Trapezunti" (Venice, 1478), but no such edition of Aristotle's Rhetoric was found. Hoffman may have confused Trapezuntius' own five book treatise on rhetoric with Aristotle's work which was or has been divided into three books.

PLATE FORTY

first two folios of the 1477 Paris edition

courtesy of the Bibliothèque Municipale, Bourges

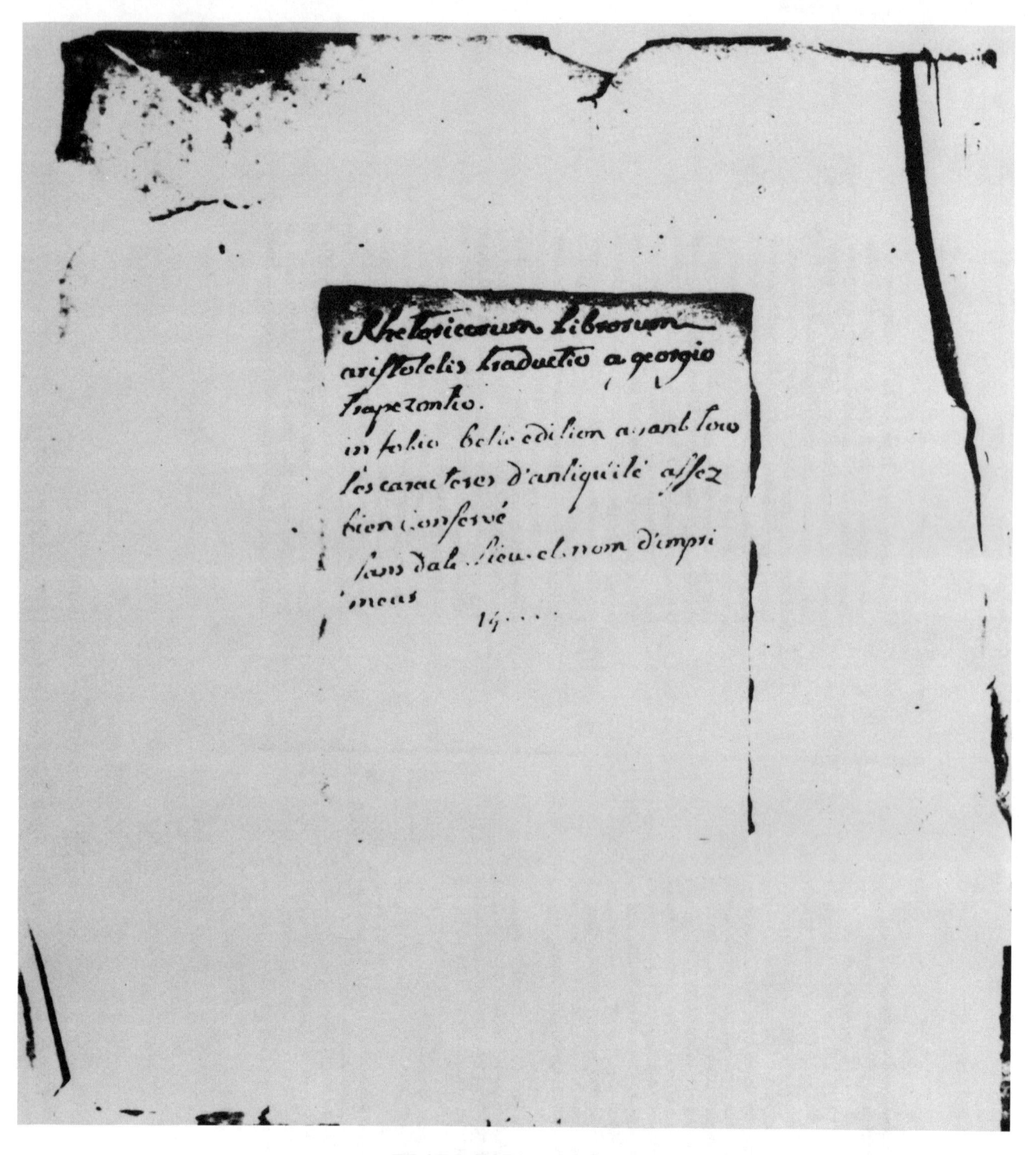

PLATE FORTY-ONE

handwritten title page in the Bourges copy of the 1477 Paris edition

courtesy of the Bibliothèque Municipale, Bourges

Early Printings

mss.81/Ia.(Victor-
ius) removed pp.
161-234;these pp.
are found under
2oA.gr.coll.mss.
81/Ib. Also 2oA.gr.
coll.22/I with
annotations in a
hand not that of
Victorius
Ohio:PA3484 M3 v.1
RomeCas:Q.V.51
Stanford:Z239.9 A36
 M28r
St.G:OE.a.Fol.22.
 Inv.37.Res.
UCBanc:fPA3484 M35
Vat:Barberini CCC.
 IV.16
Venice:392.D.57-58
Vienna:22.M.30. (1)
Yale:Beinecke Lib.
 Ge12.011

1515 BM:519.i.40
      BN:Res.X.271
      Bodleian:K.1.20.Art
       + A.20.5.Th.
       (imperfect)
      Col:PN173.A7 1968
      Flor:5C.1.34
      Harv:facsimile
       Ga.112.504.40
      Ill:X881 a8rh.
      Yae
      Maz:139*
      MilanB:F.F.15
      Munich:2°A.gr.b.172
      Naples:S.Q.XXX.C.
       211
      Ohio:PA3890 A9 1515
      RomeAles:B.i.23
      RomeBNC:68.2.E 12/3
       + 9.18.E.26
      RomeBV:S.Borr.H.IV
       90(2)
      St.Gal:Ink.132
      Tub:Cd 1086.Fol.
      UNC Folio
       PN173.A7 A4 1515a
       (facsimile)
      Vat:Barb.38
       Credenz.Tasso
      Vienna:71.F.19
      Wolf:Lg 4o 13.1

TITLE PAGE: Rhetorica Aristotelis
cum fundatissimi artium &
theologie doctoris Edigij de Roma
luculentissimis comentarijs nunc
primum in luce₃ [m] editis;necnon
Alpharibij compendiosa
declaratione. Addita eiusdem
Aristotelis poetica cum magni
Averroys in eā[n]dē[m] sū[m]ma

Venice: O.Scoti (Octavianus Scotus)
& Sociorum, 1515 on colophon

[Some copies,including the 1968
reprint,have a page reading:
Rhetorica Aristotelis cum
fundatissimi artium et theologie
doctoris Egidii de Roma
luculentissimis comentariis nunc
primu in lucez editis:necnon
Alpharabii compendiosa
declaratione.

in 4°
Bks:One=1r-48r;Two=48r-90v;Three=90v-
 118v
Edited by Alexander Achillinus
Reissued in Frankfurt in 1968. Facimile
 by Minerva of Frankfurt.
118 folios set up in 2 cols. per page:
Got copy lost,presumably in WWII
 following an air attack by British
 planes
This Moerbeck edition is interspersed
with Edigio's commentary. The commentary
is longer than the text.
This edition is a printing of BN MS.
N.A.Latin 1876, a 14th century MS from
the Phillipps collection. See Plates
11-16 for details of the formats.

| ～～～ | ～～～ | Egidio commentary |
| ～～～ | ～～～ | Latin of Moerbeck |

| 〰〰〰 | Latin of Moerbeck |
| 〰〰〰 | Egidio commentary |

Gesamt 6,6369

Ind Aur 2,165
107.828

Primo 6,5825

NUC 21,18;
0403882

Hoffman 336

Schwab 2950,
3002(errs
in dating
1525)

Cranz 107.828

---

ca.   Basel:C.B.II.14.No.5
1515 Camb:U.Lib.Rel.b.
       51.2(3) + Rel.b.
       51.2.(2)
      Gennadius:GC 3284.2
      Got:4°Auct Gr.IV
       656
      Munich:2°L.eleg.g.11
      Newberry:Case Y9867.
       931
      RomeAng:IV.12.16
      Yale:Gfa 84 + Mf 515

TITLE PAGE:Ad revendissimum In
cristo Patrem ac dominum dominu[m]
[dominorum] Fratrem de padua
domini nostri papae thesaurarium
dignissimum Georgij trapezumcij
in Rhetoricarum [sic]
aristotelis libros traductionis
prefatio

Paris: Gilles de Gourmont,ca.1515

in 4°
chaps:a=15;b=26;g=19
Bks:One=aijrecto-bvverso;Two=bvverso-
 diijverso;Three=diijverso-evirecto
pages not numbered
Trapezuntius' own rhetoric precedes A's
R. in the Gennadius,Cambridge and Newberry copies
Index on final leaves gives only reference to Bks One & Two.
ICN date of 1519 in NUC is error. Newberry, in letter of 6/3/72,so acknowledged

Primo 6,6723

NUC 21,18;
0403880

not in Gesamt

Editions limited to commentaries will not be reported, with a few exceptions.
One of those is an early 1500 commentary entitled "Laurentianus Florentinus in
Librum Aristotelis de Elocutione (impressus impensis dñi [domini] Andree
Torresani de Asula), printed in Venice by Simonem de Luere on January 8, 1500.
        (footnote continued on next page)

	Metten:Inc.I.6
	MAmb:1074
	Munich:2°Inc.C.A.
	  1020M + 2°A.gr.b
	  171[rubr]
	Naples:S.a.V.F.41
	RomeAles:Inc.452
	RomeAng:In.564
	RomeCas:Vol.Inc.
	  2005
	Stockholm:Ink.103
	Stuttgart:Inc.fol.
	  821
	U.Pa:INC.4282F
	Venice:Incun.180
	  + Inc.342
	ViennaUB:II,137,910
	Weimar:Inc.64(n.a)
		two columns of Latin
		per page
			Alemannus rather than to Moerbeck.
			Pollard & Sholdered wrongly attribute
			Latin tr. to Herman. Gesamtkatalog &
			Goff are accurate. Schwab is cautious,
			saying R. & R. from Arabic into Latin
			by Hermann Alemannus with Dec. by Al-
			pharabi.
			Emmanuel(Camb) and Got.lack title page.
			Folios not numbered by printer, so
			librarians have often handlabeled.
			Contents are as follows:
			  Folio 1r-9v....Decleratio(Alfarabi)
			  Folios 10r-49r..Moerbeck's tr.
			  Folios 50r-63v .Hermann Alemanus'
			    tr. of Averroes com-
			    mentary on Poetics
			This book is a printing of BN MS.Latin
			16673.
				Hoffman 336
				
				Brunet I,476
				
				Mitarelli Ap-
				pendix 11-12
				
				Hain 1681 +
				*821
				
				Proctor 4282

c.
1499
	Bamberg:Inc.Typ.
	  M.III.3
	Bodleian:Auct.O.
	  inf.2.23
	Dresden:Ink.1005(2°)
	Gdansk:Cc4760 4°
	Gorlitz:Inc.138.5
	Leipzig:Arist.19a
	Manch:Christie 2ab
	Olomouc:48387
	Regensburg:4°Inc.207
	WroclawU:XV F987,5
	Uppsala:Ink.35b.167
		TITLE PAGE: Aristotelis Stagirite
		et philosophi oim℈[omniumque]
		spiratissimi et oratoris eloque[n]-
		tissimi tria rhetorico℈ [rum]
		volumia [sic] incredibili suauitate
		et rhetorice artis ubertate insig-
		nia; quibus pluria splendidissimi
		facultati rhetorice adiumenta at-
		quis ornamē[n]ta subministrasse
		cognoscitur [no period]
		
		folio 1r: Liber primus rhetoricorum
		aristotelis . . .
		
		The printer's mark on the colophon
		identifies the printer as Jacobus
		(Jakob) Thanner of Leipzig. The
		Bodleian determined that the type
		points to circa 1499 as date of
		publication.
			in 4°
			Book One has 27 paragraphs;Book Two,
			46 paragraphs;Book Three,23 paragraphs.
			Bks:One=48ff;Two=46ff;Three=33ff
			no pagination or foliation
			contains only Latin tr. by Moerbeck ex-
			cept for 6 lines of Latin verses by
			Dottanius
			copy at Dessau destroyed in WWII;
			Zittau does not have
				Hain 1679
				
				Proctor 3086
				
				Gesamt 6,6368
				
				Gesamt der
				Wiegendrucke
				2,2479

1504	Bodleian:Byw.A.5.1 Vienna:118.239-C	TITLE PAGE: Aristotelis Varia Opera Novissime Traducta . . . Rhetoricorum Aristotelis ad Theodecten Libri tres: Georgius Trabezuntius [sic] e graeco in latinum convertit. gggi: Rhetoricorum Aristotelis ad Theodecten Libri tres Georgius Trapezuntius in latinum transtulit. Venice: Bernardinus Venetus de Vitalibus, 1504 (on colophon)	in 2° chaps:A-19;B=28;G=19 Bks:One=27pp;Two=28pp;Three=20pp.Pp. not numbered. Total of 77 folios. Vienna copy lacks date	Hoffman 314 Ind Aur 2,155 107.721 Gesamt 6,6013 Cranz 107.721

1508	BM:686.i.5,6 + 835.
	  1.2 + 835.1.1 + 73.
	  g.13,14 + G.8499,
	  8500
	BN:Res.X.273
	  & Res.X.611
	Bodleian:Auct.
	  1R.4.3
	Camb:Trinity N.4.33-
	  34 + N.4.36(2)
	Gennadius:GC 3889
	Got:4oA gr I 3490
	Harv:*IC.M.3194
	  508r (Harvard
	  Film A19 does not
	  contain the R.)
	Ill:882 M31r
	Leid:1366 B 3
	Morgan:E28F
	Munich:2oImpr.c.n.
		TITLE PAGE: RHETORES IN HOC
		VOLUMINE HABENTUR HI.
		
		index on title page:Aristotelis
		Rhetoricorum ad Theodecten Librii
		tres.
		
		page 161: ΑΡΙΣΤΟΤΕΛΟΥΣ ΤΕΧΝΗΣ
		ΡΗΤΟΡΙΚΗΣ ΤΩΝ ΕΙΣ ΤΡΙΑ
		ΤΟ ΠΡΩΤΟΝ.
		
		Venice:Aldus Manus,1508-9 on
		colophon
			in 4° but somewhat small
			Bks:One=pp.161-187;Two=188-215;Three=215
			  234
			Because this edition is bound with other
			rhetorics, it often is not catalogued
			under "Aristotle" but under "Manuzio,
			Aldo Pio," the editor and printer, or
			as "anonymous" under "Rhetores Graeci."
			It should not be confused with its
			successor, Rhetorum Graecorum Oration-
			es published by Aldus in Venice in 1513.
			The R. & Poetics had not appeared in
			Aldus' 1495-1598 Greek edition.
			In the BN & Trinity copies, spaces were
			left for ornate capital letters never
			supplied.
			U.Chic fPA3484.M26 has only vol. 1;Stan-
			ford has only vol.1
				NUC 360,177
				under "Manu-
				zio:"
				0194257
				
				Fabricci III
				335
				
				Gesamt 6,6303
				(no loca-
				tions)
				
				Schwab 2946
				
				Hoffman 295
				
				Legrand I,82

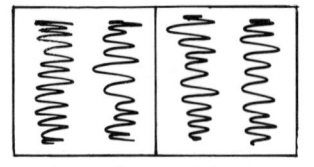

Aristotelis Stagirite et philosophi oim perspicatissimi et oratoris eloquentissimi tria rhetoricorum volumia incredibili suauitate et rhetorice artis vbertate insignia: quibus pluria splendidissime facultati rhetorice adiumenta atque ornameta subministrasse cognoscitur

Georgij bottanij menigensis Hexastichon

Excipe Aristotelem toti que contulit orbi
Stagira praeclarum lector amice iubar
Rhetorices campos peramoena fronte nitentes
Ingredere: excultos nobilis arte ducis
Collige odoriferos flores: liquidos bibe fontes
Dicendi certa lege peritus etis

PLATE FORTY-TWO

title page of the 1499 Leipsig edition

courtesy of the Universitetsbibliotheket, Uppsala Universitet, Sweden

PLATE FORTY-THREE

colophon of the 1499 Leipsig edition showing the printer's mark of Jacobus Thanner
courtesy of the Universitetsbibliotheket, Uppsala Universitet, Sweden

Early Printings

Georgii trapezuntii qui suis temporibus sopitam & tantum non mortuam Eloquentiam suscitauit Ars Rhetorica nunc primum in gallia ipressa: Et oratoribus nostri seculi maxie accommodata

Gilles de gourmont.

Parisiis apud Aegidium gourmōtiū qui in vtraqʒ lingua libros fidelissime imprimendos curat.

PLATE FORTY-FOUR

colophon of the 1515 Paris edition

courtesy of the Bayerische Staatsbibliothek, Munich

| 1523 | Basel:B.C.II.14
BM:11340.k.1
BN:Res.X.275
Bodleian:Byw.C.4.9
  + Auct.2 R.1.11
Brown:not catalogued
Camb:U.Lib. F.152.b.
  2.2;Trinity Grylls.
  11:400
Col:B881 G294 V 5
  1523
Gennadius:GC 3890
Harv:f 1C5.T1945.
  523g
Htgtn:HEH 137910
Leid:715 A 10
Lyon:343682
MAmb:S.Q.I.VII.27
  + S.Q.E.VII 14 +
  S.Q.E.VII 11 +
  S.Q.E.VII 18 +
  S.R.32
Munich:2oA.gr.C.24
Naples:S.Q.XIX.F.3
OxPem:7.d.
NYPub:*KB+1523
RomeAles:M.h.1
RomeAng:SS.6.54
RomeCas:Q.IV.20.
St.G:OE.A.Fol.
  35.Ind.54
UCLA:*Z 233 A4C768
Va:*PA3484.C65 1523
Vat:Chigi II 999
  (int.1)
Venice:Aldine 218
Vienna:22.M.5
WroclawU:363879 | TITLE IN INDEX: Aristotelis Rhe-
toricorum ad Theodecten Georgio
Trapezuntio interprete libri III

folio 109r: GEORGII TRAPEZUNTII
IN TRES RHETORICORUM ARISTOTELIS
LIBROS AD THEODECTEN TRALATIO

Venice:Aldus Manus, 1523
on colophon | in 4°
chaps:a=15;b=26;g=18
Bks:One=109r-118v;Two=118v-128v;Three=
  128v-135v
Book Three has capital letters for Chap.
9 omitted,but all of text is present.
Sometimes, as in Virginia copy,all capi-
tal letters to begin books are omitted
Jacobus Taurellus wrote preface
Contains Trapezuntius' own rhetoric along
with other rhetorics
NUC listing for American Antiquarian So-
ciety (MWA) is in error | Gesamt 6,6370
(no loca-
tions)

Hoffman 336

Schwab 2946

NUC 195,487;
0139027 +
21,18;
0403844 |
| 1529 | Bamberg:L.gr. 72
Basel:B.C.VII.36.
  No.28
Berlin:Vu 7481
  (Rarum)
Bodleian:A.S.275
BM:519.e.3
Camb:Trinity Grylls.
  7.53(3)
Got:4°A.gr.IV.515
Gotha:Phil.4° 260/d
Ill:881 A 8rh.fr.
  1529
Krakow:Gramm.2966
  & Cim.6123 &
  590003
MAmb:S.Q.T.VII.33 +
  35 (2nd copy) +
  21 (3rd copy)
Munich:4°A.gr.a.
  162/1
NYGT:RBR 185.1 AR
  460 1536/1529
OxPem:5.d.1. +
  5.d.38
Prague:65.D.3258
Princeton: Ex
  1559.383.029
RomeCas:M.VI.27
  CCC | TITLE PAGE:ΑΡΙΣΤΟΤΕΛΟΥΣ ΤΕΧΝΗΣ
ΡΗΤΟΡΙΚΗΣ ΒΙΒΛΙΑ Γ.

ARISTOTELIS DE ARTE RHETORICA
LIBRI TRES.

page 3:ΑΡΙΣΤΟΤΕΛΟΥΣ ΤΕΧΝΗΣ
ΡΗΤΟΡΙΚΗΣ ΤΩΝ ΕΙΣ ΤΡΙΑ ΤΟ
ΠΡΩΤΟΝ.

Basel:in officina Frobeniana
per Hieronymum Frobenium et
Ioannem Hervagium (Hieronymius
Froben and John Herwagen),1529,
Augusto. (see colophon for
details) | in 4° but small for quarto
Bks:One=3-58;Two=58-115;Three=116-156
only Greek
Munich copy preceded by Aristophanes;
Cambridge-Trinity copy bound with Poli-
tics & Ethics dated 1556 and 1560 res-
pectively. Trinity copy well annotated.
Fabricii links 1508 Aldo Pio edition
with editions of 1520,1529, and 1530
Schwab links Paris 1530;Venice 1537;
Basel 1546 and Argentorati 1547
Peabody Library of Johns Hopkins does
not have. | Gesamt 6,6304

NUC 21,11;
0463705

Ind Aur 2,174
107.904

Adams 1939

Fabricii III
335

Schwab 2937

Cranz 107.904 |

The preface is dated 1498. The work in 4° contains a Latin commentary by Petrus Trinitus Laurentiano in four books, bound with Aigidii [sic] on the Prior Analytics. See Hain 9947 & Coppinger, part 2, vol. 2, 270. Among the libraries holding this work are Harvard Nov.1499.7 or Inc.5624 (two entries for the same volume) and Bodleian Byw.G.6.19.

Year	Library	Title	Format	References
	Tub:Cd 2196.8⁰ + Ce 105.4⁰ ang. U.Pa:GrC Ar466 22 1529 Vat:Barb.I.111. 48 int.2 Yale:Gfa84 m529			
1530	BM:518a.34.(1.) + 518.a.36 BudapestNB:Ant.6109 MAmb:S.Q.S.II.28 Maz:20302 Princeton:2599.383. 030 Vat:R.G.Classici V.493	TITLE PAGE: ΑΡΙΣΤΟΤΕΛΟΥΣ ΤΕΧΝΗΣ ΡΗΤΟΡΙΚΗΣ ΒΙΒΛΙΑ Γ. ARISTOTELIS DE ARTE RHETORICA LIBRI TRES. page 1: ΑΡΙΣΤΟΤΕΛΟΥΣ ΤΕΧΝΗΣ ΡΗΤΟΡΙΚΗΣ ΤΩΝ ΕΙΣ ΤΡΙΑ ΤΟ ΠΡΩΤΟΝ. Paris: ex officina Gerhardi Morrhii (Gerard Morrhy) Campensis apud collegium Sorbonnae, 1530. Date on colophon and on title page.	in 16⁰ Bks:One=96pp;Two=96pp;Three=69pp pages not numbered only Greek in BM copy, R. first, followed by other works; BM catalogue says another 1529 edition	NUC 21,11; 0403706 Hoffman 296 Cranz 107.926 Ind Aur 2,176 107.926 not in Gesamt Schwab 2973
1530	Bodleian:St.Am.119 Maz:20302 RomeCas:N.XII. 46 in CC U Amst:O 67-1 Vat:R.G.Classici V.493	TITLE PAGE: ARISTOTELIS RHEtoricorum ad Theodecten,Georgio Trapezuntio interprete,libri III. page 2: GEORGII TRAPEZUNTII ab Pape Thesaurarium prologus in tres Rhetoricorum Aristotelis libros ad Theodecten,a se tralatos Paris:Simon de Colines,1530	in 8⁰ but small chaps:a=15;b=26(index gives 25);g=19 Bks:One=4r-47v;Two=47v-92r;Three=92r-123r only Latin Tours copy burned in fire of 1940	Legrand III, 333 Ind Aur 2,176 107.923 Hoffman 336 Schwab 3003 Cranz 107.923
1531	Augsburg:2⁰LG 37 Bamberg:L.gr.f.5 Basel:B.C.I.1 BM:30.G.7. + C.45.i.14 + 520.L.1.(2.) Bodleian:K 6.15 Art BudapAkB:ANT.937 BudapEK:vet 31/20 BudapNB:Ant.73 + 851 Camb:U.Lib.Peterboro A.5.23;Gonville-Caius G.32.5 Col:Gonzalez-Lodge 1531 Ar 46 Flor:5.1.149 Geneva:no call # Got:2⁰A.gr.IV.4 Halle:AB 65 137 Harv:*fNC5.Er 153,	TITLE PAGE: ΑΡΙΣΤΟΤΕΛΟΥΣ ΑΠΑΝΤΑ. ARISTOTELIS SUMMI SEMPER VIRI,ET IN QUEM UNUM uim suam universam contulisse natura reru(m) uidetur, opera,quaecunque impressa hactenus extiterunt omnia, summa cum vigilantia excusa page 121,vol.2:ΑΡΙΣΤΟΤΕΛΟΥΣ ΤΕΧΝΗΣ ΡΗΤΟΡΙΚΗΣ ΤΩΝ ΕΙΣ ΤΡΙΑ ΤΟ ΠΡΩΤΟΝ. [Desiderius] Erasmus of Roterdam [sic] & Simon Grynaeus (S.Gernusaeus), eds. Basel: Io.Beblium (John Bebel), 1531	in 4⁰ Bks:One=121r-130r;Bk Two=130v-139v;Bk Three=139v-146v Two vol. set; R. in vol.2; vol 1 has 335 folios:vol 2 has 253 folios only Greek text with type reset from Aldo Pio Camb.U.copy from library of Th.Greaves, M.D.ornately bound with leather clasps Fabricii links 1531 with 1539 Schwab quoting Brunet said reissue of 1508 with some changes by Grynaeus Lilly Library copy at Indiana has different paginations:One=202-218;Two= 218-531;Three=532-246 Yale and Prague (65.C.347) have only vol.one;Kiel,Bonn, and Berlin 2⁰Vt.423 + 2⁰Vt.8 lost in WWII;Munster does not have	Ind Aur 2,177 107.928 Gesamt 6,5894 NUC 20,583; 0400612 Primo 6,5313 Fabricci III 319 Adams 1730 Hoffman 288 Schwab 382

Hoffman, 295; Fabricci III, 335; Brunet I, 475 in note, and Panzer all indicate a 1520 Aristotelis Rhetorica et Poetica published in Basel by Frobenius. No such edition was found. Perhaps one index erred, transcribing 1529 to 1520, and other indexers copied that error. Or perhaps there is a 1520 edition not found by this research.

The 1521 edition of Aristotle's works listed in NUC 20,583, published in Paris by Colinae and housed at the library of the College of Physicians of Philadelphia does not contain the Rhetoric. Source is a letter of May 23, 1980, from the College of Physicians that included a copy of the title page enumerating the contents.

Monfasani (1984, 698) noted that the Trapezuntius translation underwent a revision when it appeared in Paris in 1530, and that these changes continued in subsequent editions. The initiator of these changes is unknown. Therefore only the first four published Trapezuntius editions are true to the translator's original version.

ΑΡΙΣΤΟΤΕΛΟΥΣ
ΤΕΧΝΗΣ ΡΗΤΟΡΙΚΗΣ ΤΩΝ ΕΙΣ
ΤΡΙΑ ΤΟ ΠΡΩΤΟΝ.

PLATE FORTY-FIVE

first page of the 1531 Basel edition showing the use of the Alphabet of the Dead

courtesy of the Universitätsbibliothek, Marbourg

ΑΡΙΣΤΟΤΕΛΟΥΣ ἍΠΑΝΤΑ,

ARISTOTELIS

SVMMI SEMPER VIRI, ET IN QVEM VNVM
uim suam uniuersam contulisse natura rerū uidetur, opera,
quæcunq impressa hactenus extiterunt omnia,
summa cum uigilantia excusa.

PER DES. ERAS. ROTERODAMVM
φιλολόγȣ καὶ βιβλιοπώλȣ διάλογ^ο.

Φιλ. Τὸν τοῦτον κομίζεις; βίβλον; βιβ. ὐδ' ἀμῶς. Φιλ. τί δή
Ειβ. Χρυσȣ ῥεῖθρα. Φιλ. Ναὶ σὺ πλȣσίως λέγεις,
Παχύτορον εἰπέ. βιβ. τὸν Σταγιρίτην λέγω,
ὃν ἔλαθεν ὐδέν τῶν μαθημάτων, ἱερός
Οὗτος γ' ἀνέκαθ' ὡς πρὸς τὸ πολὺ καλλίων.
Φιλ. Λέγεις ἀληθῶς τ' ἀμαλθείας κέρας,
Βιβ. Οὐ μὴν γ' ὀπώρας μεστόν, ἀλλ' ἀμφνόνων.
Φιλ. Καὶ τίς ὁ τοῦτον πλȣτον ἡμῖν ἐμφέρει;
Βιβ. Τοῦτόν γε παρέχει φιλόπονος Βιβέλιος.
Φιλ. Χρυσέμπορος γοῦν ὅδε ἢν, ὃ λογέμπορος;
Βιβ. Ναί, κεἴτι χρυσȣ τῶν λόγων προφερέστερον,
θέας δὲ σοφίας οὐδὲν ἐς αὐτ' ἀξιον.

PALMA BEB.

Indicem librorum, id est, longum diuitis thesauri
catalogum, octaua pagina continet.

BASILEAE, APVD IO. BEB.
ANNO M. D. XXXI.
Cum gratia & priuilegio Cæsareo.

PLATE FORTY-SIX

title page of the 1531 Basel edition

courtesy of the Universitätsbibliothek, Marbourg

	531a + fOGC Ar46, 531 Ill:uncatalogued Ind:PA389U .A2 1531 Leipsig:fol.Arist.1 Lyon:107184 Marburg:IV A 41(2) Maz:3468 + 3469 Munich:2⁰A.gr.b.74 Naples:84.M.5 Newb:CASE fY 642.A805 Nurn:Philos.56.2⁰ OxPem:6.c. RomeCas:L.III.5-6 RomeBNC:69.4.G.35 U.Okla:Hist.of Sci. Collections-un-catalogued Yale:Gfa 84 + A531 Vat:R.G.Classic.II 16;R.G.Classic II 92 + Mai XI.K.X.16 Vienna:71.b.12 + another Wf.ALVENSLEBEN Ca 10 2⁰ WroclawU:464.742			Brunet I,458 Cranz 107.928
1534	Edinb:D.N.S.474 Ill:881 a 8rh.Lg Ind:Spec.PA389.3 Z563 Munich:A.gr.b.640 Newb:CASE Y642.A8937 Nurn:Philos.1.8⁰ UNC:PA 3893.Z5	TITLE PAGE: ARISTOTELIS RHETORICORUM AD THEOdecten, Georgio Trapezuntio interpret, libri III page 5: RHETORICORUM ARISTOTELIS AD THEODECTEN. LIBER PRIMUS. Basel:in officina Frobeniana, 1534(date also on colophon)	in 8⁰ chaps:a=15;b=26;g=19 Bks:One=5-77;Two=77-151;Three=152-205 only Latin	Ind Aur 2,178 107.940 Gesamt 6,6371 Hoffman 336 NUC 21,19; 0403885 Cranz 107.940 Legrand III, 352
1536	BM:518.a.35 + 165.d.10 + 111824.aa.32.(1) + G.7921 BN:X.16674 + Res. X.2147 Bodleian:8⁰E.7.BS. + Byw.K.3.8 Flor:3.C.6.90 Gennadius:GC 3213 Got:8⁰A Gr IV 517 & 518(2 copies) Ill:881 A8rh 1536 Ind:PA3893.R3 1536 Iowa:xPA3893 R3 1536 MilanB:&&.VI.92 Munich:A.gr.b.626 (defective) (Victorius' bookmark) RomeAles:O.e.103 RomeAng:TT.21.78 RomeBNC:6.6.B.64 RomeCas:p.V.17.1 Vat:Ross.5543 + Chigi V.1464 + Barb.J.II.83	TITLE PAGE:ΑΡΙΣΤΟΤΕΛΟΥΣ ΤΕΧΝΗΣ ΡΗΤΟΡΙΚΗΣ ΒΙΒΛΙΑ Γ. ARISTOTELIS DE ARTE RHETORICA LIB. TRES folio 1r:ΑΡΙΣΤΟΤΕΛΟΥΣ ΤΕΧΝΗΣ ΡΗΤΟΡΙΚΗΣ ΤΩΝ ΕΙΣ ΤΡΙΑ ΤΟ Α. Venice:in aedibus Bartholomari Zanetti (Bartholomaeus Zanettus). 1536 (January)	in 8⁰ but small Bks:One=1r-68r;Two=68r-138r;Three=138r-186v R. is in first 186pp; edition includes Poetics and ad Alexandrum Munich copy lacks final pp. after 149 pages not numbered,only printer's marks only Greek. Fabricii links with 1546 Venice edition;Schwab with 1546 and 1551 editions Munich copy heavily annotated by Victorius Florence copy has One=cc.1r-34r;Two=34r-69r;Three=69r-93r RomeAng copy has One=2iir-6ivr;Two=6ivr-5iiir;Three=5iiir-wiiir Trincavelli's marginal variant readings are not frequent. RomeBNC copy formerly owned by the Society of Jesus.	NUC 20,595; 0400905 + 0400907 Gesamt 6,5992 Primo 6,5345 Ind Aur 2,180 107.955 Hoffman 295 Fabricci III 335 Schwab 2947 Brunet I,475 Cranz 107.955

Early Printings 103

Venice:121.D.191
+ 214.C.132
Vienna:214.C.132

1537
BM:520.i.8
Bodleian:Byw.D.63
Naples:XXV.E.64
RomeAles:C.d.42
RomeCas:L.IV.1
RomeBNC:8.26.H.16/1
RomeV:S.Borr.H.IV.90(1)

TITLE PAGE: Magni philosophi Augustini niphi Medicis Suessani Expositio atquis interpretatio lucida in Libros artis Rhetorice Aristotelis. Nouiter ab ipso authore in lucem edita, ad Antonium Carlonium Allifanorum Principem.

Venice: apud Octauianum Scotum(Octavianus Scotus), 1538. Date on colophon is 1538

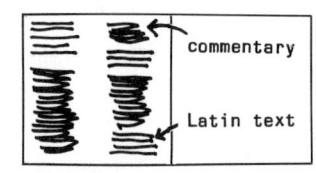

[diagram showing commentary and Latin text layout]

in 4°
Bks:One=2r-71v;Two=71v-123r;Three=123r-153v
The editor made random editorial changes in the Moerbeck text, seemingly as he wished. Of course there was nothing to prevent an editor from adopting an ancient text, editing or not editing the text, and issuing it under his own name. In 1537 there was little familiarity with the varying Latin versions of the Rhetoric, so appropriation of texts was easy, convenient, and possibly profitable.
Rome BV, RomeCas, and Bodleian copies have 1538 on the colophon, which may be that the book was reissued in the following year.

Primo 6,6724

not in Gesamt

1538
Augsburg:2°LG 40
Bamberg:L.gr.f.7
Basel:B.C.I.12
Brown:1538 Ar4 2-Size
BudapNB:Ant.103
Camb:Jesus Eil.24
Col:B888 Ar51 JP8
Erl:VII,9
Flor:5.2.2227
Minn:288Ar41 fJV837
Munich:2°A.gr.b.86
Nurn:Philos.58.2°
Oregon:MF 473 D688
OxPem:1.i.4
PhilAPS:885.Ar 4°
Prague:5.A.25
Sibiu:u III 228
Tub:Cd 911
Vienna:17.A.1
WroclawU:463037
+ 463038

TITLE PAGE, vol. 1: ARISTOTELIS STAGIRITAE, PHILOSOPHORUM OMNIUM FACILE PRINCIPIS,OPERA quae quidem extant omnia , . . .

page 242,vol.two: ARISTOTELIS STAGIRITAE RHETORICORUM AD THEODECTEN LIBER primus,Georgio Trapezuntio interprete.

TITLE PAGE, vol.2:OPERUM ARISTOTELIS STAGIRITAE,PARTIM AD GRAECUM EXEMPLAR DILIGENtissimé recognitorum,partim nunc primum latinate donatoru, TOMUS SECUNDUS. Adiectae estuita Aristotelis, de ✠ [que] genere philosophiae, ac scriptis eiusdem,commentatio doctissima,PER PHILLIPUM MELANCH.

Basel: J(ohn) Oporinus, 1538

in 4°
chaps:a=15;b=26;g=19
Bks:One=242-264;Two=264-287;Three=287-303 (pages sometimes irregularly numbered
two vols.can be bound together;R.in vol.2 ed. Philippus Melanchthonus with notes by Simon Grynaeus
Olomouc III.27410 has only vol.one
Colophon says Sept.,1538,with publisher identified by his mark

NUC 20,590;
0400784;
20,591;
0400786

Gesamt 6,5959

Ind Aur 2,
181-182;
107.968

Cranz 107.968

1538
Bodleian:Antiq.f.F.1538/1
Brown:uncatalogued
Ghent:CL1273
Ill:uncatalogued
Limoges:L696 in 8°
Madrid:2/69949
Roanne:R 8° 140
U.Pa:GrC Ar466 22 1538 (2 copies)
Vat:R.G.Classici V282

TITLE PAGE:ΑΡΙΣΤΟΤΕΛΟΥΣ ΤΕΧΝΗΣ ΡΗΤΟΡΙΚΗΣ ΒΙΒΛΙΑ ΤΡΙΑ.

ARISTOTELIS DE arte Rhetorica libri tres.

page 3:ΑΡΙΣΤΟΤΕΛΟΥΣ ΤΕΧΝΗΣ ΡΗτορικῆς τῶν εἰς τρία τὸ πρῶτον.

Paris:Chr.Wechelius (Chrestien Wechel),1538

in 8°
Bks:One=3-80;Two=81-161;Three=162-216
some readings in the margin
only Greek
BN does not have
Annonay copy burned in library fire

Ind Aur 2,182
107.976

not in Gesamt

Hoffman 296

NUC 21,11;
0403707

Cranz 107.976

1539
Alleg:Tf 888.5 Ar 4ae
Augsburg:2°LG 41
Basel:B.C.I.2
BN:R698-699
Bodleian:Antiq.c.GS.1539.2

TITLE PAGE: Αριστοτέλους ἅπαντα

ARISTOTELIS SUMMI SEMPER VIRI,ET IN QUEM UNUM UIM suam universam contulisse natura rerum videtur . . .

in 4°
Bks:One=202-218;Two=218-235;Three=235-246
only Greek in two vols;R. in vol.two lines numbered 10,20,30,40,50
Copies in Camb U Lib and in Genadius

Gesamt 6,5895

Primo 6,5314

Adams 1731

	BudapEK: 39/66
	Camb:U.Lib.Bury 1.
	  12-13;Gonville-
	  Caius G.32.10;Kings
	  K.20.22;Clare Q.3.
	  9.;St.Johns Dd.1.
	  32;Pembroke 9.17.13
	Col:Spec.Col.B88Ar51
	  JP8
	Cornell:RARE PA3890
	  A2tt 1539
	Gennadius: GC 3128
	Got:4°A.gr.IV.6
	Harv:Ga 112 105F*
	  (2 copies A & B
	  under same number)
	Leid:758 A 7;706 A
	  3;758 A.8
	Leipsig:fol.Arist.2
	MAmb:S.R.509 + S.R.
	  582 + S.Q.Z.VIII.
	  3-4
	Marburg: IV A 42
	Maz:3470
	Munich:2oA.gr.b.75
	Nurn:Philos.57.2o
	OxPem:8.b.8
	Olomouc:III.27765
	PhilAcad:QH41/.A71
	  Pre-Linnean Col.
	RomeAng:TT.19.16
	RomeBNC:71.3.F.2 +
	  69.4.G.34 +
	  71.3.F.1
	RomeBV:S.Borr.VII.1
	St.Gen:R.fol.26
	  inv.21
	U.Pa:fGrC Ar 466 1
	  1539
	Vat:Barb.J.X 3-4
	  + Barb.J.X.5-6
	Vienna:71.b.13
		page 202,vol.2:ΑΡΙΣΤΟΤΕΛΟΥΣ ΤΕΧΝΗΣ ΡΗΤΟΡΙΚΗΣ ΤΩΝ ΕΙΣ ΤΡΙΑ ΤΟ ΠΡΩΤΟΝ.
		
		ed.[Desiderius] Erasmus of Roterdam [sic] with notes by Simon Grynaeus
		
		Basel: Io. (Joannes) Bebelius and Michel Isingrinius, [1539]
			dated. Date written in ink on fly leaf of vol. one of BN copy. Harvard copy A has title page saying MCXXXIX with 1539 written in pencil; in 2nd Harvard copy B, lacking title page, many inked-in annotations
			Some use of Hans Holbein the Younger's woodcuts for capital letters, known as "Alphabet of the Dead." See A.B.Chamberlain, Hans Holbein the Younger, 2 vols. (London: George Allen, 1913) BN Estampes Yb33.2063. The alphabet spread Protestant doctrine,using 24 letters with no "J" or "U" as would be expected. It appeared as early as 1524. Block prints for 1531 and 1539 editions vary.
			Life of Aristotle by Guarinus.
			Kiel copy burned in WWII;Griefswald copy is lost;Wurzburg copy L.gr.f.108 missing since 1963;WroclawU copy missing after WWII.
				Ind Aur 2,183
				107.980
				
				NUC 20,583;
				0400613
				
				Schwab 54,
				383
				
				Hoffman 288-9
				
				Brunet,Supp.
				59
				
				Cranz 107.980

1540	Munich:A.gr.b.2o 174	TITLE PAGE: ANTONII BERNARDI MIRANDULANI CASERTAE EPISCOPI, aetate sua Philosophi celeberrimi, IN LIBRUM RHET. ARIST. EGREGIA EXPLICATIO. page 9: ANTONII BERNARDII MIRANDULANI CASERTAE EPISCOPI In primum, & secundum Cap.lib. primi.Rhetoricorum Aristotelis, expositio. Bononiae (Bologna): apud Michaelem Berniam (Michel Berni), 1540	in 2° Bks:One=9-94;Two=94-156;Three=156-186 The editor made some editorial changes in the Moerbeck version, and added his commentary.	
1540	Besancon:BN X.156672 BN:X.16672 Col:Spec.Col.	TITLE PAGE: Aristotelis rheTORICORUM AD THEODECTEN,GEORGIO	reprint of 1530 edition chaps:a=15;b=26;g=19 Bks:One=ff.4r-38r;Two=38r-72v;Three=72v-96v	Cranz 107.990 Ind Aur 2,184 107.990

A popular commentary on the Rhetoric, published in Paris by Conradus Neobarius in 1539 entitled Aristote de arte rhetorica libri III gr. com commentariis anonym is a commentary. The single volume, in Greek in 4o, contains 82 folios, with the commentary on the Rhetoric on the first eighty folios. The Greek title is ΕΙΣ ΤΗΝ ΑΡΙΣΤΟΤΕΛΟΥΣ ΡΗΤΟΡΙΚΗΝ ΥΠΟΜΝΗΜΑ ΑΝΩΝΥΜΟΝ. Locations are numerous: BM 519.i.36; Camb.U.Lib. Cc.l0.6(1) + R.2.35(1)(c); Camb.Trinity N.4.36 + II.6.30; Camb.Clare I.6.5. + E.6.4; Camb. St. Catharine's F.III.61; Camb.Emmanuel S.11.2.37; Camb. St. Johns Cc.3.33; Camb. Peterhouse S.140(1); Morgan E28F; Munich 2oA.gr.b.175; U.Pa. GrC Ar466 (T)22 1539; Bodleian P.1.13 Med; Illinois xq 881 A 8rh 1539. For documentation, see Fabricci III, 335; Adams 1960; Schwab 293, 3047; Ind.Aur. 107,985; & Primo 6,5699.

Early Printings

	B88Ar51 VB40 Edinb:K.32.6 Maz:20303 U.Pa:GrC Ar66 Ef 22 1540 ViennaUB:I 161.814	TRAPEZUNTIO interprete,libri III. page 3: GEORGII TRAPEZUNTII ad Papae Thesaurarium prologus in tres Rhetoricorum Aristotelis libros ad Theodecten a se tralatos. Paris:Simon de Colines,1540	WroclawU copy missing after WWII	Legrand 3,394
1541	Bodleian:Antiq.f.F 1541/2 Flor:5.BC.8.56 Ill:UNCAT 77:1116 Padua:135a101 RomeBNC:6.6.F.4 + 6.6.F.48/1	TITLE PAGE: ARISTOTELIS RHETORICORUM AD THEODECTEN LIBRI TRES, Georgio Trapezuntio interprete page 4: RHETORICORUM ARISTOTELIS AD THEODECTEN LIBER PRIMUS. Lyon:Sebastian Gryphius, 1541	in 8° but small chaps:a=15;b=25;g=19 Bks:One=4-=64;Two=64-125;Three=125-167 only Latin Brunet, I, 458 linked loosely to the 1550 edition which he said underwent some revisions	Primo 6,6725 Ind.Aur 2,186 108.015 Baudrier VIII 155 Cranz 108.015
1542	Augsburg:2°LG 43 Bamberg:L.gr.f.8 Basel:B.C.I.15 Berlin:2°Vt.424a RARA BM:C.76.f.5 BN:R695-697 BudapNB:1916 Camb:Trinity copy could not be located in 1981; St.Johns Cc.8.9 Cath:C.L.185.1 A717 Erl-Nurn:2°Phil. VII 10 Folger:PA3890 A2 L7 1542 Cage Lyon:107187 Munich:2°A.gr.b.87 Naples:84.M.6-7 + XXX.3.14-17 + XXXVIII.5.79 + B.Branc.4.4.H.34 (incomplete) OxAS:i.1. Prague:5.A.25 Princeton:Ex 2599. 2542q RomeV:S.Borr.H. VII.2 St.Mary:B 406 1542 Folio UCBanc:B406 1542 Wolf:Lg 2o 9 WroclawU:GK VI: 6960 Vat:St.Barbarini Cr.Tasso 40	TITLE PAGE,vol 1: ARISTOTELIS STAGIRITAE,PHILOSOPHORUM OMNIUM FACILE PRINCIPIS, OPERA quae in hunc unqs[usque] diem extant omnia (some titles vary) page 293,vol.3: ARISTOTELIS STAGIRITAE RHETORICORUM AD THEODECTEN LIBER primus Georgio Trapezuntio interprete. Basel:[J.Oporinus],1542	in 4° chaps:a=15;b=26;g=19 Bks:One=293-314;Two=315-340;Three=340-358 lines numbered 10,20,30,40,50 three vol. set bound in 2 or 3 covers; Trapezuntius' tr. in vol.3 Running heads confusing,sometimes saying "Ethicorum ad Evdemum Lib II," sometimes "Rhetorica ad Alexandrum." vol.1 dated 1538 Munich copy marked "Bibliotheca Palatina." Munich has only vols. 1 & 2. Catholic U copy in Clementine Collection, after library of Pope Clement. Munster does not have;BudapestNB has only vol.3;Prague has this 1542 vol. 3 joined with first 2 vols. of 1538 edition	Adams 1742 Primo 6,5779 Gesamt 6,5960 NUC 20,591; 0400787 Ind Aur 2,188 108.033 Cranz 108.033
1545	Bordeaux:B3h89 Brescia:8° F.X.13 Madrid: 27460 Maz:20305 MilanB:&& VI.100 U.Chic:PA3895.R3 G35 1545 Vienna SB:71 M.20(2) Venice:114.D.172.1	TITLE PAGE: RHETORICORUM ARISTOTELIS AD THEODECTEN LIBRI TRES. GEORGIO TRAPEZUNTIO interprete. page 4: RHETORICORUM ARISTOTELIS AD THEODECTEN LIBER PRIMUS. Lyon:Sebastian Gryphius,1545	in 8° Bks:One=4-64;Two=64-125;Three=125-171 total of 248 pp. including R. ad Alex Princeton copy lost	NUC 21,19; 0403891 Gesamt 6,6375 Primo 6,6728 Ind Aur 2,46 108.102 Baudrier VIII, 193 Cranz 108.102

Year	Locations	Title	Notes	References
1546	BM:518.a.37 + 2nd. copy BN:Res.p.x.429(original number changed to reserve room) Bodleian:Byw.K.3.9 + second copy Flor:11.F.8.124 Gennadius: GC 3214 Ill:Uncat 64 Ind:PA3893.R3 1546 Munich:A.gr.b.623 + A.gr.b.624 + A.gr.b.625 (with Victorius' bookmark) Naples:38.A.46 1/2 RomeBNC:36.9.A.32 + 6.6.A.17 + 6.5.B.17 + 71.2.B.18 + 71.2.B.26 U.Chic:PA3893.R3 1546 Venice:219.C.163 Vienna:46.Mm.137 WroclawA:XVI.O.8715	TITLE PAGE: ΑΡΙΣΤΟΤΕΛΟΥΣ ΤΕΧΝΗΣ ΡΗΤΟΡΙΚΗΣ ΒΙΒΛΙΑ Γ. ARISTOTELIS DE ARTE RHETORICA LIBRI III. page 1: ΑΡΙΣΤΟΤΕΛΟΥΣ ΤΕΧΝΗΣ ΡΗΤΟΡΙΚΗΣ ΤΩΝ ΕΙΣ ΤΡΙΑ ΤΟ Α. Venice:Johannes Gryphius excudebat, 1546	in 8° but small Bks:One=3-91;Two=89-178;Three=179-240 Some maginal annotations, but not many. Alphabet of the Dead supplied to begin Bk One, but not for Bks Two or Three Title page in NY Pub missing, supplied from BM by photostat. Therefore the Lyon, 15-- edition, listed at the NY Pub in NUC 21,11, may be this 1546 edition, and the lack of date in the NUC attributable to lack of title page. NY Pub Rare Bk Rm could not trace the NUC entry to any other edition in their collection only Greek BM falsely attributed 518.a.36 copy to Aldus, 1537, on title page	Ind Aur 2,197 108.112 Adams 1940 Gesamt 6,6305 Primo 6,5700 Hoffman 296 NUC 21,11; 0403708 + 0403704 Cranz 108.112
1546	Augsburg:LG 196 Basel:BcVII 692 BM:C.19.f.5 + 518.a.36 BN:X.16676 Bodleian: 8°D.128.Art Camb: U.Lib. W.6.41 Col:Spec.Col.Gonzalez-Lodge 1546 Ar 463 Mich:PA3893.R3 1546 MAmb:S.Q.T.II.36 + S.Q.S.II.9 MilanB:&&.VI.94/1 NYPub:*KB 1546 RomeCas:p.XIX.28 UCBanc:PN173 A73R1 1546 U.Pa:GrC Ar466 22 1546 Ven:133.D.212.1 Wolf.Lg 298	TITLE PAGE: ΑΡΙΣΤΟΤΕΛΟΥΣ ΤΕΧΝΗΣ ΡΗΤΟΡΙΚΗΣ ΒΙΒΛΙΑ Γ. ARISTOTELIS DE ARTE RHETORICA LIBRI TRES. page 3: ΑΡΙΣΤΟΤΕΛΟΥΣ ΤΕΧΝΗΣ ΡΗΤΟΡΙΚΗΣ ΤΩΝ ΕΙΣ ΤΡΙΑ ΠΡΩΤΟΝ. Basel:apud Isingrinium, 1546	in 8° but BN copy small;Primo says in 16o Bks:One=3-91;Two=91-178;Three=179-240 Got copy lost in WWII only Greek, although Greek & Latin on title page some variant readings in the margins Bodleian links to 1536 edition with Rh. ad Alex pages irregularly numbered	NUC 20,595; 0400907 Primo 6,5347 Ind Aur 2,197 108.121 Hoffman 295 Schwab 2947 Gesamt 6,5993 Cranz 108.121
1547	Munich:A.gr.b.627 + A.gr.b.2247	TITLE PAGE: ΑΡΙΣΤΟΤΕΛΟΑΣ ΤΕΧΝΗΣ ΡΗΤΟΡΙκῆς βιβλία γ́. ARISTOTELIS DE ARte dicendi, libri tres. page 1: ΑΡΙΣΤΟΤΕΛΟΥΣ ΤΕΧΝΗΣ ΡΗΤΟΡΙΚΗΣ ΤΩΝ ΕΙΣ ΤΡΙΑ τὸ πρῶτον. Argentorati(Strasbourg): W.Rihelius (W.Rihel), 1547 (on colophon)	in 16° Bks:One=2r-47r;Two=47v-93v;Three=93v-125r only Greek date penned in on title page, but appears on colophon folios sometimes numbered irregularly Munich copy bound with other works	Gesamt 6,6306 Hoffman 296 Ind Aur 2,199 108.133 Cranz 108.133
1548	Basel:B.C.I.17 Berlin:2° Bibl.Diez. 326-327 BN:R.70 BudapestAkB:Ant.932 BudapNB:Ant.294 Camb:Corpus Christi G.3.4;Pembroke 9.17.15;Peterhouse M.7.14	TITLE PAGE,vol.1: ARISTOTELIS STAgiritae,,Philosophorum omnium FACILE PRINCIPIS,OPERA,QUAE IN hunc usɜ̃ɜ̃ [usque] Diem Extant omnia page 278,vol.3: ARISTOTELIS STAGIRITAE RHETORICORUM AD THEODECTEN LIBER primus, Georgio Trapezuntio interprete.	in 4° chaps:a=15;b=26;g=19 Bks:One=278-299;Two=299-321;Three=322-337 lines numbered 10,20,30,40,50 only Latin R. in vol.3 of 3 vol. set editor Hier. Gemusaeus BN & Corpus Christi title pages differ Corpus Christi copy does not give name of publisher	Ind Aur 2,199 108.137 Adams 4,10,31 Gesamt 6,5961 NUC 20,591; 0400789

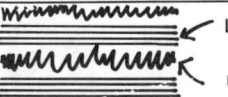

	Erl:2º Phl.VII,14
	Harv:*61.807F
	Munich:2ºA.gr.b.88
	  1-2-3
	Olomouc:27412
	PhilCP:Cage-Zy-4-
	  1548
	Vienna:70.C.5
	Wolf:Lg 2º (3)
	WroclawU:415094
		Basel:ex officina Ioan.Oporini
		(John Oporinus), 1548
			U.Pa. copy fGrC Ar 466 Ef1 1548 lacks
			vol.3;Augsburg does not have; Prague,both
			S.A.27 and Sa.31(I-II) do not have vol.3
				Cranz 108.137

1548	BM:520.k.11 + 73.h.9
	BN:R.253
	Bodleian:G.5.8.Art
	  + Byw.G.4.15
	Camb:Jesus E.2.25;
	  Magd:I.2.15;St.C.
	  E.III.45;St.J.C6.
	  8.23;Trin.T.6.23
	  + T.17.6-12; Trin
	  H. E.3.29
	Cornell:RARE PA3893
	  R3 1548
	Edinburgh:K.31.a
	Flor:3.301
	Got:4ºA.gr.IV 607
	Harv:Smyth 2893.10
	Htgtn:371272
	Ill:xq 881 A8rh.Yve
	  1548
	Ind:PA3893.R4 V592
	  1548
	MAmb:S.T.N.X.17
	MilanB:&&.10.54
	Maz:135
	Munich:2ºA.gr.b.167
	  + A.gr.b.168
	  (Victorius;
	  bookmark) +
	  2ºA.gr.b.169
	Naples:38.F.3 +
	  S.Q.XXII.E.4
	Newb:CASE fY
	  642.A8945
	OxCC:A.B.3.4
	RomeAng:YY.16.18
	RomeBNC:31.2.H.6
	RomeBV:S.Borr.H.
	  VIII.74
	St.Gen:X.fol.138
	  Inv.240 Res.
	Stanford:RBC
	  KB1548 V4f
	U.Chic.fPN 185.V6
	U.Pa:gGrC Ar466 22
	  1548
	UCBanc:fB450 B39
	  1548
	Vat:R.I.II.333 +
	  Chigi II.675 +
	  Barber.J.X.9
	Venice:149.D.8 +
	  69.D.92
		TITLE PAGE: PETRI VICTORII
		COMMENTARII IN TRES LIBROS
		ARISTOTELIS DE ARTE DICENDI.
		POSITIS ANTE SINGULAS
		DECLARATIONES GRAECIS VERBIS
		AUCTORIS
		
		page 1: PETRI VICTORII
		DECLARATIONE IN ARISTOTELIS
		RHETORICES LIBRUM PRIMUM.
		
		Florence:in officina Bernadus
		Juncta,1548 (details on colophon)
			in 4º
			Bks:One=1-234;Two=235-450;Three=451-637
			Trinity T.17.6-12 given by Sir J.E.
			Sandys, fellow at St. Johns in 1922
			gilt on leaves of copy two in BN and
			in Camb.U.Lib.
			1547 editions listed in NUC as held at
			PPL and PPULC are in error. Must have
			occurred because the introduction to the
			1549 edition says it was written in Flo-
			rence in September of 1547
			Part I of Staats Bib. in Munich: "Cata-
			logue #733-825 'Codices ex bibliotheca
			Petri Victorii"
			2oA.gr.b.177 & 178 have Victorius' book-
			mark & 177 appears to have some of his
			notes
			At Edinburg there are a number of books
			on the shelf number other than this edi-
			tion
			The Greek text and the commentary are
			interspersed
			
			←Latin commentary by Victorius
			←Greek text by Victorius
				Primo 6,5701
				Adams 1941
				Hart I, 141
				NUC 21,11;
				0403710
				Hoffman 296
				Schwab 3049

1549	Bamberg:L.r.f.9
	BN:Res.R.156
	  + R.254
	Bodleian:D.5.10 Art
	Edinburgh:K.31.a
	Ill:q881 A8rh.Yve
	  1549
	Leid:707 A.57 +
	  13 f.1
	Maz:134
	Munich:2oA.gr.b.176
		TITLE PAGE: PETRI VICTORII
		Commentarij longe doctissimi,in
		tres libros Aristotelis de Arte
		dicendi,nunc primum in Germania
		editi. Cum locuplete rerum et
		verborum in ijsdem memorabilium
		Indice.
		
		page 2: PETRI VICTORII
		DECLARATIONES IN ARISTOTELIS
			in 4º
			Bks:One=cols.1-308;Two=309-613;Three=
			  614-871
			lines numbered 10,20,30,40,50
			type set in 2 cols per page
			BN R.254 not in BN catalogue;found by
			observing that the numbers R.253 and
			R.255 pertained to A. and by taking
			a chance in requesting R.254
				NUC 21,11;
				0403711
				Hoffman 296
				Schwab 3059

PETRI VICTORII
DECLARATIONES,
IN ARISTOTELIS
RHETORICES

LIBRVM PRIMVM.

Ἡ ῥητορική ἐστιν ἀντίστροφος τῇ διαλεκτικῇ.

RIMAM hanc huius libri partem, summos uiros, qui ipsam interpretentur habere, constat: M. Ciceronem & Alexandrum Aphrodisiensem: quorum alter, cum ingenuas etiam alias artes didicisset, huius maxime stud.; atq; artificij peritissimus merito semper est habitus: alter uero ita accurate cunctos Aristotelis libros euoluit, ac tantum ingenio ualuit, ut omnia obscuriora sensa eorum & percipere ipse, & alijs declarare potuerit. Dissidere tamen hi inter se in loci huius explicatione uidentur. quare sententias amborum proferam, &, quid utrunq; secutum esse suspicer, ostendam. Ciceronis igitur ex oratore uerba hæc sunt. Atq; etiam ante hunc Aristoteles, principio artis rhetoricæ, dicit illam artem quasi ex altera parte respondere dialecticæ. ut hoc uidelicet differant inter se: quod hæc ratio dicendi, latior sit: illa loquendi, contractior. Hæc autem è libro primo Academicarum quæstionum ad Varronem. Huic quasi ex altera parte, oratoria uis dicendi adhibebatur: explicatrix orationis perpetuæ, ad persuadendum accommodatæ: eundem enim hunc locum manifesto intelligit, quamuis sententiam hanc Aristotelis esse: ut in oratore fecerat, non ostendat. Alexander uero in primum librum Topicorum, de dialectica loquens, inquit. Τοιαύτην δ᾽ οὖσαν αὐτὴν, εἰκότως καὶ ἀντίστροφόν φησιν ὁ Ἀριστοτέλης εἶναι τῇ ῥητορικῇ, ἐπειδὴ κἀκείνη περὶ τὰ πιθανά: ἃ, τῷ ἐνδόξα εἶναι καὶ αὐτά ἐστι τοιαῦτα: τὸ γὰρ ἀντίστροφον ἀντὶ τοῦ ἰσόστροφόν τε καὶ περὶ τὰ αὐτὰ στρεφομένην καὶ καταγινομένην, λέγει. Cum tradat hic scilicet Aristoteles dialecticam esse antistrophon rhetoricæ: sit autē dialectica qualem illic descripsit Alexander, recte ipsum fecisse. Rhetorica nanq; circa res ad persuadendum accommodatas uersatur, quæ huiuscemodi sunt, ac naturam eam habent, quia conueniunt opinionibus hominum: quicquid enim sensibus iudicijsq; hominum conuenit, id etiam ad persuadendum appositum est. nam quod ad uim nominis pertinet, ἀντίστροφον pro ἰσόστροφον positum ab eo esse uult. id autem nihil aliud est, nisi quæ uersatur circa easdem res, & in illis tractandis tota occupatur. intelligit autem quæ ex opinionibus hominum sunt, & ἔνδοξα ob eam causam uocantur. Et sententiam igitur Aristotelis, & uim uerbi, unde omnis controuersia orta est, expressit Alexander. Sed ad Ciceronem reuertamur, qui, ut liquido intelligitur, aliam primæ partis huius nominis rationem esse credidit: est enim manifesto duplex, è duobusq; nominibus iunctum nomen. Non igitur, ut Alexander postea fecit ἀντί Cicero hic ἴσον significare putauit: quo intellectu sæpe prisci Græci capiebant, & quam uim in multis iunctis uerbis habet, sed è regione & contra: hoc enim significare apud ipsum ex altera parte, perspicuum est: alijs nanq; etiam plurimis in locis, ita Cicero locutus est, & in orationibus, & in libris, quos de philosophia scripsit: exemplis enim in re plana, & quæ passim obuia sit, supersedebo. Videtur igitur ita locum hunc Cicero accepisse, tanquam discriminis etiam aliquid inter has artes esse, significare hic uoluerit Aristoteles: nam similes illas esse: affinesq; multum inter se, optime ipse intelligebat. id enim manifesto significauit, cum appellarit antea dialecticam, uicinam atq; finitimam rhetoricæ. Sed etiā uerbo idem indicasse uidetur, quo hic usus est, cum inquit ipsam respōde. eo.n. prorsus similitudo quædā declaratur. nihil igitur protulit, si diligenter attendimus, quod uerum nō sit, & notioni eius nominis, & naturæ rei, nō quadret: Alexander.n.

A

PLATE FORTY-SEVEN A

page one of the 1548 Victorius Florence edition

courtesy of the Library of the University of Illinois at Champaign-Urbana

PETRI VICTORII DECLARA-
TIONES IN ARISTOTELIS
Rhetorices Librum Primum.

Ἡ ῥητορική ἐστιν ἀντίστροφος τῇ διαλεκτικῇ.

Primam hanc huius libri partem, summos uiros, qui ipsam interpretentur habere, constat: M. Ciceronem, et Alexandrum Aphrodisiensem: quorum alter, cum ingenuas etiam alias artes didicisset, huius maxime studij atq; artificij peritissimus merito semper est habitus: alter uero ita accurate cunctos Aristotelis libros euoluit, ac tantum ingenio ualuit, ut omnia obscuriora sensa eorum & percipere ipse, & alijs declarare potuerit. Dissidere tamen hi inter se in loci huius explicatione uidentur. quare sententias amborum proferam, & quid unumq; secutum esse suspicer, ostendam. Ciceronis igitur ex Oratore uerba haec sunt: Atq; etiam ante hunc Aristoteles, principio artis rhetoricae, dicit illam artem quasi ex altera parte respondere dialecticae, ut hoc uidelicet differant inter se, quod haec ratio dicendi, latior sit: illa loquendi, contractior. Haec autem e libro primo Academicarum quaestionum ad Varronem. Huic quasi ex altera parte, oratoria uis dicendi adhibebatur, explicatrix orationis perpetuae, ad persuadenda accommodatae. eundem enim hunc locum manifesto intelligit, quamuis sententiam hanc Aristotelis esse, ut in Oratore fecerat, non ostendat. Alexander uero in primum librum Topicorum, de dialectica loquens, ita ait: Τοιαύτην δ᾽ οὖσαν αὐτήν, εἰκότως καὶ ἀντίστροφόν φησιν ὁ Ἀριστοτέλης εἶναι τῇ ῥητορικῇ, ἐπειδὴ καὶ αὕτη περὶ τὰ πιθανά, ἅ τῷ ἐνδόξα εἶναι καὶ αὐτά ἐστι ταῦτα, τὸ δ᾽ ἀντίστροφον αὐτῇ τὸ ἰσόστροφόν τε καὶ περὶ τὰ αὐτὰ στρεφόμενην καὶ καταγινομένην λέγει. Cum tradat hic scilicet Aristoteles dialectica esse antistrophum rhetoricae, sit autem dialectica qualem illic descripsit Alexander, recte ipsum fecisse. Rhetorica nanq; circa res ad persuadendum accommodatas uersatur, quae huiusce modi sunt, ac natura eam habent. quia conueniunt opinionibus hominum, quid enim sensib. iudicijsq; hominum conuenit, id etiam a persuadendum appositum est. nam quod ad uim nominis pertinet ἀντίστροφον pro ἰσόστροφον positum ab eo esse uult, id autem nihil aliud est, nisi quae uersatur circa easdem res, & in illis tractandis tota occupatur. intelligit autem, quae ex opinionibus hominum sunt, et ἔνδοξα ob eam causam uocantur. Et sententiam igitur Aristotelis, & uim uerbi, unde omnis controuersia orta est, expressit Alexander. Sed ad Ciceronem reuertamur, qui, ut liquido intelligatur, aliam prioris partis huius nominis rationem esse credidit. est enim manifesto duplex, è duobusq; nominibus iunctum nomen. Non igitur, ut Alexander postea fecit, ἀντί, Cicero hoc uerbo significare putauit: quod intellectu saepe prisci Graeci capiebant, & quam uim in multis iunctis uerbis habet, sed è regione et

contra. hoc enim significare apud ipsum ex altera parte, perspicuum est. alijs naq; etiam plurimis in locis ita Cicero locutus est, & in Orationibus, & in libris quos de philosophia scripsit: exemplis enim in re plana, & quae passim obuia sit, supersedebo. Videtur igitur ita locum hunc Cicero accepisse, tanquam discrimins etiam aliquid inter has artes esse, significare hic uoluerit Aristoteles. nam similes illas esse, affinesq; multum inter se, optime ipse intelligebat: id enim manifesto significauit, cum appellarit antea dialecticam, uicinam atq; finitimam rhetoricae. Sed etiam uerbo idem indicasse uidetur, quo hic usus est, cum inquit ipsam respondere: eo enim prorsus similitudo quaedam declaratur. nihil igitur protulit, si diligenter attendimus, quod uerum non sit, & notioni eius nominis, et naturae rei non quadret. Alexander enim quoq; cum similitudinem harum artium illic ostendisset, quibus rebus illae discrepant inter se, tradit: tria autem affert, ut facile ex uerbis ipsius intelligere licet. At si nus quoq; qui dam non ignobilis rhetor, eodem intellectu, quo ceperit hic Cicero, ἀντίστροφον usurpauit, dicens perorationes habere se ἀντιστρόφως procœmijs. cum enim eadem sic tractentur & in principijs, orationum et in perorationibus, modo tamen mensuraq; illa discrepare dicit. Contra ijs autem in locis & tanquam e regione illa collocata esse, manifestum est, cum principium orationis procœmium sit: peroratio autem, finis et extremum. Nihil tamen hic apud Aristotelem legitur, quod ad differentiam ullam harum artium indicandam pertineat: nisi in prima parte huius nominis id latet. uerum si hoc docere nunc uoluisset, uerisimile uidetur accuratius eum id, apertiusq; traditurum fuisse, nec tam obscure, nomineq; demum quod aliter quoq; sumi posset, id declaraturum fuisse. Cuncta sane quae infra ab eo traduntur, similitudinem potius affinitatemq; ingentem rhetoricae artis, cum differendi ratione significant. nunc enim ipsam μόριον dialectices, nunc ὁμοίωμα, nunc παραφυές uocat: ut cum quasi hunc ipsum locum interpretans, inquit: ἔστι γὰρ μόριόν τι τῆς διαλεκτικῆς καὶ ὁμοίωμα, καθάπερ καὶ ἀρχόμενοι εἴπομεν. quod secutus Alexandrum, arbitror eum quem antea ostendi sensum ex his uerbis elicuisse. quamuis quod ad sententiam potius eius loci, quam uerborum explanandi pertineat, illic protulit Aristoteles. Verbum sane ipsam multiplex est, et non à diuersis tantum, sed ab ijsdem quoq; scriptoribus aliter alijs in locis usurpatum. quae res intellectu huius loci obscuriorem reddidit. Inde autem uidentur & uariae notiones eius nominis, et ea de causa diuersae latins interpretationes manasse, quod non unus, semper primus pos huius iuncti nominis significat, sed longe aliud atq; diuersum, non seorsum tantum posita, sed cum eodem etiam uerbo copulata.

A

PLATE FORTY-SEVEN B

page one of the 1549 Victorius Basel edition

courtesy of the Library of the University of Illinois at Champaign-Urbana

	+ 2oA.gr.b.177 + 2oA.gr.b.869 Naples:38 F.12 + 38.F.5 Olomouc: 23176 PhilLC:Log 521.F UCBanc:fB450 V39 1549 U Amst:474 A 16 1 Vat:R.G.Class.II. 101 Venice:147.D.1 Wis:X32Y A8 R YV64	RHETORICES LIBRUM PRIMUM. Basel:ex officina J.Oporini (John Oporinus), 1549 (publisher, date on colophon)	⬅ Latin commetary by Victorius ⬅ Greek text by Victorius	
1549	Bamberg:L.gr.f9 Berlin:4°4 W 220 RARA BN:R.84 Camb:Clare Q.2.15; Gonv-C.G.9.16-17 Lyon:22536 Maz:20305 Munich:2°A.gr.b.89 Naples:III.7.21 RomeAng:TT.22.15 RomeBNC:8.39.M.17-18 + 71.2.F.16-17 + 12.3.H.7-8 Vat:R.Gen.Class.I.88	TITLE PAGE,vol 1: INDEX ALPHABETICUS OMNIUM OPERUM ARISTOTELIS STAGIRITAE. TITLE PAGE,vol.2: ARISTOTELIS STAGIRITAE OPERUM Tomus Secundus. col.1088,vol.2:ARISTOTELIS STAGIRITAE RHETORICORUM ad Theodecten,Liber Primus. Georgio Trapezuntio Interprete. Lyon:apud Ioannem Frellonium [Jean Frellon],1548	in 4° chaps:a=15;b=26;g=19 Bks:One=cols.1087-1222;Two=1223-1260; Three=1259-1284 lines numbered 10,20,30,40,50,60 two vols, with R. in vol. 2 Latin only with block prints for capital letters pp. not cut in Gonville-Caius copy Bodleian has only index	Baudrier V, 214 Ind Aur 2,202 108.160 Adams 1744 Gesamt 6,5962 Primo 6,5780
1549	Basel:C.C.VI 18 Nr.2 Berlin:Vu 7494 BM:1607/4688 + 11805.aaa.9 (def) BN:X.20484 Bodleian:8° St.Am. 195 and 8°Rawl 505,506 BostPub:*Res. 4979. 36 Camb:St.J.CC.16.2 Folg:PA3893 R3 1549 Cage Got:8°A.gr.IV 521 Ill:Baldwin 2154a MAmb:S.Q.S.III.26 Munich:A.gr.b.628 (with Victorius' bookmark) + 2° A. gr.b.176,179 OxQ:BB.f.190(cnly Greek) RomeAng:TT.21.73 RomeBNC:71.3.A.4 + 6.16.I.2 U.Chic:PA3893.R3 1549 UNC:PA3893.R3 1549 Vat:Barb.J.I.61 + R.G.Classici V 501 Venice:216.C.102 ViennaSB:71.L.36(2) Yale:Gfa 84.m545 1 & 2	TITLE PAGE:ΑΡΙΣΤΟΤΕΛΟΥΣ ΤΕΧΝΗΣ ΡΗΤΟΡΙΚΗΣ ΒΙΒΛΙΑ ΤΡΙΑ. ARISTOTELIS DE ARTE DICENDI LIBRI TRES. Ad Fidem uetustiss. codicum accuratissima diligentia a Petro Victorio correcti & emendati. Iide[m] Latinitate donati per Hermolau[m] Barbaru[m]. folio 2r:ΑΡΙΣΤΟΤΕΛΟΥΣ ΤΕΧΝΗΣ ΡΗτορικῆς τῶν εἰς τρία τὸ πρῶτον. (no Latin title on folio.2r of Greek text) Paris:apud Vascosanum (Michel de Vascosan),1549 (Latin translation) TITLE PAGE: ARISTOTELIS DE ARTE DICENDI LIBRI III.HERMOLAO BARBARO INTERPRETE. folio 4r: ARISTTOTELIS [sic] RHETORICORUM LIBER PRIMUS Hermolao Barbaro interprete.	in 8°;Primo says in 16o;Yale, in 4° chaps:a=41;b=46;g=33 Bks for Greek:One=2r-41r;Two=41v-82r; Three=82v-110r Bks for Latin:One=4r-52r;Two=52r-98r; Three=98v-131v Munich,Bodleian lack Latin;BN & UNC lack Greek;Latin edition reads "Aristotelis de arte dicendi libri III. Hermoleo Barbaro interprete." (on title page) Yale has 2 copies of the Barbaro commentary bound separately in 16o Primo says R. in Greek from Victorius; Latin from Barbaro Bonn copy destroyed in WWII BM lacks Latin WroclawU copy missing since WWII	Ind Aur 2,202 108.166 Hoffman 296, 337 Schwab 2984; 3007 Brunet I,475 Gesamt 6,6307 + 6,6376 Primo 6,5702 + 6,6730 NUC 21,11; 0403712 + 21,19; 0403893 Adams 1943 Cranz 108.166

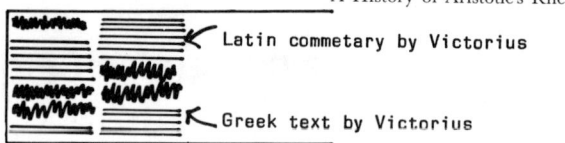

IACOBI BROCARDI IN TRES libros Aristotelis de arte rhetorica Paraphrasis. call. no.in Venice: 104.D.229. Paris: apud Jacobum Dupuys, 1549. 1=15 chaps;2=26 chaps;3=19 chaps. Book One=35-154;II=155-288;III=289-376. Well done paraphrase, not infrequently found in library collections.

| 1550 | Berlin:2o Bibl Diez. 319-324
BM:28.f.4-10
BN:R.181--191 + Res.R.322-328
Bodleian:A.2.1-6.Art + Toynbee 3673
BudapAkB:55.743
Camb:Christs 18.20.1;Kings K.2;Trin.T.6.17 + N.1.15 + N.1.16(vols.4-7);U.Lib.M.2.31
Flor:16.1.14 + 5.1.148
Got:4o A.gr.IV.78
Gotha:Math.2o 131a
Harv:*OGC Ar.46. E550 vols.2 & 3 + *56-1780F
Leid:681 A.2-9
Lyon:107189
Maz:3477-3481
MAmb:S.T.P.IX.13-16 + IV.St.C.XVI.17-21
MilanB:B.XVI.5975/1-8
Munich:2oA.gr.b.90 + A.gr.b.fol.90a
Naples:XXIV.F.21 + XXIV.5.3
Newb:CASE fY 642.A8 1978
NotreD:Rare Bk Rm B406 B147
OxPem:6.D.3
OxQ:BB.y.51-56
Princeton:Ex2599.2552
RomeAles:B.d.25
RomeAng:TT.15.23
RomeCas:L.X.13
RomeBNC:37.31.d.12-18 + 68.9.F.14-19
U.Chic:fPA3895.A49 1550
U.Pa:fGrC Ar466 Ef1 1552 vols.2-3
Vatican:Barberini J. IV.39 + Theologia Filos.32(1-7)
ViennaSB:71.C.2
Wolf:98-103 Quod.2o
Yale:Gfa 84 +af550 1 | TITLE PAGE,vol 1: ARISTOTELIS STAGIRITAE OMNIA QUAE EXTANT OPERA . . . AVERROIS CORDUBENSIS IN EA OPERA OMNES QUI AD NOS PERVENERE COMMENTARII . . .

TITLE PAGE,vol.2: ARISTOTELIS STAGIRITAE DE RHETORICA, ET POETICA LIBRI, CUM AVERROIS CORDUBENSIS IN EOSDEM PARAPHRASIBUS: QUORUM NUMERUM VERSA PAGINA MONSTRAT.

verso of title page of vol.2: ARISTOTELIS Artis Rhetoricae libri Tres, Georgio Trapezuntio interprete.

folio 1r,vol.2: ARISTOTELIS STAGIRITAE PERIPATETICORUM PRINCIPIS ARTIS RHETORICAE LIBER PRIMUS Georgio Trapezuntio interprete.

Venice:apud Iuntas,1550-1552 | in 4o
chaps:a=15;b=27;g=19
Bks:One=ff.1r-11r;Two=11v-22r;Three=22r-29r
lines numbered 10,20,30,40,50
eleven vols. issued between 1550-1552. R. in vol.2,dated 1550.
Two cols per page, only Latin tr. by Trapezuntius
vols.1,7,8,9,10 dated 1552. Although vol. 2 predates vol.1,the table of contents of vol.1 accurately reflects citations to vol.2
BM 11 vols. bound in 7;R. in vol.2 of 28.f.5
Harvard copy *56-1780 bound by Samuel Mearne
Got has 9 vols. bound in 6
ed. I.B.Bagolinus
Augsburg does not have;Wisconsin has only vol. 1; NUC entries for Mass. Hist. Society and St. Mary's College are in error. At Wolfenbutel, the R is in 99 Quod 2o | Schwab 401
Gesamt 6,5963
Adams 1745
Primo 6,5781
NUC 20,591; 0400797
Ind Aur 2,205 108.193
Cranz 108.193 |
| 1550 | Basel:B.C.I.3 + Frey-Gryn.L.I.20
BerlinH:11:Vt 49 2o + 4o Vt 21a
Bodleian:Vet.D.1 c.39
BM:C.76.f.4 + 518.m.1 + 31.g.5
BN:R632-633 + R.703-704
Brno:R.M.f.5
BudapEK:Vet.50/56
Camb:CorpusC.G.3.1; Christs.H.7.36; Jesus E.1.22;St. Johns CC.2.25;Trin. T.6.15;U.Lib.L.8.21
Col:Spec.Col.Gonzalez Lodge 1550 Ar 463 | TITLE PAGE: Ἀριστοτέλους ἅπαντα.

ARISTOTELIS SUMMI SEMPER PHILOSOPHI . . . per Des[iderium] Eras[mus] Roterodamum

page 184,vol.2:ΑΡΙΣΤΟΤΕΛΟΥΣ ΤΕΧΝΗΣ ΡΗΤΟΡΙΚΗΣ ΤΩΝ ΕΙΣ ΤΡΙΑ ΤΟ ΠΡΩΤΟΝ.

Basel:Io Bebelius (John Bebel) & Michel Isingrinius,1550 | in 4o
chaps:a=15;b=27(but 26 skipped);g=19
Bks:One=184-200;Two=200-217;Three=217-228
Α,Β,Γ,Δ,Ε,Ζ every 10 lines down left hand inside margin recto with Η,ΤΗ,Ι,Κ,V, M down inside margin verso margin
Simon Grynaeus' mark on colophon of vol. 2
2 vols.in one;R.in vol.2
only Greek text
edition states that several editors were consulted for this edition, e.g., Iustus Valsius, Petri Victorius, Matthies Flaccius Illyrious, and Cunradus Gesnerus uses same wood blocks to begin books as 1539 edition; some printers marks and some variant readings in margins
Kiel and Bonn copies destroyed in | NUC 20,584; 0400615
Ind Aur 2,203 108.174 1550
Gesamt 6,5896
Primo 6,5315
Adams 1782
Hoffman 289
Schwab 387
Cranz 108.174 |

Ἀριστοτέλης ἅπαντα.

ARISTOTELIS
SVMMI SEMPER PHILOSOPHI, ET IN

quem unum uim suam uniuersam contulisse natura rerum uidetur, opera quæcunqɜ hactenus extiterunt omnia: quæ quidem ut antea integris aliquot libris supra priores æditiones omnes à nobis aucta prodierũt, ita nunc quoqɜ, lucis & memoriæ causa, in capita diligenter distincta in lucem emittimus. Præterea quam diligentiam, ut omnibus æditionibus reliquis, omnia hæc exirent à nostra officina emendatiora, adhibuerimus, quoniam uno uerbo dici non potest, ex sequenti pagina plenius cognoscere licebit.

PER DES. ERAS. ROTERODAMVM
φιλολόγυ καὶ βιβλιοπώλυ διάλογ⊕.

Φιλ. Τί νέον κομίζεις; βίβλον; Βιβ. ὀδαμῶς. Φιλ. τί δή;
Βιβ. Χρυσᾶ ῥέεθρα. Φιλ. Ναὶ σὺ πλησίως λέγεις,
Ταχύτερον εἰπέ. Βιβ. τὸν Σταγειρίτην λέγω,
Ὃν ἔλαθεν ὀδὲν τῶν μαθημάτων μέρ⊕.
Οὗτ⊕ γ' ἀνέζηο, ὡς περὶ τῶ πολὺ καλλίων.
Φιλ. Λέγεις ἀληθῶς τὸ ἀμαλθείας κέρας.
Βιβ. Οὐ μὼν γ' ὀπώρας μεςόν, ἀλλ' ἀμεινόνων.
Φιλ. Καὶ τίς τοσοῦτον πλοῦτον ἡμῖν ἐμφορεῖ;
Βιβ. Τοῦτόν γε τὸ ἔχει φιλόπον⊕ Βεβέλι⊕.
Φιλ. Χρυσέμπορ⊕ γοῦν ὅςιν, ὂ λογέμπορ⊕;
Βιβ. Ναὶ, κἤτι χρυσᾶ καὶ λίθων πολυφορέςρον·
Θείας τε σοφίας ὀδὸν ἐς' αὐτάξιον.

BIBLIOTHECA REGIA MONACENSIS

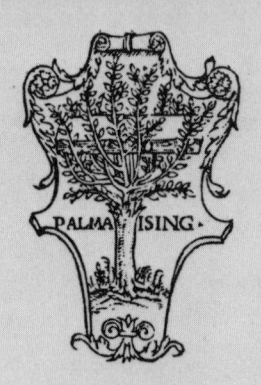

Indicem librorum, id est, longum diuitis thesauri catalogum, octaua pagina continet.

Cum gratia & priuilegio Cæsareo.

BASILEAE, PER IO. BEB. ET MICH.
ISING. ANNO M. D. L.

PLATE FORTY-EIGHT

title page of the 1550 Basel edition

courtesy of the Bayerische Staatsbibliothek, Munich

Early Printings

Erl:2°Phil.VII,16
Flor:5.1.148
Folg:Pa3890 A2 1550 Case
Got:2°A.gr.IV.8
Gotha:Phil.2°9/1
Griefs:2°CW 154
Halle:Ce 1692.2°
Harv:Smyth 2286.20
Ill:UNCAT
Lyon:22537
MAmb:S.Q.B.III.13
Maz: 3471*
MilanB:XVI.5972
Munich:2° A.gr.b.76
Naples:85.N.2 + XXIV. H.27
OxAS:i.1.
OxQ:BB.y.50
ParisArs: S&A253
PhilLC:Log 347.F
Prague:C.122
Princeton:Ex2599. 1550.2q
RomeAles:C.q.2
RomeCas:A.II.76, in C.C.
Stanford:Barchas Collection
Tub:Cd 855
U.Pa:fGrC Ar466 1 1550
Venice:133.D.5
ViennaUB:III 192. 229/1.2
Vienna:71.c.8
Wolf:Lg 2o 4
WroclawU:415093 + 363534
Yale:Gfa 84 + a531c
Zurich: Z 23.5

WWII; Augsburg does not have
Wolfenbutel has only vol.2
seemingly the first Greek edition
divided into chapters

1551 Basel:B.C.I.35
BM:520.k.2
BN:R.753
Bodleian:A.27.Art + Byw.4.1.
Camb:U.Lib. P*7.36 (C)
Ill:xq881 ABrh.Yb
Maz:136(1p)
Munich:2°A.gr.b. 176,177 + 2°A.gr.b. 1021 + A.gr.b.292
Naples:107.K.7 + S.Q.XX.B.5
OxPem:6.h.15
RomeAles: L.H.39
U.Pa:fGrC Ar46 22
Vat:R.G.Classici II 255 + Palatinus II 546
Venice:134.D.25
Wolf:Lg 4o 26

TITLE PAGE: MARTINI BORRHAI Studardiana in tres Aristotelis de Arte dicendi libros Commentaria. HERMOLAI BARBARI, EORUNDEM VERSIO,CUM GRAECO textu . . .

page 1:ΑΡΙΣΤΟΤΕΛΟΥΣ ΤΕΧΝΗΣ ΡΗΤΟΡΙΚΗΣ ΤΩΝ ΕΙΣ ΤΡΙΑ ΤΟ ΠΡΩΤΟΝ.

page 1: ARISTOTELIS RHETORICORUM LIBER PRIMUS, Hermoleo Barbaro interprete.

Basel:ex officina Iacobi Parci, Impensis Ioannis Oporini, Sept. 1551 (publisher,date on colophon)

in 4°
Bks:One=1-166;Two=167-335;Three=336-436
NUC says also appeared in 1555 and 1559, but no such editions located
omits chapter divisions found in previous Barbaro editions
Greek + Barbaro Latin translation & Borrhaii commentary
Munich 2° A.gr.b.177 in same binding as one of the copies of Victorius' 1549 Basel edition

— Greek text
— Latin by Barbaro
— Borrhai's commentary

Primo 6,5703
NUC 21,11; 0403713
Hoffman 296
Schwab 3051

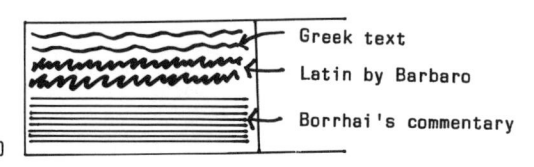

1551 BerlinSPK:Ald.Ren. 150.5
BM:C.19.bb.11-16 + G.7888-93 + 165. d.13-17 + 519.b. 1 + 980.e.2
BN:X.16677 + Res.R. 2248

TITLE PAGE,vol.1:ΑΡΙΣΤΟΤΕΛΟΥΣ ΑΠΑΣΑΝ ΛΟΓΙΚΗΝ, ΡΗΤΟΡΙΚΗΝ, ΚΑΙ ΠΟΙΗΤΙΚΗΝ ΠΡΑΓΜΑΤΕΙΑΝ ΠΕΡΙΕΧΩΝ ΤΟΜΟΣ Α.

ARISTOTELIS OMNEM LOGICAM, RHETORICAM, ET POETICAM DISCIPLINAM CONTINENS,TOMUS I

in 8°
Bks:One=443-494;Two=494-546;Three=546-581
lines numbered 1,2,3,4 every ten lines in some copies; does not appear in BN, BM, & Trinity copies
different type setting from 1536 edition
R. in vol. 1 of 5 vol. set;UCBanc,Berlin

Cranz 108.218
NUC 20,595; 0400614
Brunet I,458
Gesamt 6,5897

	Bodleian:Auct.i.R.6. 24-41 + Auct.1.R.6. 1 + Byw.J.8.4-9 Camb:Trin.N.1.11 Col:Spec col. Gonzalez-Lodge 1551 Ar465 Edinburgh:K.37.g Erlangen:VII,39 Flor:Nencini Ald. 2.1.4 + Ald.2/1 4-5 + Ald.2.1.66-69 Gennadius:Gc.3129 Got:8⁰ A gr IV 10 Halle:AB W 790L(1) Harv:*OGC Ar46 551, vol. 1 Ill:X881 A8 1551 Leid:679 1-4 Leip:8 Aldin 158-162 Maz:42195 Mich:999 A8 C18 MAmb:S.Q.I.VI.30-31 MilanB:AP.XV.42-46 Morgan:E 25 B Munich:A.gr.b.528 Naples:S.Q.XX.B.5 Newb:CASE 3A 2689 Nwtn:Sp.Col. 1551 Ar OxAS:i.10 OxCC:e.4.41 OxPem:3.c (2 sets) RomeAng:TT.21.58 RomeBNC:68.6.C.1-2 Sibiu:uI.415 St.Gen:DE.a.8o 160-165 Res.Inv.377-382 U.Chic:PA9890.A363 1551 U.Pa:GrC Ar466 1 1551 UCLA:Z233 A4A7 1551 Vat:Barberini CCC. III.4-9 + 5 other copies Venice:395.D.218-223 Vienna:22.S.1 WroclawU:457986	page 441,vol.1:ΑΡΙΣΤΟΤΕΛΟΥΣ ΤΕΧΝΗΣ ΡΗΤΟΡΙΚΗΣ ΒΙΒΛΙΑ Γ. ARISTOTELIS DE ARTE RHETORICA LIB. TRES. page 443,vol.1:ΑΡΙΣΤΟΤΕΛΟΥΣ ΤΕΧΝΗΣ ΡΗΤΟΡΙΚΗΣ ΤΩΝ ΕΙΣ ΤΡΙΑ ΤΟ Α. Venice:apud Aldi Filios,1551	W, & Got have 6th vol. by Theophrastus BN has one vol. 1 bound with set, and X.16677 bound by itself; BN copy on reserve because of ornate binding spaces left for block capital letters at beginning of each book, but never supplied for Bks Two & Three only Greek Camb:U.Lib.missing vol.1;Trinity has only 4 vols Schwab linked to 1536 and 1546 Venice editions Vienna has only vols. 1 and 2;U.Chic. has only vol. 1; Got bound in 6 vols. Griefswald's copy cannot be located; Munster & Augsburg do not have;Bonn & Kiel copies destroyed in WWII	Renouard 150 Primo 6,5316 Hoffman 289 Schwab 385 + 2947 Ind Aur 2,207 108.218
1558	Caen:Res.B 712/4	TITLE PAGE: Aristotelis Rhetoricorum ad Theodecten, Georgio Trapezuntio interprete,libri III page 2: Georgii Trapezuntii,ad Papae Thesauriarum prologus in tres Rhetoricorum Aristotelis Libros ad Theodecten, a se translatos Paris:Thomas Richard, 1558	in 4⁰ Bks:One=3-33;Two=33-65;Three=65-86 colophon says Paris, 1548, but there is no evidence that such an edition, other than the Basel publication,was ever issued	Monfasani 700 Legrand IV,73
1559	Antwerp:B2114 BM:671.d.3 BN:X.3052;X.3053(1); X.1939(10) all incomplete Bodleian:Byw.K.3. 14(1)(2) Camb:Trinity Grylls. 7:53	TITLE PAGE:ΑΡΙΣΤΟΤΕΛΟΥΣ ΤΕΧΝΗΣ ΡΗΤΟρικῆς, βιβλία τρία. ARISTOTELIS DE ARTE dicendi Libri tres. page 3:ΑΡΙΣΤΟΤΕΛΟΥΣ ΤΕΧΝΗΣ ῥητορικῆς, τῶν εἰς τρία τὸ πρῶτον.	in 4⁰ Got, BN, Princeton copies have no chapters GK:Bks:One=3-52;Two=61-120;Three=113[sic] -153 for total of 153 pp.+ readings in Greek LAT:Bks:One=1-55;Two=57-108;Three=109-145 Princeton has only Greek; Chicago copy includes Latin; pp. are erratically numbered	Gesmt: 6, 6378;6,6308 Ind Aur 2, 222;108.392 Cranz 108. 392 Primo 6,5704

Hoffman (296) cited a 1558 Basel edition as a repeat of the 1551 Basel edition. No copy of such an edition was found.

Aristotelis Rhetoricorum ad Theodecten, Georgio Trapezuntio interprete, Libri III.

NVNC RECENS AD GRÆ-
cam veritatem recogniti, & doctissimis
argumentis, singulis capitibus
præfixis illustrati.

PARISIIS.

Ex Typographia Thomæ Richardi sub Bibliis
aureis, è regione collegij Remensis.
1 5 5 8.

PLATE FORTY-NINE

title page of the 1558 Paris edition

courtesy of the Bibliothèques de la Ville de Caen

	Got:8ºA gr IV 523 Ill:Baldwin 2154 MAmb:S.Q.S.VII.9 Naples:67.k.29(3 Princeton:Ex2599. 383.059 U.Chic:PA3893.R3 1559 Wash.U:PA3893 R3 1559	Paris:Guil.Morelium (Guillaume Morel), 1559	Cambridge-Trinity copy begins on p.3, but other pp.do not match those given above; all three BN copies defective e.g.,X.1939(10) has no book Two and no Book Three,but index gives Bk Two as having 36 pp. & Bk Three as having 33 pp. Gives varient readings from Victorius Berlin Vu 2884.3(graece) lost in WWII	Hoffman 296' 337 NUC 21,11; 0403714 + 0403715 + 0403716 Schwab 2974 + 3007
1560- 1562	Arizona:PA3895.A4 1560 BN:R.1621 Bodleian:8ºA.14 Art Seld. + Toynbee 688-689 Bonn:Da 907/40 Brno:R.M.I.b.9 Camb:Emmanuel S6.4. 2-11;Clare J .2.3; St.Johns Kk.10.33; St.Catharine's KV 79-89,in vol. 3 Col:Spec.Col.B88 Ar51 JP7 1560 + Film F888 Got:8ºA gr IV 80 Gotha:Phil.32/1 Griefswald:8ºCW 155 Harv:*56-1790 + Film A26 Leid:649 T 12-22 Lyon:338656 MAmb:Villa Pernice 1914,1-15 + S.M. X.VII.35 Marburg:IV.C.192 Munich:8oA.gr.b.535/1 Naples:24.D.22 + XXIV.B.19/30 Prague:5.G.38 RomeBNC:6.41.G.6-1C U.Pa:GrC.Ar466.Efl. 1560,vol. 3 USC: 185 A 71 L UWash:888.5 AAL Wolf:Lg 277	TITLE PAGE: OMNIA OPERA, ARISTOTELIS STAGIRITAE OMNIA,QUAE EXTANT,OPERA TITLE PAGE,vol.3: ARISTOTELIS STAGIRITAE PERIPATETICORUM PRIN-CIPIS,QUI RHETORICORUM LIBROS AD ARTEM dicendi attinentes folio 1r of Bk One,vol.3: ARISTOTELIS STAGIRITAE PERIPATE-TICORUM PRINCIPIS,ARTIS RHETOR-ICAE LIBER PRIMUS. Georgio Tra-pezuntio interprete. cum Aver-rois Cordubensis paraphrasi. Abramo de Balmes interprete. Venice: Cominus de Tridino, Montisferrati,1560 [publisher on colophon]	in 8º chaps:a=15;b=27;g=19 Bks:One=1r-19r;Two=19v-38v;Three=39r-52r R is first 52 folios of vol.three Harvard film,copy of BN holding, has 11 vols.on 6 reels;Trapezuntio's tr.followed by Averroes commentary on ff.52r-116r; bound with Poetics vol.12 is a thesaurus by Antonii Posi Bodleian & U.Pa. have all 11 vols; Camb. has only vol. 2; Harvard has vols.2,3,5, 10,11,13;Prague has 2,3,9,10,11;Budapest NB 4935 has only 1,2,5;Venice has only 5; Marburg lacks Thesaurus;U.S.C.has vols. 1,3,8 whereas their Hoose Library has 11 vol.set; Budapest EK Hb.4135 has only vol. 1 Augsburg and Villanova do not have R.	Adams 1746 Primo 6,5783 Gesmt 6,5964 NUC 20,591-2 0400805 + 0400810 + 0400812 Ind Aur 2 225;108.423 Cranz 108.423
1561	BN:R.705-706 Camb:U.Lib.L.9.5 Munich:2oA.gr.b.91	TITLE PAGE, vol. 1: ARISTOTELIS STAGIRITAE OPERA, post omnes quae in hunc usque diem prodierunt editiones,summo studio emaculata, & ad Graecum exemplar diligenter recognita. TITLE PAGE, vol.2: ARISTOTELIS STAGIRITAE OPERUM Tomus Secundus. cols.1087-88,vol.2:ARISTOTELIS Stagiritae Rhetoricorum ad Theodecten,Liber Primus,Georgio Trapezuntio Interprete. Lyon:apud Ioannem Frellonium [Jean Frellon], 1561	in 4º chaps:a=15;b=26;g=19 Bks:One=cols.1087-1122;Two=1123-1160; Bk Three=1160-1184 lines numbered 10,20,30,40,50,60 same as 1563 edition in Munich and UPa. copies except vol.one dated 1561 2 vols, R in v.2; bound together at Got Tours copy burned in 1940 fire	Baudrier V, 253 Gesamt 5, 5965 Adams 1747 Ind Aur 2, 226;108.429 Cranz 108.429

Early Printings

1561	Flor:5.Magl.1V.11.301 Lyon:800371 Munich:A.gr.b.536/6 (i.e.vol.6) Naples:B.branc.81.A.46-52 NurnN:L.2459.z5 Rome BNC:204.8.A.24 + 68.11.A.13.2 + 6.37.B.3 U.Chic:PA3895.A.49 1561 UCBanc:tPN173 A73 R1 1561 Vat:Chigi.VI.1705(6) + Barber J.I.(38-44) + Chigi VI.186 (6) + Chigi IV.1636	TITLE PAGE,vol.1: ARISTOTELIS STAGIRITAE, ORGANUM, QUOD LOGICAM APPELLANT. Tomus Primus TITLE PAGE,vol.six:ARISTOTELIS STAGIRITAE RHETORICORUM Artisque POETICAE libris . . . page 3,vol.6: ARISTOTELIS STAGIRITAE PERIPATETICORUM PRINCIPIS ARTIS RHETORICAE LIBER PRIMUS. GEORGIO TRAPEZUNTIO interprete. Lyon:apud haeredes Iacobi Iuntae (Jacques Guinta), 1561 (for volume six)	in 32° chaps:a=15;b=27;g=19 Bks:One=3-66;Two=67-130;Three=131-175 Berlin Vt.459 missing after WWII R in vol.6 of six vol. set Augsburg does not have R ad Alex. by Francesco Philelpho bound with Rhetoric Lyon has only vol.with R.+ Index under 813181 Berlin Vu.459 lost in WWII	Primo 6,5784 + 6,5782 Gesamt 6,5966 Cranz 108.430 Ind Aur 226 108.430
1561	Got:2oA.gr.IV.82 MilanB:XVI,5971/1-2 Munich:2oA.gr.b.94 Naples:B.Branc.81.F.44/45 + XXIV.F.8-9 RomeAles: B.h.24 Wroclaw:363536	TITLE PAGE,vol.1: ARISTOTELIS STAGIRITAE OPERA,post omnes quae in hunc usque diem prodierunt editiones,summo studio emaculata, & ad Graecum exemplar diligenter recognita. TITLE PAGE,vol.2:ARISTOTELIS STAGIRITAE OPERUM Tomus Secundus. cols.1087-108,vol.2: ARISTOTELIS Stagiritae Rhetoricorum ad Theodecten, Liber Primus, Georgio Trapezuntio Interprete. Lyon:Antonius Vincentius [Antoine Vincent], excud. Symphorianus Barbier, 1561		
1562	Bamberg:L.gr.g73 BM:74.D.4 BN:X.1393(10) (incomplete) Bodleian:A.1.10 Linc. + Auct.S.2.29 Camb:Trinity T.23.14¹ Flor:5.5.63 Ill:X881 A8rh 1562 MAmb:S.Q.T.VII.36 Munich:4°A.gr.b.235(m) + 4°A.gr.b.408 Naples:87.K.29 (c3) (raised) UCLA:PA3049.C723D Venice:113.D.73.1	TITLE PAGE:ΑΡΙΣΤΟΤΕΛΟΥΣ, ΤΕΧΝΗΣ ΡΗΤΟρικῆς βιβλία τρία. ARISTOTELIS DE ARTE dicendi Libri tres. page 3:ΑΡΙΣΤΟΤΕΛΟΥΣ, ΤΕΧΝΗΣ ῥητορικῆς τῶν εἰς τρία τὸ πρῶτον. Paris:Guil.Morelis (Guillaume Morel),1562	in 4° Bks:One=3-58;Two=61-120;Three=113[sic]-153. Pages erratically numbered BN X.3053(1)and BN.3053(2) bound together with this 1562 edition so that this Greek version,Barbaro's Latin issued in 1559, and Barbaro's Latin issued in 1562 are in the same cover BN X.1393(10) contains same 58 pp.as 1559 Morelium edition plus Barbaro's Latin complete dated 1562 as X.3053(1) On p.167,the date M.D.LIX shows that the 1562 edition is only a reprint of the 1559 edition Illinois copy bound with 1559 edition editions not bound with the Barbaro Latin are only in Greek	Primo 6,5704 Adams 1942 Ind Aur 2,228 108.454 Gesamt 6,6309 Hoffman 296 Schwab 2974 NUC 21,11; 0403717 Cranz 108.454

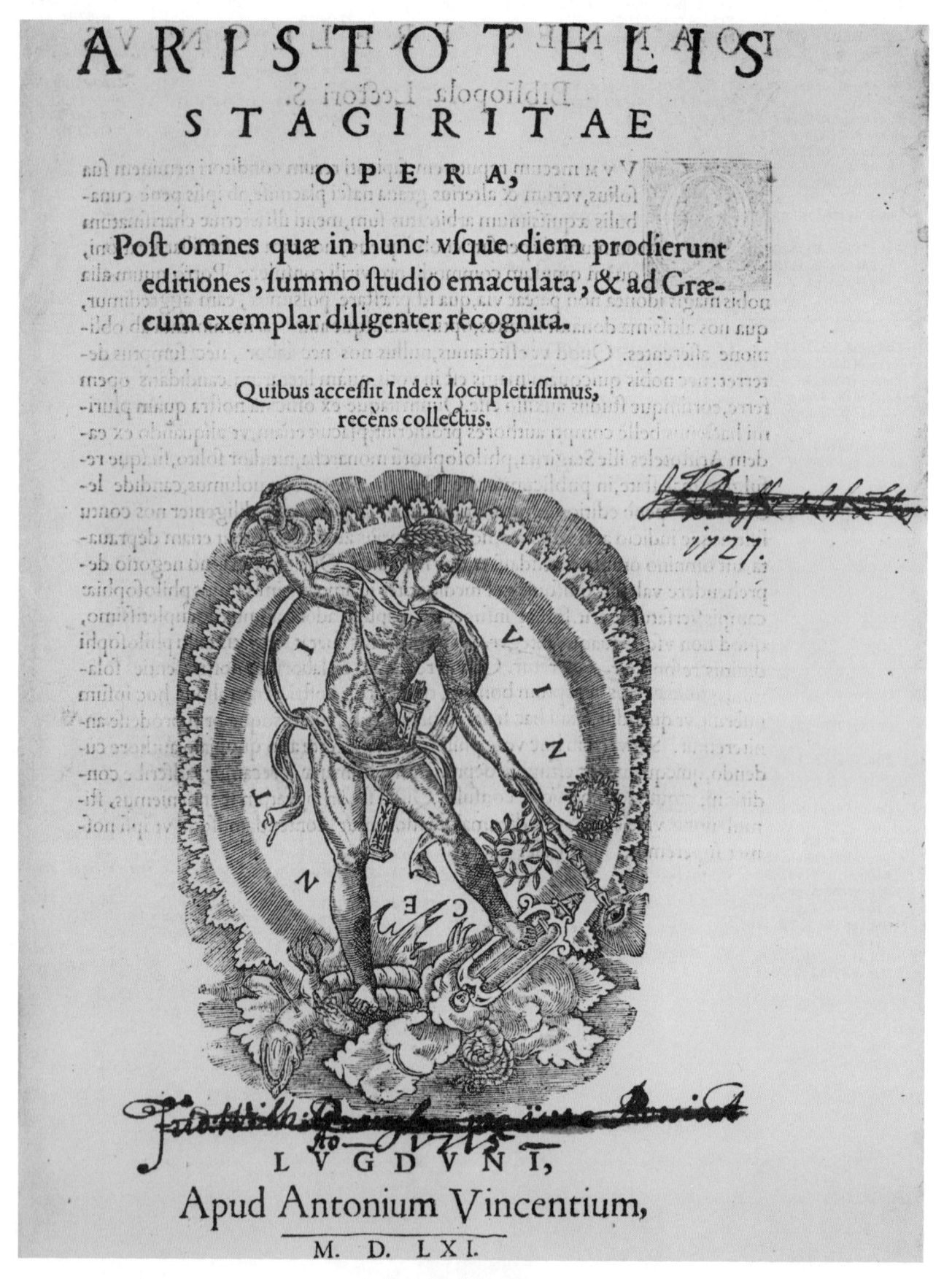

PLATE FIFTY

title page of volume one of the 1561 Lyon edition attributed to Antonius Vincentius

courtesy of the Niedersachsische Staats-und-Universitäts-Bibliothek, Göttingen

ARISTOTELIS
STAGIRITAE
OPERVM

Tomus Secundus.

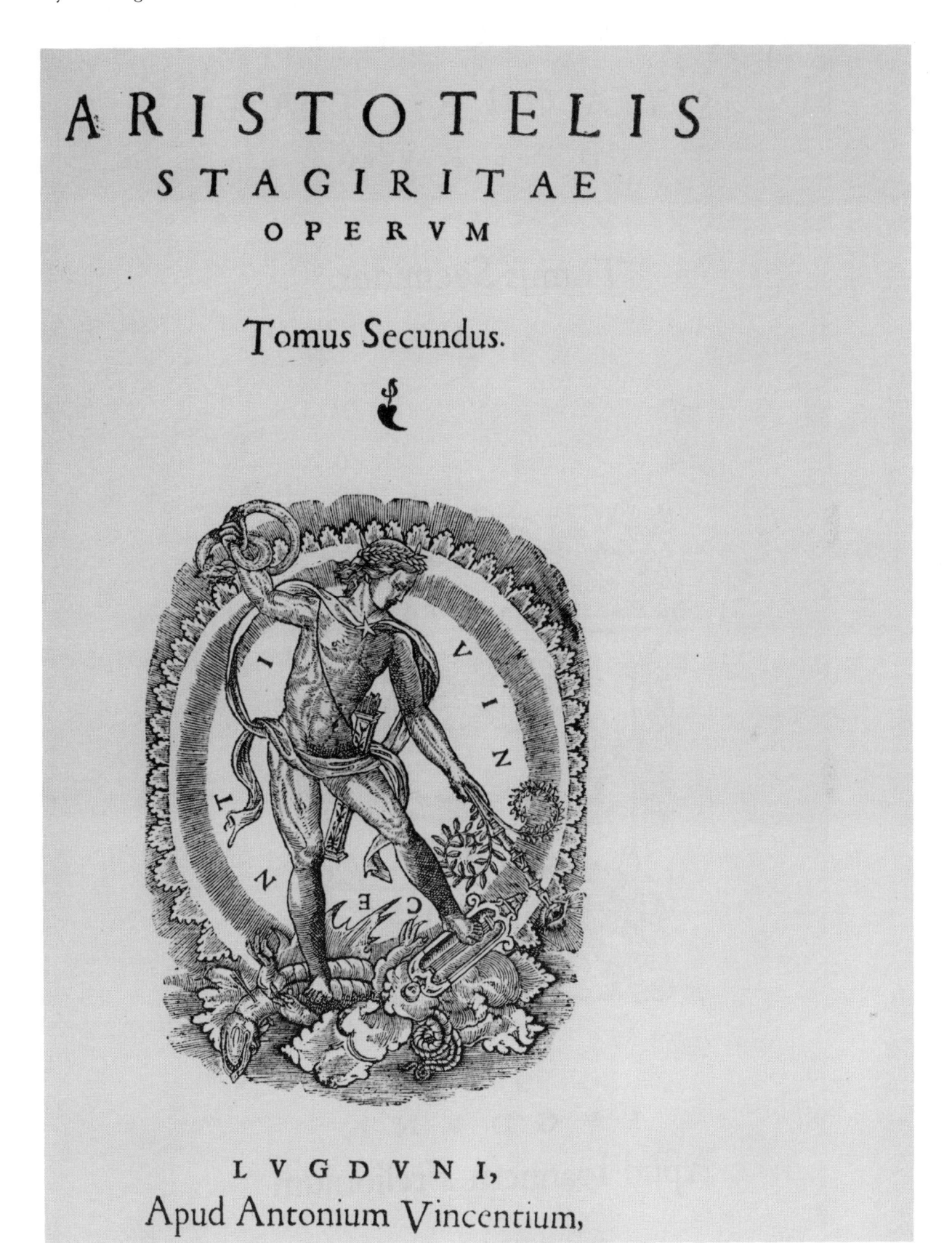

LVGDVNI,
Apud Antonium Vincentium,

PLATE FIFTY-ONE

title page of volume two of the 1561 Lyon edition attributed to Antonius Vincentius

courtesy of the Niedersachsische Staats-und-Universitäts-Bibliothek, Göttingen

ARISTOTELIS
STAGIRITAE
OPERVM

Tomus Secundus.

LVGDVNI,
Apud Ioannem Frellonium

PLATE FIFTY-TWO

title page of volume two of the 1561 Lyon edition attributed to Jean Frellon

courtesy of the Bayerische Staatsbibliothek, Munich

Early Printings

1563 MilanB:TRIV B439 TITLE PAGE: ARISTOTELIS STAGIRITAE
   Munich:2oA.gr.b.92 OPERA, post omnes quae in hunc
   Pom:XL 44 usque diem prodierunt editiones,
   RomeBNC:14.12.G. summo studio emaculata, & ad
   13-14 Graecum exemplar diligenter
   Tours:Res.77863 recognita.
   U.Pa:fGrC Ar466 Efl
   1563b TITLE PAGE,vol.2:ARISTOTELIS
    STAGIRITAE OPERUM Tomus
    Secundus

    cols.1087-1088,vol.2:ARISTOTELIS
    Stagiritae Rhetoricorum ad
    Theodecten,Liber Primus,Georgio
    Trapezuntio Interprete.

    Lyon:apud Ioannem Frellonium,1563
    (for vol. 1)

1564 (all three deposi- Rhetoricorum liber primus. Com
   tories located were prooemio Joan(nis) Casellii
   destroyed in WWII)
    Vitebergae (Wittenberg on the
    Elbe),1564

1570 Augsburg:LG 209 TITLE PAGE: ARISTOTLIS
   Berlin: Vu 7500 RARA RHETORICORUM libri III. IN
   BM:52.k.4. LATINUM SERMONEM conversi, &
   BN:X.16682 Scholis breuioribus explicati
   Bodleian:Crynes a JOANNE STURMIO.
   541 + Argent.
   1570.8o folio 1r: ARISTOTELIS DE ARTE
   BudapestEK:Hb.451 RHETORICA Liber Primus.
   Camb:U.Lib L.12.44;
   Gonville-Caius F. Argentoriatei(Strasbourg):
   20.19;St.Johns G. Theodosius Rihelius
   12.18;Pembroke 9. (T.Rihel),1570
   19.49;Emmanuel
   S6.4.44
   Edinburgh:K.32.g
   Gennadius:G.C.3217
   Got:8oA.gr.IV 525
   Halle:AB 42 10/k,12
   Ill:Baldwin 2153
   Ind:Spec.PA 3893.R3
   1570
   Krakow:Phil.gr.235
   Munich:A.gr.b.629
   Neuberg:8oOZ.Ant.27i
   Olomouc:28002
   OxPem:9.c.15
   RomeAng:TT.21.80
   Prague:5.I.86
   Torun:Ob.6.II +
   Ob.II.1314
   U.Chic:PA3893.R3 1570
   U.Pa:GrC.Ar466.22
   1570
   UCLA:PA3893 R3 1570
   Vienna:71.L.71
   WroclawA:XVI.O.9695
   WroclawU:316768 +
   450327
   Yale:Gfa 84 M570
   Vat:Barb.J.II.86
   + RG Class.V.1292
   Venice:118.D.192

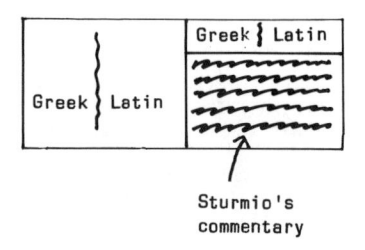

[Diagram: Page layout showing "Greek | Latin" columns, with second panel showing Greek | Latin header above text lines, arrow pointing to Sturmio's commentary]

Hoffman 296 + 337

Schwab 2936

Cranz 108.558

1573	Flor:1199.6 Pisa:Misc.310.10	TITLE PAGE:ΑΡΙΣΤΟΤΕΛΟΥΣ ΤΕΧΝΗΣ ΡΗΤΟΡΙΚΗΣ ΒΙΒΛΙΑ ΤΡΙΑ. ARISTOTELIS DE ARTE DICENDI LIBRI TRES. page 7:ΑΡΙΣΤΟΤΕΛΟΥΣ ΤΕΧΝΗΣ ῥητορικῆς, τῶν εἰς τρία τὸ πρῶτον. Florence:In officina Iunctarum, 1573	only a fragment first 50 pp. of Greek was uncovered for this study	
1575	Bodleian:Antiq.e.F. 1575/1 Got:8°A.gr.IV 527 Ill:Baldwin 2154	TITLE PAGE:ΑΡΙΣΤΟΤΕΛΟΥΣ ΡΗΤΟΡΙΚΗΣ ΤΕΧΝΗΣ ΒΙΒΛΙΑ ΤΡΙΑ ARISTOTELIS DE ARTE DICENDI Libri tres page 3:ΑΡΙΣΤΟΤΕΛΟΥΣ ΤΕΧΝΗΣ ῥητορικῆς, τῶν εἰς τρία τὸ πρῶτον. Paris:apud Ioannem Benenatum, 1575.	in 8° same books as 1559 edition reprint of 1559; at conclusion,"Excudebat Guil.Morelium in Graecis Typographus Regius,M.D.LIX."	Gesamt 6,6312
1576	BM:521.a.37 Brno:A.IV.P.m.16 + R.M.II.dd.33 Camb:St.Johns Smith a.5 Flor:11.9.398 + B. 17.8.34 MAmb:S.I.F.I.18 Munich:A.gr.b.538 Naples:112.A.80 RomeBNC:12.18.A.18 St.Ben:B406 1576 U.Pa:GrC.Ar466.Efl. 1576 Yale:Gfa 84 Af576	TITLE PAGE:ARISTOTELIS STAGIRITAE PERIPATETICORUM PRINCIPIS OPERA OMNIA in partes septem divisa; TITLE PAGE, vol.6: ARISTOTELIS STAGIRITAE, Rhetoricorum . . . PARS SEXTA. page 3,vol.6:ARISTOTELIS STAGIRITAE,PERIPATETICORUM PRINCIPIS,ARTIS RHETORICAE LIBER PRIMUS,GEORGIO TRAPEZUNTIO interprete. Venice:Gaspar Bindonis, 1576	in 16° chaps:a=25;b=27;g=19 Bks:One=3-66;Two=67-130;Three=131-175 seven vol. set,R. in vol. 6 only Latin BN has only vols.2,5,6;Vienna 71.L.25 has only vol.5;Rome BNC has only vol.1; Kiel copy burned in WWII;NUC in error in designating copy at UCBancroft Munich has 6 vols,missing vol.3;RomeBNC has 7 vols,missing vol.2,one duplicate Florence B 17 8 34 has vols.3,6,index	Gesamt 6,5974 Primo 6,5792 Ind Aur 2,243 108.610 NUC 20,593; 0400850 + 20, 608;0401202 Cranz 108.610

Bodleian Byw.G.6.12 has a tabular paraphrase entitled TABULAE RHETORICAE RAPHAELIS CYLLENII ANGELI published in Venice by Iordanus Zillettus in 1571. It is noted here because it varies decidedly in format from other sixteenth century paraphrases.

Early Printings

1577	Augsburg:an LG 1222 Berlin:Vu 7511 RARA BM:G.16787 Got:8°A.gr.IV.529 Halle:Ce 2320 Leipsig:8 Arist.162 Munich:A.gr.b.630 Wf:ALVENSLEBEN Cb 203(3) WroclawA:XVI.O.161 + XVI.O.236	TITLE PAGE: ΑΡΙΣΤΟΤΕΛΟΥΣ ΤΕΧΝΗΣ ΡΗΤΟΡΙΚΗΣ ΒΙΒΛΙΑ Γ. Aristotelis de arte dicendi libri tres, opera & studio Ioannis Casely . . . page 3: ΑΡΙΣΤΟΤΕΛΟΥΣ ΤΕΧΝΗΣ ΡΗΤΟΡΙΚΗΣ ΤΩΝ ΕΙΣ ΤΡΙΑ ΤΟ ΠΡΩΤΟΝ. Rostochii(Rostock):ex officina Iacobi Lucii,1577.	in 16.° Bks:One=3-95;Two=96-192;Three=193-256 preface dated 1576 only Greek,edited by Joannis Caselly who consulted Victorius bound with other of A's works Got copy heavily annotated with pages of notes inserted	Gesamt 6,6313 Ind Aur 245 108.625 Hoffman 296 + 337 Schwab 2975 + 3307 + 3056 errs in citing 1571 Cranz 108.625
1578	Got:2°A.gr.IV.90 RomeBNC:14.11.G.12 Venice:113.D.13-14	TITLE PAGE: ARISTOTELIS STAGIRITAE OPERA,Post omnes quae in hunc usque diem prodierunt editiones, summo studio emaculata,& ad Graecum exemplar diligenter recognita. Ab. A.Iacobo Martino. Doctore Medico ac Philosopho. cols.1087-1088,vol.2: ARISTOTELIS Stagiritae Rethoricorum [sic] ad Theodecten,Liber Primus, Georgio Trapezuntio Interprete. Lyon:Stephanus Michaelis(Etienne Michal),1578	in 4° chaps:a=25;b=26;g=19 Bks:One=cols.1087-1122;Two=1123-1160; Three=1160-1184 columns numbered 10,20,30,40,50,60 2 vols. bound in one;R in vol. 2 Martino has somewhat modified the Latin Trapezuntius version vol. 1 dated 1579 on title page, & 1577 on colophon; vol.2 dated 1578	Ind Aur 2,245 108.629 Gesamt 6,5976 Primo 6,5794 Cranz 108.629
1579	BM:520.k.12 + G.8030 BN:Res.R.157;R.255; X.1177 Bodleian:Meerm.107 + Godw.272 Camb:U.Lib P*.89(C) + L.8.23;Trinity T.6.26 ;Peterhouse K.3.12;St.Cathar- ine's D.II.58 Columbia:Spec.Col. B88 Ar51 VZ v2 Edinburgh:K.31.a Flor:5.1.35 + 1.B. 3.2.12 Got:4°A.gr.IV 616 Ill:xq881 A8rh.Yva 1579 Krakow:Graeca 3644 Maz:135 A. Munich:2°A.gr.b.170 N'wstn:L881 A8 V44v Naples:38.F.5 OxAS:i.3 OxPem:8.d. OxQ:BB.y.76 RomeAles:L.g.8 RomeAng:XX.15.13 RomeCas:L.IV.48 U.Chic:fPA3893.R3 1579 U.Pa:fGrC Ar466 22 1579 Vat:Chigi II.675 Venice:17.T.1. Yale:Gfa84 tmy 548c	TITLE PAGE: PETRI VICTORII COMMENTARII In tres libros Aristotelis de arte dicendi. Positis ante singulas declarationes,valde studio & nova cura ipsius auctas,Graecis verbis auctoris,usque fideliter Latine expressis.Cum vetere exquisito indice,cui multa addita sunt,modo animaduersa. page 1: PETRI VICTORII DECLARATIONES IN ARISTOTELIS RHETORICES LIBRUM PRIMUM. Florence:ex officina Iunctarium (Philippua Juncta,minor),1579	in 4° BksS:One=1-270;Two=271-538;Three=539-756 Yale copy being transferred from Sterling to Beinecke Library where number will be changed says new edition:introduction dated Sept. 1579. AS return to format of 1548 edi- tion, except this edition has 756 pp. + index,with Victorius' Latin translation. RomeBV does not have. ← Greek text ← Latin text ← Latin commentary	Adams 1945 Primo 6,5705 Hoffman 296 Schwab 3050 NUC 21,11; 0403719

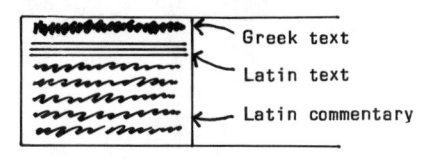

ΑΡΙΣΤΟΤΕΛΟΥΣ ΤΕΧΝΗΣ ΡΗΤΟΡΙΚΗΣ ΒΙΒΛΙΑ Γ

Aristotelis de arte dicendi libri tres, opera & studio Ioannis Caselij, quàm emendatissimè editi, & quàm diligentissimè correcti, iuxta eam, que vna omnibus ceteris præstat, editionem Petri Victorij, qui exemplaribus & pluribus, et vetustissimis, & optimis vsus fuit.

ὀρθίῳ
ἀθωᾶς
νόμῳ

ROSTOCHII. ex officina Iacobi Lucij.
Anno M. D. LXXVII.
Sum Ioh. Georgij a Werdenstein, 1578.

PLATE FIFTY-THREE
title page of the 1577 Rostock edition
courtesy of the Bayerische Staatsbibliothek, Munich

PETRI VICTORII
DECLARATIONES
IN ARISTOTELIS
RHETORICES
LIBRUM PRIMUM.

Ἡ ῥητορική ἐστιν ἀντίστροφος τῇ διαλεκτικῇ.

Rhetorica versatur in iisdem rebus, in quibus dialectica.

PRIMAM hanc huius libri partem, summos viros, qui ipsam interpretentur habere, constat, M. Ciceronem, & Alexandrum Aphrodisiensem: quorum alter, cum ingenuas etiam alias artes didicisset, huius maxime studij atque artificij peritissimus merito semper est habitus: alter vero ita accurate cunctos Aristotelis libros euoluit, ac tantum ingenio valuit, vt omnia obscuriora sensa eorum, & percipere ipse, & aliis declarare potuerit: dissidere tamen hi inter se in loci huius explicatione videntur. quare sententias amborum proferam, &, quid vtrumque secutum esse suspicer, ostendam. Ciceronis igitur ex oratore verba haec sunt. Atque etiam ante hunc Aristoteles, principio artis rhetoricae, dicit illam artem, quasi ex altera parte respondere dialecticae, vt hoc videlicet differant inter se, quod haec ratio dicendi, latior sit: illa loquendi, contractior. Haec autem è libro primo Academicarum quaestionum ad Varronem. Huic quasi ex altera parte, oratoria vis dicendi adhibebatur, explicatrix orationis perpetuae, ad persuadendum accommodatae: eundem enim hunc locum manifesto intelligit, quamuis sententiam hanc Aristotelis esse, vt in oratore secerat, non ostendat. Alexander vero in primum librum Topicorum, de dialectica loquens, inquit. Τοιαύτην δ᾽ ἡγητέον αὐτὴν, εἴ τινος καὶ ἀντίστροφόν φησιν ὁ Ἀριστοτέλης εἶναι τῇ ῥητορικῇ, ἐπειδὴ τὰ αὐτὰ τοῖς τὰ πιθανὰ: ἅ, τῷ ἐνδόξῳ εἶναι, καὶ αὐτά ἐστι τοιαῦτα : τὸ γὰρ ἀντίστροφον ἀντὶ τοῦ ἰσοστρόφου τι καὶ πρὸς τὰ αὐτὰ ἐπιφερόμενον καὶ καταγινόμενον, λέγει. Cum tradat hic scilicet Aristoteles dialecticam esse antistrophon rhetoricae: sit autem dialectica qualem illic descripsit Alexander, recte ipsum fecisse; rhetorica namq; circa res ad persuadendum accommodatas versatur, quae huiuscemodi sunt, ac naturam eam habent, quia conueniunt opinionibus hominum: quidquid enim sensibus iudicijsq; hominum conuenit, id etiam ad persuadendum appositum est. nam, quod ad vim nominis pertinet, ἀντίστροφον pro ἰσοστρόφον positum ab eo esse vult. id autem nihil aliud est, nisi, quae versatur circa easdem res, & in illis tractandis tota occupatur. intelligit autem, quae ex opinionib. hominum sunt, & ἔνδοξα ob eam causam vocantur. Et sententiam igitur Aristotelis, & vim verbi, vnde omnis controuersia orta est, expressit Alexander. Sed ad Ciceronem reuertamur, qui, vt plane intelligitur, aliam primae partis huius nominis rationem esse credidit: est enim manifesto duplex, è duobusq; nominibus iunctum nomen. Non igitur, vt Alexander postea fecit, ἀντὶ Cicero hic, ἴσον significare putauit: quo intellectu saepe prisci Graeci capiebant, & quam vim in multis iunctis verbis habet, sed è regione & contra: hoc enim significare apud ipsum ex altera parte, perspicuū est: aliis namq; etiam plurimis in locis, ita Cicero locutus est, & in orationibus, & in libris, quos de philosophia scripsit: exemplis enim in re plana, & quae passim obuia sit, supersedebo. Videtur igitur ita locum hunc Cicero accepisse, tamquam discriminis etiam aliquid inter has artes esse, significare hic voluerit Aristoteles: nam similes illas esse; affinesq; multum inter se, optime ipse intelligebat: id enim manifesto significauit, cum appellarit antea dialecticam, vicinam atq; finitimam rhetoricae. Sed etiam verbo idem indicasse videtur, quo hic vsus est, cū inquit ipsam respondere: eo enim prorsus similitudo quaedam declaratur. nihil igitur protulit, si diligenter attendimus, quod verum non sit, & notioni eius nominis, & naturae rei, non quadret. Alexander enim quoq; cum similitudinem harum artium illic ostendisset, quib. rebus illae discrepant inter se, tradit. tria autē affert, vt facile ex verbis ipsius intelligere licet, A psinus quoq;

A   quidam

PLATE FIFTY-FOUR

first page of the 1579 Florence Victorius edition

courtesy of the Library of the University of Illinois at Champaign-Urbana

Year	Locations	Title Page	Details	References
1579	Bologna:A.IV.TT. VII.26 BudapestNB:Ant.8580 Flor:02.10.31 + Magl. 22c.6.8(lacks vol. two) + 3.P.8.645 (lacks index) Harv:*56-1805 MAmb:M.5237 Munich:8°A.gr.b.539/6 Olomouc: 27719 Prague:5.L.34/6 RomeAles:A.a.15-21 RomeBV:S.Borr.H.V.II Sibiu:u I 309 St.Gen:R.8^C58 inv. 1438 Tub:Cd 2375. Vat:R.Gen.Class.VI. 205(1-7)	TITLE PAGE,vol.1: ARISTOTELIS STAGIRITAE ORGANUM,QUOD LOGICAM APELLANT. Tomus Primus. TITLE PAGE,vol.6:ARISTOTELIS STAGIRITAE RHETORICORUM . . . page 3,vol.6:ARISTOTELIS STAGIRITAE PERIPATETICORUM PRINCIPIS ARTIS RHETORICAE LIBER PRIMUS. GEORGIO TRAPEZUNTIO INTERPRETE. Lyon:apud haeredes [Ioannam] Iacobi Iuntae F. (Jacques Guinta filius), 1579	in 16° chaps:a=15;b=27;g=19 Bks:One=3-66;Two=67-130;Three=131-175 set appeared between 1579 & 1603 R. at Harvard & Munich in vol 6;7 vols. in all only Latin Trapezuntius version Harvard KC 15757 (6 vols) is as bastard set; vol. 3 & the index belong to this 1579 edition; other vols. issued by Cardon in Geneva in 1614-18. Apparently a bookseller put together a set & bound them together. The index refers accurately to references in the R. published in 1579 and the index is dated 1579 Augsburg does not have; Prague UK has all 7 vols,but the publishers differ. Prague has a second set,but it lacks vol.6; Marburg IV C 208 lacks vol. 6; Budapest AkB 551.862 has only vols.1 & 5; Munster does not have Lyon has only index; RomeAles & RomBV have 7 vols.	Primo 6,5793 Ind Aur 2,246 108.636 Baudrier VI,69 + X,289 NUC 20,593; 0400815 Gesamt 6,5976 Cranz 108.636
1580	Augsburg:LG216 Basel:B.C.VIII.40 BM:974.a.1 Bodleian:Vet.D.1 f.129 Geneva:S 22511 Harv:*56-1806 Krakow:Class.gr.205 Morgan: 1851-57 Ohio St:PA3895 A4 1566 RomeCas:L.XIII.7 Vat:R.Gen.Classici VI 79(1-6) WroclawA:XVI.O.8180	TITLE PAGE:vol.1: ARISTOTELIS STAGIRITAE OPERA OMNIA . . . TITLE PAGE,vol.6: ARISTOTELIS STAGIRITAE RHETORICORUM,Artisque Poeticae libri, atq: . . . page 3,vol.6: ARISTOTELIS STAGIRITAE PERIPATETICORUM PRINCIPIS ARTIS RHETORICAE LIBER PRIMUS. GEORGIO TRAPZEUNTIO interprete. Lyon:Iacobus Berjon (Jacques Berion),1580	in 16° chaps:a=15;b=27;g=19 Bks:One=3-66;Two=67-130;Three=131-175 R. in vol. 6 Trapezuntius tr. in Latin Bodleien set of 7 vols. has index has vol. 7;UCBanc has only index;Illinois has only vol. 1;BN has only vol. 5; Munich 8°A.gr.b.540 lacks vol. 6;Ohio State has vols. 1,2,3,6,7;Prague has only vols.1,2,3;Erlangen has only vol. 4;Augsburg,Bamburg do not have Like 1579 Lyon edition, except not divided into parts 1 & 2. Type reset from 1579.	NUC 20,592; 0400819 Primo 6,5795 Schwab 2957 Ind Aur 2,247 108.644 Gesamt 6,5977 (does not give locations) Cranz 108.644
1581	BM:8464.h.9 Camb:St.Johns Cc.1. Halle:AB84303 Kenyon:Locker folio 888.5 A4 1581 Lyon:22538 Marburg:IV A45 N'wstn:L881.A8.JLm RomeBNC:8.23.F.16	TITLE PAGE: ARISTOTELIS STAGIRITAE OPERA . . . cols.1088-1089: ARISTOTELIS Stagiritae Rethoricorum [sic] ad Theodecten,Liber Primus,Georgio Trapezuntio Interprete. Lyon: Stephanus Michaelis (Etienne Michal),1581	in 4° chaps:a=15;b=26;g=19 Bks:One=cols.1088-1121;Two=1124[sic] -1160;Three=1160-1184 lines numbered 10,20,30,40,50,60 only Latin with 2 cols per page two vols bound in one, R in vol. 2 vol. 1 at St. Johns lacks title page.St. John's catalogue says vol.1 issued in Basel by Bourgetius in 1577 Berlin 2°Vt.484 lost in WWII;Rome BNC 8.23.F.16 has only vol.1 without the R. ed. Iacobus Martinus WroclawU copy missing since WWII	Gesamt 6,5979 Primo 6,5796 Adams 1750
1581	Berlin:4°Vt.484(a) BM:8464.h.9 Gotha:Phil.2° 10/5 Ill:q881 A8 1581 Prague:5.A.24 Wolf:ALVENSLEBEN Ca.11 2o	TITLE PAGE,vol.1: ARISTOTELIS STAGIRITAE OPERA,Post omnes quae in hunc usque diem prodierunt editiones,summo studio emaculata, & ad Graecum exemplar diligenter recognita ab A.Iacobo Martino Doctore Medico ac Philosopho	in 4° chaps:a=15;b=26;g=19 Bks:One=1087-1122;Two=1123-1160;Three= 1160-1184 lines numbered 10,20,30,40,50,60 only Latin Marburg does not have 2 vols in one; R in vol.2	Gesamt 6,5978 Baudrier IV, 139 Ind Aur 2,248 108.652

The Sorbonne lists a 1580 Lugduni edition, published by S. Gryphius in 1580 under the call number L.C. 6 62.12o in 12o. However, a letter from the Sorbonne dated 9/14/81 stated that, although they show such a listing, the book is not on the shelf at the Sorbonne and cannot be located. Moreover, the Sorbonne reported that, since Gryphius died in 1556, and his heirs stopped publishing in 1564, they concluded that their entry was a mistake and that there was no such 1580 edition.

ARISTOTELIS
STAGIRITÆ
OPERVM,
TOMVS ALTER.

Nuper auctus libr. Nono ac Decimo POLITICORUM
per KYRIACUM STROZAM.

LVGDVNI,
Apud Bartholomæum Honoratum.

M. D. LXXXI.

PLATE FIFTY-FIVE
title page of volume one of the 1581 edition attributed to Bartholomew Honoratus
courtesy of the Library of the University of Illinois at Champaign-Urbana

ARISTOTELIS
STAGIRITÆ
OPERA,

Post omnes quæ in hunc vsque diem prodierunt editiones, summo studio emaculata, & ad Græcum exemplar diligenter recognita ab A. Iacobo Martino Doctore Medico ac Philosopho.

Nuper autem noua accessione Theologiæ seu Philosophiæ mysticæ, & Noni ac Decimi Politicorum lib. locupletata, vt octaua ab hinc pagina patet.

Quibus accessit Index locupletissimus recens collectus.

LVGDVNI,
Apud Bartholomæum Honoratum.

M. D. LXXXI.

PLATE FIFTY-SIX

title page of volume two of the 1581 edition attributed to Bartholomew Honoratus

courtesy of the Library of the University of Illinois at Champaign-Urbana

Early Printings

ARISTOTELIS
STAGIRITÆ
OPERVM,
TOMVS ALTER.

Nuper auctus libr. Nono ac Decimo POLITICORVM
per KYRIACVM STROZAM.

LVGDVNI,
Apud Stephanum Michaëlem.
M. D. LXXXI.

PLATE FIFTY-SEVEN

title page of volume two of the 1581 edition attributed to Stephanus Michaelis

courtesy of the Chalmers Memorial Library, Kenyon College

		cols.1087-1088,vol.2: ARISTOTELIS Stagiritae Rhetoricorum ad Theodecten,Liber Primus,Georgio Trapezuntio Interprete. Lyon:(Barthelemy)Honoratus (Honorat),1561		NUC 20,593; 0400852 Cranz 108.652
1582	Bodleian:B.13.2. Linc. Princeton:Ex 2599 383.082 RomeBNC:1.58.E.30/2	TITLE PAGE:ΑΡΙΣΤΟΤΕΛΟΥΣ ΡΗΤΟΡΙΚΗΣ ΤΕΧΝΗΣ ΒΙΒΛΙΑ ΤΡΙΑ. ARISTOTELIS DE ARTE dicendi Libri tres. page 3:ΑΡΙΣΤΟΤΕΛΟΥΣ ΤΕΧΝΗΣ ῥητορικῆς, τῶν εἰς τρία τὸ πρῶτον. Paris:Steph.Preuosteau (Etienne Prevosteau),haeredis Guil. Morelij,1582	in 8° Bks:One=3-52;Two=61-120[sic];Three=113--153[sic] only Greek,except for Barbaro's commentary as spublished by Morelius in 1559 pages numbered erratically reprint of 1559 gives variant readings from other printed editions	Primo 6,5706 NUC 21,11 0403721
1584- 1596	Augsburg:4oLG 62 BerlinH:Vt 55 Berlin:Vu 7521 BM:11805.f.1(not part of a set) + + 671.d.2 + 30.i.3-11 + G.7958-63 BN:X.3054;R.1593; R.1597 Bodleian:St.Am.19-23 + Francof.1584--7.4o + Byw.J.8. 10-14 + Saville R.5. shelved by itself Bonn:Da 860 10 BostonPub:**H.72.20 Camb:Emmanuel S6.3. 4-12;Pembroke 9. 18.7;Peterhouse D. 5.19;Selwyn E.6.2; St.Catharine's D IX 3;U.Lib.L.10. 42-48 but vol.8 with R at S.13.16 Columbia:Spec.Col. Gonzalez-Lodge 1584 Ar46 Cornell:RARE PA3893 R3 1584 Erl:4oPhil.VII,6ai Flor:5.4.83 Gennadaius:GC.3130 Got:8oA.gr.IV.13 + 8oA.gr.IV.531 Gotha:Phil.4o 4/1 Griefswald:8oCW 154 (1-11) Halle:Cc 1694 Harv:*OGC.ar46.584. v2 Hldbg:D.2697;Hauser 245 Htgtn:357923 Ill:UNCAT Leid:570 E 21-30 + 757 D.25-31 Leipsig:4 Arist.113 Maz:14210 B & B* MAmb:S.Q.T.VII.12-21 MilanB:2EE.II.1-10	TITLE PAGE TO INTRODUCTORY VOLUME ΑΡΙΣΤΟΤΕΛΟΥΣ ΤΑ ΕΥΡΙΣΚΟΜΕΝΑ. ARISTOTELIS OPERA QUAE EXSTANT. TITLE PAGE,vol.with Rhetoric: ΑΡΙΣΤΟΤΕΛΟΥΣ τέκνης ῥητορικῆς βιβλία γ. Aristotelis Artis Rhetorica libri III. page 3,vol. with Rhetoric: ΑΡΙΣΤΟΤΕΛΟΥΣ ΤΕΧΝΗΣ ῥητκορικῆς, τῶν εἰς τρία τὸ πρῶτον. Frankfurt:Andreae Wecheli,Claudius Marnius,& Joannes Aubrius, 1584-1596	in 4° but small,closer to standard 8° chaps:a=15;b=26;g=19 Bks:One=3-58;Two=58-116;Three=117-156 lines numbered 5,10,15,20,25 only Greek with Rh. ad Alex. #'s refer to pp. in 1559 and 1562 editions,but no #'s in Princeton copy chapters marked with Greek letters in margins volumes not numbered by editors,so binders and libraries have often assigned varying volume nos. However,in the general preface to vol.one,Sylburg listed the ten vols. of his edition, and this order is generally followed with the R. in volume two. However, the BN,Erlangen have R in vol. 9;Camb U.Lib. as vol. 8; Emmanuel as vol.5;Northwestern as vol.1 vol.3, beginning with the Physica, was reissued in 1596, evidently to resupply the vol.3 issued in 1586 Virginia has only vol. with Physica, *PA3890.A6 1584; Columbia has 2nd set B88Ar5l IB84 with only vols. 8-11;Boston Public has only vol. with the R.;Heidelberg has 2 vols dated 1584 and 1587 including the comprehensive title page. UCBanc has only volume one. Naples S.G.XVII.101 is defective One of Northwestern vols. bears stamp of Heidelberg University. Munster, Berlin & N.Y.Academy of Medicine do not have;Kiel copy burned in WWII. Got 8°A gr.IV.936 and 8°A.gr.IV.2827 do not contain the R. The chaps. match Roemer's chaps.,following Trapezuntius' chapter headings. The edition uses some readings from Victorius. Tub Cd 1946 has 5 vols, no R ed. Frederick Sylburg Htgtn has 11 vol. set bound in 12 with vol.3 bound in two. Vol. 2 with R has date of 1584 after each work, this edition gives variant readings, and then the Sylburg index in Greek & Latin for that work, e.g., Greek: ἔντεχνοι πίστεις...7,21 (page 7, line 21) Latin:Demosthenes 103,6 (page 106,line 6)	NUC 20,584; 0400627 + 0400628 + 20,586; 0400914 + 0400919 Adams 1734 + 1757 Gesamt 6, 5898 + 6, 5997 Primo 6, 5317 Hoffman 290 -291 + 295 + 297 Schwab 386; 2953 Brunet I,458 Supp.59-60 Ind Aur 2,249 108.664 Cranz 108.664

Aristotelea

ΑΡΙΣΤΟΤΕΛΟΥΣ
ΗΘΙΚΩΝ ΝΙΚΟΜΑΧΕΙ-
ΩΝ ΒΙΒΛΙΑ ΔΕΚΑ.

ARISTOTELIS ETHICORVM, SIVE DE MORIBVS, AD NICO-
MACHVM LIBRI DECEM.

Opera doctißimi viri Petri Victorij emendati.

Additæ in fine præter Varias lectiones à Victorio adnotatas, aliæ quoque scripturæ diuersitates, è Basiliensi, Veneta, & aliis editionibus; emendationes etiam nonnullæ ex doctorum virorum obseruationibus. Ad hæc Index capitum; & rerum ac verborum notatu digniorum bina Inuentaria; alterum Græcum, alterum Latinum.

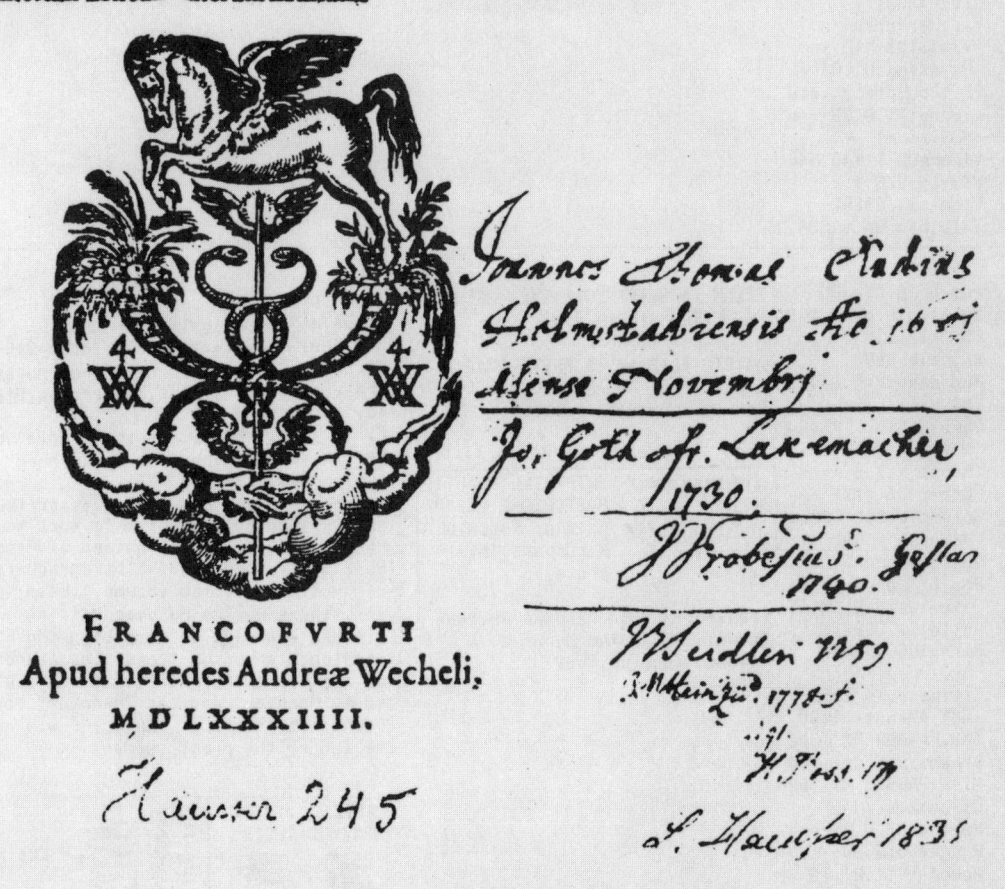

FRANCOFVRTI
Apud heredes Andreæ Wecheli.
M D LXXXIIII.

PLATE FIFTY-EIGHT

title page of the 1584 Sylburg Frankfurt edition

courtesy of the Universitätsbibliothek Heidelberg

Munich:4°A.gr.b.164
Nurn:Solg.1822-
 1825a.b.c
Okl:Hist.of Sci.
 Col(no call #)
OxAS:i.7.
OxCC:A.B.54 + V.3.
 1 + A.D.2.5
OxPem:1.d
OxQ:Sel.e.224-233
ParisArs:S & A 261
PhilLC:Log343.Q
Princeton:Ex 2599.
 1587
RomeAng:TT.22.20
St.Gen: R307
Tub:Cd 1755.4°
Turun:Ob.6.II.3020
U.Chic:John Crerar
 6615,R in vol.two
 of 11 vol. set;
 PA3893.R3 1584 is
 R by itself;PA
 3890.A2S9 begins
 with A's biog,ends
 with R
U.Pa:Founders 128
 Q (complete set) +
 Gr C Ar466 22 1584
 (bound separately)
UCLA:PA3893 07 1585
 (by itself)
Vat:Barberini J.
 VIII.103-112 +
 Palatina N.103 +
 3 incomplete sets
Vienna:71.G.39 (in
 MSS.room)
ViennaUB:I 148.544
Wf: Lg 276.1
Wroclaw:353262
Yale:Gfa 84 a 584 2

1588 Augsburg:LG 220
      Bamberg:L.gr.o.168
      BM: 714.b.6
      BN: X.19980
      Bodleian:Vet.D.1f.
       83
      Camb:U.Lib.L.19.64
       + w.3.48; Peter-
       house K.7.5
      Coburg: A 1871
      Columbia:Spec.Col.
       B88Ar51 VB88
      Gdansk:Cc 4733 8°
      Got:8°A.gr.IV.533
      Griefswald:8°CW175
      Halle:Ce 2322
      Harv:*OGC Ar46W
       588
      Ill:Baldwin 2156 +
       881 A7rh.ri 1588
      Ind:PA3893 R3 1588
      Krakow:Phil.gr.234
      Mich:PA3893 R3 1588
      OxPem:3.c.
      Naples:38.B.32
      Prague:5.G.88
      RomeAng:TT.21.79
      RomeBNC:6.8.F.2
      RomeBV:S.Borr.D.I.
       202
      St.Gen:X8°530 Inv.
       1065
      U.Pa:GrC Ar466 Ef22
       .9 1588

TITLE PAGE:ΑΡΙΣΤΟΤΕΛΟΥΣ ΤΕΧΝΗΣ
ΡΗΤΟΡΙΚΗΣ βιβλία γ΄.

ARISTOTELIS ARTIS RHETORICAE
LIBRI TRES; AB ANTONIO RICCOBONO
Latine conversi.

page 1:paired Greek/Roman titles

| ΑΡΙΣΤΟΤΕΛΟΥΣ ΤΕΧΝΗΣ ΡΗΤΟΡΙΚΗΣ τῶν εἰς τρία τὸ πρῶτον. | ARISTOTELIS ARTIS RHETORICAE LIBER primus; Antonio Riccobono interprete. |

Frankfurt: apud heredes Andreae
Wecheli, Claudium Marnium, &
Ioannem Aubrium,1588

in 8° but small
chaps:a=15;b=26;g=19
Bks:One=1-105;Two=106-215;Three=216-288
Riccobono is said to have incorporated
the work of Victorius,Maioragius,Sigon-
io, and Mureto
R. is first 288 pp. of the single vol.
Berlin Vu8384,Bonn, and Braunsberg
copies destroyed in WWII
An error in the BN catalogue attribu-
ting a 1588 edition of this work to
Hanover (BN X.19980) instead of Frankfurt has caused other bibliographers who
did not consult the volume itself to
err. There was no Hanover edition. The
mistake was made in compiling the BN
catalogue when the typesetter glanced
at the following entry that was published in Hanover, and set "Hanover" for the
Frankfurt edition. The error was not detected by the proof readers.

Primo 6,5707

Cranz 108.697

Ind Aur 252
108.697

Adams 1946

Gesamt 6,6314

NUC 21,30;
0403905 + 21
0403723

Hoffman 337

Schwab 2987 +
3006 + 3061

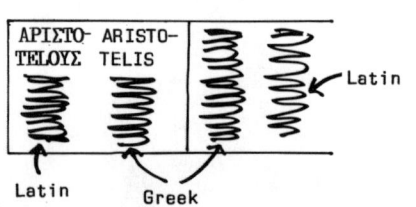

| ΑΡΙΣΤΟ-ΤΕΛΟΥΣ | ARISTOTELIS | | ←Latin |

↑Latin   ↑Greek

Vat:Chigi V 1038
Vienna:71.L.72
Wolf:54 Rhet.(1) +
  Lg 299 + ALVERS-
  LEBEN 388 (1)
WroclawA:XVI.9048 +
  XVI.O.8451
WroclawU:3167699 +
  450416

1590 Basel:B.c.I.4
      Berlin:2°Vt 38a
        RARA
      BerlinH:Vt.60 2°
      BM:456.g.i + 517.
        m.1
      BN: R.85-86
      Bodleian:B.3.13 Art
      Brno: ST 4-315
      Brown:PA3890 =A2
        1590 *
      BudapestEK:Hb2r136
      Camb:U.Lib.Yorke
        a.2;Kings K.19.27;
        Corpus Cristi G.2.
        1;Trinity T.6.11
      CathU:C.L. 1851
        A717 1590
      Edinburgh:K.370.c.
      Erl:2°Phil.VII.26a
      Geneva:Ca 249
      Got:Auct.Gr.IV.15
      Gotha:P 2° 176
      Griefswald:2°CW 154
      Halle:Ce 1595.2°
        + AB 177787
      Harv:*56-1812F
      Htgtn:374808
      Ill:UNCAT
      Leipsig:fol.
        Aristot.3
      MilanB:25.5.N.8
      Munich:2°A.gr.b.77
      Naples:V.9.2 +
        84.N.17-18 + B.
        Branc.81.g.13
      NYAcMed: RB
      Lyon:22-539
      Prague:5.A.94
      Princeton:Annex
        V2599.1590q
      RomeAles:C.p.2
      Sibiu:u V 34
      Tub:Cd 856
      Tulane:RARE 888
        A 717 xca
      U.Chic:fPA3890.A2
        1590
      U.Pa:fGrC Ar466 1
        1590
      Vat:Barb I.X.17
        + Palatina S 19
      Vienna:248.189 D
      Wolf:1.4.Quod.2o
      Wroclaw: 463041
        + 557535

TITLE PAGE, vol.1: ΑΡΙΣΤΟΤΕΛΟΥΣ
ΤΟΥ ΣΤΑΓΕΙΡΙΤΟΥ ΤΑ ΣΩΖΟΜΕΝΑ.

OPERUM ARISTOTELIS STAGIRITAE PHI-
LOSOPHORUM OMNIUM LONGE PRINCIPIS,
NOVA EDITIO,Graece & Latine . . .
ex bibliotheca Isaaci Casauboni

Title page,vol 2: Operum Aristotelis Tomus II

page 289,vol 2 :ΑΡΙΣΤΟΤΕΛΟΥ
ΤΕΧΝΗΣ ΡΗΤΟΡΙΚΗΣ ΤΩΝ ΕΙΣ ΤΡΙΑ
ΤΟ ΠΡΩΤΟΝ.

ARISTOTELIS ARTIS RHETORICAE LIBER
PRIMUS. Antonio Riccobono interprete.

Lyon: apud Iacobus Bubonium (Jacques Bubonius), 1590

In some copies,vol.one designated as "apud Guillaume Laemarium,1590," e.g., BM,Bodleian,
Budapest,Edinbug,rGottingen,
Harvard & Munich. Halle has
copies of both, one marked "Bubonium" and the other
"Laemarium."

in 4°
chaps:a=15;b=26;g=19
Bks:One=289-310;Two=310-332;Three=332-347
lines labled A to H and A to G
2 vols, R in vol. 2
no indication of source of Greek text
variant readings noted in margins
Primo listing for RomeBNC is in error;Vi-
enna 248.189-D has only vol.1;Braunsberg,
Bonn, and Kiel copies destroyed in WWII;
BudapestEK has marked as lost a second
copy, HB IVret 149;Marburg IV A43 missing vol.2; NUC entry for USC is in
error
RomeAles has vol.2 attributed to
Laemarius

```
┌─────────┬─────────┐
│ ≷  A    │ ≷  A    │
│ ≷  B    │ ≷  B    │
│ ≷  C    │ ≷  C    │
│ ≷  D    │ ≷  D    │
│ ≷  E    │ ≷  E    │
│   etc.  │   etc.  │
└─────────┴─────────┘
  ↑    ↑    ↑    ↑
Greek  Latin  Greek
```

NUC 20,584;
0400629 +
0400623

Schwab 387

Adams 1736 +
1737 + 1738

Baudrier
I,239-240

Gesamt 6,
5899 + 6,
5900

Primo 6,5318

Ind Aur 2,253
108.708

Hoffman I,291

Cranz 108.708

The 1590 Antonii Bernardi Mirandulani Casertae Episcopii . . . in Tertium Librum
Rhetorica Aristoteles Egregia Explicatio. (Bononiae:
Michael Berman, 1590), Adams 741, Camb. U. Lib. Ff.9.54, is a commentary. Can be
listed under Bernardi della Mirandala, Antonio de and Bernadus, Antonius.
There appears to have been more than one edition of this commentary, because the
British Library under C.80.c.5 lists a 1595 edition issued in Bologna by V.
Benalius.

ΑΡΙΣΤΟΤΕΛΟΥΣ
ΤΟΥ ΣΤΑΓΕΙΡΙΤΟΥ
ΤΑ ΣΩΖΟΜΕΝΑ.
OPERVM
ARISTOTELIS
STAGIRITAE PHILOSO-
PHORVM OMNIVM LONGE
PRINCIPIS; NOVA EDITIO,
Græcè & Latinè.

Græcus contextus quàm emendatißimè præter omnes omnium editiones est editus adscriptis ad oram libri & interpretum veterum recentiorúmque & aliorum doctorum virorum emendationibus: in quibus plurima nunc primum in lucem prodeunt, ex bibliotheca
ISAACI CASAVBONI.

Latinæ interpretationes adiectæ sunt quæ Græco contextui meliùs responderent, partim recentiorum, partim veterum interpretum: in quibus & ipsis multa nunc emendatiùs quàm antehac eduntur.

Accesserunt ex libris Aristotelis, qui hodie desiderantur, FRAGMENTA quædam.
Adiecti sunt etiam INDICES duo perutiles: quorum alter nomina auctorum qui in Aristotelem scripserunt, continet: alter quid sit à quoque in singulas libroum eius partes scriptum indicat, necnon alius INDEX rerum omnium locupletissimus.

LVGDVNI,
Apud Guillelmum Læmarium.
M. D. XC.

248.189-D

PLATE FIFTY-NINE

title page of volume one of the 1590 edition attributed to Laemarius

courtesy of the History of Science Collection, John Hay Library, Brown University

OPERVM
ARISTOTELIS
TOMVS II.

IBRORVM ARISTOTELIS QVÆ
non extant, FRAGMENTA quædam.

ITEM,

ndices duo: quorum prior nomina eorum continet qui in Aristotelem scripserunt: alter quid sit
à quoque eorum in singulos Aristotelis libros scriptum, indicat.

Alius INDEX rerum omnium locupletissimus.

LVGDVNI,
Apud Guillelmum Læmarium.
M. D. XC.

PLATE SIXTY

title page of volume two of the 1590 edition attributed to Laemarius

courtesy of the History of Science Collection, John Hay Library, Brown University

ΑΡΙΣΤΟΤΕΛΟΥΣ
ΤΟΥ ΣΤΑΓΕΙΡΙΤΟΥ
ΤΑ ΣΩΖΟΜΕΝΑ.
OPERVM
ARISTOTELIS
STAGIRITAE PHILOSO-
PHORVM OMNIVM LONGE
PRINCIPIS, NOVA EDITIO,
Græcè & Latiné.

*cuius contextus quàm emendatißimè præter omnes omnium editiones est editus:
adscriptis ad oram libri & interpretum veterum recentiorúmque &
aliorum doctorum virorum emendationibus: in quibus plurima
nunc primùm in lucem prodeunt, ex bibliotheca*
ISAACI CASAVBONI.
*Latinæ interpretationes adiectæ sunt quæ Græco contextui meliùs responderent,
partim recentiorum, partim veterum interpretum: in quibus & ipsis
multa nunc emendatiùs quàm antehac eduntur.*
Accesserunt ex libris Aristotelis, qui hodie desiderantur, FRAGMENTA quædam.
Ixecti sunt etiam INDICES duo perutiles: quorum alter nomina auctorum qui in Aristotelem scripserunt, continet: alter quid sit
à quoque in singulas librorum eius partes scriptum indicat. necnon alius INDEX rerum omnium locupletißimus.

LVGDVNI,
Apud Iacobum Bubonium.
M. D. XC.

PLATE SIXTY-ONE

title page of volume one of the 1590 edition attributed to Bubonius

courtesy of the Library of the University of Illinois at Champaign-Urbana

RHETORICORVM LIB. I.   289

eos, possent ne facere promissum? Qui cùm posse se affirmarent, non ille quidem loco mouit procuratorẽ, tributa verò, quæ æstimatione ipsi sua subiecerant, exigi iussit. Neque igitur constituto abs se honorem detrahere videbatur, neque præfectis maiora tributa imponere quàm ipsi constituissent, cùm ad sese multiplex pecunia perueniret. ¶Pythocles Atheniensis, Atheniensibus consilium dedit, vt plumbum Tyrium respublica à priuatis ad se reciperet, eo precio quo venibat, nimirum duobus denariis, vt ciuitas deinde illud venderet, constituto precio denariorum sex. ¶Chabria coactis ad naues centum viginti quantum satis esset hominum, cùm Tao non pluribus quàm sexaginta opus esset, iussit vt reliqui iis, qui in sexaginta nauibus essent, duorum mensium stipendium soluerent, aut nauigare ipsos. At hi cupientes remanere apud sua, dederunt quod imperauerat. ¶Antimenes ea quæ condi solebant propter vias regias à satrapis compleri iubebat, secundum regionis illius legem. Quoties autem inopia laborabat vel exercitus, vel alia multitudo, absque rege, aliquo abs se misso vendebat, ea quæ condita erant. ¶Cleomenes, accedente luna noua, cùm stipendium esset dandum militibus, accessit de industria nauigio. Et deinde abeunte mense discedens nauigio stipendii persoluebat. Postea sequente mense differebat solutionem vsq; ad alteram nouam lunam. Milites autem, quòd paulò antè stipendium accepissent, quieti erant: itaque ille vnum in anno mensem præteriens, vnius mensis stipendium militibus subtrahebat. ¶Stabelbius cùm deberet militibus stipendium, conuocatis ductoribus, sibi priuatis nihil prorsus opus esse dixit: & quoties indigeat militibus, si illorum cuique argentum dederit, ita ad conducendum externum militem eos posse ablegari. Et ea stipendia, quæ militibus persoluere cogatur, se eis libentius esse daturum. Iussit igitur dimittere suos vnumquemque ita vt manipulatim ex illa regione discedant. Ductores cùm ea ex re lucri aliquid se facturos esse arbitrarentur, milites ita, quemadmodum Stabelbius præceperat, dimiserunt. Modico autem interposito tempore, congregatis ipsis: neque tibicinis absque cœtu Musico, neque ductoris absque militibus vsum esse dixit, iussitque eos regione illa excedere. ¶Dionysius circum fana obiens, sicubi cerneret propositam mensulam auream aut argenteam, Boni euentus, cùm infunderet iussisset, præcepit illam auferri. Quæ simulacra autem erant eiusmodi, vt extensa manu præferrent pateram, eam adimere iussit, quòd diceret se accipere. Pallia etiam aurea & coronas de simulacris detrahebat, dicebátque eis sic & leuiora & melius odorata dare velle, atque ita illis pallium linteum & coronas violaceas circundabat.

ΑΡΙΣΤΟΤΕΛΟΥΣ ΤΕΧΝΗΣ
ΡΗΤΟΡΙΚΗΣ, ΤΩΝ ΕΙΣ ΤΡΙΑ ΤΟ ΠΡΩΤΟΝ.

ARISTOTELIS ARTIS RHE
TORICAE LIBER
PRIMVS.
Antonio Riccobono interprete.

CAPVT I.
De Rhetorica similitudine cum Dialectica, & de vtilitate.

RHETORICA conuenientiam habet cum Dialectica: ambæ enim in eiusmodi rebus versantur, quæ communiter quodammodo cognoscuntur ab omnibus, & nullius sunt scientiæ definitæ. Quamobrem etiam omnes quodammodo ambarum participes sunt. Omnes enim quadamtenus & exquirere & sustinere rationem, & defendere, & accusare conantur. Ac ex imperita quidem multitudine alij temere hæc faciunt: alij consuetudine, & habitu. Quoniam verò vtroque modo contingit manifestum est licere eadem etiam facere certa via, & ratione. Cur enim finem consequantur, tum qui hæc faciunt consuetudine, tum qui casu, causam intueri contingit. Iam verò omnes confessi fuerint huiusmodi esse artis munus. Ac nunc quidem qui artes orationum componunt, exiguã ipsarũ particulã confecerunt. Fides.n. artificiosa est solũ: alia verò additamẽti sunt loco. At hi nihil quidẽ de enthymematib. dicũt, id qõ est robur fidei: de iis verò, quæ sunt extra re, plurima tradũt. Criminatio.n. & misericordia, & ira & huiusmodi animi perturbationes

---

PLATE SIXTY-TWO

the *Rhetoric* in volume two of the 1590 Lyon edition, with the parallel Greek text and the Riccobono Latin
courtesy of the Library of the University of Illinois at Champaign-Urbana

1591	Arizona:PA3893.R3 1591 BM:74.h.2 + G.8031 + 520.K.3 Bodleian:4:Δ.269 Camb:U.Lib.L.9.20; Peterhouse C.2.9 CathU:CL 185.1 Coburg: A 2090 Flor:5.C.1.36 Gennadius:GC.3219.2 Got:4oA.gr.IV.621 Halle:Ce 2323.4o Harv:Ga112.438F* Leipsig:Kirchen bibliothek 406 + fol.Arist.7 Lyon:107617 MilanB:&&.X.31 Maz:138* Naples:107.K.6 OxPem:7.c.10 OxQ.BB.y.75 Prague:5.B.113 RomeAles:L.h.33 RomeBNC:9.19.M.15 St.G:X.Fol.Sup. 7.Res. U.Amst:458 A 4o U.Pa:gGrC Ar466 22 1591 Va:*PA3893.R34M3 1591 Venice:148.D.19	TITLE PAGE: ARISTOTELIS STAGYRITAE [sic] De Arte Rhetorica Libri Tres,CUM M. ANTONII MAIORAGII COMMENTARIIS. folio 1r: M.ANTONII MAIORAGII COMMENTARIUS IN PRIMUS ARISTOTELIS LIBRUM, De Arte Rhetorica. Venice:Franciscus de Franciscis Senensis,1591	in 4° chaps:a=49;b=49;g=49 Bks:One=1r-110r;Two=110v-202v;Three=203r -270v lines numbered 10,20,30,40,50 270 ff. + index ornate graphic at beginning title page says new chapter beginnings Greek text from Maioragius,with some adaptations from Victorius;Latin text by Maioragious, with some changes from earlier editions Berlin 2°Vu 7525 lost in WWII tries to resemble the 1579 Victorius except divided into chapters Greek Latin commentary	Ind Aur 2,254 108.714 Primo 6,5708 Gesamt 6,6315 Hoffman 297 + 337 Schwab 2985 NUC 21,12; 0403725 Cranz 108.714
1592	Olomouc:27902 Wf:44.1.2 Rhet.	TITLE PAGE: Aristotelis RHETORICORUM AD THEODECTEN LIBRI TRES, EX PETRI VICTORII TRALATIONE LATINI page 1: ARISTOTELIS RHETORICES LIBER PRIMUS ed. Martin Marstaller Bardi: Pomeraniae: ex officina ducalis, 1592.	in 8° isolated indications of chapters Bks:One=1-128;Two=129-264;Three=265-355 lines numbered 10,20 adaptation from Victorius by Martin Marstaller date of Wolfenbütel copy somewhat confusing, indistinct,could read 1594; Wolfenbütel catalogue says "1594"	Ind Aur 2,254 108.715 Cranz 108.715
1593	Basel:Frey-Gryn L VII 5 BudapestAkB:551.575 BudapestNB:Ant.7516 + Ant.7302 Erl:Phils VII, 65 Ill:X881 A8.L 1593 Krakow:Auct.gr.1792 Leid:Th. 1235 MAmb:S.L.S.I.64-68 Munich:A.gr.b.542,1 OxPem:12.b.7 Olomouc:600.709 Prague:5.I.92 RomeAles:B.f.33 Tüb:Cd 2377 U.Pa:GrC Ar466 Ef 2 1593 UCBanc:B 406 1593 Vienna:71.L.72+ Wolf:297.3 Quod WroclawU:405.199	TITLE PAGE,vol.1: ARISTOTELIS OPERUM QUOTQUOT EXTANT,LATINA EDITIO. TITLE PAGE TO VOLUME WITH RHETORIC ARISTOTELIS II TOMUS LOGICUS . . . page 3,vol.with Rhetoric: ARISTOTELIS ARTIS RHETORICAE LIBER PRIMUS,Antonio Riccobono interprete. Frankfurt:apud Andreae Wecheli heredes,Clauidium Marnium & Io. Aubrium,1593	in 8° chaps:a-15;b=26;g=19 Bks:One=3-49;Two=49-97;Three=97-129 R.in part 2 of vol.one; vols not always numbered and sometimes the two parts of vol. one are bound together UChic does not have;UNBanc copy bound with Rhet ad Alex, Poetics, Categories, etc. Berlin Vt.504-T.log u V + 504a have only vol. 1; Vienna 71.L.72 has only vol. 1;Bodleian Vet.D1 e.105 has only vol.1. volumes not numbered by the printer; Ox Pem has 11 vol. set; Tüb has 3 vol.set	Hoffman I, 320 Primo 6,5798 NUC 20,593; 0400855 + 596,0400926 Gesamt 6,5982 Ind Aur 2,255 108.721 Cranz 108.721

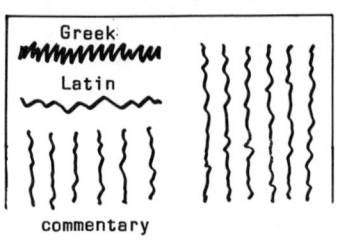

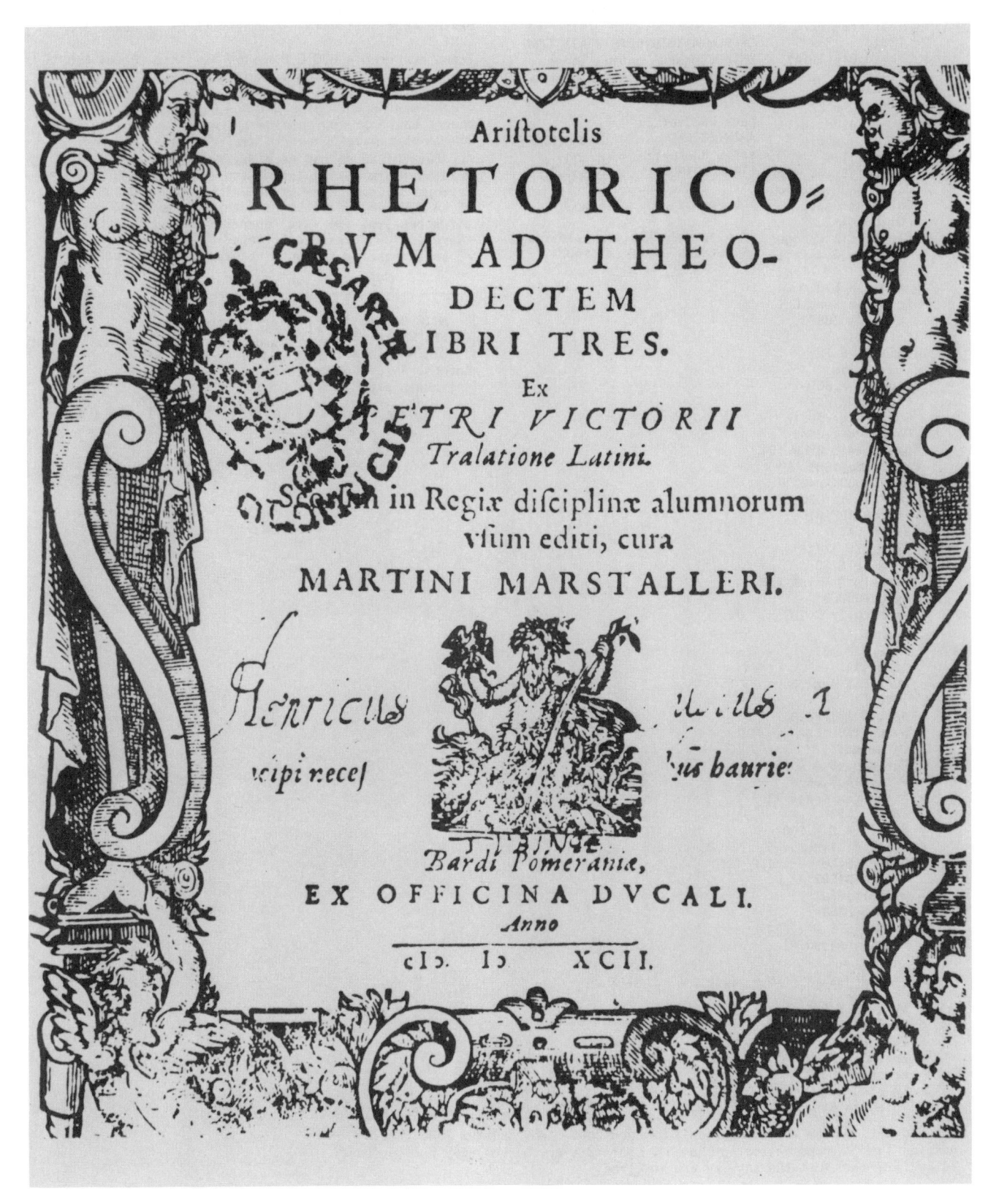

PLATE SIXTY-THREE

title page of the 1592 Pomeranian edition

courtesy of the Státní Védecká Knishovna, Olomouc

1597 Bamberg:L.gr.o.103   TITLE PAGE;ΑΡΙΣΤΟΤΕΛΟΥΣ ΤΟΥ   in 8°   Gesamt 6,5901
      Basel:B.C.III.gb.U.   ΣΤΑΓΕΙΡΙΤΟΥ ΤΑ ΣΩΖΟΜΕΝΑ.   chaps:a=15;b=26;g=19
      10 + Frey Gr L V   Bks:One=602-649;Two=649-698;Three=698-   Adams 1739
      13,14   OPERUM ARISTOTELIS STAGIRITAE   731
      Berlin:Bibl.Diez.   PHILOSOphorum omnium longè   lines numbered A,B,C,D,F, every 10 lines   Primo 6,5319
      2143-44   principis nova editio,Graece   Greek & Latin for each work in 2 vols.,
      BerlinH:Vt 72   & Latine.   R. in vol. 2   Hoffman 291
      BM:1477.bb.39   Greek version on inside columns,Ricco-
      Bodleian:Vet.E.1e.   page 602,vol.2:   bono's Latin tr. on outside columns   Ind Aur 259
      53,54 + Antiq.e.   ARISTOTELIS   ΑΡΙΣΤΟΤΕΛΟΥΣ   Bonn,Kiel copies burned in WWII;Vienna,   108.755
      F.1597.1-4   artis Rhetoricae   τέχνης   Augsburg,Milan do not have;Stanford and
      BudapestEK:Hb.4127   LIBER PRIMUS   ῥητορικῆς,   Griefswald (8°CW154) lack vol.2   NUC 20,584;
      BudapestNB:Ant.6804   Antonio Riccobono   τῶν εἰς τρία   Erlangen 71 copy says EXCUDEBAT PETRUS   0400634 +
      Budapest Raday: interprete   τὸ πρῶτον.   DE LA ROVIERE (on title page on vol.one)   0040636 +
      0.2240/1-2   title page,vol.two says "apud Guillemum   0040637
      Camb:U.Lib Brough-   Lyon:apud Guillelmum Laemarium   Laemarium" whereas the Erlangen Phil.VII
      ton 37-;Gonville-   (Guillaume Leymarie),1597   72 has Laemerius for both volumes   Baudrier
      Caius G.14.71-2;   I,240
      Clare N:5:J   page 602,vol.2:
      Columbia:Spec.Col.   Cranz 108.755
      B88Ar51 IB97
      Erl:Phl.   ARISTOTELIS   ΑΡΙΣΤΟΤΕΛΟΥΣ
      VII,71 & 72   artis Rhetoricae   τέχνης ῥητορικῆς,
      (2 copies)   LIBER PRIMUS   τῶν εἰς τρία
      Flor:15.7.369   Antonio Riccobono τὸ πρῶτον
      Geneva:Ca.251   interprete
      Got:8°A.gr.IV.17   κεφάλαιον α.
      Gotha:Phil.26/2   CAPUT I
      Griefswald:8°CW 154
      Halle:Ce 1696
      Harv:*OGC.Ar46.
      597(A) + *OGC.
      Ar.46.597(B)
      Ill:UNCAT
      Leid:679 17/18 +
      679 19 & 20
      Leipsig:8 Arist.158
      Lyon:400006
      Marburg:IV C 193
      Maz:66.157
      MilanB:B.XII.
      516311
      Munich:8°A.gr.b.
      529
      Naples:XXIV:B.3
      NYPub:*KB 1597
      OxPem:4.f.
      ParisArs:S & A 256
      Prague:5.G.36
      Princeton:Annex II
      2599.1597
      RomeAles:C.c.100
      RomeBNC:31.2.C.4-5
      RomeBV:S.Borr.H.II.2
      Stanf:KB1597 A7
      Stras:C1082
      Tüb:Cd 2160
      U.Amst:616 J 13/14
      U.Chic:PA3890.A2
      1597
      Vat:Barb.I.vii
      66 & 67
      Ven:105.D.142-143
      Vienna:71.L.5
      ViennaUB:I 148.489/2
      Wolf:Lg 276.2
      Wroclaw:450403-4 +
      335540
      Yale:Gfa 84 a597P

Hoffman 291, Schwab 388, Schweiger I,51, and Chaix 146 report a 1596 Geneva
edition in 2 volumes following the 1590 Lyon edition, but no copy can be found.
It would appear that the entries are in error.

Crameria, Danielis. (1597) SYNOPSIS TRIUM LIBRORUM RHETORICORUM ARISTOTELIS. no
place: Impensis Henrici Osthausy Bibliop. Maz:20495.

Early Printings   141

| 1598 | Augsburg:LG.224
Berlin:Vu 7528
BM:518.a.32.(1,2)
BN:X.16683
Bodleian:Byw.K.3.18
BostonPub:H.75.16
BudapestEK: 08513
Camb:U.Lib.W.4.
  14.
Coburg: A2693
Cornell:RARE PA
  3893 R3 1598
Gdansk:Cc 4736 8o
Got:8°A.gr.IV.535
Ill:X881 A8rh.po
  1598
Krakow:Auct.gr.248
Leid:679 T.30
Maz:20301
OxAS:i.10.8
OxCC:O.X.3.25
OxPem:4.b.
Princeton:Ex 2599.
  383.098
Wurzburg:L.gr.o.M8
WroclawU:335458 | TITLE PAGE:ΑΡΙΣΤΟΤΕΛΟΥΣ ΤΕΧΝΗΣ
ΡΗΤΟΡΙΚΗΣ, βιβλία τρία.

Aristotelis Artis Rhetoricae,sive
de Arte Dicendi,Libri III,AM.
AEMILIO PORTO, FRANCISCI PORTI
Cretensis F. in antiquissima, &
celeberrima Heidelbergensi Academia
ordinario linguae Graecae
Professore . . .

page 1: ARISTOTELIS DE ARTE
RHETORICA LIBER PRIMUS ex nova
AEMILII PORTI,FRANCISCI PORTI,
Cretensis F. interpretatione.

Speyer (Bern):apud Bernardum
Albinum(Bernard Weiss),1598 | in 16°
chaps:a=48;b=47;g=34
Bks:One=1-171;Two=172-351;Three=352-487
information on place,publisher,date on
  on colophon
only 1 vol.
Bonn,Kiel copies destroyed in WWII
Clare College,Cambridge,may have copy

Greek Latin   Greek Latin | Ind Aur 2,261
108.770

Adams 1948

Gesamt 6,6316

NUC 21,12;
0403727

Schwab 2988 +
3065

Brunet I,475

Cranz 108.770 |
| 1599 | Naples:B.Branc.81.
B.78 | TITLE PAGE: ARISTOTELIS ARTIS
RHETORICAE LIBRI TRES. Latina
versione e regione Graeci sermonis
posita.

page 3:

ΑΡΙΣΤΟΤΕΛΟΥΣ   ARISTOTELIS
ΤΕΧΝΗΣ ῥητορικῆς   artis Rhetoricae
τῶν εἰς τρία τὸ   L.B.I.Antonio
πρῶτον.   Riccobono
                      Interprete.

Avenione(Avignon): ex typographia
Bramereau(Jacques Bramereau),1599 | in 16°
chaps;a=25;b=26;g=19
Bks:One=3-95;Two=95-190;Three=190-254
254 pp.

Greek   Riccobono   Greek   Riccobono
ΑΡΙΣΤΟΤΕΛΟΥΣ   ARISTOTELIS
ΤΕΧΝΗΣ   artis Rhetoricae
ῥητορικῆς   LIB. I
τῶν εἰς τρία   Antonio Riccobono
τὸ πρῶτον.   Interprete. | Primo 6,5709 |

Porto, Aemilio.. Artis Rhetoricae, Sive, de Arte Dicendi Libri III. a Emilio
Porto Noua Interpretatione . . .   Speyer: B. Albinus, 1598.   Berlin Vu 7528.
Can be entitled FR. PORTI CRETENSIS COMMENTARII IN TRES ARISTOTELIS RHETORICAE,
SIVE DE ARTE DICENDI Libros, ab AEMILIO PORTO, Fr. P.C.F.

LATIN TRANSLATIONS BY MAIORAGIUS

Year	Locations	Title	Format/Details	References
1550	BM:1492.d.64 Bodleian:Byw.K.3.12 Columbia:Gonzalez- Lodge 1550 Ar 463 Cornell:RARE PA 3893 R3 1550 Ill:Baldwin 2151 MAmb:S.C.X.II.13 Munich:8ºA.gr.b.645 U.Chic:PA3895.R3C75 1550	TITLE PAGE: ARISTOTELIS STAGIRITAE RHETORICORUM LIBRI III,QUOS M. ANTONIUS MAIORAGIUS vertebat. page 3: ARISTOTELIS STAGIRITAE, RHETORICORUM LIBRI I.M.ANTONIO MAIORAGIO INTERPRETE Mediolani(Milan):Valerius & Hieronymus Metius,fratres,1550	in 8º but small Bks:One=3-90;Two=91-180;Three=181-240 only Latin	NUC 21,19; 0403894 Ind Aur 2,204 108.179 Gesamt 6,6377 Cranz 108.179
1552	Basel:B.C.17.50 Bodleian:Antiq.f.I. 1552/I Ill: X881 A8rh.Lm Maz:20306 Mich: 888 A8r M23 Naples:38.A.46c2 RomeBNC:202.9.B.30 U.Amst:2003 C 21 1) U.Pa:Ar466 Ef22 1552 Venice:209.D.144	TITLE PAGE: ARISTOTELIS STAGIRITAE, RHETORICORUM LIBRI III, QUOS M. ANTOINIUS MAIORAGIUS vertebat page 3: ARISTOTELIS STAGIRITAE, RHETORICORUM LIBRI I. M.ANTONIO MAIORAGIO INTERPRETE. Venice:per Ioannem Patavinum (Johannes Ruffincellus of Padua), 1552	in 8º Bks:One=3-83;Two=84-164;Three=165-22 only Latin	NUC 21,19; 0403895 Primo 6,6731
1562	Bamberg:L.gr.o.105 (3) BM:520.c.1-11 BN:R.1752-3 + R. 25526 for vol. 2 + R.1631 Bodleian:Antiq.e. 1562 2-12 Columbia:Spec.Col. B88Ar1 IB62, vol 1, c.1 Harv:*56-1791 + Ga. 112.120(reprint) Ill:Baldwin 2152 LC:PA3895.A4 1562 (reprint) Maz:53819,1-11 Naples:84.B.31-32 OxCC:W.q.7.1 OxPem:3.f.1-11 RomeAles:B.f.24 RomeCas:L.I.4 RomeBNC:68.10.G g- 18 + 6.30.G.27 + 6.42.F.6 U.Pa:PA3895 A4 1562a (reprint) + GrC. Ar466. Ef1. 1562 Venice:43.D.181-192	TITLE PAGE, first part of volume one which is divided into 3 parts: Primum Volume. ARISTOTELIS STAGIRITAE Organum. AVERROIS CORDUBENSIS IN EO COMMENTARIA Epitome, Quaesita nonnulla,ac Epistola una. TITLE PAGE,vol.2: Secondum Volume. ARISTOTELIS DE RHETORICA ET POETICA LIBRI, cum AVERROIS IN EOSDEM PARAPHRASIBUS Venice:apud Iunctas,1562	in 8º chaps:a=15;b=27;g=19 Bks:One=1r-25v;Two=26r-51r;Three=51v-68v lines designed A,B,C,D,E,F,G,H,I on inner and outer margins only Latin of Maioragius set in 2 cols. Reprint says: "Aristotelis Artis Rhetoricae . . . M. Antonio Maioragio interprete (Minerva: G.M.B.H.,Frankfurt am Main,Universänderter Nachdrunk,1962) BN says 11 vols in 13,but can be 12 vols. in 14;R. in vol. 2 Harv has vol.One(Part 3);vol.2,vol.8;Berlin Vt 462-1,1.2/4.6/10 TAB lost in WWII; Brno copy 2 KL.I.13 does not contain the R.;BudapestNB 3458 has only vol.4;BM 520.c.1-11-rhet c.3,but it is vol.2. RM R. is in 520.c.3, which is vol.2 of 520.c.1-11 R in vol.2 of RomeBNC copy; in another BNC set, 6.41.H.4, R also in vol.2 but library catalogues it as vol.5 Berlin Vt.462-1,1.2/4,6/10 TAB lost in WWII	Gesamt 6,5968 Ind Aur 2,228 108.456 Primo 6,5786 NUC 20,592; 0400815 Cranz 108.456
1563	Antwerp: B 727 Augsburg:LG48 Basel:B.c.I.18 BerlinH:Vt 1009 Berlin:Vt. 465a BM:8464.g.2 (microfiche) Brno:St.3-86. 538 +	TITLE PAGE: ARISTOTELIS STAGIRITAE TRIPARTITAE PHILOSOPHIAE OPERA OMNIA ABSOLUTISSIMA . . . cols.427-428,vol.1: ARISTOTELIS DE ARTE DICENDI LIBER PRIMUS, M. ANTONIO MAIORAGIO INTERPRETE. Basel: per Ioannem Heruagium	in 4º chaps:a=15;b=23;g=22 Bks:One=cols.430-473;Two=473-518;Three= 518-547 R. in vol. 1 of four vol. set but can all be bound together as in Tub & Leipsig left col. is Maioragius' commentary; right col. is Maioragius' tr. of R. many printed marginal comments	Primo 6,5788 Gesamt 6,5969 NUC 20,592; 0400816 Cranz 108.457

Early Printings

R III.b.4831 +
NRA.III.1759
BudapestNB: 614
Camb:U.Lib.P*.8.3;
  St.Johns 8.Cc.11
Columbia:Spec.Col.
  B88Ar51 JP2 F
Erl:2°VII,22
Göt:4°A.gr.IV.86
Gotha:2° 10/4
Halle: ASB 92 787
Ind:PA 3893.08 1563
Leid.706 A.8
Leipsig:49 A 283
Marburg:IV A 445
Maz:20301
Munich:2oA.gr.b.93
Naples:XXV.4.6(3
Nurn:Philos.
  61.2
Pommersf:L VI 20
RomeAles: C.g.36-37
RomeBNC:8.52.H.12-
  13 + 71.2.F.18
  + 14.7.G.14
UCBanc:fB406 1563
  Fontana
U.Pa:fGrC Ar466 Ef1
  1563
Vienna:71 C 3
Wolf:45.1 Quod.2o
WroclawU:552789
Yale:Gfa 84 taf 563
	(John Herwagen),1563	occasionally chapters divided into
		subparts by Roman numerals
		"B's" in middle of columns one-half
		way down the page
		Munster,Bonn,Braunsberg do not have
			Ind.Aur.2,229
			108.457

1571

BN:X718
Naples:XXXV.4.7
  + 38.A.45(2
RomeBNC:32.2.H.15
UCBanc:fPN173 A73
  R2 1571
Vat:R.G.Classici
  II,292
ViennaUB:II 148.851
Wolf:SCHULENBURG
  LA 16
Yale:Gfa 84 +My571
	TITLE PAGE: M.ANTONII MAIORAGII IN
	TRES ARISTOTELIS LIBROS de Arte
	Rhetorica QUOS IPSE LATINOS FECIT,
	EXPLANATIONES.
	
	folio 1r: M.ANT.MAIORAGII
	COMMENTARIUS IN PRIMUM ARISTOTELIS
	LIBRUM, De Arte Rhetorica.
	
	Venice:apud Franciscum de
	Franciscium Senensem(Franciscus
	de Franciscium Sensnsis),1571
		in 4°
		BKS:One=1-186;Two=187-341;Three=342-458
		lines numnbered 10,20,30,40,50
		Schwab 3000 cited a 1547 edition apud
		Frs.Franciscum, in 4°,but no copy was
		found
		Krakow Phil.gr.357 is in Italian
		
		[diagram: Latin text with lines numbered 10, 20, 30, 40, 50, and Latin commentary indicated by arrows]
			Primo 6,6735
			
			NUC 21,19;
			0403899

1572

BM: 72.g.13
BN: R.261 + X.1059
BodLeian:H.1.14.Art
Camb:U.Lib P*.9.5.
  (C)
Columbia:B88 Ar51
  VZM
Ill:xq 881 A 8rh.
  Yma
Leid:707.A.7
Munich:A.gr.b.2o.
  173
Naples:118.I.12
Oregon:MF884 AR46r
  LM
RomeAng:XX.15.17
RomeCas:Q.IV.46
RomeBNC:9.18.E.27
U.Chic:PA3895.R3C75
  .R3C75 1572
U.Pa:fGrC Ar466
  Ef22 1572
	TITLE PAGE: M.ANTONII MAIORAGII IN
	TRES ARISTOTELIS LIBROS,De Arte
	Rhetorica,QUOS IPSE LATINOS FECIT
	Explanationes.
	
	page 1: M.ANT.MAIORAGII COMMEN-
	TARIUS IN PRIMUM ARISTOTELIS
	LIBRUM. De Arte Rhetorica.
	
	Venice:Franciscus Franciscis
	Senensis,1572.
		in 4°
		Bks:One=1r-186v;Two=187r-341v;Bk Three=
		  342r-458v
		lines numbered 10,20,30,40,50
		Rome BNC has both 1571 and 1572 copies
		exactly alike except for date
		UCBanc does not have,has Sigonio
		edition instead
		Text & commentary are interspersed
			Gesamt 6,6382
			
			NUC 21,19;
			0403901
			
			Hoffman 296,
			337
			
			Schwab 2985
			
			Primo 6,6736

144

Vat:Stamp.Barb.J.
IV.76 + R.I.II.
558
Venice:78.D.47

Year	Library holdings	Title page	Notes	References
1575	BN:X.16684 Bodleian:Byw.K.3.13 Munich:A.gr.b.646 Naples:1107.A.18 Olomouc: 27751 RomeAles:O.e.47 RomeAng:RR.21.76 RomeBNC:6.4.B.51 RomeCas:p.IX.11 U.Chic:PA3895.R3C75 1575 Vat:Racc.I.V.41	TITLE PAGE: RHET[ORICAE] ARISTO-TELIS AD THEODECT[EN] LIBRI III. Quos M.Ant[onius] Maioragius vertebat. EIUSDEM LIBER ED ALEXAN-DRUM CUM Expositione Ioannis Marinelli. page 8:ARISTOTELIS STAGIRITAE RHETORICORUM LIBER I M.ANTONIO MAIORAGIO Interprete. Venice:ex.officina Victoriae,apud Ian.Valgrisium(Johannes Valgrisius),1575	in 8° but small Bks:One=8-117;Two-118-242;Three=243-336 pagination at the beginning is confusing bound with R. ad Alex tr. by Francesco Philelpho Latin commentary by Ioan Marinelli in italics;Latin tr. in standard print Berlin Vu 7900 lost in WWII no chapters but frequent subheads WroclawU copy lost in WWII	Gesamt 6,6382 Primo 6,6737 Hoffman 337 Schwab 3011 Ind Aur 2,242 108.601 Cranz 108.601
1575	BM:C.65 bb 14 Bodleian:Byw.K.3.13 Olomouc:600.543 + 600.560 RomeBNC:6.4.B.51 Vienna:*38.X108	TITLE PAGE: RHET[ORICAE] ARISTOTELIS AD THEODECT[EN] LIBRI III. Quos M.Ant(onius) Maioragius vertebat . . . cum expositione Ioannis Marinelli page 8: ARISTOTELIS STAGIRITAE RHETORICORUM LIBER I. M. ANTONIO MAIORAGIO Interprete. Venice:apud I.A. (Johannes Antonio)Bertanus,1575	in 8° Bks:One=3-117;Two=118-242;Three=243-336 bound with R. ad Alex Marinelli's commentary interspersed in Maioragius' Latin translation RomeBNC gives Venice:Valgrisius,1575 Wroclaw copy lost in WWII	Gesamt 6,6381 Ind Aur 2,242 108.600 Cranz 108.600
1584-1585	BM:521.a.39 BudapestNB:Ant.8084 Flor:B.17.8.33 Harv:Ga112.113.10* (7 vols.) + Ga.112.113.11* for vol.8 MAmb:S.N.U.I 38=44 Munich:A.gr.b.541, vol.2 Naples:S.G.XVII.101 + F.Aosta bis XXV. A.44-51 + XXIII.c.105 OxPem:3.a Sibiu:u I 271 RomeBV:VI.7.A.34 U.Pa:GrC.Ar466.Ef1. 1585,vol.2 Vat:Chigi VI 591 (1-8) + R.Gen. Class.VI.10 Yale:Gfa 84 mf565 e 2	TITLE PAGE,vol.1: ARISTOTELIS STAGIRITAE PERIPATETICORUM PRINCIPIS operum omnium PARS PRIMA,QUAM LOGICAM, . . . TITLE PAGE,vol.2: ARISTOTELIS STAGIRITAE RHETORICORUM Ad Theodect(en) Libri III. Quos Carolus Sigonius, & M.Anton Maioragius vertebat page 3,vol.2: ARISTOTELIS PERIPATETICORUM Principis Artis Rhetoricorae LIBER PRIMUS Carolo Sigonio & M. Anton(ius) Maioragio interpretibus. Venice:Nicolaus Moretius,1584-1585. Bruniolus' name (Joachimus Bruniolus) appears on the title page to vol.one but Moretius' name shows on the colophon. Sometimes, as in vol.four,Bruniolus appears on the title page and in some volumes, and Moretius' name does not appear on the colophon.	in 16° Bks:One=5-252;Two=253-474;Three=475-619 The dated 1584 and 1585 also appear on the colophon. The two Latin tr. by Sigonio & Maioragius are offered side by side followed by a commentary by Ioan Marinelli. Gesamt gives Bruniolus as publishing the same 6 vols in 1584-1585 U.Pa. has 8 vol. set; R. in vol. 2;Vienna 71.L.26 is only vol.1; BM 1481.dd.25 lacks vol.2; LC has only vol.6. UCBerk has only vol.1	Gesamt 6,5980 + 6,5981 Primo 6,5797 Schwab 3012 gives a 1585 Brixiae edition,but none has been located NUC 20,593; 0400853 Ind Aur 2,250 108.669 Cranz 108.669

1591 see main entry

1595 see Muret for use of Maioragius' third book

RHET.
ARISTOTELIS
AD THEODECT.
LIBRI III.

Quos M. Ant. Maioragius vertebat.

EIVSDEM

LIBER AD ALEXANDRVM

CVM

Expositione Ioannis Marinelli.

Index rerum omnium copiosissimus.

CVM PRIVILEGIIS.
VENETIIS, MDLXXV.
Apud Ioan. Antonium Bertanum.

PLATE SIXTY-FOUR

title page of the 1575 Maioragius Venice edition

courtesy of the Státní Védecká Knishovna, Olomouc

RHET.
ARISTOTELIS
AD THEODECT.
LIBRI III.

Quos M. Ant. Maioragius vertebat.

EIVSDEM

LIBER AD ALEXANDRVM

CVM

Expositione Ioannis Marinelli.

Index rerum copiosissimus.

CVM PRIVILEGIIS.
VENETIIS, MDLXXV.
Ex Officina Victoriæ. Apud Ioan. Valgrisium.

PLATE SIXTY-FIVE
title page of the 1575 Maioragius Venice edition
courtesy of the Bayerische Staatsbibliothek, Munich

Early Printings   147

LATIN TRANSLATIONS BY SIGONIO

1565	Ven:116.D.191	TITLE PAGE: ARISTOTELIS DE ARTE RHETORICA LIBRI TRES. CAROLO INTERPRETE. page 1: ARISTOTELIS ARTIS RHETORICAE, Carolo Sigonio Interprete, LIBER PRIMUS. Venice:Ex Officina Stellae Iordani Ziletti,1565	in 8° Bks:One=1-97;Two=97-196;Three=197-262 no chaps, but major subheadings and someone has penned in the Trapezuntius chapters in the Florence copy, i.e., a=15;b=25;g=19	
1565	BN:R.1710 Bodleian:4°K.27 Art + Byw.K.3.15 Camb:U.Lib T.14.19 Krakow:Greka 367 Munich:4°Jur.is.52 OxAS:i.9.15 RomeBNC:204.10.D.23 + 68.9.D.15.1 + 71.3.D.52 RomeBV:S.Borr Q.V. 39(3) RomeCas:Vol.360 UNC:Pa3895.R3 1565 U.Pa:GrC Ar466 Ef22 1565 Vat:Barb.J.I.63 + R.G.Class.V.184 Venice:214.C.89 + A.es.21.T.135	TITLE PAGE: ARISTOTELIS DE ARTE RHETORICA LIBRI TRES. CAROLO SIGONIO INTERPRETE page 9: ARISTOTELIS ARTIS RHETORICAE, LIBRE TRES, Carolo Sigonio Interprete,LIBER PRIMUS. Bononiae(Bologna):ex officina Alexandri Bennatti (Alexander Benacius),1565	in 4° Bks:One=9-78;Two=79-149;Three=150-195 Latin translation only Schwab also indicated a 1557 edition, but no copy was found	NUC 21,19; 0403897 Gesamt 6, 6379 Hoffman I,337 Adams 1949 Primo 6,6733 Ind Aur 2,231 108.488 Cranz 108.488 Schwab 3009
1566	BM:11824.aa.32.(2.) BN:X16681 Camb:U.Lib.W.14.8 Columbia:Gonzalez-Lodge 1566 Ar463 Flor:3.C.6.123 Ill:991 A8rh.Ls JohnsH:PB1895.R3 55 Lyon:347156 MilanB:&&.VI.97 Munich:8°L.eleg.g. 132/1 Naples:38.B.63 OxPem:4a + 4b Princeton:EXTRAN 2599.383.566 RomeAng:TT.21.75 RomeBNC:6.8.F.33 Torun:ob.6.II.522 U.Pa:GrC Ar466 Ef22 1566 Vat:Barb.J.I.63 Vienna:46 M 8 Wolf:473 Quod (2) WroclawU:316770	TITLE PAGE: ARISTOTELIS DE ARTE RHETORICA LIBRI TRES.CAROLO SIGONIO INTERPRETE. page 1: ARTISTOTELIS ARTIS RHETORICAE, Carolo Sigonio Interprete,LIBER PRIMUS. Venice:ex officina Stellae Iordani Zilleti (Jordanus Ziletus,1566	in 8° Bks:One=1-97;Two=97-196;Three=187-262 Latin translation only Schwab also gives a 1567 edition, but no copy found at U.Pa.bound with other rhetorics; at BN,Vienna, and Cambridge,bound by itself; Berlin Vu 7896 lost in WWII	Adams 1950 Gesamt 6,6380 Primo 6,6734 Hoffman 337 Ind Aur 2,233 108.516 Cranz 108.516 NUC 21,19; 0403898
1572	Harv:Ga112.120* Munich:8°A.gr.b.537 Prague:5.L.133 RomeAng.XX. 8.46 Tub:Cd 2376 UCBanc:tPN173 A73 R1 1572 Ven:220.C.214	TITLE PAGE,vol.1: ARISTOTELIS STAGIRITAE PERIPATETICORUM PRINCIPIS OPERA OMNIA in partes septem divisa TITLE PAGE,vol.2: ARISTOTELIS STAGIRITAE PERIPATETICORUM PRINCIPIS RHETORICORUM	in 16° Bks:One=3-66;Two=67-133;Three=134-176 R. in vol.2 of 7 vols. + index but pagination for each work starts with page one Sigonio's chapter summaries in large print with his Latin translation below in Munich,R.in vol.2 of seven vol. set Brno (Mn.VIII.8.18) does	Gesamt 6,5972 Primo 6,5790 Schwab 3010 Ind Aur 2,239 108.549

Year	Location/Shelfmark	Title/Imprint	Notes	References
	ViennaUB:I.148.538	page 3: ARISTOTELIS STAGIRITAE PERIPATETICORUM Principis Artis Rhetoricae LIBER PRIMUS,Carolo Sigonio interprete Venice:ad signum Seminantis,1572	not contain vol.2 Tub has complete set; in Venice, R in vol.2 of 8 vol.set	NUC 20,592, 0400820 Cranz 108.549
1574	BM:519.c.4 + G.7907 -18 BN:R.9421 + Res.R. 1704 + R.9418-9 Bodleian:Savile S. 1.(2) BudapestRaday: O.1585/3 Cornell:RARE PA3895 A4 1575 v.2 Flor:Rinasc.A.233 + 5.11.303 Harv:*OGC.Ar46.E573 Ind:PA3890.A2 1574 (11 vols in 17 covers) + PA3893.R3 Maz:27457-277470 1574(only vol.two) MilanB:XVIII 6.336/ 1-9,v.III Naples:XXII.b.7 OxCC:O.f.4.1 OxPem:4.d PhilLC:Six Aris. 50629.D RomeBNC:6.42.F.3-15 RomeBV:S.Borr.H.II. 7 U.Pa:GrC Ar466 Ef1. 1575 v.2 Wis:765683-97	TITLE PAGE,vol.1 dated 1574: ARISTOTELIS STAGIRITAE ORGANUM. TITLE PAGE,vol.2: ARISTOTELIS DE RHETORICA ET POETICA LIBRI Cum AVERROIS [sic] IN EOSDEM [sic] PARAPHRASIBUS page 6,vol.2: ARISTOTELIS ARTIS RHETORICAE,Carolo Sigonio Interprete,LIBER PRIMUS. Venice:apud Iuntas,1574(vol.2)	in 8° chaps;a=15;b=27;g=19 Bks:One=6r-25v;Two=25r-46v;Three=47r-64v lines numbers A,B,C,D,E,F,G,H,I,K,L,M eleven vols;vol 1 has part one,part two and part three,all dated 1584;the R in vol.2 is therefore the 4th tome in BN & BM, but 2nd tome in Vienna BM missing vol.5; vols 6-11 under 520. c.7-11;NUC entries for LC,Case-Western Reserve,Johns Hopkins in error. Library College of Phil has only vol.2; Ca. State Library does not have RomeBV has all 11 vols,with vols. 7 & 9 dated 1573, index 1575 Florence 20.6.216 does not have Rhetoric U.Wash & Denver U do not have.	Gesamt 6,5973 Ind Aur 2,241 108.599 Primo 6,5791 NUC 21,19; 0403902 + 29,592; + 0400821 + 0400831 + 0400832 + 0400833 + 0400845 Cranz 108.599
1577	Krakow:Cim.262 Uppsala:Script. Graeci [Aristoteles] 230 Vat:R.I.V.1040 int.2 WroclawA:XVI.O.161 + XVI.O.236 Wroclaw:316778	TITLE PAGE: ARISTOTELIS ARTIS RHETORICAE,Carolo Sigonio Interprete. page 1: ARISTOTELIS ARTIS RHETORICAE,Carolo Sigonio Interprete,LIBER PRIMUS. Cracoviae:ex officina Stanislai Scharffenbergij,1577	in 8° Bks:One=1-82;Two=82-144,146-168; Three=176(should be 169)-231 Schwab also gives a 1578 edition, but no example was found Vatican copy bound with other works subheads inserted Leningrad does not have;Kiev does not answer inquiries no chapters,but a long series of subheads within the books	Cranz 108.618 Ind Aur 2,244 108.618
1577	Gotha:Phil.690/3 Rara	TITLE PAGE: ARISTOTELIS DE ARTE RHETORICA LIBRI TRES. CAROLO SIGONIO INTERPRETE. page 1: ARISTOTELIS ARTIS RHETORICAE, Carlo Sigonio Interprete,LIBER PRIMUS. Rostochii (Rostock):ex officina Jac.Lucius,Transylvanis,1577	in 8° chaps:a=32;b=20;g=14 Bks:One=1-104;Two=105-210;Three=211-282 286 pp. I.A.lists WroclawU, but it said it had no copy	Ind Aur 2,245 108.626 Schwab 3007 Gesamt 6,6383 Cranz 108.626
1584	Brescia CINQ.II.7 RomeCas:p.XXIV.29.	TITLE PAGE: ARISTOTELIS DE ARTE RHETORICA LIBRI TRES. CAROLO SIGONIO interprete. page one: ARISTOTELIS ARTIS RHETORICAE,Carolo Sigonio Interprete,Liber Primus.	in 16° chaps:a=15;b=27;g=19 Bks:One=1-84;Two=85-172;Three=173-228	Hoffman 337 Schwab 3012

Early Printings

Brixae(Brescia,Italy):ex officina.
Petri Marie Marchetti (Petrus
Maria Marchettus),1584

1584 see main entry

LATIN TRANSLATIONS BY MURET

1577	Princeton:Ex 2599. 383.577 RomeAng: II.1.19 RomeBNC:21.2.D.10 Vat:R.I.IV.1046	TITLE PAGE: ARISTOTELIS DE ARTE DICENDI LIBER SECUNDUS M.ANTONIO MURETO INTERPRETE Rome:apud heredes Antonij Bladij (Antonius Bladus),Impressores Camerales,1577	in 4° only Book Two, pp.7-48 RomeBNC copy had belonged to the Jesuits and is heavily annotated in Greek and Latin	Primo 6,6740 NUC 21,19; 0403903
1585	Bodleian:Byw.K.3.17 Camb:Emmanuel 323. 6.32 Gennadius:GC.3219 Got:8°A gr IV,700 Htgtn:374795 Mich:888.A85 tM Munich:A.gr.b.648-649 (2 copies) Oberlin:o94.2 1585 Ar45 RomeAles:O.b.125 RomeAng:TT.21.17 RomeBNC:6.5.B.24 + 6.5.A.5 RomeBV:S.Borr.Q.I. 212 U.Pa:GrC Ar466 Ef22 1585 Vat:Barb.J.I.62 + R.I.V866 Venice:116.D.185 + 67.D.190	TITLE PAGE: ARISTOTELIS RHETORI-CORUM LIBRI. DUO. M.Antonio Mureto Interprete. page 1: ARISTOTELIS ARTIS RHETORICAE LIBER PRIMUS. M. ANTONIO MURETO Interprete. Rome:apud Bartholomaeum Grassum(Bartholomaeus Grassius), 1585	in 8° but small Bks:One=1=88;Two=89-180;no book Three as if it were spurious Because of damage,RomeBV copy ends with p. 176;Michigan copy dated 1595 in NUC is in error;Berlin Vu 7920 lost in WWII	Schwab 3013 Hoffman 337 Ind Aur 2,251 108.679 Primo 6,6739 Gesamt 6,6385 Adams 1952 NUC 21,19; 0403904 + 21,20; 0403907 Cranz 108.679
1594	Asch:K=761 Bamberg:L.gr.o.169 Krakow:Phil.gr.236	TITLE PAGE: ARISTOTELIS RHE-TORICORUM LIBRI TRES:PRIORES DUO M.ANTONIO MURETO,TERTIUS M.ANTONIO MAIORAGIO, interpretibus. page 7: ARISTOTELIS ARTIS RHETORICAE LIBER PRIMUS,M. ANTONIO MURETO Interprete Coloniae Agrippinae (Cologne); In Officina Birckmannica, sumptibus Arnoldi Mylij,1594	in 8° chaps:a=25;b=26;g=22 Bks:One=7-87;Two=88-172;Three=173-234 234 pp. Berlin Vu 7924 lost in WWII;1st two books by Mureto;third by Maioragius	Gesamt 6,6386 Schwab 3013 Ind Aur 2,256 108.729 Cranz 108.729

LATIN TRANSLATIONS BY RICCOBONO

| 1577 | Venice:215.c.81
RegEm:B G 116/3 | TITLE PAGE: ARISTOTELIS ARTIS RHETORICAE, ANTONIO RICCOBONO INTERPRETE. Liber primus.

page 1: ARISTOTELIS ARTIS RHETORICAE, ANTONIO RICCOBONO INTERPRETE,Liber Primus.

Patavii(Padua):Laurentius Pasquatus excudebat,1577 | copy is a fragment consisting of ff.1r-29v
some guides to readers in margins
centered subheads in caps | |

ARISTOTELIS
RHETORICORVM
LIBRI. DVO

*M. Antonio Mureto
Interprete.*

ROMAE,
Apud Bartholomaeum Graſſum.
M. D. LXXXV.

PLATE SIXTY-SIX

title page of the 1575 Muret Rome edition

courtesy of the Library of the University of Michigan

Early Printings

| 1579 | BN:X.16685
Bodleian:8⁰.T.20.
  Art + Byw.K.3.10
BudapestNB:Ant.13.
  469
Camb:U.Lib W.5.60
Ind:PA3893.R3 1579
Maz:20403
MilanB:&&.VI.99 +
  EE.VI.97
Munich:A.gr.b.647.
RomeAles:M.f.60
RomeBNC:6.5.B.16
RomeCas:Z.XXIII.7
St.Gen:X.8o 534
  Inv.1069
Sibiu:U I 2254
UPa:GrC Ar466
  Ef22 1579
Vat:Racc.Gen.
  Classici V.459
Venice:19.T.239 | TITLE PAGE: ARISTOTELIS ARS RHETORICA AB ANTONIO RICCOBONO RHODIGINO I.C.HUMANITATEM in Patavino Gymnasio profitente latine conversa.

page 1: ARISTOTELIS ARTIS RHETORICAE, ANTONIO RICCOBONO Interprete,Liber Primus.

Venice:Paulus Meiettus,1579 | in 16⁰ but large
Bks:One=1-71;Two=73-148;Three=149-198
Begins with Latin text matching the Latin of the 1588 Riccobono edition followed by p.201-345 entitled "Antonio Riccobono Rhodigini in Artem Rhetoricam Aristotelis Liber," but this commentary does not appear to match the 1588 commentary
Poetics is same volume
Berlin VU.7910 lost in WWII
In MilanB, R is vol.1 of 4 vol. set
The old call number in Munich A.gr.b. 647 was A.Gr.Vet.8⁰.Arist.6. | Hoffman 296 + 337

Gesamt 6,6384

Primo 6,5852 + 6,6738

Adams 1951

Ind Aur 2,246 108.640

Schwab 2952 + 3006

Cranz 108.640 |

1588 see main entry

1590 see main entry

1593 see main entry

| 1594 | Vienna: *38 X 72 | Aristotelis Artis rhetoricae libri tres. Ab Antonio Riccobono Latine conversi

Vice[n]tiae:Paulus Meiettus, 1594 | in 8⁰
chaps:a=15;b=26;g=19
Bks:One=ff.1-46;Two=47-94;Three=95-128 | Gesamt 6,6387

Ind Aur 2,257 108.738

Cranz 108.738 |

1597 see main entry

1599 see main entry

LATIN TRANSLATIONS BY BARBARO

| 1544 | Augsburg:4⁰LG48
BM:520.g.11 +
  + C.77.d.18
Bodleian:4⁰D.4.Art
BostonPub:Acc.
  80-192
Columbia:B88 Ar51
  VP44
Flor:A.6.12
Harv:*OGC Ar46W
  E544
Ill:881 ABrb.Lba
  1544
Krakow:Graeca 358
Maz:20304
MilanB:B.IV.3614/2
Munich:4⁰A.gr.b.241
Princeton:EXTRAN
  2599.383.544
RomeAles:O.g.28
RomeAng:TT.22.40 | TITLE PAGE: RHETORICORUM ARISTOTELIS LIBRI TRES,INTERPRETE HERMOLAO BARBARO PP.V.COMMENTARIA IN EOSDEM DANIELIS BARBARI.

page 2: ARISTOTELIS LIBRORUM Rhetoricorum primus incipit. Interpret Herm.Barb.Proemium. Cap.primum. De similtudine Rhetoricae, & dialecticae.

Venice:Cominus de Tridine,1544 | in 8⁰
chaps:a=41;b=46;g=33
Bks:One=2v-86r;Two=86v-144r;Three=144v-202v
begins with proemium,followed by intermingling of Barbaro "condensation" in large letters with Danielis Barbaro's commentary on the R. in small print
both the 1544 Venice & the 1544 Lyon are bound together at the Bodleian
NUC in error for St. Mary Seminary;Berlin Vu 7880 lost in WWII | NUC 21,19; 0403888

Schwab 3004

Ind Aur 2,45 108.094

Gesamt 6,6373

Primo 6,6727

Hoffman 336-7

Cranz 108.094 |

RomeBNC:6.8.E.5 +
6.40.I.13 +
204.20.B.28
RomeCas:BB.X.80
U.Chic:PA3893.R3
1544
U.Pa:GrC Ar466 Ef22
1544
Vat:R.I.IV IIII
Venice:134.D.118
Vienna:+38.X.47

1544	Besancon:202323 BN:R.9484 + X.16678 Bodleian:4º.D.4 Art Folger:PA3903 A1,B3 1544,CAGE Grenoble:F.3701 Lyon:347180 + 349380 MAmb:M.3734 MilanB:&&.III. 133 Maz:20304 Mich:PA3893 R4 B23 1544 Munich:A.gr.b.641 + A.Gr.B.642 Naples:38.B.31 RomeAles:M.d.49.f. 2o RomeBNC:1.20.A.3 + 6.5.C.18 + 71.2.C.23 RomeCas:p.xx.17 U.Pa:GrC Ar466 Ef22 1544b Vat:Ferraroli V. 1289 Venice:16.C.183 Vienna:*38.X.47	TITLE PAGE: DANIELIS BARBARI IN TRES LIBROS RHETORICORUM ARISTOTELIS COMMENTARIA page 18: ARISTOTELIS RHETORICORUM LIBER PRIMUS. Lyon:Seb(astien) Gryhius,1544	in 8º chaps:a=41;b=40;g=33 Bks:One=18-236;Two=236-367;Three=367-524 contains Herman Barbaro's Latin tr. interspersed with Daniel Barbaro's commentary BM and Gdansk do not have;Frankfurt does not have,destoyed in WWII	NUC 21,19; 0403887 Schwab 3005 Baudrier VIII 185 Primo 6,6726 Gesamt 11, 1619 Ind.Aur.3,132 112.847
1545	Basel:B.c.VI 49 Berlin:Bibl.Diez 2109 BudapestEK:Vet 15/33 Gennadius:G.C.3214 Ill:881 A8rh.Lbar 1545 Htgtn:382062 Munich:A.gr.b.643 + A.gr.b.644 Neuberg:8º BW 17 OxPem:5.c.12 Olomouc: 601842 Prague: 5.K.241 RomeAng:TT.21.74 Tub:Cd 2450.8º UCBanc:PN173 A73 R2 1545 Vat:R.G.Classici V. 402(1-2) Venice:114.D.168 Vienna:527.770-A ViennaWS:A45.236 Wolf:Lg 297 WroclawU:450500	TITLE PAGE: ARISTOTELIS Rhetoricorum LIBRI TRES, HERMOLAO BARBARO Patricio Veneto interprete. DANIELIS BARBARI in eosdem libros Commentarij. p.8: ARISTOTELIS RhetoricorUM LIber primus. Basel: ex off.Bartholmaeus V[W]estermerus (Barthomew Westheimer),1545. Publisher,dates on colophon.	in 8º chaps:a=41;b=40;g=32 Bks:One=8-332;Two=333-539;Three=540-679 (679 is printer's error for 769) Barbaro's tr. followed by Danielis Barbaro's commentary interspersed among the books Got lost in WWII Augsburg does not have.	Primo 6,6729 Gesamt 6,6374 Schwab 3005 Ind Aur 2,45 108.098 NUC 21,19; 0403890 Cranz 108.098 Hoffman 337

Early Printings

1548	Avignon:8°10.515 Basel:Frey Gryn.O. V.23 Nr1 Ill:881 A8rh.Lba Newberry:CASE Y 642.S8935	TITLE PAGE: RHETORICORUM ARIS- TOTELIS LIBRI TRES,INTERPRETE HERMOLAO BARBARO P.V. p.3: ARISTOTELIS LIBRORUM RHE- toricorum primus incipit, In- terprete Herm.Barb.PROOEMIUM. Lyon:apud Theobaldum Paganum,1548	in 8° chaps:a=41;b=40;g=33 Bks:One=3-150;Two=151-291;Three=292-391	Ind Aur 2,200 108.142 Baudrier IV, 241 NUC 21,19; 0403892 Cranz 108.142
1549	see main entry			
1551	see main entry			
1558	Avignon:Calv.10 516 RomeBNC:6.8.B.11	TITLE PAGE: RHETORICORUM ARISTOTELIS LIBRI TRES,INTERPRETE HERMOLAO BARBARO P.V. page 3: ARISTOTELIS LIBRORUM RHEtoricorum primus incipit, Interprete Herm[olao] Bar[baro] P.V. . . . Lyon:apud Theobaldum Paganum,1558	in 8° chaps:a=41;b=46;g=33 Bks:One=3-138;Two=139-267;Three=268-359	Cranz 108.349 Ind Aur 2,219 108.349 5 Primo 6,6732 Baudrier IV, 277
1559	Antwerp:B2114 Berlin:Vu 2884.3 (graece) BM:671.d.3(2.) BN:X.1939(11) + X.3053(2) Bodleian:Byw.K. 3.14 Göt:8°A.gr.IV,653 Ill:Baldwin 2154 Krakow:Phil.2194 Princeton:Ex2599. 383.082 St.Gen:Res.X.4°429. Inv.417.Res. U.Chic:PA3893.R3 1559	TITLE PAGE: ARISTOTELIS DE ARTE DICENDI LIBRI III. HERMOLAO BARBARO INTERPRETE. page 1: ARISTOTELIS RHETORICORUM LIBER PRIMUS, Hermolao Barbaro interprete. Paris:apud Guil.Morelium (Guillaume Morel),1559	in 8° chaps:a=41;b=46;g=33 Bks:One=1-55;Two=57-108;Three=109-145 Ornate caps to begin the books, similar to ones found in manuscripts, + inserted guides to chapters Berlin Vu 2884.3(graece) does not have the volumes to examine to see if the Latin volume was once a part of their collection.	NUC 21,19 0403896 Gesamt 6,6378 Ind Aur 2,222 108.392 Cranz 108.392

```
┌─────────────────────────────────────────┐
│ CONTRARIA ESSE SERVANDA DISSUAdentibus  │◄─┐
│                                         │  │
│              Cap XVII                   │  │
│                                         │  │
│ XXXXXXXXXXXXXXXXXXXXXXXXXXXXXXXXXXXXX   │  │
│ XXXXXXXXXXXXXXXXXXXXXXXXXXXXXXXXXXXXX   │  │
│ XXXXXXXXXXXXXXXXXXXXXXXXXXXXXXXXXXXXX   │  │ chapter
│ XXXXXXXXXXXXXXXXXXXXXXXXXXXXXXXXXXXXX   │  │ headings
│                                         │  │
│ DESCRIPTIO BONI, ET ENUMERATIO BONO-    │◄─┘
│ rum, ceterorum quae efficientia sunt    │
│ occasiones ve bonorum.                  │
│                                         │
│              Cap XVIII                  │
│                                         │
│ XXXXXXXXXXXXXXXXXXXXXXXXXXXXXXXXXXXXX   │
│ XXXXXXXXXXXXXXXXXXXXXXXXXXXXXXXXXXXXX   │
│ XXXXXXXXXXXXXXXXXXXXXXXXXXXXXXXXXXXXX   │
│ XXXXXXXXXXXXXXXXXXXXXXXXXXXXXXXXXXXXX   │
└─────────────────────────────────────────┘
```

Schwab 3007 listed a 1577 Barbaro edition published in 4° in Rostock. It seems
possible that Schwab confused the 1577 Sigonio edition with a 1577 Barbaro
edition.

LIST OF LIBRARIES INDEXED IN TABLE THREE

Aarau	Aarganische Kantonabibliothek Obervorstadt,5001 Aarau,Switzerland
Alleg	Pelletier Library,Allegeny College,Meadeville,Pa.16335,USA
Antwerp	Stad Antwerpen Museum Plantin-Moretus en Pretenkabinet,Vrijdagmarkt 22-23,200 Antwerpen,Belgium
Arizona	University Library,U.of Arizona,Tucson,Ariz.85721,USA
Asch	Hofbibliothek,Schloss Johannisburg,8750,Aschaffenburg,W.Germany
Augsburg	Staats-u.Staatbibliothek,Schaezlerstrasse 25 Postfach 11 19 09,D-8900,Augsburg,W.Germany
Avignon	Bibliothèque Municipale,2 bis rue Laboureur,8400 Avignon,France
Bamberg	Staatsbibliothek Bamberg,Neue Residenz,Domplatz 8, D-8600 Bamberg,W.Germany
Basel	Universitätsbibliothek Handschriften-Abteilung, Schönbeinstrasse 18/20,CH-4056 Basel,Switzerland
Berlin	Deutsche Staatsbibliothek,Unter den Linden 8 Postfach 1312,DDR-1086,Berlin,E.Germany
BerlinH	Humboldt Universitätsbibliothek,Clara-Zetkin Strasse 27,DDR-1080,Berlin,E.Germany
BerlinSPK	Staatsbibliothek Potsdamstrasse 33,D-Berlin 30,W.Germany
Besançon	Bibliothèque Municipale,1 rue de la Bibliothèque,Besançon,France
BM	British Library,Dept.of Printed Books,Great Russell Street,London WC13 3DG,England
BN	Bibliothèque Nationale,58 rue Richelieu 75084,Paris,France
Bodleian	Bodleian Library,Dept.of Printed Books,Oxford,OX1 3BG,England
Bologna	Biblioteca Universitairia,via Zamboni 35,40100,Bologna,Italy
Bonn	Universitätsbibiothek,Adenaueralle 39-41 Postfach 2460 D-5300 Bonn 1,W.Germany
Bordeaux	Bibliothèque Municipale,3 rue Mably,33075,Bordeaux,France
BostPub	Boston Public Library,666 Boylston Court Box 286,Boston,Mass.02117,USA
Bourges	Bibliothèque Municipale,8 Place des Quatre-Piliers, B.P.69,28002 Bourges,France
Brescia	Biblioteca Queriniana,via Mazzini 1,Brescia,Italy
Brno	Státní Vědecká Knihovna,Leninova 5-7,601 87,Brno,Czechoslovakia
Brown	John Carter Brown Library,Brown U.,Providence,R.I.02912,USA
Budapest AkB	Magyar Tudományos Akadémia Könyvtáva,Acadèmia u.2,1361 Budapest,Hungary
Budapest EK	Eotvos Lorad Tudományegyetem Egyetemi Könyvtar Karoly Mihaly u.10,10553 Budapest,Hungary
BudapestNB	Országos Széchényi Könyvtár,Múzeum-Körút 146.1827 Budapest,Hungary
Budapest Raday	Református Egyházkerület Ráday Gyüjtéménye Ráday utca 28,1092 Budapest,Hungary
Caen	Bibliothèques de la Ville de Caen,Place Louis Guillouard,14027 Caen,France
Camb. Christs	Christs College Library,Cambridge CB2 3BU England
Camb.Clare	Clare College,Forbes Library,Cambridge CG2 1TL,England
Camb.Cor-pus Christi	Corpus Christi College Library,Cambridge CB2 1RH,England
Camb. Emmanuel	Emmanuel College Library,Cambridge CB2 3AP,England
Camb.Gon-ville-Caius	Gonville & Caius College Library,Library CB2 1TA England
Camb.Jesus	Jesus College Old Library,Cambridge CB2,England
Camb.Kings	King's College Library,Cambridge CB2 1ST,England
Camb. Pembroke	Pembroke College Library,Cambridge CB2 1RF,England.
Camb. Peter-house	Peterhouse Ward Library,Cambridge CB2 1RF,England.
Camb.St. Catha-rine's	St.Catharine's College Library,Cambridge CB2 1RL,England
Camb.St. John's	St.John's College Library,Cambridge CB2 1TP England
Camb. Selwyn	Selwyn College Library,Grange Road,Cambridge CB3 9DQ,England
Camb. Trinity	Trinity College Library,Cambridge CB2 1TQ England

Early Printings

List of Libraries (continued)

```
Camb......Cambridge U.Library,West Road,Cambridge
  U.Li-    CCB3 9DR,England
  brary
Cath......Clementine Library,Catholic University,Washington,D.C.20064,USA
Coburg....Landesbibliothek Coburg,Schloss Ehrenburg,D8630 Coburg,W.Germany
Col.......Butler Library,Columbia U.,NY,NY 10027,USA
Cornell...Cornell U.Library,Cornell University,Ithaca,NY 14853,USA
Dresden...Sächsische Landesbibliothek,Marienallee 12
          Postschliessfach 467/468 DDR-8060 Dresden,E.Germany
Edinburg..National Library of Scotland,George IV Bridge
          Edinburg EH 11EW,Scotland
Erl.......Universitätsbibliothek Erlangen,Universität-
          strasse 4,8520 Erlangen,W.Germany
Erl-Nürn..Universitätsbibliothek Erlangen-Nürnberg
          Egidienplatz 23,8500 Nürnberg,W.Germany
Flor......Biblioteca Nazionale Centrale,Piazza dei
          Cavalleggeri IA,50100 Firenze,Italy
Folg......Folger Shakespeare Library,Washington,D.C.20003,USA
Gdansk....Polska Akademia Nauk,Biblioteka Gdańska ul.
          Walowa 16,Gdańsk,Poland
Geneva....Bibliothèque Publique et Universitaire
          Promenade des Bastions,CH 1211 Geneva 4,Switzerland
Gennadius.Gennadius Library,American School of Classical
          Studies,Athens 140,Greece
Gent......Rykuniversiteit Centrale Bibliotheek
          Rozier 9,9000 Gent,Belgium
Görlitz...Oberlausitzische Bibliothek der Wissenschaften
          Bei den Städtischen Kunstsammlungen Görlitz
          Neisstrasse 30,DDR 8900 Gorlitz,E.Germany
Göt.......Niedersächsische Staats-und Universitäts-bibliothek Göttingen,34
          Göttingen,Prinzenstrasse 1,W.Germany
Gotha.....Forschungsbibliothek Gotha,Schloss Fiedenstein
          Postfach 30,DDR 5800 Gotha,E.Germany
Grenoble..Bibliothèque d'Etude et d'Information,Boulevard
          Maréchal Lyautey 6e,B.P.38021,Grenoble,France
Griefs....Bibliothek Ernst-Moritz-Arndt-Universität,DDR-22,
          Griefswald,E.Germany
Halle.....Universitäts-und Landesbibliothek Sachsen-Anhalt
          Martin Luther Universität,August Bebel
          Strasse 13u.50,DDR-401,Halle,E.Germany
Harv......Houghton Library,Harvard U.,Cambridge,Mass.02138,USA
Hldbg.....Universitätsbibliothek,Plöck 107-109,6900,Heidelberg,W.Germany
Htgtn.....Huntington Library,1151 Orford Rd,San Marino,California 91108,USA
Ill.......U.of Illinois Library,1408 W.Gregory Drive,Urbana,Ill.61801,USA
Ind.......Indiana U.Library,Indiana U,10th & Jordan Ave.
          Bloomington,Ind.47405,USA
Iowa......U.of Iowa Library,Iowa City,Iowa 52242,USA
JohnsH....George Peabody Library,Johns Hopkins University
          17 E.Mount Vernon Place,Baltimore,Maryland 21202,USA
Kenyon....Chalmers Memorial Library,Kenyon College,Gambier,Ohio 43022,USA
Krakow....Uniwersytet Jagielloński,Biblioteka Jagiellońska
          Al.Mickiewicza 22,30-059 Krakow,Poland
L.C.......Library of Congress,Washington,D.C.20540,USA
Leid......Universiteitsbibliotheek Leiden,Witte Singel 27, Leiden,The
          Netherlands
Leipsig...Karl Marx Universität,Universitätsbibliothek,
          Beethovenstrasse 6,DDR 7010 Leipsig,E.Germany
Limoges...Bibliothèque Municipale,6 Place de l'Ancienne
          Comédie,87032 Limoges,France
Lyon......Bibliothèque de La Ville de Lyon,30 Boulevard
          Vivier Merle,69431 Lyon,France
Madrid....Biblioteca Nacionale,Paseo de Recoletos 20,Madrid 1,Spain
Mainz.....Landeshauptstadt Mainz, 42 Stadtbibliothek
          Rheinallee 3B,D-6500 Mainz,W.Germany
MAmb......Biblioteca Ambrosiana,Piazzo Pio XI 2,20100,Milan,Italy
Manch.....John Rylands University,Library of Manchester,U.of
          Manchester,Manchester M13 9PL,England
Marburg...Universitätsbibliothek,Wilhelm Röpke Strasse 4
          3550 Marburg,W.Germany
Maz.......Bibliothèque Mazarine,23 Quai Conti,75006,Paris,France
Metten....Bibliothek der Abtei Metten,St.Michaels-Gymnasium
          mit Schülerheim, D-8354 Metten,W.Germany
Mich......University Library,U.of Michigan,Ann Arbor,Michigan 48109,USA
MilanA....Archivio Storico Civico e Biblioteca
          Trivulziana,Castello Sforzesco,20121 Milan,Italy
```

List of Libraries (continued)

```
MilanB.....Biblioteca Nazionale Braidense,via Brera 28
           20121,Milan,Italy
Minn.......U.of Minnesota Library,Minneapolis,Minnesota 55455,USA
Morgan.....Pierpont Morgan Library,29 East 36th St.,
           NY,NY 10016,USA
Munich.....Bayerische Staatsbibliothek München,Postfach 150
           D-800 München 34,W.Germany
Naples.....Biblioteca Nazionale Vittorio Emanuele III
           Palazzo Reale,80100 Napoli,Italy
Neuberg....Staatliche Provinzialbibliothek,Karaplatz A17
           D-8858 Neuberg,W.Germany
Newberry...Newberry Library,60 W.Walton St.,Chicago,Ill.60610,USA
NotreD.....University Libraries,U.of Notre Dame,Notre Dame,
           Indiana 46556,USA
Nürn.......Stadtbibliothek Nürnberg,Egidienplatz 23,D-8500,1,W.Germany
NürnN......Bibliothek des Germanischen Nationalmuseums,
           Kornmarkt 1,8500 Nürnberg,W.Germany
N'wstn.....University Library,Northwestern U,Evanston,Illinois 60201,USA
NYAcMed....New York Academy of Medicine,2 East 103rd St.,NY,NY 10029,USA
NYGT.......St. Mark's Library,General Theological Seminary
           175 9th Ave.,NY,NY 10011,USA
NYPub......New York Public Library,5th Ave & 42nd St.,NY,NY 10018,USA
Oberlin....Oberlin College Library,Seeley G. Mudd Learning
           Center,Oberlin,Ohio 44074,USA
Ohio.......Ohio State U.Libraries,1858 Neil Ave.Mall,Columbus,Ohio 43210,USA
Olomouc....Státní Vĕdecká Knishovna nositelka Rádu práce
           Bezručova 2,Olomouc,Czechoslovakia
Oregon.....U.of Oregon Library,Eugene,Oregon 97403,USA
OxAS.......All Souls College,Codrington Library,Oxford OX1 4AL,England
OxCC.......Christ Church College Library,Oxford,England
OxPem......Pembroke College Library,Oxford,England
OxQ........Queens College Library,Oxford,England
Padua......Biblioteca Universitoria,via S.Diagio 7,35100 Padua,Italy
ParisArs...Bibliothèque de L'Arsenal,1 rue de Sully,75004 Paris,France
ParisInst..Palais de L'Institut de France,23 Quai de Conti,75006 Paris,France
PhilAcad...Academy of Natural Sciences,Wolf Room Collection
           19th & Parkway,Philadelphia,Pa.19103,USA
PhilAPS....Library,American Philosophical Society,105 South
           5th St.,Philadelphia,Pa.19106,USA
PhilCP.....Library of the College of Physicians of Philadelphia
           19 South 22nd St.,Philadelphia,Pa.19103,USA
PhilLC.....Library Company of Philadelphia,1314 Locust St.
           Philadelphia,Pa.19107,USA
Pisa.......Biblioteca Universitaria,Via Curtatone,Montanara,15,56100
           Pisa,Italy
Pommers-...Graf Von Schönborn'sche Schlossbibliothek,
felden     D-8602 Pommersfelden,W.Germany
Prague.....Státní Knihovna CSR,Klementinum 190,Praha,Czechoslovakia
Princeton..Princeton U.Library,P.O.Box 190,Princeton,N.J.08544,USA
Reg........Biblioteca Municipale A Panizzi,Via Farini 3
  Emilio   4210 Reggio Emilia,Italy
Regensburg.Fürst Thurn und Taxis Zentralarchiv-Hofbibliothek
           Postfach 110246,D-8400 Regensburg 11,W.Germany
Roanne.....Bibliothèque Municipale,42 Roanne,France
RomeAles...Biblioteca Universitaria Alessandrina,P.Aldo
           Moro 5,00185,Roma,Italy
RomeAng....Biblioteca Angelica,Piazza S.Agostino 8,00186,Roma,Italy
RomeBNC....Biblioteca Nazionale Centrale,Vittorio Emmanuele
           II,00185,Roma,Italy
RomeBV.....Biblioteca Vallicelliana,Piazza Della Chiesa
           Nuova,18,00186 Roma,Italy
RomeCas....Biblioteca Casanatense,Via S.Ignazio 52,00186,Roma,Italy
Sibiu......Biblioteca Muzeului Brukenthal,Piaţa Republicii 4,Sibiu,Roumania
Stanford...Stanford U.Libraries,Stanford,Calif.94305,USA
St.Ben.....Library,St.Benedict's Abbey,Atchison,Kansas 66002,USA
St.Gal.....Stiftsbibliothek Klosterhof 6,CH-9000,St.Gallen,Switzerland
St.Gen.....Bibliothèque Sainte-Geneviève,10 Place du
           Panthéon,75005 Paris,France
St.Mary....Library,St.Mary of the Lake Seminary,Mundelein,Illinois 60060,USA
Stockholm..Kungl.Biblioteket,Box 5039,102 41 Stockholm,Sweden
Strasbourg.Bibliothèque de la Ville de Strasbourg,3 rue
           Kuhn,67 Strasbourg,France
```

Early Printings

List of Libraries (concluded)

```
Stuttgart..Württembergische Landesbibliothek,Konrad-Adenauer
           Strasse 8,Postfach 769,7 Stuttgart 1,W.Germany
Torun......Biblioteka Glówna,Uniwersytetu Mekotala Kopernika,Torún,Poland
Tours......Bibliothèque Municipale,Place A,37042 Tours,France
Tüb........Universitätsbibliothek,Wilhelmstrasse 32,7400,Tübingen,W.Germany
Tulane.....Howard Tilton Memorial Library,Tulane U,New Orleans,La.70118,USA
U.Amst.....Universiteitsbibliotheek Amsterdam,Singel 421-425,NL-1012 WP,
           Amsterdam
UCBanc.....Bancroft Library,U.of California,Berkeley,California 94720,USA
UCLA.......University Research Library,University of California at Los
           Angeles,405 Hilgard Ave.,Los Angeles,California 90024,USA
UChic......Joseph Regenstein Library,1100 East 57th St.,Chicago,Illinois
           60637,USA
UOkla......University of Oklahoma Library,History of Science
           Collection,401 W.Brooks,Norman,Oklahoma 73019,USA
UPa........Charles Patterson Van Pelt Library,U.of Philadelphia,Pa.19104,USA
Uppsala....Universitetsbiblioteket,Uppsala Universitet
           Box 510,S-751 20 Uppsala,Sweden
UNC........Rare Book Room,Wilson Library,U.of N.C.,Chapel,Hill,N.C.27514,USA
USC........University Library,U.of S.California,Los Angeles,Calif.90089,USA
UWash......Suzallo Library,U.of Washington,Seattle,Washington 98195 USA
Vat........Biblioteca Apostolica, Porta S.Anna,Cortile de
           Belvedere,1-00120 Citta del Vaticano,Italy
Venice.....Biblioteca Nazionale Marciana,S.Marco 7,30124,Venezia,Italy
Vienna.....Osterreichische Nationalbibliothek,Josefsplatz,Vienna I,Austria
ViennaSB...Bibliothek der Benediktinerabtei U.L.Fr.z.d.
           Schotten,A-1010 Vienna 1,Austria
ViennaUB...Universitätsbibliothek Wien,Fernleihe,Dr.Karl
           Lueger-Ring 1,A-1010 Vienna,Austria
ViennaWS...Magistrat der Stadt Wien,Wiener Stadt-u.Landes-
           bibliothek,1082 Vienna,Austria
Va.........Library,U.of Virginia,Charlottesville,Va.22904,USA
Warsaw.....Biblioteka Uniwersytecka w Wartszawie,Krakowskie
           Przedmieście 26-28,00-927,Warsaw,Poland
Wash.......Library,Washington University,St.Louis,Mo.63130,USA
Weimer.....Nationale Forschungs-und Gedenkstäaten,Der
           Klassischen Deutschen Litgeratur in Weimar
           DDR 53,Weimer,E.Germany
Wolf.......Herzog August Bibliothek,Lessingplatz 1,3340
           Wolfenbüttel,W.Germany
Wis........Memorial Library,U.of Wisconsin,728 State St.
           Madison,Wisconsin 53706,USA
WroclawA...Biblioteka Zakladu Narodowego im Ossolińskich
           ul.Szewska 37,50-139 Wroclaw,Poland
WroclawU...Universytet Wroclaw,Biblioteka Uniwersytecka
           ul.K.Szajnochy 10,50-076,Wroclaw,Poland
Würzburg...Universitätsbibliothek Am Hubland,D-8700,Würzburg,W.Germany
Yale.......Beinecke Rare Book & Manuscript Library,Box
           1603,Yale Station,New Haven,Connecticut 06520,USA
Zittau.....Christian Weise-Bibliothek,Stadt-u.Kreisbiblio-
           thek,DDR 88,Zittau,E.Germany
Zurich.....Zentralbibliothek,Zähringerplatz 6,8025,Zürich,Switzerland
```

BIBLIOGRAPHY OF SOURCES CONCERNING MEDIEVAL AND RENAISSANCE SCHOLARS

ALFARABI

De Boer, T.J. (1967). The History of Philosophy in Islam, New York.

Encyclopedia Britannica. (1967). vol.9, p.66. London.

Hammont, Robert. (1947). The Philosophy of Alfarabi and Its Influence on Medieval Thought, New York: Hobson Book Press.

Sandys, J.E. (1921). A History of Classical Scholarship, vol.1, pp.563-4, Cambridge, England.

Steinschneider, Moritz. (1869). "Alfarabi (Alpharabius), Des Arasbischen Philosophen Leben und Schriften . . . ," Mémoires de L'Académie Impériale des Sciences de St. Pétersbourg, VIIe séries, 13, 4, 1-268.

AVERROËS

De Boer. (See Alfarabi).

Encylopedia Britannica. (1910). 11th ed, vol.3, p.58. London.

Franklin, Alfred. (1875). Dictionnaire des Noms, Surnoms et Pseudonymes Latins de L'Histoire Littéraire du Moyen Age (1100-1530), Paris: Firmin-Didot,

Gauthier, Leon. (1948). Ibn Rochd (Averroës), Paris: Presses Universitaires de France.

Renan, Ernest. (n.d.). Averroes et l'Averroisme, 8th ed., Paris: Calmann-Levy.

Yūssif, Alī Abdullah. (1939). Averroës: The Philosopher of East and West, n.p.,n.pub.

BARBARO

Dizionario Biografico Delgi Italiani. (1960-   ), vol.6, 96-99, Rome: Institute della Enciclopedia Italiani.

Encyclopedia Britannica. (1910). vol.3, p.382. (see Averroës)

Franklin. (See Averroës).

Franck, Adolphe. (1875). Dictionnaire des Sciences Philosophiques, 2nd ed., 1, 711, Paris: Hachette.

Michaud, Louis-Gabriel. (1842-1865). Bibliographie Universelle, vol.3, pp.69-70. Paris: A. Thoisnier Despeaces.

Nicéron, Jean Pierre. (1727-1745). Mémoires pour Servier à L'Histoire des Hommes . . ., vol.14, 1-34, Paris: Briasson.

Sandys, vol.2, pp.83. (see Alfarabi).

COLONNA, EGIDIO

Dizionario Enciclopedico Italiano. (1955-1961). vol.4, p.282 Rome: Istitute della Enciclopedia Italiana. (listed under Egidio Romano).

La Grande Encyclopédie. (1885-1901). vol.11, p.1119. Paris: Société Anonyme de la Grande Encyclopedie.

Michaud. vol.8, p.660. (see Barbaro). Listed as Colonne, Gille.

Murphy, J.J. (1969). "The Scholastic Condemnation of Rhetoric in the Commentary of Giles of Rome on the Rhetoric of Aristotle," in Arts Libéraux et Philosophie au Moyen Age (Acts du Quatrième Congrès Internationale de Philosophie Médiévale), 833-841. Montreal.

Bibliography of Sources concerning Medieval
and Renaissance Scholars (continued)

Nouvelle Biographie Générale. vol.2, cols.292-3.

Sandys, vol.1, p.587. (See Alfarabi).

HERMANNUS ALEMANNUS

Boggess, W.F. (1965). Averroës Cordubensis Commentarium Medium in
  Aristotelis Poetriam. Unpubl. diss. University of North Carolina.

Boggess, W.F. (1968). Hermannus Alemannus's Rhetorical Translations,"
  Viator: Medieval & Renaissance Studies, 2, 227-350.

Historische Commission bei der König. Akademie der Wissen-Schaften. (1875-
  1912). Allegemeine Deutsche Biographie, vol.12, p.163, Leipsig: Duncker &
  Humblot.

Luquet, G.H. (1901). Herman L'Allemand: Mémoire Presenté au Congrès
  International d'Histoire des Réligions en Séance de Section, le 3 Sept.
  1900, Revue de l'Histoire des Réligions (Annales du Musée Guimet), 44,
  3, 407-22.

Michaud. vol.19, p.280. (see Barbaro)

Nouvelle Biographie Générale. (1862-1898). vol.24, col.257. Paris: Firmin
  Didot, Frères.

Sandys, vol.1, p.569. (see Alfarabi).

MAIORAGIUS

Enciclopedia Italiana. (1929-1939). vol.21, p.969. Rome: Istituto della

  Enciclopedia Italiana.

La Grande Encyclopédie. vol.22, p.1028. (see Colonna).

Nouvelle Biographie Générale. vol.32, p.987. (see Hermannnus).

Sandys, vol.2, p.147. (see Alfarabi)

MOERBECK

Franck. p.661. (see Barbaro)

Franklin. p.391. (see Averroes).

Historische Commission. vol.22, p.215. (see Hermannus)

Nationaal Biografisch Woordenboek. (1972). vol.5, p.610. Brussels: Palais
  der Academïen.

Nouvelle Biographie Générale, vol.34, p.710. (see Hermannus)

Paquet, Jean Noel. (1763-1700). Mémoires pour Servir à L'Histoire Littéraire
  des Dix-Sept Provinces des Pays-Bas . . ., vol.13, 89-99, Louvain: Imprimerie
  Académique.

Sandys, vol.1, pp.585-6. (see Alfarabi).

Verbeke, Gérard. (1953). "Guillaume de Moerbeke Traducteur de Proclus,"
  Revue Philosophique de Louvain, 51, 349-373.

Verbeke, Gérard. (1955). "Guillaume de Moerbeke et sa Méthode de Traduction,"
  Medioevo e Rinascimento: Studi in Onore di Brune Nardi, vol.2, 781-800,
  Florence: G.C.Sansoni.

Bibliography of Sources concerning Medieval
and Renaissance Scholars (concluded)

MURET

Dejob, Charles. (1881). Marc-Antoine Muret, un Professor Français en Italie
. . . , Paris: E. Thorin.

Encyclopedia Britannica. (1910). vol.19, p.34. (see Averroës)

La Grande Enclopédie. vol.24, p.575. (see Colonna)

Nouvelle Biographia Générale. vol.36, col.997. (see Hermannus)

Sandys, vol.2, pp.148-152. (see Alfarabi).

RICCOBONO

Enciclopedia Italiana. vol.29, p.252. (see Maioragius)

Michaud. vol.35, p.566. (see Barbaro)

Nouvelle Bibliographie Générale. vol. 42, col.149. (see Hermannus)

SIGONIO

Enciclopedia Italiana. vol.31, p.761. (see Maioragius).

Encyclopedia Britannica. (1910). vol.25, p.82. (see Averroes).

La Grande Encyclopédie. vol.30, p.17. (see Colonna).

Nouvelle Biographie Générale. vol.43, col.985. (see Hermannus).

Sandys, vol.2, pp.143-5.

TRAPEZUNTIUS

Franck. p.613. (see Barbaro)

Franklin. 574. (see Averroës)

La Grande Encyclopédie. vol.18, p.817. (see Colonna)

Nicéron, vol.14, pp.322-339. (see Barbaro)

Monfasani, John. (1976). George of Trebizond, Leiden: E.J. Brill.

Monfasani, John. (1984). Collectanea Trapezuntiana, Binghamton,
N.Y.: Renaissance Society of America.

Sandys, vol.2, p.63. (see Alfarabi).

VICTORIUS

Bandini, Angiolo Maria. (1759). Victorius, Sue de Vita et Scriptis Petri
Victori, Florence, n.pub.

Michaud. vol.43, p.69. (see Barbaro).

Niccolai, Francescoo. (1914). Pierre Vettori (1499-1585), Florence:
Libreria Internazionale, Florence.

Rudiger, Wilhelm. (1896). Petrus Victorius aus Florenz, Halle: Max Niemayer.

Sandys, vol.2, pp.135-40. (see Alfarabi).

CHAPTER FOUR

IMPROVEMENTS IN THE GREEK TEXT DURING THE NINETEENTH AND TWENTIETH CENTURIES

The previous chapter concerned what had happened to the *Rhetoric* during the fifteenth and sixteenth centuries. The seventeenth and eighteenth centuries did not see major developments in the Greek text. The years between 1600 and 1820, however, developed numerous Greek and Latin editions, including in 1619 the first publication of the treatise in England by Edward Goulston. The seventeenth and eighteenth centuries also saw a number of translations of the *Rhetoric* into English and the vernaculars of the continent.

THE BIPONTE EDITION OF THE RHETORIC (1793)

The period was climaxed in 1791-1800 by the publication of the popular five volume edition of Aristotle's works in Greek and Latin under the editorship of Theophilus Buhle. This set, interrupted by the French Revolution, claimed to have incorporated into its text the most recent improvements, but the Greek texts did not result from a vigorous collation of the manuscripts that were then discoverable in the major libraries of Europe. If Buhle had intended to include a collation of manuscripts together with his references to previous printed editions, the turbulence of the French Revolution and the Napoleonic wars interfered.

The introduction to the Biponte edition (1793, xiv), in clarifying its editorial method, referred to manuscript sources only through the corrections made to Victorius' manuscript sources and via its consultations with Trapezuntius and Barbaro whose Latin translations, the Buhle preface pointed out, were based upon manuscripts. As Kassel noted, the Aldus Manutius edition of 1508 was also based upon manuscripts, so Buhle had indirect primary source access via the 1508 edition as well. But Buhle, with the exception of the instances in which he attempted to clarify by reference to primary sources [*Excussi igitur non solum edd. Aldinam, Venetam, Basileenses, Spirensem, Riccobonianam and Maioragianam, sed etiam diligentius, quam a Morelio factum est, ex Victorii commentario varietatem lectionis e Codd. MStis enotatam in animadversionibus criticis congessi* (1793, xiv-xv)], used only secondary sources.

In his introduction (1793, xiv), Buhle explained: "I have considered it my duty to compare anew with the Sylburg edition as many editions of the *Rhetorica* as I have been able to find; some reading(s) have been incorporated from these editions, in order that I might deliver into the hands of learned men a text that is as correct as possible. For this reason, I have examined not only the Aldine, Venetian, Basileensian, Spirensian, Riccobonian and Maioragian editions, but also, with more care than Morelius, I have gleaned from the critical notes some readings from codices and manuscripts, which I have taken from the commentary of Victorius."

As popular and useful as the 1793 edition was, it did not make even a moderate contribution to the establishment of a critical Greek edition. The impact of the Buhle edition, however, was considerable, as is witnessed by the number of editors between 1837 and 1926 who referenced their texts to the numbering system used by the Biponte edition. The lineal numbers in the text of the Biponte edition served to correlate the Greek text at the top of the page with the Latin given at the bottom of the page. However, editors of later editions who furnished only a Greek or a Latin text used the Biponte numbers in their margins, so readers could compare their text with the familiar Biponte. (see Tables One and Two)

Therefore, prior to 1820, the improvements in the Greek text since Victorius had been minimal. The stage was set for a major leap forward. The Napoleonic wars had ended. Europe, except for the Franco-Prussian War of 1870, was to be in comparative peace for almost one hundred years. It was the English and German scholars, with the assistance of Dufour of France and Tovar of Spain in the twentieth century who seized, and who have continued to seize, the opportunity of providing as authentic a Greek text of the *Rhetoric* as the evidence permits. What resulted was almost like a tennis match, with the English winning the first set, the Germans the second, and so forth, back and forth across the North Sea. Instead of being rivals, however, the scholars contributed materially to each other, and one built upon the developments of his predecessors.

THE 1820 GAISFORD EDITION

Who was to begin? The English made the first move. In 1820 in Oxford, Thomas Gaisford (1779-1855) published in two volumes his *Aristoteles, de rhetorica libri tres, ad fidem manuscriptorum recogniti, cum versione latina*. Gaisford, who had been appointed Regius professor of Greek at Oxford in 1812 and assumed the role of Dean of Christ Church between 1831-1855, was active in producing Greek texts of a number of classical works. Undoubtedly his curiosity about what the manuscripts of the *Rhetoric* might show was stimulated by his duties as official curator of the Bodleian.

There is a minor mystery as to why Gaisford's name does not appear in his edition. To this day, neither the Bodleian nor the British Library acknowledges Gaisford in their catalogue entries, although numerous sources since l820 have recognized his editorship. Inquiries to the Bodleian have so far been fruitless. Nevertheless, Gaisford was the editor of the 1820 edition, a major step forward since it acknowledged manuscript sources and not secondary sources.

Gaisford's edition was highly indebted to Buhle. He reproduced Buhle's introduction to the 1793 edition as well as Vater's 1794 "prooemium." He also followed the Buhle text, noting, where he thought it important, the manner in which the l793 edition varied from the following sources.

A = Parisinus 1741 = Ac Bekker
B = Parisinus 1869 = Bekker Gb
C = Parisinus 1818 = (not used by Bekker)
D = Parisinus 2038 = (not used by Bekker)
E = Parisinus 2116 = (not used by Bekker)

If Gaisford preferred the reading of one of the manuscripts he consulted rather than the Buhle text, he used the manuscript version, footnoting the Buhle edition. If he preferred to keep the Buhle reading where his manuscripts differed, he footnoted the variant manuscript reading.

It was in "Libri Tres" (usually found in a second volume) that Gaisford offered the variant readings of Portus, Victorius, Buhle, Morel, Maoiragius and others. "Libri Tres" cannot be distinctly categorized as either philological or critical, because it is often both. Gaisford was much interested in quoting passages from Cicero and from other works of Aristotle to clarify passages in the *Rhetoric*.

For the Latin translation entitled *Aristotelis Librorum Trium de Arte Rhetorica Liber Primus*, Gaisford used the Biponte Latin which, in turn, had appropriated some of Sigonio's Latin phraseology.[1] The borrowed Latin version is divided into the same number of chapters as the Greek text, with the Biponte Latin numbers subdividing each chapter.

THE BEKKER EDITION

German scholars picked up the gauntlet thrown down by the English. In 1831, Immanuel Bekker published his two volumes of Aristotle's works in Greek as part of what became by 1870 a five volume set issued by the *Academia Regia Borussica* of Berlin. Bekker's methodology established a format for referencing the *Rhetoric* that remains in use today How did Bekker and his colleagues proceed?

Bekker (1785-1871), who was born and died in Berlin, himself examined in excess of 400 manuscripts during his visits to various places on the continent (Sandys, 85), sometimes working under the sponsorship of the Berlin Academy and sometimes on his own. It was from what he discovered on these expeditions that Bekker chose the most promising MSS. to serve as the basis for his edition of all of Aristotle's works. It is said that Bekker was a poor teacher but an inexaustible scholar who inspired many others to productive work.

What transpired specifically in the case of the editing of Aristotle's works? First, to establish the texts of the entire works, Bekker selected over 100 manuscripts, assigning each one a Roman letter, e.g., Parisinus Grec 1741 was assigned the letters Ac and Marcianus Grec 200 was assigned the letter Q. It is not altogether clear why Bekker assigned Ac to Parisinus 1741. The simplest answer is that Bekker began using the letters of the alphabet to name the manuscripts he consulted, possibly in the order in which he saw them. When he ran out of letters of the alphabet, he went to Ab, Bb, Cb, etc., and, when that series was exhausted, to Aa, Ab, Ac, Ad, etc. Parisinus 1741 was therefore somewhat at random assigned the letters Ac. It is clear that the "c" does not indicate any particular scribe involved in the production of Parisinus 1741, which results in some confusion later on when editors of critical editions tend to use subscripts to refer to corrections in the first hand, corrections in the second hand, etc.

Second, for each particular work of Aristotle, Bekker selected the texts he considered most productive for collation. In the case of the *Rhetoric*, Bekker chose the following:

Q = Marcianus 200
Yb = Vaticanus 1340
Zb = Palatinus 23, now Vaticanus 23
Ac = Parisinus 1741

Third, the text was then established by collation. Variations from the text were footnoted. Therefore, only these four manuscripts appear in the annotations to the text. Conspicuous by their absence are the Latin translations and Cantabrigiensis Ff.5.8.

In order to facilitate referencing, Bekker numbered the pages of the volumes he edited. Each page was set up in two columns, with anywhere from 30 to 40 lines per column. The left hand column was known as column "a" and the right hand column as column "b." Therefore, to cite the Bekker text of the *Rhetoric*, the citation is first to the page number of the two volumes of the Greek, e.g., page 1354, then to column "a" or column "b," e.g., 1354b, and third to the number of the line in that column, e.g., 1354b25.

A third volume of the series also appearing in 1831 contained the works of Aristotle in Latin as translated by various scholars including the Riccobono version of the *Rhetoric* on pages 695-727. The Latin text also appeared in two columns, with cross-referencing to the Greek text in volume two, using the page, column and line in the Greek corresponding to Riccobono's Latin. A fourth volume containing the *scholia*, edited by Christianus Augustus Brandis, was issued in 1836. The fifth volume, appearing in 1870, included Aristotelian fragments and additions to the 20 *scholia* appearing in volume four plus the *Index Aristotelicus* by Hermannus Bonitz. Additional Aristotelian works have appeared since 1831, e.g., the pastiche of the *Athenian Constitution*, but, generally speaking, the Western world after 1831 has had an excellent basis for its research on the works of Aristotle following the Bekker collations.

Bekker issued a second edition of the *Rhetoric* in 1843 and a third edition in 1859. His third edition of 1859 has been preferred by some scholars because it presents Bekker's reflective conclusions. The 1859 edition was reprinted in octavo in 1873.

THE OXFORD EDITION OF BEKKER'S TEXT

The older references in the literature to an "Oxford edition" refer to the first two volumes of the Bekker edition reissued in England in 1837 in eleven volumes under the title, *Aristotelis Opera. ex Recensione Immanuelis Bekkeri*, with the addition of the 1584 indexes of Friedrich Sylburg at the conclusion of each of Aristotle's separate works.

The editors of the 1837 edition realized that they needed an index, so they turned to the Greek and Latin indexes that accompanied the 1584 Sylburg edition. However, the Sylburg edition was over two hundred years old and not readily available. It was the 1791 Biponte edition that readers were consulting more frequently. Therefore, the editors took the Sylburg index items, made some changes in what was indexed, and, instead of referencing them to the 1584 edition, cited first whether the term could be found in book one, two or three; second cited which Trapezuntius chapter the item could be found in; and third, cited the readers to the subsection of the Biponte edition, numbers which the Biponte edition had used to correlate its Greek text with its Latin text. What resulted could be summarized as follows:

a. a reprinting of the Bekker edition, in one column instead of two
b. an appropriation of the terms indexed by Sylburg with minor additions
c. for each term indexed, a substitution of the book, chapter, and section of the Biponte edition for the page and line number of the 1584 edition.

Therefore, the 1837 has indebtedness to the Bekker, the Sylburg, and the Biponte editions. (see Table One)

The text of the *Rhetoric* for the Oxford edition was based upon the same manuscripts as was the Bekker's *Rhetoric* with the following additions:

Na = Marcianus 215
Vb = Palatinus 260
Bc = Urbinus 47
Parisinus 2038 & 2039
Vaticanus 265

Gaisford had referenced Parisinus 2038.

THE SPENGEL CONTRIBUTION

In 1867, Leonard von Spengel (1803-1880)[3] published his two volume *Aristotelis Ars Rhetorica Cum Adnotatione*. Spengel had studied at Munich and Berlin where one of his instructors had been Bekker. Spengel became a professor at the University of Munich in 1835, where he served until his death, except for six years at the University of Heidelberg between 1841-1847.

Spengel (1867, xii-xiii) stated his method of operation as follows. "We have faithfully presented the ancient codex A [Parisinus 1741] from which we have noted that these works [by Brandis, Bonitz, Behlen, Thurot] are especially derived; those readings that differ from this [i.e., Codex A] may be consulted, as they are given in the margin [i.e., the apparatus criticus]. At the beginning of the note [i.e., for a particular passage or phrase or word], the Greek readings, which are arranged in accordance with the greater Bekker edition [1859 or third edition], present the readings offered by the lesser manuscripts, for the most part without comment. Other readings, that are necessary to clarify the meaning, are expressly added; but many more are omitted, as they are worthless and fruitless. A few conjectures of which we are reasonably certain, once they came to our attention, we did not hesitate to retain, e.g., 1402b19 ἀεί [which] was first noted by Behlen, or 1414b27 οἰκεῖον changed to κοινόν, following Bonitz. I have no doubt that much remains to be corrected by men of more acute perspective [than I]."

Spengel's objective, therefore, was to produce what he considered to be the most authentic Greek text. He appears first to have contrasted Parisinus 1741 with the Bekker third edition of 1859, for there are notes pointing out where his Greek version differs from the 1859 Bekker. He then consulted the lesser manuscripts and comments of the critics, and chose from them what readings he wished to incorporate into his text and which he wished to footnote. But largely he does not share with his readers the sources of his variant readings or those that he changed because he sensed a different reading from that given in Bekker. For example, at 1377b9-11, Bekker changed the text to retain the first person plural of both verbs:

ἀξιοῦμεν . . . . . ἐμμενοῦμεν
(which had read ἐμμένουσιν)

Spengel, on the other hand, changed the first verb, and retained the original reading of the second verb, thus:

ἀξιοῦσιν . . . . . ἐμμενοῦσιν

In his commentary in his volume two, Spengel specifically mentioned this modification (1967, II, 206), but in his comments in volume two, he did not often make such clarifications.

Spengel endeavored to produce what he considered to be the most authentic Greek text. Although the edition was highly praised in its time and is still consulted, because of its lack of documentation, it is less useful now than it was in the late nineteenth and early twentieth centuries. Spengel sensed the subjectivity of his work, for he was right in saying that much remained to be corrected "by men of more acute perspective" than the one adopted by him.

Spengel then produced in volume one the Moerbeck Latin text (which he labeled the Vetusta, 178-342). For his printing of the Moerbeck Latin translation, Spengel footnoted references to Monacensis 307, Victorius, and the 1546 Venice edition, as well as comparisons with the Greek MSS of the Bekker and Gaisford editions.

To correlate his Greek text with other editions, Spengel followed the Bekker style of citations, i.e., page in the Bekker edition, but not columns since his edition was set up in one column, with every fifth line numbered in rough correspondence to the line numbers in the Bekker edition.

To elaborate on the implications of the Greek text, to present further variant readings, and to refer to works by Aristotle and others, Spengel offered in a second volume of 456 pages a philological and critical commentary in which he explained certain passages, noted variant readings mostly from other printed editions, and made cross references to other Aristotelian works and to classical and modern treatises, such as Plato, Isocrates, Demosthenes, the Latin texts, and Brandis. Volume two did not amplify the Moerbeck text, except in making comparisons between the readings of the Greek and Moerbeck texts.

Spengel's other works included an edition of the Aldine edition of 1513 (*Rhetores Graeci*, 3 vols, Leipsig, 1853-1856) as well as his *Ueber die Rhetorik des Aristotles* issued in Munich in 1851.

COPE'S COMMENTARY AND GREEK EDITION

In 1867, in preparation for issuing his version of the Greek text, Edward Meredith Cope had published an *Introduction to Aristotle's "Rhetoric."* As was noted above, Spengel also published his Greek text in 1867. John Edwin Sandys, who edited and completed Cope's three volume text, stated that Cope had continued to work on his version of the Greek text in the two years that followed the publication of his introduction (Cope, 1877, vii) during which time Cope "only occasionally consulted and quoted Spengel's edition, refraining purposefully from incurring any such indebtedness as would prevent his own edition remaining a perfectly independent work." (Cope, 1877, viii) When Cope died, his brothers asked Sandys to complete the work, which was issued in three volumes in 1877.

Trinity College made available to Sandys two copies of the Bekker edition in which Cope had made notes. Sandys concluded that it was Cope's intention to accept, on the whole, the text as he found it "in the earlier editions with which he was familiar." (Cope, 1877, x) Therefore, Sandys chose to adopt as the text of the commentary the 1873 reprint of Bekker's third edition (octavo, 1859), noting in the footnotes "the instances in which the evidence of his translation or notes... pointed clearly to some other reading as the one which he deliberately preferred to that of Bekker's third edition, or in which he was at any rate content to acquiesce." (Cope, 1877, x) Sandys inserted in the margins not only the appropriate page, column and line to the 1831 editions but also the page, column and line appropriate to the 1859 edition. Therefore, the Cope three volume edition resembled the sixteenth century publications described in Chapter Three, in which the commentary far exceeded the text itself. Cope did not cite manuscripts in his notes, but frequently referred to other works of Aristotle as well as to articles on Aristotle and historical allusions. Thus, Cope proposed that "an editor's main duty was explanation in its widest sense and accordingly...[devoted] himself mainly to questions of exegesis, to elucidation of subject matter, to illustration of verbal expression, and to matters of grammatical and lexicographical interest...." (Cope, 1877, x)

THE BERLIN EDITION COMPLETED IN 1870

Although the 1831 Leipsig edition of sixteen volumes in 16° with the *Rhetoric* in volume 12 claimed to have been newly edited, it failed to furnish scholars with the revised text they needed to complete their knowledge of Aristotle's texts. Therefore, when Bekker published three volumes in 1831 comprising the Greek and Latin texts of Aristotle's works, and in 1836 there appeared the *scholia* of Aristotle collected by Christianus Augustus Brandis, what was needed to make available a collated, comprehensive edition of Aristotle's works was a collection of the Aristotelian fragments and an index that would assist readers in associating the ideas in one of Aristotle's treatises with the discussions of those same terms in other of Aristotle's works. The latter was supplied by Bonitz in 1870 and will be discussed in the next section. The fragments were edited by Valentinus Rose, together with a supplement to the *scholia* edited by Hermann Usener.

This five volume set, published in Berlin by G. Reimer, was sponsored by the *Academia Regia Borussica*. The first two volumes and the Bonitz *Index* were reissued in Darmstadt in 1960 by the Wissenschaftliche Buchgesellschaft and all five volumes in Berlin between 1960 and 1978 by Walter de Gruyter.

BONITZ' INDEX ARISTOTELICUS

In the years before the computer, the appearance of an index was a major event. Therefore when Hermann Bonitz (1814-1888) published his comprehensive index to the complete works of Aristotle, he provided Aristotelian scholars with an important research tool. The Royal Borrusican Academy had long promised readers the Bonitz *Index* (Bonitz, iii) so its appearance in 1870 was a major event in classical scholarship.

After studying in Dresden and Berlin, Bonitz taught classical philology in Vienna between 1849 to 1867, assisting Austria in the reorganization of its schools and lecturing on Sophocles, Homer, Plato and Aristotle. When in 1866 Austria and Prussia became active enemies, Bonitz returned to Berlin where he completed his index. Bonitz himself had ambitions to produce a new text of Aristotle, but never achieved his goal.

When Bonitz undertook the task of preparing an index for the Academy, he requested that he be permitted to find a partner to assist him in such a major undertaking. J. B. Meyer, who had achieved prominence for his knowledge of Aristotle's zoological works, began to help Bonitz, but after Meyer had completed the research for the letter α, he had an opportunity to take a post at another university and so asked to be excused from assisting further with the index. Bonitz replaced Meyer with Bernard Langkravel who worked with Bonitz until the task was completed. (Bonitz, iii)

Naturally the Bonitz *Index* used the numbering system originated by Bekker to cite the Aristotelian works to which the terms refer, e.g., for πίστεις ἄτεχνοι, Bonitz cited Pa15.2.1355b35, the "P" standing for the *Rhetorica*, the "a" for Book One, the "15" for Chapter

15 (the main location of the comments on the πίστεις ἄτεχνοι), the "2" for Chapter Two (a secondary but earlier reference to πίστεις ἄτεχνοι). Both the "15" and the "2" were references to the usual chapters found in the Trapezuntius Latin edition. Some Trapezuntius editions were not so chaptered, because there were no chapters in the Greek manuscripts and editors were free to make whatever changes they wished when they printed the Trapezuntius edition. Presumably Bonitz concluded that it was necessary to offer researchers working in both Greek and Latin some assistance, so he chose to reference the Trapezuntius chapter divisons for they were the chapter divisions most widely used in the Latin translations. (see Table Two) Users of his index working in Greek could locate specific passages, whereas users working in Latin could locate the chapter(s) of the Trapezuntius text where a reference to the subject could be found. The 1355b35 *supra* is a citation to page 1355 of the Bekker edition, column b, line 35. In his preface, Bonitz explained his method of citing the Bekker edition, and the manner in which he distinguished in his entries the several works of Aristotle and the several books within a given work, but he gave no indication in his preface that he included chapter references.

Bonitz called his work an index, not a concordance, because he did not cite all instances where a given term appears in Aristotle's works, but only provided citations to areas of the works where topical uses of the terms could be found. It was up to the researcher to follow up by making a more intensive study of the passages in the area of the reference. In his preface Bonitz stated that "if one should list every occurrence of each word in Aristotle, it could well be that the work would grow too large to be useful." (Bonitz, iv) Furthermore, Bonitz limited his index to those words that were peculiar to Aristotle. Such limitations of his research were not serious, particularly when we remember that, prior to his work, there had been no extensive index whatsoever, only those limited indexes offered as appendices to certain editions. Bonitz in his preface explained that "I would have my judges, if they be just, remember that this is an index, not a lexicon of Aristotle, and brevity would seem to require that the various usages be listed, not for interpretation, but for collecting the locations of words and distinguishing their usages in due order." (1870,iv)

At least four other aids to Aristotelian research have appeared since the Bonitz lexicon of 1870. In 1894, Matthias Kappes published his *Aristoteles-Lexikon; Erklarung der Philosophischen Termini Technici des Aristoteles in Alphabetischer Reihenfolge*. This somewhat short guide to certain of Aristotle's terminology also pointed the reader to the location of the term in the Latin edition of Trapezuntius as well as in the Bekker Greek edition. It was reissued by Burt Franklin of New York in 1971. In 1949, Troy Organ issued his *An Index to Aristotle in English Translation*. In his introduction, Organ proposed that, although the Bonitz *Index* was of great help to advanced students of Aristotle, it was of little help to the student "interested in attaining a well-rounded view of Aristotle's analysis of a particular subject." (Organ, v) Organ listed the English translation of the Greek terms, followed in some instances by the original Greek, and ending with a reference to the term where it appeared in the Bekker edition. More recently, in 1962, Thomas P. Kiernan edited the *Aristotle Dictionary*. Kiernan began his work by summarizing the several works of Aristotle, and then selected certain of Aristotle's concepts for delineation. For each concept chosen, Kiernan gave in English translation one or more quotations from Aristotle, each of which is referenced to the Latin book and chapter, and to the Greek location in the Bekker edition.

The most recent aid to scholars is André Wartelle's 1982 *Lexique de la Rhétorique d'Aristote*. Wartelle said that his work hoped to fill in gaps left by Bonitz and to correct errors that had appeared in the 1870 Index. The index lists Greek terms, followed by citations to where these terms appear in the Bekker edition, e.g., for πιστεις, Wartelle gave almost an entire page of references, in comparison to the more limited listings by Bonitz. The contribution is major, and will be helpful to all Greek scholars of the *Rhetoric*.

THE ROEMER TEXTS OF 1885 AND 1898

After Cope's three volume set appeared, the forum returned to Germany. Adolf Roemer (1843-1913) spent the majority of his life as professor of classical philology and education at the University of Erlangen. After taking his degree at the University of Heidelberg, Roemer established himself as one of the world's authorities on Homer. He made numerous friends among the scholars at Munich. In 1866 he was required to serve time as a soldier, but such duties did not slow down his studies because in 1868 he passed his examinations in philology. In 1869 he became an assistant at the gymnasium in Speyer, and in 1877 assumed the post of rector of the gymnasium in Munich. In 1893 he took the positions at Erlangen that he held until his death.

Unlike Cope and Spengel, Roemer elected to present his own version of the Greek text with citations to sources noted in the footnotes. His expanded method of footnoting a number of variations was as follows:

1. except when he wished to call particular attention to the Ac [or Parisinus Grec 1741], he used the symbol π when he wanted to refer to the four sources cited by Gaisford and the symbol θ when he wished to refer to the three sources for the Bekker edition.

2. when Roemer wished to refer to a particular one of the MSS referred to by Gaisford or Bekker, he used the following symbols:

Ac = Parisinus 1741
B = Parisinus 1869
C = Parisinus 1818
D = Parisinus 2338
E = Parisinus 2116
Q = Marcianus 200
Yb = Vaticanus 1340
Zb = Vaticanus 23

3. Roemer also used the following symbols:

Tr = Moerbeck(as in Spengel,Vetusta)
Ald = 1508 Aldus Manutius edition
Venet = 1546 Gryphius edition
Vict = 1548 & 1579 Victorius editions
Bas.Isingr = 1550 Basel edition
Morel = 1562 Paris edition
Sylburg = 1584 Frankfurt edition
Buhle = Buhle Zweibrücken edition
Gaisford = 1820 edition
Bekker = 1831 edition
Bekker 3 = 1859 third edition
Paris = 1848 Firmin Didot edition
Spengel = 1867 edition
Cope = 1877 3 vol. edition
Muretus = 1585 Muret

4. there are references as well to the *scholia* and other works.

The first edition appeared in Leipsig in 1885, but scholars generally cite the revised edition of 1898. Roemer's editions were a material step forward in establishing an improved text. They remained the leading collation for more than fifty years.

THE FREESE LOEB LIBRARY EDITION OF 1926

When the Loeb Classical Library, under the editorship of E. Capps, T.E. Page, and W.H.D. Rouse, elected to issue in London a "pocket-sized" set of volumes covering all of the major works of antiquity, they chose the relatively obscure John Henry Freese to furnish the Greek text with an English translation. In keeping with other classical works previously issued for their edition, the editors of the Loeb Classical Library wanted a Greek text coordinated in some manner with an English translation so that the two could be published with the Greek on the verso and the English on the recto, enabling the reader to following the *Rhetoric* in both languages with minimal difficulty.

In his introduction, Freese said that his text made "no pretense of being a critical one" (Freese, 1926, xxvii) but that he had incorporated numerous alterations (supposedly to the Bekker text) proposed by Roemer and others, some of which he footnoted. Freese also referred to other English translations to annotate his English version, and cited such sources as Homer and Euripides to clarify the Greek or the English texts.

Although the Freese edition is certainly not as assiduously done as some of the others referred to in this chapter, it should not be ignored because it is particularly helpful in coordinating the Greek text with the English translation.

THE CONTRIBUTIONS OF FRANCE AND SPAIN

The tennis match between England and Germany was interrupted in the first half of the twentieth century by the appearance of two Greek editions by Dufour and Tovar.

Médéric Dufour (1866-1933) published in 1938 both a Greek and French text of the *Rhetoric* following the Freese format, except that the Greek text was on the recto and the French on the facing verso. It was difficult to locate any biographical details on Dufour, particularly to determine if he had had legal training, because he was not listed in the biographical references and no obituary appeared either in the *Revue des Etudes Grecques*, the *Revue de Philologie*, or in the *Bulletin de l'Association G. Budé*. Fortunately one his outstanding students, l'Abbé André Wartelle of the *Institut Catholique de Paris*, undertook to furnish us with some details of of his life, finding that the records on Dufour had been transferred to the *Archives Nationales* in Paris. In a letter dated October 1, 1985, Wartelle reported that Dufour had had no specific training in law, and had been a teacher of classics at Lille from 1891 to his death in 1933. Apparently the *Rhetoric* was the only work of Aristotle for which Dufour published a translation.

In his introduction, Dufour noted the hierarchy of certain of the Latin and Greek manuscripts and listed the following sources as those on which his Greek and

French texts were based:

    A = Parisinus 1741
    A(1) or A.ead.man. = corrections on the 1741 by the first hand
    A rec = corrections on 1741 in the second hand
    A sup.lin. = corrrections in 1741 between the lines
    A marg = corrections or additions to 1741 in the margins
    X = references to the Vetusta Latin translation
    Guil. = references to the Moerbeck translation

π
    [B = Parisinus 1869
    [C = Parisinus 1818 . . . . the Gaisford MSS
    [D = Parisinus 2038
    [E = Parisinus 2116

θ
    [Q = Marcianus 200
    [Y = Vaticanus 1340
    [Z = Vaticanus 23

    Fragm.Monac. = Monacensis 313
    Monac. = Monacensis 176
    X = *scholia*
    Ald. = 1508 Aldus version
    Venet. = 1546 Venice Gryphius version
    Vict. = 1548-1579 Victorius versions
    Bas.Isingr. = 1560 Basel Isingrinius version
    Morel = 1562 Morelius version
    Sylburg = Frankfurt 1584 edition
    Gaisford = Gaisford 1820 edition
    Bekker = 1831 Bekker edition
    Bekker(3) = Bekker 3rd edition
    Spengel = 1867 Spengel edition
    Cope = Cambridge 1877 edition

The cumulative effect of the preceding Greek editions is evident from the list of sources footnoted by Dufour. By 1938, most of the primary and secondary sources that could be of service in establishing a text were known to scholars. The only major source that Dufour did not consult was the Cambridge MS that was to be used in 1971 by Kassel.

Dufour is meticulous in his annotation of the Greek text. His French translation tends to be literal rather than expansive. For example, in distinguishing ἄτεχνοι and ἔντεχνοι πιότεις, Dufour (1967, I, 76) said "Entre les preuves, les unes sont extra-techniques, les autres techniques." About the "extra-techniques," Dufour said that he understood them to be those that were not developed "par nos moyens personnels" (by means of our own efforts) but "étaient préablement données" (were already available).

Dufour's work made available in French a serviceable translation that can also be of guidance to anyone attempting further translations in any language.

In 1953, Antonio Tovar issued a Spanish translation of the *Rhetoric* in a format similar to the English version offered by Freese and the French version offered by Dufour. A second edition was issued in 1971. Antonio Tovar (1911-) began his teaching career as professor of Latin at the University of Salamanque. Between 1963 and 1967 he was on the faculty of the University of Illinois. From 1967 to 1985, he was professor of comparative linguistics at the University of Tübingen. He has recently retired from his position at Tübingen and has returned to Spain.

Since Tovar had specific instruction in law which he wrote us that he completed to please his father, we asked Tovar what influence his knowledge of law had had upon his translation. In a letter dated Sept. 3, 1985, from his place of retirement in Madrid, Tovar said that it was difficult to tell what effect his three years of the study of law had had upon his work on Aristotle, but that they were of some use to him, "even for some political adversities."

What assistance can Tovar's work be to scholars seeking a clarification of the meaning of the *Rhetoric*? In contrast to Dufour, Tovar is considerably less literal in his interpretation, emphasizing more Aristotle's flow of ideas and deemphasizing the literal meaning of Aristotle's words. The expansiveness of Tovar's treatment is indicated in his preface to the work when he said that "without the trace of a doubt Aristotle was voicing in this text the opinion of the entire Academy." (1953, xxiv) It is possible, therefore, that Tovar had no doubt but that Aristotle's *Rhetoric* was influential in its day, and voiced the opinion of the Peripatetic School.

Concerning the division between what in chapter five we term evidence and argument, Tovar's translation avoided placing the use of evidence outside the scope of the art of rhetoric. The Spanish reads: "De los argumentos retoricos unos son sin arte y otros propios del arte." (1953, 10) An appropriate translation would be "As for rhetorical arguments, some are artless and others require art." Tovar continued by saying: "Llamo sin arte a los que no son logrados por nosotros, sino que preexisten, como los testigos, confesiones en tormento...objeto del arte, los que mediante el método y por nosotros pueden ser dispuestos, de manera que es preciso de aquéllos servirse, estos inventarlos." (1953, 10) This passage could be interpreted as "I term artless those that are not created by us, but which preexist, as the presentations of witnesses, confessions under torture...the nature of arguments entailing art, those achieved by method and design, so that it is necessary to seek out the former, but to invent the latter." Evidence therefore is in Tovar's translation not extra-

Nineteenth & Twentieth Centuries

neous to the art of rhetoric, but simply proofs to be discovered and used rather than invented.

Tovar divided the manuscripts of Aristotle's *Rhetoric* into three families:

first, Parisinus 1741
second, Marcianus 214
third, the manuscripts used by Gaisford and Bekker, which are in turn divided into two subgroups:

π....B or Parisinus 1869
     C or Parisinus 1818
     D or Parisinus 2038
     E or Parisinus 2116

θ.....Z or Vaticanus or Palatinus 23
      Y or Vaticanus 1340
      Q or Marcianus 200

Tovar also recognized the contribution of Monacensis 313.

THE ROSS EDITION OF 1959

The fascination with the text of the *Rhetoric* returned from the continent back to Oxford in 1959 when Ross published his *Aristotelis Ars Rhetorica*. A Scotsman, Sir William David Ross studied classics at Oxford, and was tutor, lecturer and finally professor of moral philosophy at Oxford until 1928. Ross edited the Oxford translations of Aristotle's works between 1908 and 1954. Prior to World War II and during the war years, Ross served the British government extensively on numerous boards and commissions.

Ross chose to follow Roemer's methodology, establishing what he considered to be the preferred text and annotating the sources that varied from his decisions. Ross retained a number of the symbols used by Bekker and Roemer, but added some new ones of his own, choosing to distinguish among what he termed the original, second, and third hands on Parisinus Grec 1741. The sources that he referred to in his notes were as follows:

A = Parisinus 1741 = Bekker Ac
A2 = corrections in the second hand
A3 = later recensions in A
s.l. = above the line corrections
m = marginal corrections
B = Paris 1869   ]
C = Parisinus 1818   ] = θ
D = Parisinus 2038   ] or Gaisford
E = Parisinus 2116   ]
Q = Marcianus 200   ]
Y = Vaticanus 1340 = Bekker Yb]π or
Z = Vaticanus 23 = Bekker Zb   ]Bekker
X = Moerbeck

G = Moerbeck translation
Monac. = Monacensis 176
Frag. = Monacensis 313
X = *scholia*

Ross continued the page designations of Bekker, allowing an easy comparison of Ross with Roemer and the previous Greek collations.

For an evaluation of Ross's contribution, see George Kennedy's review in the 1961 *American Journal of Philology*.

THE KASSEL & SCHNEIDER EDITION

Following the appearance of the Ross edition, the Germans found the ball in their court, and elected to respond with effective publications by Rudolf Kassel and Bern Schneider.

Kassel (1926-   ) began his career as a lecturer at the University of Würzburg. In 1962 he instructed at Oxford, and then in 1963 assumed the post as professor at the *Seminar für Klassiche Philologie im Institute für Altertumskunde* at the Free University of Berlin. Since 1975, Kassel has been a professor at the *Institut für Altertumskunde* at the University of Cologne where he continues to teach and research.

In preparation for his Greek text, Kassel published *Der Text der Aristotelischen Rhetorik* (1971) which was frequently cited in Chapters Two and Three. Then in 1976 appeared his *Aristotelis Ars Rhetorica*. The Kassel text is notable for the following reasons:

1. for the first time, the collation used the second oldest of the MSS, Cantabrigiensis Ff.5.8.
2. the text references all three of the old Latin translations
3. the number of Greek MSS cited has been considerably expanded, in particular to two MSS. in Florence as well as MSS. in Tübingen, Dresden, Madrid and Yale.

Kassel used basically the same technique established by Roemer and Ross. He established his text and footnoted it with variations and their sources. He noted in the left hand column the page, column and lines of the Bekker edition, and, in the right column, he gave the Trapezuntius chapter numbers subdivided by the numbers that the Biponte edition had used to coordinate its Greek and Latin editions.

The thoroughness and detail provided by the Kassel collation make it a major contribution. For all practical purposes, we now have a definitive Greek text of the *Rhetoric*. For an evaluation of Kassel's contribution, see Solmsen's review in the 1979 issue of *Classical Philology*.

In 1971 Bern Schneider, one of Kassel's pupils,

issued his *Die Mittelalterlichen Griechisch-Lateinischen Ubersetzungen der Aristotelischen Rhetorik* which established the hierarchy of the Latin manuscripts of Aristotle's *Rhetoric* and their relationship to Kassel's conclusions concerning the Greek MSS. Schneider edited the Vetus and Moerbeck translations, and revealed his discovery of a fragment of a third edition that Schneider named the Antiqua version.

For his 1971 study, Schneider used the following:

Vetus	Moerbeck	Antiqua
LATIN	LATIN	LATIN
Rq=Parisinus 16673	Oz=Etonensis 129	Bibl.Ducalis 488 Helmst.
Tx=Toletanus 47	Tz=Toletanus 47	
Ck=Chicagiensis Newberrianae,f.23,1	P=Parisinus 16583	
	W1=Guelferbytanus 488	
	W=Vidobonensis 125	
	P(2)=variant readings of P selected from the Antiqua version	
GREEK	GREEK	
A=Parisinus 1741	A=Parisinus 1741	
F=Cantabrigiensis 1298	F=Cantabrigiensis 1298	
H=Marcianus 214	H=Marcianus 214	
ε {Laurentianus {Conv.Sopp.AF {2755 {Tübingensis {Mb 15 {Laurentianus {60	ε=same MSS.noted for the establishment of the Vetus text	
Y=Vaticanus 1340 (rarely cited)	V=Vetus translation	
G=Moerbeck tr.		
G(1)=antiqua tr.		
G(2)=revisions in 2nd hand		

Then, in 1978, Schneider published two Latin editions of Aristotle's *Rhetoric*: the Vetus version and the Moerbeck version. For both Latin texts, Schneider provided as footnotes the relationship of his text to selected Greek sources, and then, in a separate set of footnotes, the relationship of his text to selected Latin sources. For example, in annotating the Anonymous edition, at 1376a6, Schneider used the reading "fatuus qui patrem perimens pueros derelinquit." In the Latin footnotes at the bottom of the page, Schneider indicated that the manuscript he examined at Toledo reads "patre." On that same page, for that same passage, in his Greek footnotes, Schneider observed that the passage "patrem...pueros" could be found in certain Greek texts (those indicated by rell. or, relliqui codices) as "πατέρας..υἱοὺς."

In his appendix, Schneider gave both Greek-to-Latin and Latin-to-Greek indexes. The referrals are found under the former, e.g., under "πίοτεις" in the Greek to Latin index, Schneider gives references using the Bekker system to where such terms as "fides," "credulitas," and "persuasio" may be found in both the Anonymous and the Moerbeck Latin translations. However, under "fides" in the Latin to Greek index, Scheider gives only a cross-reference to "πίοτεις" so that the reader must return to the Greek to Latin index to find where "fides" is used in the Anonymous and Moerbeck translations.

In the process of comparing the Greek and Latin manuscripts, Schneider noted certain trends that he presented in his appendices. The first appendix entitled "I. Lectiones Codicis e Selectae," produced variant readings of codex E (i.e., not in common with others) which, while different from the Greek archetype, agree with readings of Greek texts supplied by the Anonymous translation and by the William of Moerbeck translation and which are not acknowledged in the critical appendix of the edition of Rudolf Kassel.

Appendix II, entitled "Supplementum Lectionum in Editionmem Translationis Guillelmi (G)," enumerates readings of Parisinus 1741 which differ from the text as it has been restored. When these readings are marked by no abbreviation, they are offered by both P1 and P2, which are groupings of the Latin manuscripts. When these readings are designated either P1 or P2, they indicate readings existing only in the first or the second group. Evidently, in comparing the translations, Schneider noted certain trends in the Latin manuscripts, trends that shifted as the manuscripts progressed. Schneider noted 12 different groups of the manuscripts, which he called Pecia I, Pecia II, etc. [Part I, Part II, etc.] Therefore, he continued to regroup the manuscripts, from Part I through Part XII, as he noted shifts in what the manuscripts had in common. For further information about the groupings of the manuscripts, see Schneider's preface.

For establishing his texts, Schneider used the follow-

Nineteenth & Twentieth Centuries
ing sources:

Anonymous	Moerbeck
LATIN	**LATIN**
Rq,Tx,Ck supra	Oz,Tz,Pa,Wl,Wm supra
g=corrections to Moerbeck in first hand	g=corrections to Moerbeck in the first hand
G=corrections to Moerbeck in second hand	G=corrections to Moerbeck in the second hand
	V=Anonymous tr.
GREEK*	**GREEK***
A=1741 with A2 variations	A=1741 with A2 variations
H supra	H supra
F supra	F supra
Co supra	Co supra
Tu supra	Tu supra
La supra	La supra
ε=CoTuLa (in the appendix are readings of codices ε not cited by Kassel but included in this edition	ε=CoTuLa (see Anonymous for meaning of ε
Γ=a lost Greek codex derived from Moerbeck	Γv=Greek text restored with the aid of the Vetusta (Anonymous) tr.
Γg=a codex using an earlier recension	
ΓG=a codex using a later recension	rarely cited:
	Y=Vaticanus 1340
Γv=Greek text which can be restored by the use of the anonymous tr.	schol=Greek scholia from Hugo Rabe's edition
rarely cited:	Ar=Arabic tr
Y=Vaticanus 1340	rell: see Anonymous translation
schol=Greek scholia edition (from the edition of Hugo Rabe)	*refers the reader to Latin in Graeco-Latin appendix; in Latin appendix, * precedes readings that agree with one or another of the Greek readings
rell(relliqui codices): refers only to MSS. acknowledged at the beginning of the appendix	
*=refers the reader to the Latin in the graeco-Latin index and to the graeco-latin in the Latin index	v=comes before listed variant readings in the Graeco-Latin index;indicates readings in agreement with Greek text which can be restored from the Anonymous translation

SUMMARY

The purpose of this chapter was not to offer a critical evaluation of the editions briefly described above. The trends of the translations in developing their systems of referencing the readers are summarized in Table Two.

Each edition made its own contribution and deserves its own place. The purpose of this chapter was to point out that sufficient attention has been given to the establishment of an accurate Greek text so that modern students of the *Rhetoric* can examine the work with the confidence that what should have been done has been done. Although sometime in the future, undoubtedly the English will feel that it is again their turn to develop yet another edition, perhaps using the interpretations of the Paris Arabic edition, the work on the Greek and Latin texts has been thoroughly enough accomplished so that scholars can assume that, unless new evidence proves valuable, the text has been established to a fine proficiency.

BIBLIOGRAPHY

Academia Regia Borussica, ed. (1831-1870). *Aristotelis Opera*. 5 vols. Berlin. Volumes I and II containing the Greek text as established by Bekker appeared first in 1831 under the title, *Aristotelis Graece ex Recensione Immanuelis Bekkeri*. In 1831 also appeared as Volume III *Aristotelis Latine Interpretibus Variis edidit Academia Regias Borussica*, containing the Latin texts responding to Bekker's Greek. The fourth volume of the series, containing the *scholia, Scholia in Aristotelem*. Collegit; Christianus Augustus Brandis, edidit Academia Borussica, was issued in 1836. It was not until 1870 that the fifth volume appeared containing additional *scholia*, some fragments, and the Bonitz *Index*. Its official title was *Aristotelis Qui Ferebantur Librorum Fragmenta. Scholiorum in Aristotelem Supplementum. Index Aristotelicus*. A second edition of the *Index Aristotelicus* by Bonitz was issued by the *Akademische Druck-U. Verlagsanstalt* of Graz in 1955. In 1837 there appeared in England *Aristotelis Opera ex Recensione Immanuelis Bekkeri Accedent Indices Sylburgiani*. 11 vols, Oxford. Vol XI is entitled "Aristotelis de Rhetorica Libri III; de Rhetorica ad Alexandrum; de Poetica, ex Recension Immanuelis Bekkeri."

Aristoteles. (1619). Ἀριστοτέλους Τέχνης Ῥητορικῆς βιβλία τρία. *Aristotelis de Rhetorica seu arte Dicendi Libri tres, Graecolat. Contextu Graeco, ad exemplaria selectiora emendato;*

Latino, Paraphrasi, vbi opus, intertexto.... ed. Edward Goulston, London.

Bekker, I. (1859). *Aristotelis Rhetorica et Poetica: ab Immanuele Bekkero tertium edite*. 2 vols, Berlin.

Bonitz, H. (1870). *Index Aristotelicus*, Berlin.

Brandis, C. (1849). "Uber Aristoteles' Rhetorik und die Greichischen ausleger derselben," in *Philologus, Zeitschrift für das Klassische Alterthum*, ed. F. Schneidewin 4, 1-47 (Göttingen)

Buhle, T., ed. (1793). *Aristotelis Opera Omnia Graece ad Optimorum Exemplarium Fidem Recensuit, Annotationem Criticam, Librorum Argumenta, et Novam Versionem Latinam*... vol. 4, *Rhetorica*, Biponte (Zweibrücken).

Cope, E. (1867). *An Introduction to Aristotle's Rhetoric*, Cambridge, England.

Cope, E. (1877). *The Rhetoric of Aristotle*. ed. J.E.Sandys, 3 vols, Cambridge, England.

Dittmeyer, A.L. (1883). Quae ratio inter vetustam Aristotelis Rhetoricorum translationem et graecos codices intercedat. Diss. Würzburg, Munich.

Dufour, M. (1938). *Aristote Rhétorique*, 3 vols, Paris.

Freese, J.H.. (1926). *The "Art" of Rhetoric*, London, Loeb Classical Library Edition.

Gaisford, T. (1820). *Aristoteles, de Rhetorica Libri Tres, ad Fidem Manuscriptorum Recogniti, cum Versione Latina*, 2 vols, Oxford.

Hill, F.I. (1972). "The Rhetoric of Aristotle," in *A Synoptic History of Classical Rhetoric*, ed. J.Murphy, 19-76, New York.

Kappes, M. (1894). *Aristoteles-Lexikon: Erklarung der Philosophischen Termini Technici des Aristoteles in Alphabetischer Reihenfolge*, Paderborn.

Kassel, R. (1971). *Der Text der Aristotelischen Rhetorik*, Berlin.

Kassel, R. (1976). *Aristotelis Ars Rhetorica*, Berlin.

Kennedy, G. (1961). "Review of W.D. Ross, ed. 'Aristotelis Ars Rhetorica,'" *American Journal of Philology* 82, #2, 201-205.

Kiernan, T.P. (1962). *Aristotle Dictionary*, New York.

Margoliouth, D.S. (1897). "On the Arabic Version of Aristotle's Rhetoric," in *Semitic Studies in Memory of Alexander Kohut*, ed. G.Kohut 376-387, Berlin.

Murphy, J.J. (1972). *A Synoptic History of Classical Rhetoric*, New York.

Niebuhr, B.G. (1842). *Romische Geschichte*, new ed., tr. W. Smith & L. Schmitz. ed. M.Islee, London.

Organ, T.W. (1949). *An Index to Aristotle in English Translation*, Princeton, N.J.

Rabe, H. (1896). *Anonymi et Stephani in Artem Rhetoricam Commentaria*, Leipsig.

Ross, W. (1959). *Aristotelis Ars Rhetorica*, Oxford.

Roemer, A. (1885). *Aristotelis Ars Rhetorica, cum Nova Codicis Ac et Vetustae Translationis Collatione*, Leipsig.

Roemer, A. (1898). *Aristotelis Ars Rhetorica*, Leipsig.

Roemer, A. (1884). "Zur Kritik der Rhetorik des Aristoteles," *Rheinisches Museum für Philologie* 39, 491-510.

Sandys, J. (1908). *A History of Classsical Scholarship*, 3 vols, Cambridge, England.

Schneider, B. (1971). *Die Mittelalterlichen Griechisch-Lateinischen Ubersetzungen der Aristotelischen Rhetorik*, Berlin.

Schneider, B. (1978). *Aristotelis Latinus: Rhetorica*, Leiden.

Solmsen, F. (1979). "Review of R. Kassel's 'Aristotelis Ars Rhetorica,'" *Classical Philology* 74, #1, 68-72.

Spengel, L. (1867). *Aristotelis Ars Rhetorica cum Adnotatione*, 2 vols, Leipsig.

Spengel, L. (1853-1856). *Rhetores Graeci*, 3 vols, Leipsig.

Spengel, L. (1851). *Ueber die Rhetorik des Aristoteles*, Munich.

Thurot, Ch. (1860). *Etudes sur Aristote: Politique, Dialectique, Rhétorique*, Paris. For additional reference to works of Thurot on the *Rhetoric*, see Spengel 1867, xii, n.5

Tovar, A. (1953). *Aristótelis Retórica. Edición del Texto con Aparato Crítico, Traducción (en Español), Prólogo y Notas*, Madrid.

Tovar, A. (1954). "Notas Críticas a la Rhetórica de Aristóteles," *Emerita* 22, 1-34.

Vahlen, I. (1861). "Zur Kritik der Rhetorik des Aristoteles," *Reinisches Museum für Philologie* 9, 555-567.

Vahlen, I. (1861). "Rhetorik und Topik," *Rheinisches Museum für Philologie*, 22, 100-110.

Wartelle, A. (1982). *Lexique de la Rhétorique d'Aristote*, Belles Lettres, Paris.

Wecklein, Nikolaus. (1914-1918). "Adolf Roemer" in *Biographisches Jahrbuch für die Altertumswissenschaft*, 90-98.

NOTES

Quare si in omnibus esset judiciis, perinde ac in nonnullisque nunc est civitatibus,et praesertim bene constitutis,nihil haerent,quod dicerent. Omnes enim partim censent, ita leges oportere iubere,partim vero etiam observant,et prohibent. extra rem dicere; quemadmodum etiam in Areopago; recte ita statuentes,

Quare,si in omnibus judiciis eveniret quemadmodumetiamnum in nonnullis evenit civitatibus, & maxime in iis, quae legibus bene temperatae sunt,nihil haberent,quod dicerent. Omnes enim partim arbitrantur,cavere sic leges oportere;partim vero etiam id observant, & prohibent extra rem dicere,sicut quoque in Areopago;recte ita statuentes.

TABLE ONE

Relationship between Selected Indexes and Editions

SYLBURG GK & LATIN INDEXES 1584	BIPONTE EDITION (no index) 1791	OXFORD GK & LATIN INDEXES 1837	BONITZ INDEX 1870
uses Trapezuntius chaps in Greek text but does not use them in indexing; uses its own pages & line beginning anew in each volume	uses interlineal #'s beginning anew in each chap to corelate Gk at top of page with Latin at bottom of page & Trapezuntius chaps	uses Sylburg Index referenced to Biponte interlineal numbers & Trapezuntius chaps	uses Bekker page, column, line system with Trapezuntius chaps
p. 316 (usually in vol.2 but varies as as to how library catalogued the unnumbered volumes)	vol.4, p.149, chap.15, interlineal #1, line 1, text reads as follows:	vol.11, p.281 of index that follows the Greek text of the Rhetoric:	vol.5, p.119 column two
ἄτεχνοι πίστεις page 7, line 19 page 53, line 10 of the Rhetoric as it appeared in the Sylburg edition pages numbered every 5 lines. Latin index less extensive than Gk & does not always index same terms	περὶ δὲ τῶν ἀτέχνων (this reference does not give chap.15, because this reference begins the chapter.	ἄτεχνοι πίστεις i.2,2 referring to Bk One, Chapter 2, Biponte section two + ἄτεχνοι πίστεων πέρι i.15,1 referring to Bk One, Chaps 15 and 1 so that some cites are limited to book & chapter only	πίστεις ἄτεχνοι Pa 15.2.1355b35 Pa referring to the Rhetoric, Bk a, Chaps 15 and 2, with the 1355b35 indicating the cite in chapter 2.

TABLE TWO

THE DEVELOPMENT OF DIVIDING THE TEXT OF THE RHETORIC INTO CHAPTERS
AND OF DEVELOPING NUMBERING SYSTEMS TO INDICATE SECTIONS OR LINES
OF THE TEXT

MANUSCRIPT OR PRINTED EDITION	GREEK or LATIN TEXT	CHAPTERS	BIPONTE NUMBERS WITHIN CHAPTERS	BEKKER EDITION BK,PAGE,LINE ANNOTATION
???? Aristotle's own MSS	Greek	none		
10th cent 1741 Parisinus	Greek	none		
1256 16097 Parisinus	Latin	varied (9,232)		
15th cent. 4564 Vatican	Latin	15,25,19		
15th cent. 1735 Parisinus	Latin	15,25,19		
15th cent. 43 Hamel Berlin	Latin	15,25,19		
1477 Trapezuntius	Latin	15,26,19		
1481 Moerbeck	Latin	7,6,6		
1499 Moerbeck	Latin	27,46,23		
1504 Trapezuntius	Latin	19,28,19		
1508 Aldine	Greek	none		
1515 Moerbeck	Latin	none		
1515 Trapezuntius	Latin	15,26,19		
1523 Trapezuntius	Latin	15,26,18		
1530 Trapezuntius	Latin	15,26,19		
1544 Barbaro	Latin	41,46,33		
1550 Maioragius	Latin	none		
1562 Maioragius	Latin	15,27,19		
1565 Sigonio	Latin	none		
1577 Muret	Latin	none		
1579 Riccobono	Latin	none		
1584 Sylburg	Greek text	none		
1584 Sylburg index	Greek & Latin	none, only refers to page & line in Sylburg; Gk & Latin indexes do not always		

			reference same terms		
1791 to 1800	Biponti	Greek & Latin texts	15,26,18	irregular marginal numbering within chapters to correlate Greek & Latin texts	
1818	Taylor	English	16,28,19	no Biponte numbers	
1820	Gaisford	Greek	15,26,19	Biponte numbers in margins	
1831	Leipsig	Greek text	15.26.19		
1831	Bekker	Greek in vols.1-2; Latin in vol.3	15,26,19		numbers to page column & line
1837	Oxford	Greek text	15,26,19	followed Biponte irregular numbers	did not use Bekker system
1837	reprint of the 1584 Sylburg index	Greek & Latin	added bks & chaps to Sylburg numbers	Gk & Latin index to book, chapter and Biponte sub-	
1843	Bekker 2nd edition of Rhetoric (seorsim editae)	Greek	15,26,19		did not use Bekker system
1848	Didot*	Greek & Latin text	15,25,19		
1859	Bekker 3rd edition of Rhetoric	Greek	15,26,19		used Bekker system in one margin & numbers lines of this edition 5,10,15,20,25,30 in other margin **
1867	Spengel	Greek & Latin in vol.1;	15,26,19		used Bekker system
1870	Bonitz Index	Greek	15,26,19 index may refer to primary and secondary chaps		used Bekker system
1877	Cope	Greek	15,26,19	used Biponte numbers in left margin	used Bekker system in right margin
1886	Welldon	English	15,26,19		used Bekker

Nineteenth & Twentieth Centuries

					only in ftnotes; marginal numbers are to comparative pages in Welldon
1894 Buckley	English	15,26,19	in left margin		
1894 Roemer	Greek	15,26,19			uses Bekker system
1909 Jebb	English	15,26,19	in left margin		
1926 Freese	English	15,26,19	in left margin of Greek text		uses Bekker in left margin
1932 Cooper	English	15,26,19			uses only Bekker
1953 Tovar	Greek & Spanish	15,26,19			uses only Bekker
1954 Roberts	English	15,25,18			uses only Bekker
1959 Ross	Greek	15,26,19			uses only Bekker
1976 Kassel	Greek	15,26,19			uses only Bekker
1980 Grimaldi	Greek commentary of Bk.I	15 chaps			uses only Bekker

*uses numbers within Greek & Latin texts offered in parallel columns so that the reader can compare the two versions with facility.

**the index at the conclusion of the 1859 edition refers to page and line of that edition, not page and line of the 1831 edition, e.g., περὶ τῶν ἀτέχνων 49,13 to page 49 of the 1859 edition and line 13 on page 49.

CHAPTER FIVE

PERSPECTIVES ON A NEW TRANSLATION OF ARISTOTLE'S RHETORIC

In organizing his thoughts on rhetoric, Aristotle set out to accomplish what so many contemporary philosophers seek to do, namely, to improve on the efforts of their predecessors. Aristotle found the prior treatments of rhetoric inadequate for two reasons: first, because they had emphasized forensic persuasion to the exclusion of other forms [1354b22] and second, because they had concentrated on appeals to the emotions rather than on presenting the logic or reasoning upon which the decision makers could reach a rational conclusion. [1354a14]

Aristotle attempted to correct the first inadequacy by resorting to his customary method of categorization. By asking himself what could be the occasions in which persuasion might be used, Aristotle arrived at his three categories of demonstrative, forensic, and epideictic speaking. In order to enhance the import of his expanded treatment, Aristotle proposed that political persuasion was a more worthy subject than forensic persuasion. [1354b22-27]. Yet, in developing his treatment of rhetoric, Aristotle was often preoccupied with forensic oratory. What reasons might account for this preoccupation? First, the rules and procedures for forensic oratory were more developed in Greece than were the methodologies for demonstrative and epideictic speaking. That is true today. In looking for precepts, therefore, Aristotle would have been likely to turn to law. Second, and this is a matter of speculation because we have amazingly little information about who Aristotle's students were or whether they were few or as many as two thousand (Lynch, 1972, 129), such students as Aristotle had, would likely have wanted to improve their presentations before the courts of law,[1] whereas the number of statesmen who might need his advice would probably be few. Established speakers seldom seek the advice of academics. Demosthenes consulting Isaeus is the exception that proves the rule. (Bonner, 1927, 260) Young men who wished to use the law as a springboard for their political aspirations were more likely subjects.

In an attempt to rectify the second inadequacy of a lack of reasoned discourse, Aristotle held that "proofs are the only things that have a proper place in persuasion; all else is extraneous." [1354a13-14] Furthermore, he added that "the introduction of prejudice, compassion, anger and other such emotions has no connection with the issue at hand, but is directed only to the trier of fact." [1354b16-18] In Athens, the trier of fact, the δικαστής, held a position similar to three other types of decision makers: first, the citizen judges in Rome within certain classes at certain times (Enos, 1975, 381); second, the present citizen judges in Vermont; third, *die Geschwornen* in West Germany.[2] These modern lay judges sit along side the trained judge in trials for minor offenses. In Germany they can interrogate the accused and the witnesses and vote along with the trained judge. The citizen judges in Athens, known as the dicasts, about which more will be said later, were not "jurors" in the typical sense because they performed the role of both judges and jurors. The inference in the *Rhetoric* for which Aristotle offers no proof is that such persons might be susceptible to irrelevant emotional arguments, e.g., a contemporary attorney might argue to citizen judge-jurymen: "Members of the court, have compassion on this poor man, not necessarily because his cause is just, but because he has a wife and six children to support."

In opposing vigorously the introduction of irrelevant material into rhetorical discourse, Aristotle was undoubtedly continuing a battle that has persisted into modern times.[3] But Aristotle knew that all argument and evidence with strong emotional appeals could not be excluded from rhetorical discourse, e.g., in modern courtroom practice, the victims of a cutting may be permitted to display their healing wounds to the jury, and women may exhibit children to demonstrate fatherly likeness. But there are always litigants who attempt to introduce emotion when its accompanying argument or evidence is irrelevant. Therefore Aristotle rejoiced that, in his time, there were courts that banned irrelevant pleas to the emotions. As an example, he pointed to the highest criminal court in Athens, convening on the hill of Ares, hence known as the Ἄρειος πάγος. At one point Aristotle said that irrelevant speaking was banned there because of νόμος,[4] which could be translated as "because of custom" or "because of the common law."[5] Although the lack of readily available transcripts of prior cases contributed to keeping common law in Greece from achieving the place that it assumed in England after the invention of the printing press, there is no reason to think that "common law"[6] in the form of a custom could not have excluded certain forms of emotional argument in courts with which Aristotle was familiar.[7] There need not have been a "statute" banning such presentations. Local custom could have excluded it. Indeed, in his *Politics* (1319b40-1320a1), Aristotle encouraged as a means of insuring stability the "enactment" of both written and unwritten laws, i.e., statutes and the common law. Also, in his *Metaphysics* (995a3-4), Aristotle found that "the power of custom is clearly seen in the laws, in which the mythical and childish beliefs prevail over our knowledge about them, because of custom." Although, as Bonner (1927, 181) pointed out, Athenian tribunals were not bound by precedent, still the reliance upon doing what was customary was strong. Aristotle himself recommended the citation of previous cases familiar to the court, and Bonner noted that "in the extant speeches cases are not infrequently cited." (1927, 181). Still it would have been by custom rather than by case law that untoward emotion would have been banned from the courts. "By unwritten law," said Cronin, "[Aristotle] means all the unwritten principles which are supposed to be acknowldged everywhere." (1936, 21) Undoubtedly Aristotle would have been pleased if his treatise had expanded the custom of applying unwritten or "common law" to ban irrelevant emotion from Athenian courts in general.

Therefore Aristotle set out to develop an expanded treatment of rhetoric to include what he established as the three forums for persuasion. In spite of often slipping and thereby giving undue emphasis to forensic persuasion, Aristotle was moderately successful in maintaining his tri-parte perspective on rhetoric. He also set out to confine emotional arguments in their proper place and to exclude them when they were extraneous. However, that "proper place" was not then, and is not now, too well defined, and Aristotle knew that his treatment would have to include a detailed discussion of the emotions. Aristotle desired above all things to present a comprehensive treatment of his subject, and he recognized that evidence and argument intrinsically involve emotional appeals.

If these were Aristotle's two goals in his expansion of the treatment of rhetoric, how well were they executed in the general context of the treatise? Furthermore, how successful have the English translations been in conveying Aristotle's objections and the solutions he offered? In general, how well have the translations presented concepts faithful to the collated version of the Greek text as established by contemporary scholars?

OBJECTIVES VS EXECUTION

At first we thought that these two questions could best be answered by comparing the merits of the more recent English translations, pointing out when they were faithful to Aristotle's objectives and when they missed the mark. However, as work progresssed in collating the translations, it became apparent that, according to our interpretation, all of the modern English translations had rather equally misunderstood certain basic concepts and that these misunderstandings had prevented the translations from demonstrating the changes that Aristotle had intended to make. The faulty rendition of the misleading passages could be attributed largely to the fact that none of the translators possessed all three qualities necessary to produce a faithful translation:

(1) a knowledge of Greek;
(2) the *knowledge* and *application* of the perspectives of rhetoric. both in Greece and in contemporary society
(3) the *knowledge* and *application* of the perspectives that law assumed toward communication in Greece and in contemporary law

Since Aristotle was trying to distinguish persuasion in law from persuasion in his two other forms of speaking and since he was hoping to relegate emotion to its proper sphere in court as well as in other forms of rhetorical discourse, it would take a person sensitive to the application of both rhetoric and law to keep Aristotle's perspectives straight.

We are not proposing that a reorientation of the translations properly acknowledging the legal and rhetorical implications of the *Rhetoric* would change all aspects of Aristotle's theories. What we are proposing is that, without recognizing the degree to which Aristotle drew from Athenian law and custom, major portions and concepts of the *Rhetoric* can be distorted and certain passages can either be misunderstood or not recognized for their proper implications.

It may be difficult for some to acknowledge the inadequacies of previous translators to present to us portions of the *Rhetoric*. Perhaps these comments will help. First, Aristotle was one of those few in the history of the world who have been multifaceted. In order to comprehend the *Rhetoric*, achieving the status of a Greek scholar is only one facet. Similar achievements have to be made in the fields of Aristotle's specialities. In order to approach Aristotle's position, the translators have to do more than just study rhetoric and law. They have to meet the qualifications of those professions. Society has of course seen other highly multifaceted persons such as Michelangelo. In the twentieth century, Albert Schweitzer qualified himself in medicine, music and theology. The challenge of interpreting the *Rhetoric* is formidable. One would not argue that Russian scholars who "read up" on medicine would meet the qualifications to translate a complex Soviet medical treatise. One would not hire a scholar unschooled in practicing theology to interpret the philosophies of the ecumenical movement. Nor should one expect of scholars, without meeting rigorous professional standards, to achieve the degree of expertise that would permit them to understand those concepts and passages of Aristotle's treatise that blend law and rhetoric.

Furthermore, the intensity of the study of rhetoric in modern society has only recently achieved the level that it had reached in Greece and Rome. Persons who deserve the modern appellation of "rhetorician" are not now Greek scholars who have explored the classical and post-classical literature but rather specialists who have spent years of training in examining rhetorical concepts and who have continued their studies by research and publication. The number of such classical scholars as George Kennedy, James Murphy, and Richard Enos who have also qualified themselves in rhetorical theory is highly limited.

The study of law, in the United States, Germany, and England, requires an extended period of intensive training followed by study, practice and often scholarly writing. It is the perspective on law gathered by these experiences that differentiates the lawyer from the Greek scholar who has studied the law of Athens and who has read treatises on rhetoric. Legal training emphasizes that its students learn "to think like lawyers," and rhetorical training involves a wide breadth of rhetorical study that results in students learning "to think like rhetoricians."

Therefore, as difficult as it may be for some to question their deserved respect for the previous translators of the *Rhetoric*, we ask scholars to consider at least that the previous translators of the *Rhetoric* may not have possessed all of the proficiencies that they should have had to render most faithfully the sweep as well as the nuances of certain aspects of Aristotle's *Rhetoric*. Although it will not be possible for this chapter to prove this point in every respect, sufficient examples will be given to establish at least the possibility that considerable improvement can and should be made in the existing English translations.

Instead of comparing the faithfulness of the English translations to the Greek text and thereby making judgments on what is now available, this chapter proposes to add insight into a future translation and thereby to provide guidelines for a new English text more faithful to the knowledge of rhetoric and law, a knowledge that will be demonstrated by the observations of this chapter. What is offered here is the structure on which a translation could in part be based. Again, we do not propose that the proper perspectives on rhetoric and law will radically change all phases of the translation of the *Rhetoric*. We do propose, however, that these perspectives can make fundamental changes in the treatise as a whole and in certain of its parts.

Therefore, this perspective on a new English translation will discuss three concepts that should serve as part of the foundation for a fresh treatment of Aristotle's outlook on rhetoric:

 a. a more consistent vocabulary
 b. a reorientation of certain basic concepts in the *Rhetoric*
 c. a proper recognition of certain of Aristotle's nuances

A CONSISTENT VOCABULARY

As was observed in Chapter One, the text of the *Rhetoric* we now possess most likely consists of one version of Aristotle's lecture notes or perhaps a reading that was available to those who missed his lectures. (Ross, 1942, xi) Some of the inconsistencies in terminology that do exist (and they are comparatively few, considering the opportunities for textual distortion pointed out in Chapters One and Two) can be attributed in part to the reality that we are working from less than what Aristotle would have issued had he been asked for a perfected text. As Kennedy (1980, 61) pointed out, Aristotle's *Rhetoric* is "a draft of his theories without literary adornment, intended for his own use and for his students and not for publication." Kennedy (1980, 61) proposed that the custom of footnotes and appendices being unknown to Aristotle, the insertions that Aristotle made from time to time can result in a seeming disorganization and can leave some points obscure. We assume that, when he lectured, Aristotle clarified these sections, as he clarified his vocabulary. Moreover, as we know, persons with varying expertise revised and reworked Aristotle's treatise during the Greek and Roman period. In spite of all this, Aristotle's vocabulary on basic nomenclature is remarkably consistent. The difficulty with the translations is that, before beginning their work, the authors did not establish a lexicon that would reflect with feasible consistency Aristotle's points of view on law and rhetoric. The translators often appear to have reconciled each term as it appeared in its particular context, supplying an appropriate meaning for that passage. That meaning made sense for an isolated phrase, but it may have failed to provide proper continuity with the use of that term in previous contexts. The English translators, therefore, have made Aristotle appear less direct and more fragmented than he deserves to be. Naturally Aristotle sometimes used a particular word in more than one of its meanings. And Aristotle can use more than one word to express the same concept. Therefore some of his terminology is difficult to translate without supplying varying terminology. However, in our opinion, the meanings assigned can be done with much more consistency than the English translations reflect. Some translators and commentators have been so preoccupied with the leaves and trees in the well-cut over and replanted forest of the text of the *Rhetoric* that they have lost sight of the plan of the forest that Aristotle so carefully designed. The lexicon below can be faulted for being too consistent. In an effort to achieve continuity, and in the hope of counteracting the somewhat random approach used by previous translators, these suggestions may be too restrictive. Therefore we may have fallen into the trap that Roberts assigned to Roemer. (1924, 356) The result may be a terminology that will require some softening and more pliability before being incorporated into a comprehensive translation.

τέχνη

The noun, τέχνη, is the most difficult of all of Aristotle's terms to translate. It may be best to give up, as Roberts did with πίστεις, and say that no satisfactory English term or phrase exists, although, most of the time, it should be evident to the reader what Aristotle had in mind when he used τέχνη. To the Greeks, a τέχνη was something teachable, something that possessed a methodology the application of which could result in improvement. If rhetoric was a τέχνη, a person did not have to be born with a talent for rhetoric to use it effectively, and a person did not have to acquire his abilities through the school of hard knocks. Persuasion, asserted Aristotle, had a disciplinary procedure that responded to a teachable system.

It is really not possible to contrast a τέχνη with a τριβή which can mean "knack," which is knowledge required merely through practice without instruction, e.g., a preacher might learn to use the figure of speech known as χιασμός just by preaching enough and running across χιασμοί by accident and finding that it worked and practicing it until he perfected its usage. (cf. Plato, *The Phaedrus*, 260e where Socrates does contrast in some manner τέχνη with τριβή.) The word τέχνη is not properly contrasted with τύχη, which, in Greek meant something that transpired by coincidence, i.e., two people meeting by coincidence in the market place. These same people could have planned to meet in the market place, so it did not require a knack or talent for the meeting to take place, but, when they did not so plan but just happened to run across each other, their chance meeting was a τύχη. There does not appear to be a Greek term which expresses the opposite of τέχνη. (Cf. Smith, 1985, 104.)

Interestingly enough, modern teachers are still trying to make the same point that rhetoric is a discipline that can be taught. Because children learn to speak and listen, in some fashion, through the "school of hard knocks," whereas most children learn to read and write later in life, under the supervision of teachers, society often holds that instruction in speaking and listening is not needed—indeed, that it is not even possible to teach speaking and listening. Speaking and listening, it is said, are not τέχνοι. Speaking is a τριβή, something just acquired by happenstance or through a knack that just comes naturally.

If we can visualize a society in which certain children were deaf mutes until the age of six, but were instructed to read and write early, and then at six these children had their hearing restored so that they could be instructed in speaking and listening, we might imagine a society that would insist on a systematized method of instruction in speaking and listening.

In Greece, there was a strong motivation supplied by rewards for those who could speak effectively. Those ambitious for political office in both Greece and in Rome (Enos, 1975, 394) used the law courts to perfect their style and then proceeded into politics. The means by which they perfected their oral style had to meet what Bonner (1927, 200 ff.) and Bonner and Smith (1930, 7-10) pointed out was the progressive role that trained advocates were permitted to play in the courts. Although at first litigants were supposed to represent themselves, Bonner (1927, 180) noted that "by the middle of the fourth century the practice of securing advocates is firmly established." Since so much of communication in Greece was oral, society placed much value on those who could perfect an admirable oral style. As in the barn-like French revolutionary assemblies, the speaker who commanded a powerful voice in the Greek open-air courts could make himself heard and thereby gain power. So the Athenians may have been more sympathetic than we are to Aristotle when he proposed that, even though people can speak after a fashion without instruction, there were methodologies by which they could learn to speak better. The dearth of major colleges and universities that require courses in oral rhetoric in comparison to those that require courses in written rhetoric is in part a vestige of the theory that oral speech develops "naturally" whereas written composition is a τέχνη or methodology that can be taught.

What was Aristotle trying to say in proposing that rhetoric was a τέχνη? He was proposing that persuasion is a discipline, something that can be taught, a type of learning, a methodology that can be reduced to systematic treatment. The English words "skill," "technique" and "art" all have modern connotations that can be misleading. "Skill" and "technique" imply sophistry. Aristotle himself lamented that rhetoric, unlike logic, had not a Greek term that differentiated between the ethical and unethical uses of rhetoric. [1355b18-21] The dialecticians, noted Aristotle, were contrasted with the sophists; whereas, when the Greeks said that speakers were using rhetoric, their audiences could not tell whether the term referred to the speakers' ethical or unethical use of rhetoric.

It seems best to conclude that, since modern English lacks a satisfactory rendition, the new English translation should retain the Greek term τέχνη and use a footnote to clarify the meaning.

Aristotle also used τέχνη to refer to a treatise or text on the subject of persuasion, as in ἐν τῇ τέχνῃ. [1356a10-13][8] The best translation for this usage appears to be "textbook" or "handbook." In the plural, the τέχναι or the "Arts" (Kennedy, 1963, 54 ff.; 1980, 18 ff.) included the treatises that Aristotle found objectionable. It is understood, of course, that an author only writes a text if the author relies on the premise that what is being written about is teachable.

'πίστεις' and the two divisions of 'πίστεις', 'ἄτεχνοι πίστεις' and 'ἔντεχνοι πίστεις'

The problem of interpreting what Aristotle meant by πίστεις and by the two divisions of πίστεις, ἄτεχνοι πίστεις and ἔντεχνοι πίστεις, has given scholars considerable difficulty. The solution to the problem can be simplified if we recall three concepts:

a. *Although Aristotle protested that he wanted to expand his treatise to include not only forensic speaking but also deliberative and epideictic speaking, his treatise continued to apply well-developed legal concepts to political and occasional speaking*, e.g., the discussion of the emotions often reflects the role of fear in the courtroom, a role that could be transferred to the role of fear in politics and in occasional speaking.

b. *Aristotle leaned heavily on legalistic concepts for the superstructure of his treatment of rhetoric*, e.g., the division of proofs into "argument" and "evidence" is a legal concept that Aristotle applied to all three types of speaking.

c. *Because the treatise consisted originally only of Aristotle's lecture notes and because the possibilities are great for distortion and revision of these notes by those who succeeded Aristotle, not much can be learned by relying upon how and where a given word or phrase now exists in the treatise*. For, such a word or phrase may not be where and how Aristotle placed it at all. What can be relied upon are the general trends of the treatise and the concepts that it portends.

The first two premises above require some amplification. What must be remembered is that, as Bonner said (1927, 110), the Athenians "were a nation of lawyers." Bonner (1927, 110) noted that Athenians "were extraordinarily familiar with legal processes." He pointed to the plays of Aristophanes and in particular to the *Wasps* and the *Parliament of Women*, to show that Aristophanes' jests would not have been comprehensive to the general Athenian audience if the populace had not been familiar with even the intricacies of the law. "Litigation," said Bonner, "permeated the entire citizen body to a degree quite impossible in modern communities." (1927, 110) Public officials were under continual scrutiny, and if they were sued for malfeasance, they waited their turn to sue someone else.

To go to an extreme, it might be said, as is now true in London, that the law courts were "the best show in town."

If Athenians in general were imbued with the law, Aristotle in particular must have been saturated with its detail. As an observant and responsible citizen, it was his obligation in Athens to forward the public good. He needed to know the law, not only for his students but in order to fulfill his duties as a citizen. Therefore, it should not surprise us that, when he slowly developed a theory of rhetoric to supplant "the Arts" that he scorned, Aristotle consciously or unconsciously drew from the developed precepts of law for some of the bases for his treatise. Since there were few or no superstructures or "words of art" for deliberative and epideictic speaking, Aristotle could not draw from them. He deplored the lack of treatment of these types of speaking. If there had been developed methodologies for deliberative and epideictic speaking, certainly Aristotle would have acknowledged them, or evaluated them, as he did "the Arts" developed largely for forensic speaking. True, the precepts of Gorgias could be widely applied, and Gorgias himself delivered occasional addresses to Athenian audiences which were well received. But, in some areas of rhetoric, there were no vocabularies and no superstructures for the other two types of speaking. Therefore, Aristotle drew from what he had and from what he knew so well. As he proceeded, he appeared to find the precepts of forensic speaking generally applicable to deliberative and epideictic oratory, so he had no reason to retreat from his conscious or unconscious decision to use many of the perspectives of law as bases for his discussion. If the Athenians in general were "extraordinarily familiar with legal processes," Aristotle must have been whatever would be the superlative of Bonner's conclusion. The remainder of this chapter will show how Aristotle's familiarity with law influenced his writing of the *Rhetoric*.

Assuming therefore that Aristotle's treatise often applied legal concepts to deliberative and epideictic speaking and that considerable of Aristotle's superstructure was taken directly from the accepted practices of Athenian law, what are the legalistic concepts that form some of the bases for Aristotle's treatment of rhetoric?

Aristotle was faced with the dilemma previously cited. He had witnessed enough discourse in all three of his categories to know that emotion and character played an important part in persuasion, so important in fact that the treatises existing in his time, he proposed, were largely devoted to $\mathring{\eta}\theta o\varsigma$ and $\pi\acute{a}\theta o\varsigma$. Aristotle objected to such treatises as shallow and ill-fitting. They failed, he said, to treat rhetoric as it deserved. He therefore protested that he would stress proofs to an extent far exceeding the existing treatises.

But, being a realist, Aristotle did not wish to leave out the role played by $\mathring{\eta}\theta o\varsigma$ and $\pi\acute{a}\theta o\varsigma$. Aristotle wished to lay considerable emphasis on the enthymeme which, as Grimaldi (1972, 16) pointed out, involved "the interplay of reason and emotion in discourse." To put it into the vernacular, how could Aristotle "have his cake and eat it too?"

He found the solution in the legalistic concept that rhetoricians are only obliged to "discover" the available means of persuasion, to present them to the decision makers, and to let the decision makers decide who should succeed. In short, this attitude toward persuasion was used by the adversarial system in Aristotle's time just as it is used by the adversarial system in the twentieth century.

Aristotle could excuse the speaker, in the course of his "discovering," for "inventing" ethical and emotional proofs as well as "inventing" inductive and deductive reasoning, because the speaker was not "persuading" the judges, but only presenting to them what the speaker had "discovered" for their consideration. The decision makers were to make use of what they chose of the proofs that the speaker had discovered. Grimaldi (1972, 5) arrived at the same posture when he said that "in this matter of 'persuasion' Aristotle's thesis is simply that good rhetoric effectively places before the other person all the means necessary for...decision making."

Therefore Aristotle was reinforcing the reforms of Solon as they are cited in the $\mathring{A}\theta\eta\nu\alpha\acute{\iota}\omega\nu\ \Pi o\lambda\iota\tau\varepsilon\acute{\iota}\alpha$ or Athenian Constitution (vi-xi), a work that was long considered lost but was partially restored by Kenyon with the aid of a comparatively recently discovered papyrus. Solon's code law needed interpretation. It was not to be interpreted by an oligarchy or an aristocracy, but administered by the people themselves who could be appealed to by any injured person. Aristotle repeated what he stated in the *Rhetoric*, that laws need interpretation and cited in *The Constitution* the laws of inheritance. (ix, 2) Therefore, according to Aristotle's definition, in sympathy with Solon's position, the people were to be presented with the proofs and were then free to make their own decisions.

Inherent in what should be the role of the judges and what should be the role of the speakers was Aristotle's position that men largely exercised free will. It is not possible here to explore the concepts of Aristotle's *Ethics*, but it is necessary to say that Aristotle could arrive at his definition because he believed that the judges not only had the free will to arrive at their decisions, but that they could judge the ethics of the pleaders on the basis that "both goodness and badness have to do with things where a man is himself the cause and origin of his actions." (*Eudemian Ethics*, 2, 1223a14-16) Given the proofs in which the actor clearly commits "voluntarily all the acts that he commits purposely," (*Eudemian Ethics*, 2, 1223a18-19) the judges can judge, not on the basis of fate or what the Gods ordered, but on what the litigants themselves have voluntarily done. Once presented with the proofs, the judges were free to make their decisions.

It is a truism of present law that the court decides upon questions of law and the jury decides upon questions of fact. In establishing a "judicial fact," the judge and/or jury have to take a debatable proposition, e.g., "The defendant John was at home the night of the robbery," and accept or reject it. If they accept it, it becomes a "judicial fact," whether John actually was or was not at home the night of the robbery. Since, in Aristotle's time, the judge and the jury were blended into one, the dicasts had to decide both questions of law and questions of judicial fact. The communicator, therefore, had the obligation to "discover" what the judges ought to know of the law *and* the facts, to articulate these views to the judges, and then let the judges make the decisions.

If the reaction to Aristotle's position is that he resorted to a slight-of-hand trick and that, in Aristotle's treatise, the speaker is advised not only to "discover" and "invent" but also to *interpret* what he discovers and invents in a manner that appeals most effectively (a) to the judge's reasoning, (b) to the judge's emotions, and (c) to the judge's opinions about character, we must add that the same slight-of-hand trick exists in contemporary courts of law, and that the myth of the jury deciding the facts and the judge deciding the law independently of the persuasive speaking of the lawyer remains today.

Furthermore, Roberts (1954, 351) quite rightly defended Aristotle's treatise for pointing out why attorneys should make use of arguments and evidence on both sides of the issue by reminding his readers of Aristotle's explanation that, in order to defend right properly, speakers must envisage how wrong will be argued so that they oppose wrong more effectively. For a person not skilled in law, such a qualification by Aristotle may be necessary to redeem "even the treacherous or arid ground along which the *Rhetoric* sometimes passes." (Roberts, 1954, 351) The practicality of being taught to represent both sides of the issue was pointed out by Bonner (1927, 157 ff.) who showed how Xenophon's education enabled him to switch sides in a political dispute because of his training in rhetoric.

But our present law courts would not even demand Roberts' explanation of why a student should be able to plead either side of a case, and for even a sounder reason than the one pointed out by Aristotle. The modern adversarial system holds that each party to a suit is entitled to the best case it can present and that attorneys are obligated to "discover" (i.e., to investigate) the available means of persuasion for their cases and present them to the court, whether the attorneys believe that the position they are advocating is right or wrong. It is the courts via the judges and juries that make judgmental decisions. Lawyers have no right in modern Anglo-Saxon justice to prejudge the case, for lawyers might be in error and therefore a party would be unable to find a qualified advocate to present to the court an adequate statement of proofs. The deemphasis of the professional lawyer in Athenian courts did not allow this concept to develop as fully as it has in English and American law. Aristotle did not discuss this posture, since, theoretically, each accused was in general capable of presenting his own case. Later, when hiring advocates became acceptable, the Anglo-Saxon attitude guaranteeing that every litigant is entitled to an appropriate presentation may have become operational. For this study, however, no evidence of that attitude was found.

If it is Aristotle's position that communicators are to "discover" the available means of persuasion and present them to the court, what are speakers advised via their invention to discover? They are advised to discover exactly what present-day attorneys are advised to discover: "evidence" and "argument"[9], or ἄτεχνοι πίστεις and ἔντεχνοι πίστεις. Cope exaggerated Aristotle's position in proposing that Aristotle relegated ἄτεχνοι πίστεις to an inferior position by saying that ἄτεχνοι πίστεις only need to be employed. (1877, 1, 28, n.2) Aristotle so advised because that is all that a lawyer is supposed to do with evidence. Doing anything other than "discovering" the evidence and presenting it to the court would be tampering with the evidence. Pleadors in Aristotle's time were not supposed to do anything more or any less than present-day pleaders are supposed to do with evidence. Yet the discovery and presentation of evidence were an integral part of the art of rhetoric in Aristotle's time, just as they are an integral part of rhetoric today. Although attorneys cannot "invent" ἄτεχνοι πίστεις, they have to have "a good nose" for "discovering" ἄτεχνοι πίοτεις, in ferreting out evidence and in persuading third parties to cooperate in making that evidence available to the court. As MacDowell said, "before the trial came on, each litigant had to get together the evidence which he wished to present to the jury." (1978, 242) MacDowell pointed out that μάρτυς "may mean a person who appears in court to give evidence about something." (1963, 105) Seeking out those witnesses, preparing them for trial, and quite possibly questioning them as they gave their testimony, was one of the chief obligations of the Athenian "attorney." Therefore, although ἄτεχνοι πίοτεις may not be a part of the canon of invention, it forms an integral part of what Aristotle included in his definition of rhetoric. Wartelle (1982, 172) listed "inventer" as one of the possible meanings of εὑρίσκειν together with "trouver" and "découvrir." In French, one of the meanings of "inventer" is "to discover." Therefore, the meaning of "to invent" as a translation of εὑρίσκειν is apparently more appropriate in French than it is in English. But, in his definition of rhetoric, Aristotle used the verb θεωρεῖν which to Wartelle meant "to contemplate" or "to consider." It is, therefore the responsibility of the rhetorician "to consider" all of the proofs that may be helpful in each particular case.

The Roman period can be held responsible in part for relegating evidence to an inferior position in rhetoric. In fact, it was the Roman period, not Aristotle, that began the emphasis on the term, "invention," to the exclusion of proofs other than those that the orator invented. Aristotle himself made very limited use of the term "invention" in his treatise. Bonitz did not index it in the *Rhetoric* and noted only a few instances in which the noun εὕρεσις is used in other Aristotelian works. The Wordsearch computer search of the Department of Classics at the University of North Carolina generated no usages of εὕρεσις in the *Rhetoric*. In contrast, both Cicero in his *De Inventione* (I, vii, 9) and Quintilian in his *Institutes of Oratory* (I, 12, 4) placed their stress on the search for the proofs that the orator must invent, the so-called canons of rhetoric. There was no emphasis upon the proofs that the orator had to "discover," perhaps again, because as in Greece, the Roman courts did not have to confront the intricacies of evidence faced by modern European and American tribunals. The hearsay rule with a number of exceptions was in force in Athens (Bonner, 1905, 20; Bonner, 1927, 185-186; Bonner & Smith, 1930, II, 130), but we are not as clear as we would like to be even on the functioning of the hearsay rule. Although, as Bonner (1905, 12) pointed out, "our materials for constructing the history of the law of evidence are comparatively limited," we can be certain that, because there was no judge to interpret court procedures, the need for a lawyer to "discover" evidence that would meet the requirements of the court was less demanding than what is required of contemporary lawyers.

Still, Aristotle was well aware that the "discovered" proofs needed their appropriate place, and he gave it to them. It is interesting to note that present legal concepts speak of the "rules of discovery." Whatever is "discovered" in the way of evidence is generally made available to the opposition, via contemporary rules of discovery. In criminal trials, the prosecution is obliged to reveal to the defense any relevant evidence that it has "discovered" that may be of assistance to the defense, whereas the defense in criminal trials is under no obligation to reveal to the prosecution what it may have "discovered." Aristotle's use of "discover" has, either by accident or design, maintained itself into the twentieth century.

Of course, both ancient and modern pleadors have attempted to do more than just discover and present their evidence. They try to bring out the reasoning, the emotion and the character of that evidence in a manner most favorable to their side of the case. But the contemporary judge stands as a vigilant referee, to limit the invasion of attorneys and to confine their role to that of the "discoverer" and "presenter," relegating to the courts decisions about matters of law and to the juries decisions about matters of judicial fact. But the judge's vigilance can only be so successful; and the slight-of-hand trick fails, in modern trials as it did in Aristotle's time, to limit successfully the role of the pleador. Therefore, attorneys may imbue the evidence they have "discovered" and "presented" with emotion where none may be needed, attempt to invade the independence of the witness by asking inappropriately leading questions, and, by changes in voice inflection and posture, add their own persuasive implications to the evidence they are presenting. Some courts, of course, permit more invasion by the lawyers than others. MacDowell reasoned that the judges in the Ἄρειος πάγος, being more experienced and constituting what has been estimated as two hundred in number rather than the estimated five hundred in an heliastic jury, were less susceptible to emotional arguments. (1963, 42)[10]

But the distinction between "persuading" and "discovering the available means of persuasion" solved Aristotle's dilemma, and allowed him to present in his treatise the uses that the pleador could make of emotion and character without specifically causing Aristotle to fall into the trap of his predecessors.

In his *Poetics* (1450b8-10), Aristotle gave us a clue as to how he might have conceived of the presentation of ἦθος within his definition of rhetoric. "Character," said Aristotle, "is that which reveals choice, shows what sort of thing a man chooses or avoids in circumstances where the choice is not obvious, so those speeches convey no character in which there is nothing whatever which the speaker chooses or avoids." (tr. Fyfe, 1927, 29) In the law courts, speakers choose their proofs, and therefore would use, said Aristotle, ethical proof. But it is also possible for the judges to make a choice as to what proof presented by the speaker the judges will accept. Therefore, speakers can "present" their ethical proof by choosing what they will or will not present, but the judges can exercise their choice of accepting or rejecting what the speakers have presented, thus permitting speakers to "offer" proof and the judges to accept or reject it.

Grimaldi (1980, 349-356) was sufficiently concerned about clarifying the meaning of πίστεις that, at the conclusion of his commentary, he added a special appendix to unite what had been his several remarks about πίστεις as he proceeded with his commentary. Earlier, in discussing 1354a4, Grimaldi (1980, 19) had pointed out that Aristotle used πίστεις in three different ways.[11] First, Aristotle used the concept of πίστεις to signal that a belief had been achieved. Such a usage was to be expected, and we would use a form of πίστις to indicate "a state of being persuaded." It is when Grimaldi proposed a distinction in his second and third categories of Aristotle's use of πίστεις that we differ from Grimaldi's position. On what bases are our differences with Grimaldi based?

First, Grimaldi's admirably detailed discussion of Aristotle's use of proofs in the appendix to his commentary is based upon a painstaking search of the consecutive wording of the *Rhetoric* as we now know it, attempting to rationalize phrases that appear early in the treatise with subsequent phraseology. As we pointed out in Chapter One, such an approach can lead to difficulties. We are not certain that any amount of restoration of the Greek text can restore the readings as they were in Aristotle's time. Too much opportunity has arisen for distortion to try to fix Aristotle's ideas by linking one sentence to another. Not only are we sufficiently unsure of Aristotle's original language to permit extended speculation by comparing phraseologies, but, even if we were certain that the text we now have was faithfully Aristotelian, we would have to face the reality that we are examining lecture notes and not a polished treatise. Lecture notes can frequently contain non-sequiturs that are easily explainable by the lecturer but obscure to the unassisted examiner.

Not only do we depart from Grimaldi's position on the basis of the nature of the text itself, but we cannot share Grimaldi's puzzlement as to why Aristotle does not always clarify the position of each element discussed in relation to the whole. Our position is that Aristotle had established a superstructure that was clear in his mind, and he explained that superstructure to those who listened to his treatise. The superstructure was able to provide categories for the ideas he presented. Therefore, Grimaldi's statement (1980, 351) that "identifying the πίστεις as ἐνθύμημα, ἦθος, and πάθος causes sheer confusion" can be easily explained by reminding ourselves that the πίστεις were not ἐνθύμημα, ἦθος, and πάθος, but rather λόγος, ἦθος, and πάθος, as Aristotle pointed out on lines 1356a1-4, and that λόγος has two subdivisions by which the speaker can "demonstrate" his proofs, the enthymeme and the example. Not only does such an explanation solve the dilemma Grimaldi presented on p. 351, but it also resolves his confronting the possibility that Aristotle ended up with four ἔντεχνοι πίστεις rather than three (1980, 353). What Grimaldi would classify as two types of ἔντεχνοι πίστεις are rather subdivisions of the third category, λόγος. Grimaldi (1972, 56) said that "nowhere in the *Rhetoric*, or indeed elsewhere in his writings..." did Aristotle identify the enthymeme as one of the three ἔντεχνοι πίστεις. The reason that Aristotle did not so identify the enthymeme is that, rather than being one of the three ἔντεχνοι πίστεις, it is instead a subdivision of one of the three ἔντεχνοι πίστεις:

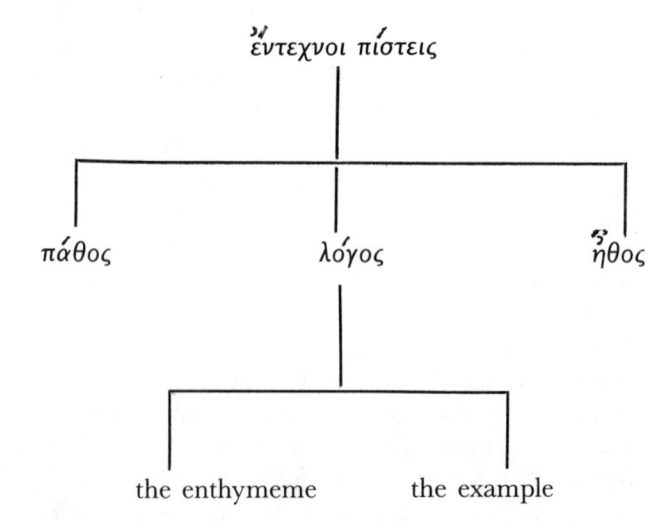

```
              ἔντεχνοι πίστεις
        ┌──────────┼──────────┐
      πάθος       λόγος       ἦθος
                   │
              ┌────┴────┐
         the enthymeme  the example
```

Our position is that Grimaldi's careful analysis led him into difficulties, not only because of the nature of the text and the attempt to create major categories for the two subdivisions of λόγος, but also because he cut off his finding a solution by associating λόγος with "the factual evidence contained in the subject" (1980, 354) rather than with the enthymeme and the example. As pointed out above, the λόγος presented by the speaker are not in the nature of "evidence" but rather in the nature of "argument" and cannot therefore be classified as "facts."

Aristotle carefully avoided using the term "fact" as a basic term on which he built his superstructure. Bonitz listed relatively few references to πρᾶγμα. Wartelle (1982, 362-363) noted several usages of πρᾶγμα in the early sections of Book One. When Aristotle does use πρᾶγμα, it is generally in the sense of "the business at hand," "the affair in hand," or "the case in hand." The term does not serve Aristotle's basic structure. Aristotle knew the pitfalls of establishing a working definition of "fact." He preferred instead to contrast the "arguments" [ἔντεχνοι πίστεις] created by the speaker with the "evidence" [ἄτεχνοι πίστεις] discovered by the speaker to complete his hierachy of categories. Modern law does speak of "facts" in two respects. First, it says that the court will listen to the argument and evidence, and establish the "judicial facts," i.e., the court will listen to what is said about whether the defendant was at the scene of the crime or not, and then establish a "fact" that the defendant was or was not there, a "fact" that operates within the context of the law. What the courts establish therefore is a "judicial fact," and, in the example given here, that fact is independent of whether the defendant was or was not actually at the scene of the crime. [cf. 1354a28] Second, it does associate "evidence," but not "reasoning," with "facts" by speaking of "facts-in-evidence" or "facts," meaning that there is a presumption that the evidence presented by both sides is truthful and therefore "factual." But these usages of the word are carefully fenced in by custom and statute, and do not cause misunderstandings in modern litigation. These attitudes toward evidence were undoubtedly operative in Athenian courts, and caused no more confusion then about what is a "fact" than they do now.

The pleaders, being biased in adversarial courts in favor of one side or the other, cannot themselves "present" evidence or "facts." Pleaders argue. They argue with reasoning, with emotional proof, and with ethical proof. Grimaldi consistently used the correct terminology to translate Aristotle's λόγος, ἦθος and πάθος in places where Aristotle is differentiating among the three types of ἔντεχνοι πίστεις or argument. When the pleador offers to the court the evidence that he has "discovered," he is supposed to offer such "evidence" without influencing its content. Ἄτεχνοι πίστεις therefore is "discoverable" (and a part of the art of rhetoric is to discover it, for it does not automatically fall into the lap of the pleador) but not "inventable." That pleadors can present their evidence entirely impartially is of course a myth. But, in present Anglo-Saxon courts, the judge sits as a referree to make certain that lawyers do not invade the providence of the evidence to the place where they distort the ability of the court to interpret the evidence without undue bias.

Aristotle had need to use the terms ἔντεχνοι πίστεις and ἄτεχνοι πίστεις consistently. He intended to establish the sort of relative terms that he discussed in the *Categories*, "when a thing's being such as it is, is explained by a genitive following or else by some phrase or expression designed to bring out the relation." (tr. Cooke, 1938, 6b6-8) The category of argument can only be understood in contrast to the category of evidence, and vice versa. The courts of his time and the courts of our time attempt to preserve the distinction between evidence and argument in so far as is possible. Although a commentary that looks at the trees may appear to detect material differences in the way Aristotle employed such terms in specific passages, in seeing the forest and in understanding the legal concepts involved, the consistency of Aristotle's superstructure emerges.

Therefore, we cannot concur with Grimaldi that Aristotle's statements at 1354a13-15 attempted to establish an approach to proof outside of his superstructure that he presented at 1355b35-1356a4. If the early phrase is Aristotelian, it had as its purpose to emphasize that the speaker ought to rely upon reasoning as the body of proof and so ties in with Aristotle's polemic aimed at his competitors who stressed emotion and character, at the expense of a constructive use of logic, based upon the use of the enthymeme and the example.

In Aristotle's time, of course, the use of induction was much more limited than it is now. There were few if any opportunities to use scientific data and to introduce the results of studies of multiple examples. But inductive reasoning could still be very effective in the courtroom. A single example [1357b30-35] can set forth the entire inductive-deductive chain of reasoning:

EXAMPLE ONE: Pisistratus asked for a body guard and then became a tryant		EXAMPLE TWO: Theagenes of Megara asked for a bodyguard and then became a tyrant
GENERALIZATION: Public figures who ask for a body guard (Major Premise)	are	public figures who may well aim at becoming tyrants
Dionysius (Minor Premise)	is	a public figure who asks for a body guard
Therefore Dionysius (Conclusion)	may	aim at becoming a tyrant

Aristotle took considerable pains to point out two aspects of this inductive-deductive chain of reasoning. First, because we are dealing with rhetoric and not with dialectic, the conclusion is one of probability and not of certainty. Therefore, the only conclusion that can be drawn is that Dionysius *may* well aim at becoming a tyrant. Second, in rhetorical discourse, the communicator does not have to state all the steps of this chain. The audience, said Aristotle, once it has been given the two examples of Pisistratus and Theagenes, in comparison with Dionysius, can follow through on its own. Therefore, although Aristotle does not say so directly, he seems certain to have concluded that inductive, as well as deductive reasoning, can be truncated.

Grimaldi was not alone in having difficulty defining πίστεις. Others have been troubled as well. In his 1924 article on Aristotle's *Rhetoric*, Roberts (1924, 354) found "proofs" as an unsatisfactory translation of πίστεις. He concluded that, "if the term 'proofs' be retained, it should be qualified by the adjective 'probable' or 'rhetorical...'" Roberts (1924, 353) proposed that the English philosophers might find a more satisfactory term. He should instead have looked to the English jurists for his answer. There is no more reason to object to the use of the term "proofs" in translating Aristotle's *Rhetoric* than there is to object to its usage in modern law treatises and in modern courts of law. Law operates on the presumption that its proof is "probable" or "rhetorical." That is why it has such dependence upon the phrases "proof by a preponderance of the evidence, "proof by the greater weight of the evidence," "proof by clear, strong, and convincing evidence," and "proof beyond a reasonable doubt." "Proof" in law is an established "word of art," and since Roberts acknowledged that Aristotle's treatise was "full of 'terms of art,'" he should have recognized πίστεις as one of those terms.

Πίστεις, unlike τέχνη, is translatable into English as "proofs" and its two subdivisions are properly translated as "evidence" and "argument."

Three other terms closely related either to the three discussed above or to each other need to clarified:

τεχνολογία	textbook
τεχνόλογος	writer on the art of rhetoric
λόγος	logical proof, reasoning, or rational proof as opposed to formal logical proof

The third of these definitions is controversial. It has been previously discussed in connection with our clarification of πίστεις, and it will be further clarified later in this chapter.

A fourth term, persuasion, is actually a complex of four terms:

πείθειν	to persuade (the verb)
πιθανός, ή, όν	persuasive (the adjective)
τὸ πιθανόν	persuasion[12] (the noun)
πιθανῶς	persuasively (the adverb)

Since these aspects of "persuasion" were used by Aristotle in the *Rhetoric* (Wartelle, 1982, 332, 337-338) and since we have chosen to refer to Aristotle's work as a treatise on persuasion, it is fair to ask why some reference to persuasion is not found in the title of the work.

To begin with, we are not even certain that Aristotle gave a title to his lectures. The manuscripts of the *Rhetoric* sometimes bear titles, but these could have been added later. Aristotle could have called his lectures by another title unfamiliar to us. But, assuming that the Greek words most frequently found on the manuscripts, ΑΡΙΣΤΟΤΕΛΟΥΣ ΤΕΧΝΗΣ ΡΗΤΟΡΙΚΗΣ, was a title established in Aristotle's time, what posture should be adopted toward the title? Should the title include the word "persuasion?"

The title offered by both Roberts (1954, 19, n.1) and Cooper (1932, 1) of "The Art of Public Speaking" is inappropriate. Aristotle was plainly writing for persons engaged in courtroom dialogue as well as for those addressing court assemblies, and even persons engaged in writing, since he saw little or no distinction between effective speaking and writing. "A litigant," observed Bonner and Smith (1930, 2, 122), "always had the right to question his opponent in court." So Aristotle was directing his remarks to dialogue as well as public presentations. The theories that Aristotle proposed could apply to conference work as well as public appearances, and certainly in Athens many settlements took place out of court, just as they do today.

Other translators are more cautious in offering titles for the *Rhetoric*, preferring versions of "Aristotle's 'Art' of Rhetoric" (Freese, 1926, 3); "The Art of Rhetoric" (Taylor, 1818, 2, 1); "Aristotle's Treatise on Rhetoric" (Buckley, 1910 (1833), title page); and "The Rhetoric of Aristotle" (Cope, 1877, Welldon, 1886, & Jebb, 1909). But we have discarded "art" as a term that can be misleading in modern English because of its sophistic connotations, and a literal translation avoids the issue. If we would like to call the treatise "Aristotle's Treatise on Persuasion," how does the term "persuasion" come in?

Aristotle inserted it himself in defining rhetoric when he said that rhetoric is the faculty of discovering in each instance or case the possible means of persuasion, το ἐνδεχόμενον πιθανόν. [1355b26-27][13] The purpose of rhetoric therefore is to enable the pleador to invent his arguments and to uncover his evidence, and by the use of these arguments and evidence, to be persuasive, i.e., to gain agreement by means of the presentation of proofs. The persistence of the ambiguity about the ethics of the speaker that results from an unqualified use of the term "rhetoric," seems best to select as the title of the treatise the goal of rhetoric, namely, training in persuasion. The most appropriate title therefore seems to be "Aristotle on Persuasion." Other possible titles could be "Aristotle's System of Rhetoric" or "The Τέχνη of Aristotle's Rhetoric."

The remaining terms need to be given consistent translations:

οἱ ἀμφισβητοῦντες	the litigants or opponents in a law suit [1354a31]
πρᾶγμα	an alleged fact (infrequently used)
ἀπόδειξις	a demonstration
ἀκροατής	any listeners; plural = audience
συλλογίζεσθαι	to reason logically
συλλογισμός	a syllogism
ἐπαγωγή	the process of reasoning by induction
ἐνθύμημα	an enthymeme
παράδειγμα	an example

A REORIENTATION OF CERTAIN BASIC CONCEPTS IN THE RHETORIC

The discussion under the section on vocabulary has stated one of the two basic reorientations necessary for a new translation of the *Rhetoric*, namely, the substitution of the dichotomy of argument and evidence for the dichotomy of artistic and non-artistic, or artificial and inartificial proofs. These translations are literal ones, e.g., when referring to things, τέχνη can mean "artificial." We propose that the excellent translators who employed the literal meanings did so because they did not possess the basic perspectives of legal pleading, and therefore followed a safe route of translation. The concept with which they should have been familiar is that what is said by the lawyer is argument and what is presented to the court in the way of witnesses, oaths, torture and the like is evidence. Lawyers cannot take the witness stand and "give" evidence. Lawyers take the evidence that they find from others and "argue" with it, reasoning logically with a logic that encompasses both emotional proof to arouse the audience and ethical proof to improve the lawyer's image with the jury. Therefore, at the end of a jury trial, lawyers present a "closing argument" to the jury. As Dufour stated, the orator in presenting his πίστεις ἔντεχνοι developes "son argumentation." (1967, 1, 39)

On the other hand, what the lawyer goes out and discovers (those proofs that would have existed whether the lawyer had ever taken the case or not) are termed evidence. The lawyer is not supposed to tamper with the evidence, but merely to present it. Therefore, what is said by witnesses or introduced in the form of pictorials, documents, recordings or real evidence (guns, clothing, etc.) is evidence and is subject to the "rules of evidence."

When presented with a case, in Greece as well as in present Anglo-Saxon courts, lawyers set out in two directions: they search for their evidence, things that they did not invent but rather that they use; then, in reflecting upon the evidence they have been able to amass, the lawyers develop their arguments, with their accompanying emotional and character aspects. To put this into context, in a murder case, the defense lawyers would use "discovery" to locate witnesses that could establish an alibi for their client; they would use chemical tests to establish that the fibers of clothing found at the scene of the crime did not match the clothing worn by the defendant, and so forth. As the discovery process continued, the lawyers would develop their "arguments," establishing by induction that five witnesses were sufficient to show that their client was elsewhere, and establishing by deduction that, since the fibers did not match, someone else and not their client must have committed the crime. The lawyer can then use the major premise (truncated or fully put), "Persons whose clothing fibers match fibers found at the scene of the crime are persons who were probably at the scene of the crime." The lawyers would "invent" the chains that link together the pieces of evidence to show the guilt or innocence of the accused.

Therefore, theoretically, lawyers invent their argument and discover their evidence. But, as was pointed out earlier in this chapter, that categorization does not always hold. Lawyers become skilled in handling their evidence to make the most of its ethical, emotional and logical components. As we have said before, Aristotle pointed out in *The Constitution* (ix, 2) that the laws are not always clear and require interpretation, and, as Aristotle explained in the *Rhetoric*, legislators cannot always foresee the exegencies of a particular case when they draft the laws. (1354b15-16). And so pleadors learn to amplify the logical, emotional, and ethical components of their evidence, interpreting it in a light most favorable to their case. In jury trials, judges stand as guardians to separate evidence from argument and they exercise controls to keep the two elements separated. But, in spite of their efforts, the two components often become meshed.[14]

Even though the categories cannot remain totally separated, the dichotomy between evidence and argument is the basis of law. Therefore, when Rhys Roberts gave us the translation "of the modes of persuasion, some belong to the art of rhetoric and some do not,"[15] he erred twice. First, he should have translated πίστεις as "proofs" and not as "modes of persuasion." Second, he should have said: "In regard to proofs, some are argumentive and some are evidential." When Aristotle said that some proofs have to be taken advantage of and other devised,[16] he was saying that the lawyer's evidence in the form of witnesses, contracts, oaths, and the like were out there somewhere when the case began, and what the lawyer had to do was to seek them out and use them to their best advantage. Then, with the aid of the evidence, the lawyer will invent arguments in the form of ethical proof, emotional proof and logical proof (or reasoning) that will put his client's case before the decision makers in its best light.

This position has not been taken by some of the prominent commentators on the *Rhetoric*. Cope proposed that the modes of proof or persuasion were πίστεις, ἦθος, and πάθος. (1867, 131). This left Cope without a comprehensive term to cover both ἄτεχνοι πίστεις and ἔντεχνοι πίστεις, for Cope had appropriated πίστεις for a subdivision of ἔντεχνοι πίστεις. What sort of umbrella term did Cope employ? Later in his commentary Cope said: "Of rhetorical proofs there are two kinds, scientific and unscientific." (1867, 150). Is "scientific" to be the umbrella term? If so, Cope would have to be translating τέχνη as "science." But Cope allied unscientific proof to ἄτεχνοι πίστεις or evidence, and ἔντεχνοι πίστεις to what we term here argument. In modern terminology and in Aristotle's time as well, "evidence" is closer to being "scientific" than argument. The terms as applied by Cope are simply inappropriate. Cope tried to justify calling ἔντεχνοι πίστεις scientific by saying that they "may be conducted and established by the processes and rules of the art, and by our own agency." (1867, 150) Cope was writing in a time when science was supposed to answer practically all of the world's problems, and so he choose terminology that was in vogue in his time. In the footnotes to his Greek text, Cope (or his editor, Sandys) (1877, 1,28,n.2 & 269,n.) referred to the position taken in the commentary, and then added some amplifications that, however, did not change his basic position.

We are highly indebted to Grimaldi for the astuteness of his detailed commentary on Book One of the *Rhetoric*. Earlier in this chapter, in presenting our meaning of πίστεις, we discussed how our interpretation of Aristotle's basic structure differs from Grimaldi's and there is no need to repeat that discussion here. A work less detailed than Grimaldi's is Hill's essay in Murphy's *A Synoptic History of Classical Rhetoric*. In presenting the major divisions of the *Rhetoric*, Hill divided the proofs into "artistic or inartistic," (1972, 23) rather than "argument" and "evidence." He stated that Aristotle's proofs are of only three kinds rather than that there are three kinds of ἔντεχνοι πίστεις and five kinds of ἄτεχνοι πίστεις. But Hill does label correctly, as did Grimaldi, the three types of ἔντεχνοι πίστεις as logical proofs, ethical proofs, and "psychological proofs" (rather than emotional proofs, but the change in terminology is not misleading). Hill does identify correctly the two instruments of logical proof as the enthymeme and the example. (1972, 23) But, from our point of view, he erred as did Cope in concluding that Aristotle found ἄτεχνοι πίστεις "outside of the art of rhetoric," rather than outside of the art of invention. No wonder, therefore, that Hill is surprised that Aristotle spent so much time on the ἄτεχνοι πίστεις when Hill concluded that they belonged outside of the sphere of rhetoric. Crem (1957, 31) took a similar position in her commentary, proposing that "inartificial [proofs] do not properly belong to the rhetorical method," this in spite of the amount of space that Aristotle devotes to them in his treatise. If Crem is correct, Aristotle certainly wrote an illogical treatise indeed.

In short, ἄτεχνοι πίστεις have a role in rhetoric outside of and parallel with the "'invented" proofs. That their discovery requires "'inventiveness" on the part of the speaker to locate them and present them should not result in a conflict of terms.

Therefore, in our interpretation, a schema of Aristotle's hierarchy would look like this:

The judge and/or jury who listen to the πίστεις or proofs discovered by the pleador and presented for the court's consideration**

proofs "invented" by the pleador or lawyer (hence "inventio") the ἔντεχνοι πίστεις or the lawyer's argument*

a. the logical proofs invented by the lawyer, the λόγοι

   (1) deductive reasoning via the enthymeme

   (2) inductive reasoning via the example

b. the emotional proofs, the πάθη

c. the ethical proofs, the ἤθεα

proofs "discovered" by the pleador or lawyer (hence a part of rhetoric but not a part of "inventio" because lawyers cannot "invent" their evidence); the ἄτεχνοι πίστεις

a. oaths

b. torture

c. witnesses

d. contracts

e. laws

(even though these are only "discovered," each has its own logical, emotional, and ethical component, e.g., a logical, vigorous, highly respected witness)

---

*Grimaldi (1972, 16) approached this use of argument when he found that "the enthymeme as the main instrument of rhetorical *argument* incorporated the interplay of *reason* and *emotion* in discourse." [emphasis added] If Grimaldi had added that "argument" incorporated the interplay of reason, emotional, AND ethos, he would have structured argument as we have in this schema.

**for an explanation of the place of "demonstration" in Aristotle's *Rhetoric*, see footnote 17.

This schema, developed independently from Kennedy's (1980, 69), agrees with the Kennedy structure, with one exception. In labeling the two main subdivisions of rhetoric, Kennedy preferred "artistic or internal modes" and "non-artistic or external modes." Our position that these subdivisions should be labeled "evidence" and "argument" has been clearly made more than once elsewhere and does not need to be repeated here. In his earlier treatise on *The Art of Persuasion in Greece*, Kennedy (1963, 88) used the term "direct evidence" to explain the term ἄτεχνοι πίστεις and to show that, in the fourth century, direct evidence was often distinguished from "argument." Kennedy (1963, 96) recognized induction and deduction as the "two processes of logic on all levels of reasoning." Therefore the position taken here may more closely parallel Kennedy's interpretation of the *Rhetoric* than the labels on his schema and our schema indicate.

Our position is that Aristotle found ἄτεχνοι πίστεις an integral part of rhetoric. Tovar's translation as discussed in Chapter Four appears close to ours. The rhetorician/lawyer has to find the ἄτεχνοι πίστεις and integrate them with the ἔντεχνοι πίστεις to present the most effective case. If there exists evidence favorable to a client's case, no one today would hire a lawyer who used only what the lawyer himself could invent. The same was true in Aristotle's time. A rhetorician/lawyer went out and located his evidence or ἄτεχνοι πίστεις, and then figured out how to introduce this evidence to establish what logical conclusions the lawyer had drawn from such evidence, what emotional influences that evidence might have on the court, and how its presentation could enhance the reputation of the pleador in the eyes of the jury. Dufour (1967, 1, 135, n.1) concurred with our position by saying that "in treating, in his study of judicial style, 'des preuves extra-technique,' Aristotle is in no way contravening what he had said in chapter one." Dufour's translation of Aristotle's definition of rhetoric made it clear that the search for evidence was an integral part of persuasion. (1969, 1, 39)

To summarize our position as to what the interpretation of πίστεις in Aristotle's categorization should be, we would say that the judge and jury attempt to sort out what proofs the lawyer "invents" from what proofs the lawyer "discovers." That system existed in Greece and also exists today. It is often so fundamental that it is not explicitly expressed. Πίστεις should therefore be translated as "proofs."

Λόγος or logical proof

This term was defined earlier as "reasoning" and further discussion of that definition was delayed until now, because the definition of "reasoning" for λόγος has a major influence on how the *Rhetoric* is translated. Having appropriated "argument" as a sub-umbrella term for all three of the non-evidential methods of supporting a case, we must seek a term (a) that properly parallels ethical and emotional proof and (b) that can be a subdivision of the umbrella term, argument. The most appropriate term is "logical proof" or "reasoning" or "rational proof." Aristotle's third category is the proper employment of the example and the enthymeme that have their counterparts in formal logic as induction and deduction. Lawyers therefore seek out examples that will suport their cases, e.g., the lawyer observes that no examples exist in the lawyer's jurisdiction[18] wherein capital punishment has been inflicted on a juvenile under eighteen years of age, and he plugs this example into an enthymeme that says: "No juvenile under eighteen has ever been executed in this state," thereby "reasoning" with the jury that the lawyer's client should not be the first exception to the following major premise: *All juvenile offenders are offenders who are not sentenced to capital crimes in this jurisdiction*. To enhance the lawyer's position and therefore to gain "bonus points," the lawyer can also hope for the arousing of emotion by this reasoning (pity for the accused, love of tradition in the law, hope for the rehabilitation of youth), and the lawyer expects his own ethical persuasion and the ethical persuasion of his client to enhance the persuasiveness of his reasoning.

How have the translators interpreted logos? The schema below interpreting 1356a3-4 summarizes the position of six of the nineteenth and twentieth century English translators. Significant is the degree of difference among the six in interpreting the same passage. Some of the translators inject more system into Aristotle's passage than he intended, e.g., they insert "the third" which must be based on an inference that Aristotle said he was going to name three types of proofs. Cope, Welldon and Buckley avoid this minor text distortion.

"Proofs" occurs only in line 1356a2 and is not repeated. Aristotle preferred to emphasis the subheading of proofs that he was discussing in the passage. The needless repetition of proofs by Cope and Roberts can be eliminated.

The translators obviously take two approaches: the first is to translate logos as "the speech itself" and the second, as "argument." Perhaps a combination of the two translations would best encompass Aristotle's meaning. We would translate 1456a3-4 as "the last, based upon logical reasoning in the speech itself, to the extent that it clarifies or appears to clarify."[19]

TRANSLATOR	DATE	PAGE	TRANSLATION
Taylor	1818	8	"and the third is the argument itself, in consequence of demonstrating, or appearing to demonstrate"
Buckley	1833 1910	12	"others in the thing itself which is said, by reason of its proving, or appearing to prove the point"
Cope	1867	109	"πίστεις, direct logical proofs which appeal to the reason"
Welldon	1886	11	"or in the speech itself by means of real or apparent demonstration"
Jebb	1909	6	"a third, a demonstration or apparent demonstration of the speech itself"
Roberts	1924 1954 1984	24-25	"the third on the proof, or apparent proof, provided by the words of the speech itself."
Freese	1926	17	"as the third upon the speech itself, in so far as it proves or seems to prove"
Cooper	1932	8	"the third appertain to the argument proper, in so far as it actually or seemingly demonstrates"

In applying our translation to the example given above concerning capital punishment, the lawyer who invented his inductive-deductive chain appears to have proved that his client should not be put to death, by reasoning logically in the way he forms the words of the speech itself that no juvenile defendant in that jurisdiction has ever been executed and that his client should be treated as have others. This is only "apparent proof" because customary law, or *stare decisis* can always be broken, and a new attitude assumed. The speaker can use ethical argument if the audience is impressed with his example, and the speaker can use emotional argument if the audience is aroused to sympathy for the client.

As researchers know, the possible meanings of λόγος in Greek are multiple. Among these multiple meanings are "reason" and "reasoning." Although such meanings cannot be applied in the *Rhetoric* injudiciously, for the most part, when Aristotle is contrasting the three types of ἔντεχνοι πίστεις, λόγος should be translated in a manner indicating that the logical or reasoning process is involved in the words that the speaker has chosen to persuade.

NUANCES AND LEGAL INTERPRETATIONS

Now that we have suggested the basic vocabulary to provide consistency in translations and have pointed out two basic perspectives concerning πίστεις and λόγος that should provide a framework for that vocabulary, let us examine a few of the nuances in the *Rhetoric* that could be made clearer by a new translation that would be conscious of the details of law and rhetoric. Then we will present a translation of one extended passage to show how much differently the *Rhetoric* can be read with the legal perspectives in mind.

In Chapter Two, in illustrating how the Latin translations have assisted the collators in clarifying the Greek text, we pointed out that the Latin sometimes reflected more clearly the legal connotations of the *Rhetoric* than did the Greek. Here are further illustrations of how the Greek text itself can be illuminated. Early in Book One (1354a24-26), Aristotle continued to berate the use of emotion to distort persuasion. In order to reduce the possibility of decisions being unduly influenced by emotion, Aristotle suggested that all laws should be drafted as clearly as possible so as to "leave as little as possible to the decision makers." (Roberts, 1954, 20) In spite of Cope's early advice to the contrary, English versions of the *Rhetoric* tend to translate ἐπὶ τοῖς κρίνουσι[20] (1354a33-34) as "judge" or "judges." Aristotle, it should be remembered, was attempting to expand the treatment of rhetoric. Saying that laws should be framed to limit the decision of the "judges" throws the emphasis back upon forensic persuasion. Aristotle did not use δικαστής here, which he used elsewhere, but preferred κριτής that has the broad meaning of "decision makers." Therefore κριτής would pertain to all types of speaking, including occasional or epideictic oratory as well as demonstrative speeches, because in Greece even epideictic speaking was often done before a panel of "judges" who awarded prizes.[21] In a footnote (1867, 137, n.1), Cope also noted that he like Victorius interpreted Aristotle's use of κρίνειν as referring to both judicial and legislative situations. Cope and Victorius reached their conclusion because, in the passage that follows, (1354b 7-8), Aristotle pointed out that both the public assembly and the dicasts must decide matters pertaining to both the present and future. "In both cases," said Cope, "there is a judgment or decision." Cope in his footnote observed other instances in which κριτής could be extended to all three forms of speaking. His position was that, in epideictic oratory, the decision took the form of criticism. Therefore, a sensitivity to law can assist not only in pointing up the legal aspects of the *Rhetoric*, but also in pointing down its legal connotations, where they confine Aristotle's meaning contrary to his intent.

Aristotle continued to show his scorn of other treatises and of practices in Greek courts by saying in 1354b31-33 that, although in deliberative oratory, the speaker need only establish the facts, "as for what goes on in the law courts is concerned, that is not enough. The listeners have to be won over."[22] Although the adjective δικανικός can and should usually mean "judicial," it can also have the unfavorable connotation of "pettifogging" and "savouring of the law courts." Aristotle's distaste of the mispractice of law at this particular point in his treatise can be more faithfully depicted by also choosing an unfavorable connotation of τὰ δικανικά, hence "as for what goes on in the law courts." Undoubtedly Aristotle intended to adopt for his treatise those aspects of Athenian law that lent themselves to ethical practice. He took pains to point out the abuses of law and warned his followers against them. Therefore, the fact that a good set of legal principles can be abused by unethical practices should not have deterred Aristotle from using the strengths of law as one of the main bases for his treatise.

In a continuation of the same thought pattern, Aristotle complained that, since those who make decisions in the court are deciding other people's fates and not their own, they are not reluctant to "turn themselves over to the litigants"[23] and let the more persuasive litigant make the choice for them, rather than rendering a decision based on their own reasoning. Here Aristotle was confining himself to forensic speaking.

Translators have used such phrases as "surrender themselves to the disputants" (Roberts, 1954, 21), "lend themselves to the more plausible speaker" (Cooper, 1932, 4) and "surrender to the pleaders." (Freese, 1926, 9) However, "litigants' seems closer to what Aristotle had in mind.[24] As was noted earlier, as time progressed, it became common practice to let oneself be represented by a "lawyer." It was in particular these "lawyers" who tried to get the courts to surrender to their persuasive arts.

In 1355a22-29, Aristotle proposed that popular audiences could not even be persuaded by instruction resulting from scientific findings but would require that the speaker use the sort of truisms that everyone can expect to believe, i.e., sayings that result in a homespun philosophy.[25] In presenting this concept, Aristotle said that the speaker must use πίστεις (proofs) and λόγος (logic or reasoning) that are shared by everyone, that are public knowledge. Some of these proofs could approach what contemporary courts recognize as established by judicial notice. How should this passage be translated? Perhaps what Aristotle meant is that all of our proofs, and in particular our logical proofs, should be founded on generally accepted principles, e.g., *the character of any man who will not look you in the eyes cannot be trusted*, or *we all know that the emotion of jealousy can cause a man to kill*, or the lawyer might reason that of course we all know that, once a man commits one crime, he is likely to commit another, particularly in this case, if he thought he had got away with his first misdeed, why should he not commit another and get by with that one as well. Therefore an acceptable translation of τὰς πίστεις καὶ τοὺς λόγους would simply mean "[our] proofs and reasoning [or rational connotations]" to be interpreted as "our proofs and in particular when we use reasoning as proofs."[26] Or we could translate the phrase as "[our] proofs and [our] speeches as a whole [as they furnish proof]," as a means of explaining why Aristotle should use the two terms πίστις and λόγος as if they were independent of each other.

Two further examples will serve to illustrate the appropriateness of translating λόγος as reasoning or rationality. First, Aristotle stated that the reasoning a speaker uses is enhanced when spoken by a credible person.[27] Thus the credibility of the speaker bolsters the impact of the use of examples and enthymemess, and vice versa. Hence, if witnesses with high credibility tell the court that the accused is very unlikely to commit further crimes, the opposition senses that the best way to undermine the reasoning of those witnesses is to destroy their credibility by impeachment.

On 1356a19-20, Aristotle was summing up the

position of each of his three types of argument. In reference to the third type that we call "logic" or "reasoning" or "rational proof," Aristotle said: "Finally, persuasion results from the logical proof(s) of the speech itself, when we demonstrate the truth or apparent truth in each situation." There are disagreements about how the text reads at this point[28], but the Greek preferred by Kassel and also by Ross both permit the interpretation preferred here.

Why should this passage be translated in the manner given above? At this point in the text, it is necessary to rationalize Aristotle's two trichotomies:

TRICHOTOMY ONE	TRICHOTOMY TWO
types of ἄτεχνοι πίστεις or argument	elements of the speaking situation
ἦθος . . . . . character	ῥήτωρ . . . the speaker
πάθος . . . . emotion	ἀκροατής . the audience
λόγος . . . . reasoning via the enthymeme & example	λόγος . . . . the speech

How can we coordinate the use of λόγος in the first triad with the use of λόγος in the second triad? That rationalization is possible if we conclude that Aristotle meant to imply when he used λόγος in trichotomy two that the persuasion came from the speech itself, of course, but also that what should be most persuasive about the speech itself was its use of reasoning or logical proof via the enthymeme and the example. Hence, our translation: "from the logical proof(s) of the speech itself, when we demonstrate the truth or apparent truth in each situation." (Cf. Cope, 1877, I, 32, n.6)

Aristotle made his position concerning the probable or apparent truth of the reasoning of the pleador not only in the *Prior Analytics*, as was pointed out earlier in this chapter, but also in the *Topics*. (101b1-2) Therefore, what the speaker generates via both trichotomies is "apparent" or "probable" truth.

All of the modern translations miss the mark in interpreting 1356a19-20.[29] If we translate λόγος just as "the speech itself" in keeping with trichotomy two without acknowledging "reasoning" or "logical proof," we lose Aristotle's carefully constructed first trichotomy of the three categories of argument; if we translate λόγος as "argument" instead of "reasoning," we are either without an umbrella term for the three types of ἔντεχνοι πίστεις or we overlap the categories and hence fail to preserve Aristotle's trichotomy one. Aristotle plainly meant to say that persuaders have three factors at their command with which to argue: their character, their arousing of the emotions, and the logic or reasoning that they can construct by means of examples (induction) and by enthymemes (deduction) contained in the speech itself. Therefore λόγος in 1356a19-20 can best be translated as "the logical proof(s) of the speech itself."

Now let us look at an extended passage to see how legal and rhetorical perspectives can make both major and minor differences in translating the *Rhetoric*.

Chapter Fifteen of Book One is concerned with Aristotle's explanation of the five types of evidence. The *Rhetoric* is concerned with only five categories of evidence: laws, witnesses, contracts, tortures, and oaths. To contemporary users of evidence, the list is most incomplete. Among the modern types of evidence missing are the following:

all forms of what is termed in law "real evidence", e.g., blood samples, clothing analyses, etc.

photographs

recordings

scientific treatises

Naturally, some of these were not a part of the "state of the arts" in Aristotle's time and therefore could not be included. But the categories of evidence were what they were in Aristotle's time, and we must deal with them as he presented them.

In Chapter 15 of Book One (1376a6-1376sa33), Aristotle concerned himself with the type of evidence that not only received considerable emphasis in Aristotle's time, but is also most important today, i.e., witnesses. The lines translated below attempt to present Aristotle's attitudes toward evidence with emphasis on both the legal and rhetorical aspects of his treatise. In the translation, as much use as possible has been made of legal and rhetorical terminology that would apply both to Aristotle's courts and to modern-day Anglo-Saxon courts. For example, in criminal trials, where the defendant does not take the stand and where the defense does not wish to "open the door" to questions about the defendant's reputation by introducing character witnesses in behalf of the defendant, the defense does as Aristotle instructed. It limited its approach to impeaching the witnesses presented by the prosecution or plaintiff. One method of impeachment is to call witnesses friendly to you to testify as to the truthfulness and veracity of the witness testifying for your opponent.

PASSAGE FROM 1376a6-1376a33 TRANSLATED TO EMPHASIZE THE LEGAL ASPECTS OF ARISTOTLE

πρόσφατοι δ' ὅσοι γνώριμοί τι κεκρίκασιν

CONTEMPORARY WITNESSES (1) INCLUDE PROMINENT PEOPLE WHO HAVE ISSUED DECISIONS

Roberts: 'Recent' witnesses are well-known people who have expressed their opinions about some disputed matter;

Cooper: Recent witnesses are [first] any notable persons who have pronounced judgment on some matter;

χρήσιμοι γὰρ αἱ τούτων κρίσεις τοῖς περὶ τῶν αὐτῶν ἀμφισβητοῦσιν

FOR THEIR RULINGS ARE USEFUL TO THOSE ARGUING SIMILAR CASES.

Roberts: such opinions will be useful support for subsequent disputants on the same points:

Cooper: their judgments are useful to those who are contending about the same issues.

οἷον Εὔβουλος ἐν τοῖς δικαστηρίοις ἐχρήσατο κατὰ Χάρητος ᾧ Πλάτων εἶπε πρὸς Ἀρχίβιον

FOR EXAMPLE EUBULUS USED, IN ATTACKING CHARES IN THE LAW COURTS, THE REPLY PLATO MADE AGAINST ARCHIBIUS

Roberts: thus Eubulus used in the law-courts against Chares the reply Plato had made to Archibius,

Cooper: Thus [the orator] Eubulus quoted in the law-court, against Chares, the saying of Plato [? the comic poet] with regard to Archibius--

ὅτι ἐπιδέδωκεν ἐν τῇ πόλει τὸ ὁμολογεῖν πονηροὺς εἶναι

THAT IT HAD BECOME A ROUTINE MATTER IN THE CITY TO CONFESS TO VICE.(2)

Roberts: "It has become the regular custom in this country to admit that one is a scoundrel'.

Cooper: that the habit of admitting rascality had made strides at Athens.

καὶ οἱ μετέχοντες τοῦ κινδύνου, ἂν δόξωσι ψεύδεσθαι

AND PARTNERS (3) IN RISK OF PUNISHMENT, IF THEY ARE POSSIBLE PERJURORS (4),

Roberts: There are also those witnesses who share the risk of punishment if their evidence is pronounced false.

Cooper: And [secondly] there are those who, if they are suspected of perjury, share [with the accused] the risks of the trial.

οἱ μὲν οὖν τοιοῦτοι τῶν τοιούτων μόνον μάρτυρές εἰσι
εἰ γέγονεν ἢ μή, εἰ ἔστιν ἢ μή,

THEY ARE APPROPRIATE WITNESSES ONLY ON CERTAIN MATTERS, SUCH AS WHETHER A DEED WAS DONE OR WAS NOT DONE, WHETHER SOMETHING IS OR IS NOT THE CASE

Roberts: These are valid witnesses to the fact that an action was or was not done, that something is or is not the case;

Cooper: All such witnesses are useful only for their evidence on such points as these: whether a thing has occurred, or not occurred; whether a thing is at present so, or not so.

New Translation

περὶ δὲ τοῦ ποῖον οὐ μάρτυρες, οἷον εἰ δίκαιον ἢ ἄδικον,
εἰ συμφέρον ἢ ἀσύμφορον·

BUT AS TO THE QUALITY OF AN ACT, WHETHER FOR EXAMPLE IT IS JUST OR UNJUST, APPROPRIATELY OR INAPPROPRIATELY (5) DONE THEY ARE NOT SUITABLE WITNESSES.

Roberts: they are not valid witnesses to the quality of an action, to its being just or unjust, useful or harmful.

Cooper: Their evidence is of no value on the quality of an act—as, for instance, whether an act is right or wrong [a question in forensic speaking], whether a policy is advantageous or the reverse [a question in deliberative speaking]. These are questions to be decided by the judges in the case or by the assembly, not by witnesses concerned in the case.

οἱ δ' ἄπωθεν καὶ περὶ τούτων πιστότατοι,

BUT IMPARTIAL PERSONS ARE VERY CREDIBLE WITNESSES, EVEN ON SUCH MATTERS AS THESE

Roberts: On such questions of <u>quality</u> the opinion of detached persons is highly trustworthy.

Cooper: On such points [for example, the quality of an act, which is related to the known character of the agent], the evidence of recent witnesses who are not concerned in the case [are remote from it, and in no danger] is very credible.

πιστότατοι δ' οἱ παλαιοί· ἀδιάφθοροι γάρ.

THOSE WITNESSES OLD IN YEARS ARE THE MOST TRUSTWORTHY, BECAUSE THEY ARE INCORRUPTIBLE. (6)

Roberts: Most trustworthy of all are the 'ancient' witnesses, since they cannot be corrupted.

Cooper: Most credible of all are the ancient witnesses, since there is no possibility of corrupting them.

πιστώματα δὲ περὶ μαρτυριῶν, μάρτυρας μὲν μὴ ἔχοντι,

IN CONFIRMING YOUR CASE BY THE TESTIMONY OF WITNESSES, IF YOU HAVE NONE,

Roberts: In dealing with the evidence of witnesses, the following are useful arguments. If you have no witnesses on your side,

Cooper: In dealing with testimony, the speaker may argue as follows: If he can call no witnesses,

ὅτι ἐκ τῶν εἰκότων δεῖ κρίνειν καὶ τοῦτ' ἔστι τὸ γνώμῃ τῇ ἀρίστῃ

THEN YOU SHOULD SAY THAT ONE SHOULD JUDGE ON THE BASIS OF WHAT PROBABLY TOOK PLACE, AND THAT IS WHAT IS MEANT BY THE JUROR'S OATH TO USE HIS BEST JUDGMENT (7)

Roberts: you will argue that the judges must decide from what is probable; that this is meant by 'giving a verdict in according with one's honest opinion';

Cooper: he may argue that the judges must decide on the basis of probabilities; that such is the meaning of [the judge's obligation to decide] 'according to my best judgment';

καὶ ὅτι οὐκ ἔστιν ἐξαπατῆσαι τὰ εἰκότα ἐπὶ ἀργυρίῳ

AND THAT PROBABILITIES CANNOT BE BRIBED,

Roberts: that probabilities cannot be bribed to mislead the court;

Cooper: that you cannot bribe probabilities to deceive [the judges—as you can bribe witnesses];

καὶ ὅτι οὐχ ἁλίσκεται τὰ εἰκότα ψευδομαρτυριῶν.
AND THAT PROBABILITIES ARE NOT SUBJECT TO PERJURY. (8)

Roberts: and that probabilities are never convicted of perjury.

Cooper: and that probabilities are never convicted of false witness.

ἔχοντι δὲ πρὸς μὴ ἔχοντα,
BUT IF YOU HAVE WITNESSES AND YOUR OPPONENT DOES NOT,

Roberts: If you have witnesses and the other man has not,

Cooper: If our speaker has witnesses that he can call, while the other side has none,

ὅτι οὐχ ὑπόδικα τὰ εἰκότα,
THEN PROPOSE THAT WHAT PROBABLY HAPPENED CANNOT BE HELD ACCOUNTABLE,

Roberts: you will argue that probabilties cannot be put on trial,

Cooper: he may argue that probabilities are not responsible beings [are not like persons, who can be tried and punished for false witness];

καὶ ὅτι οὐδὲν ἂν ἔδει μαρτυριῶν,
AND THAT THERE WOULD BE NO NEED OF WITNESSES AT ALL

Roberts: and that we could do without the evidence of witnesses altogether

Cooper: and that there would be no demand whatever for testimony,

εἰ ἐκ τῶν λόγων ἱκανὸν ἦν θεωρῆσαι
IF IT WERE SUFFICIENT TO BASE DECISIONS JUST ON SPECULATION [OR RATIONALITY].

Roberts: if we need do no more than balance the pleas advanced on either side.

Cooper: if all a case needed were argumentative speculation.

εἰσὶ δὲ αἱ μαρτυρίαι αἱ μὲν περὶ αὐτοῦ αἱ δὲ περὶ τοῦ ἀμθισβητοῦντος
THE EVIDENCE OF WITNESSES SOMETIMES CONCERNS BOTH OUR CASE AND THAT OF OUR OPPONENTS

Roberts: The evidence of witnesses may refer either to ourselves or to our opponent;

Cooper: Now the testimony of witnesses will concern either our man or his adversary;

καὶ αἱ μὲν περὶ τοῦ πράγματος αἱ δὲ περὶ τοῦ ἤθους
AND SOMETIMES CONCERNS THE FACTS OF THE CASE, AND SOMETIMES CREDIBILITY

Roberts: and either to questions of fact or to questions of personal character;

Cooper: and, again, it will bear either upon the [alleged] fact or upon the character [of an individual].

New Translation

ὥστε φανερὸν ὅτι οὐδέποτ' ἔστιν ἀπορῆσαι μαρτυρίας χρησίμης

SO IT IS EVIDENT THAT WE NEVER NEED TO BE AT A LOSS FOR USEFUL TESTIMONY

Roberts: so, clearly, we need never be at a loss for useful evidence.

Cooper: And hence it is clear that [the speaker] will never be wholly without resources in the way of serviceable testimony;

εἰ μὴ γὰρ κατὰ τοῦ πράγματος ἢ αὐτῷ ὁμολογουμένης ἢ τῷ ἀμφισβητοῦντι ἐναντίας

IF WE LACK TESTIMONY OF FACTS EITHER IN SUPPORT OF OUR OWN CASE, OR IN REBUTTING OUR OPPONENT

Roberts: For if we have no evidence of fact supporting our own case or telling against that of our opponent,

Cooper: for if you have no testimony regarding the fact from witnesses whose evidence will support your man or tell against his adversary,

ἀλλὰ περὶ τοῦ ἤθους

STILL WE CAN GET CHARACTER WITNESSES

Roberts: at least we can always find evidence

Cooper: still you can always find witnesses

ἢ αὐτοῦ εἰς ἐπιείκειαν ἢ τοῦ ἀμφισβητοῦντος εἰς φαυλότητα

THAT SUPPORT EITHER THE RESPECTABILITY OF OUR CASE OR THE WORTHLESSNESS OF OUR OPPONENT'S. (9)

Roberts: to prove our own worth or our opponent's worthlessness.

Cooper: in regard to character whose evidence will tend to establish the respectability of your man or the worthlessness of his adversary.

τὰ δ' ἄλλα περὶ μάρτυρος ἢ φίλου ἢ ἐχθροῦ ἢ μεταξύ,

OTHER MATTERS CONCERNING A WITNESS, WHETHER FRIENDLY OR HOSTILE OR SOMEWHERE IN BETWEEN

Roberts: Other arguments about a witness--that he is a friend or an enemy or neutral,

Cooper: As for other arguments [regarding testimony]--to show that a witness is friendly, hostile, or neither,

ἢ εὐδοκιμοῦντος ἢ ἀδοξοῦντος ἢ μεταξύ,

WHETHER DISTINGUISHED (EXPERT) OR UNKNOWN (LAY) (10) OR SOMEWHERE IN BETWEEN

Roberts: or has a good, bad, or indifferent reputation,

Cooper: and that he is estimable, disreputable, or betwixt and between,

καὶ ὅσαι ἄλλαι τοιαῦται διαφοραί,

AND WHATEVER OTHER DISTINCTIONS LIKE THESE COME UP

Roberts: and any other such distinctions--

Cooper: and every such distinction in character--

ἐκ τῶν αὐτῶν τόπων λεκτέον ἐξ οἷώνπερ καὶ τὰ ἐνθυμήματα λέγομεν.

WE MUST LOOK ON WHAT WAS DISCUSSED ON THESE COMMONPLACES IN CONSTRUCTIVE ENTHYMEMES.

Roberts: we must construct upon the same general lines as we use for the regular rhetorical proofs.

Cooper: the speaker must draw upon the same topics as we use in deriving enthymemes.

---

(1) Aristotle intended to compare witnesses whose active lives were contemporaneous to the events of the trial with witnesses who were perhaps alive but disinterested, or were deceased. The passage is difficult to modernize because contemporary courts would generally exclude such references as hearsay, unless they appeared appropriately in opening and closing arguments, or unless the persons themselves took the witness stand.

(2) Such a reference would be admissible today in the opening statement or closing argument.

(3) Not only have English translators frequently failed to be consistent in translating this passage so that it pertains to the evidence of witnesses and not to evidence in general, but they have missed Aristotle's point about co-conspirators. Those accused jointly of the same crime, or, if not accused, implicated in the same crime, are reliable witnesses only in certain areas, because they have too much to gain in matters calling for their opinion.

(4) The partner to a crime is certainly more suspect of making false statements than is an impartial witness. The contemporary lawyer, in following Aristotle's advice, is limited as to the questions he can ask a person who has "turned state's evidence."

(5) In other words, they cannot be trusted to make judgments.

(6) As with contemporary witnesses, modern lawyers could not introduce such statements as "evidence" unless they fell under some exception to the hearsay rule such as ancient documents or learned treatises. However, they could be incorporated into opening statements and closing arguments.

(7) See Cronin, 1936, 18: "I shall vote according to the laws and the decrees of the Athenian people and the Council of the Five Hundred, but concerning things about which there are no laws, I shall decide to the best of my judgment, neither with favor nor emnity. I shall judge concerning those things which are at issue and shall listen impartially to both the accusation and the defense. I swear these things by Zeus, by Apollo, by Demeter. May there be many blessings on me if I keep my oath, but if I break it may there be destruction on me and my family."

(8) The implication is that the judges should apply "the reasonable and prudent person" test in reaching their decision.

(9) The danger in introducing character witnesses in behalf of your client in contemporary courts is that you have "opened the door" to allow the opposition to challenge the credibility of your client. The opposition may ask your character witnesses, not only about your client's reputation for honesty and veracity, but also can question your credibility witnesses about their knowledge of your client's previous convictions and even arrests. Naturally the rules of the 51 jurisdictions in the United States differ widely on this point.

(10) It seems reasonable here to imply that Aristotle was contrasting what we now call "expert" and "lay" witnesses. In his time, the availability of expert witnesses in a wide variety of areas was not as great as it is today. So that makes it even more interesting that Aristotle makes allowances for the "expert" witness. For two cases in which expert testimony might have been used but was not, see Bonner (1905, 80).

One final illustration will be offered to show how the legal aspects of an English translation can be helpful in clarifying Aristotle's treatise. In Book Two, there is an extended discussion of the emotions. Modern treatises on rhetoric tend to omit any discussion of the emotions, and modern critics often say that an enumeration of the emotions is not helpful to persuasion. Why therefore does Aristotle treat the emotions in some detail? Our knowledge of the details of trials held in Athens is sufficiently limited that we cannot give many specifics about how the various emotions were used in Athenian courts. But we can use the knowledge of what occurs in the contemporary courtroom to interpolate why Aristotle may have dwelt particularly with the emotion of anger. In doing so, we risk error because cultural mores may have changed. But the risk is less in these instances because we are concerned with the interpretation of basic emotions whose applicability to law may quite possibly have remained fairly stable.

One of the elements that the prosecution must prove in what are commonly called first and second degree murder is malice. Although malice does not require that there be ill-will between the parties, one of the best approaches to show the court that the accused acted with malice is to show that the defendant was angry. An angry defendant is one who is quite likely to act with malice or with the sort of disregard for the safety of others that would be termed "willful and wanton." From such behavior, malice can be inferred. A person who is slighted or insulted or pained or made fun of or who has his infirmities held up to ridicule is a person who can be shown to have acted with malice.

To rebut the charge of malice, Aristotle explained how the attorney could show that the accused was not angry, but calm[30]. A calm client does not act with that degree of recklessnes that can show the hardened heart from which malice can be inferred.

The same explanation can be used to show why Aristotle detailed the emotion of fear. For, persons act in self-defense when they are afraid, and if they can be shown to be afraid of serious bodily harm or death, they can plead successfully the affirmative defense that they feared sufficiently to use even deadly force to protect themselves. In order to be able to show the judges that their client was sufficiently fearful that the client took retaliatory action, the attorney must understand the emotion of fear. Roberts (1954, 104) translated the passage on 1382a32-35 as "Such indications are the enmity and anger of people who have power to do something to us; for it is plain that they have the will to do it, and so they are on the point of doing it." The proof of such enmity and anger by person with power over a client is sufficient to plead self-defense.

SUMMARY

Although the original purpose of this essay was to compare the nineteenth and twentieth century English translations of the *Rhetoric* to guide American and English scholars in an understanding of the strengths and weaknesses of the existing versions, it became apparent that, to our legalistic way of thinking, all of the translations were equally ineffective in providing the perspectives and the vocabulary to match the approach that Aristotle had intended. The translators erred, not because they had not studied rhetoric and Greek law, but because such study was not able to provide the perspectives on rhetoric and law that intensive application provides. Aristotle was multifaceted. Not only did he know his own language as did few others of his time, but he also had a real command of rhetoric and law. As Diogenes Laerties' account of the life of Aristotle pointed out, Aristotle wrote other works on rhetoric,[31] including a history of its development.[32] He needed to be more than just familiar with the law courts, because it was there that his students were to apply his teaching in prosecuting and defending his fellow citizens. Furthermore, it is hard to avoid concluding that one as curious as Aristotle, living in Athens where the courts were active and where all Athenians were actively interested in law, could do other than frequent the trials, if for no other reason than to observe his students in action and give them comments on their presentations. None of the contemporary English translators was so multifaceted. Of the modern continental translators, Tovar comes closest because he was trained in both law and philology. Reading in the areas of rhetoric and law cannot provide the same expertise as can intensive application of the precepts of these areas. The existing translations are carefully and painstakingly done, and can assist, with their variant readings, the development of a new translation.

What should be expected of a new translation? First, it should indicate how successful Aristotle was in correcting what he considered to be the errors of the previous authors of treatises on rhetoric, i.e., the overemphasis upon emotion at the expense of proofs and the limitation of the treatises to forensic rather than including demonstrative and epideictic speaking as well. Aristotle set out to broaden his treatise to include not only forensic persuasion, but demonstrative and occasional persuasion. The new translation should reflect how successful he was in meeting this goal.

Do the precepts of forensic rhetoric continue to intrude disproportionately as the treatise progresses, in spite of Aristotle's announced position and probably his sincere vigilance in trying to keep them out? Does the superstructure that Aristotle acquired from law so dominate his treatment of rhetoric that demonstrative and occasional speaking could not have been given adequate consideration?

Second, a new translation should ascertain whether Aristotle's own treatment violates his proclaimed distaste for the irrelevant introduction of emotion in the courtroom. In the introduction to Book II, Aristotle said that the persuader should know how to put the judge into a certain frame of mind.[33] Is Aristotle successful in introducing emotion without encouraging excesses? Modern treatises on law generally ignore the role of emotion in persuasion, except to comment tersely that the judge has the right to exclude evidence if it will unduly bias the jury.[34] The law assumes that the judge cannot be so corrupted. It is commonly said that, unless relevant evidence is so highly emotional that it will actually make the jury physically sick, the judge is going to admit it. Courts generally want emotion in the lawyer's arguments carefully disguised under the more acceptable methods of presenting reasoning and character persuasion. For example, an expert witness can argue that his patient has endured much pain and suffering, and can describe in detail the agonies of the patient. Therefore emotion is injected as an expert witness with high credibility "argues" about the reactions of the patient. Modern treatments of rhetoric also tend to avoid the discussion of emotion.[35] The new translation should point out to the readers the extent to which Aristotle was able to treat emotion without violating his own distaste for introducing the extraneous to cater to the emotions of those who were making the decisions in ancient Greece.

Third, the translator should develop a consistent terminology before the work is begun and should update that terminology for consistency as the work progresses. The translator should avoid what has apparently been the procedure in the past, of choosing a meaning for a term that completes the immediate thought successfully in that isolated passage but which is not coördinated with previous translations of the same term. Naturally excesses in consistency should be avoided.

Fourth, the new translator should be well versed in the theory and practice of both law and rhetoric. It will not be enough that the translator is acquainted with these disciplines. The translator must be sufficiently familar with both subjects so that, in developing the translation, the perspectives of the two disciplines are held constantly in mind.

In such an enterprise the translator will be aided by the fact that the Greek text of the *Rhetoric* has now been firmly established and that the variant readings noted in the footnotes of the critical translations can show the translator what variations in the text are possible. The translation could use the Kassel version (1976) and be confident that the Greek had been satisfactorily followed.

It has been a number of years now since a new English translation has appeared. The time has come for a version that reflects properly the concepts of law and rhetoric.

NOTES

1. Success in the non-paid role of advocate in the law courts for friends and acquaintances was one of the surest paths to political prominence in Athens. Furthermore, if involved in litigation, persons proficient in speaking had a good chance to win their own law suits, for, early in the democratic period, Athens expected the litigants to speak in their own behalf. As Bonner (1927, i) noted, "...when about the middle of the fifth century, the theory of rhetoric was developed and systematically taught, those who had the inclination and the means to acquire the (art of persuasion), as the Greeks called oratory, had an immense advantage over their untrained opponents in the law courts." As a consequence, expert rhetoricians began to compose speeches for clients to be recited in court as their own. Many orations of these speech-writers were "published." An effective speech was a good professional advertisement for an ambitious speech-writer. Bonner explained that there were three groups of Athenians who would profit from improving their rhetorical skills: first, the advocates themselves who, in the beginning, were citizens who felt it their duty as public servants to help plead a case and later to represent their clients professionally; second, the speech writers who authored texts for the litigants to deliver before the dicasts as if the litigant had written the speech himself; and third, the prosecutors who were at first any Athenians who had standing to bring charges in behalf of justice and later who were specialized prosecutors. Bonner (1927, 72) noted that "Athenian dicasts were neither judges nor jurors in the modern sense, and yet they performed the functions of both. They were merely a cross-section of the Athenian populace selected by lot from among those who presented themselves for service without any test of their fitness for the tasks of administering justice."
2. For Vermont citizen judges, see 4 Vermont Statutes Annotated #111 (a) that follows the German system: "A county court shall be held in each country at the times and places appointed by law, consisting of one presiding judge, who shall be one of the superior

judges, and two assistant judges elected by the county, and two of whom shall be a quorum." Whereas the German citizen judges are selected from a list of names of recommended citizens, the Vermont citizen judges are elected by the voters of each county. MacDowell (1978, 36-40) has recently furnished us considerably more information about the size of the Athenian jury than what was generally available before he published his research in 1978. The typical jury seems to have been composed of 500 or more citizen jurors, although it may have been less than this as trial procedures in Athens developed. However, appearing before a citizen jury remained a speaking situation in which the communicators had to use mass communication techniques. If students of Aristotle's *Rhetoric* keep in mind the number of jurors to whom the litigants had to speak, they will be able to comprehend more fully the advice that Aristotle recommended. It is regrettable that MacDowell did not ally himself with a lawyer during his research. MacDowell said in his introduction that, because the Athenians were not professional lawmakers, he considered his own lack of knowledge of law as no serious handicap. However, MacDowell's treatise demonstrates that Athenian law became a highly developed system, and it is possible that a coauthor trained in law could have detected nuances in Athenians law that MacDowell overlooked because he was not sensitized to legal perspectives. Although the system in Athens was certainly at variance in a number of respects from modern practice, the basic perspective of the two systems has changed little.

3. In drafting the Federal Rules of Evidence, the Federal Judicial Center continued the unwritten code of jurists in not mentioning "emotion", by name, but referring to it indirectly in Rule 403: "Although relevant, evidence may be excluded if its probative value is substantially outweighed by the danger of unfair prejudice, confusion of the issues, or misleading the jury..." See Federal Rulies of Evidence for the United States Courts & Magistrates Effective July 1, 1975 (St. Paul, 1975), 24.

4. 1355a1-2: διὸ καὶ πολλαχοῦ, ὥσπερ [καὶ] πρότερον εἶπον, ὁ νόμος κωλύει λέγειν ἔξω τοῦ πράγματος. θ-π-γ-Bekker-Freese, καί; del. Ross, Kassel.

5. See 1375a28 for the phrase τῷ κοινῷ [νόμῳ]; νόμῳ appears only in certain manuscripts: [ΘΠΓ scholia = τῷ κοινῷ νόμῳ; Ross, Bekker = τῷ κοινῷ, Ac = τω κοινωι Perhaps its omission could be attributed to the fact that, even without the νομος, the phrase τω κοινω could be translated as "the common law." Cronin (1936, 21) said that "there is no doubt that Aristotle favored the use of unwritten law and equity in the settling of disputes, rather than the strict interpretation of the written law. By unwritten law," said Cronin, "he means all the unwritten principles which are supposed to be acknowledged everywhere..." Bonner noted that, after the expulsion of the Thirty Tyrants in 403 B.C., the special pleas that were introduced to argue that a case was not actionable, included *res judicata*. (Bonner 1927, 41) Therefore some reliance on precedent was certainly operative. Such unwritten principles had undoubtedly been used in previous law cases, and therefore they had become "common law" not only because they were generally acknowledged but also because courts had acknowledged them as pertinent in previous cases.

6. "Common law" has a way of developing in any legal system whether it is welcomed or not. Black stated: "As distinguished from law created by the enactment of legislatures, the common law comprises the body of those principles and rules of action, relating to the government and security of persons and property, which derive their authority solely from usages and customs of immemorial antiquity, or from the judgments and decrees of the courts recognizing, affirming, and enforcing such usages and customs..." *Black's Law Dictionary*, 3rd ed. (St. Paul, 1933), 368. There is every reason to believe that such "usages and customs" had become so much a part of the "common law" of certain Greek courts so as to exclude emotional evidence and argument that, even if relevant, could have been too prejudicial to a fair trial.

7. There is no hard evidence that Aristotle attended the law courts. MacDowell (1978, 248) reported that "the general public could stand around the outside of the enclosure which formed the court proper, to listen." Since it was one of the obligations of an Athenian citizen to assist in the administration of justice and since Aristotle could find no better laboratory than the courts to establish what contemporary practice was, it seems highly probable that not only did Aristotle go to court but that he was there frequently.

8. 1356a10-13: οὐ γὰρ ὥσπερ ἔνιοι τῶν τεχνολογούντων τιθέασιν ἐν τῇ τέχνῃ καὶ τὴν ἐπιείκειαν τοῦ λέγοντος ὡς οὐδὲν συμβαλλομένην πρὸς τὸ πιθανόν.

9. Modern treatises on evidence are quite specific in their terminology. Dean Wigmore established the dichotomy of evidence and argument as follows: "Argument and evidence, taken together, represent the means by which the tribunal is sought to be persuaded as to some fact in issue....A fact-in-evidence, or briefly, evidence, signifies any facts considered by the tribunal as data to persuade them to reach a reasoned belief upon a probandum....The remarks of counsel analyzing and pointing out or repudiating the desired influence, for the assistance of the tribunal, are termed argument." (1935, 7) Note that, like Aristotle's ἄτεχνοι πίστεις, evidence is presented to persuade the judge/jury to reach a reasoned belief, and that Wigmore substituted for "invention" the terms "analyzing and pointing out or repudiating the desired inference." Bonner (1905) consistently used the term "evidence" to refer to the types of proof Aristotle designed as ἄτεχνοι πίστεις. In discussing "challenges," Bonner (1905, 68) stated: "Chal-

lenges are not included by Aristotle among πίστεις ἄτεχνοι. It would seem that they ought to be included among the means by which statements are corroborated, and it has been proposed to add a sixth to Aristotle's five classes."

10. For the nature of Athenian juries, see the summary of the constitution in Aristotle's *Politics* and Bonner & Smith (1930, I, 346-378).

11. Earlier (1972, 58) Grimaldi had distinguished five uses of πιότεις. On 1375a10, Grimaldi noted πίστεις used as "pledge" or "word of honor," while Book Three, Grimaldi noted that πιστις was used "as the technical term for that part of a speech wherein one formally demonstrates one's thesis or proposition." There are prove" in a legal sense. Those used in the Rhetoric are:

δεικύναι/ἀποδεικύναι...Wartelle, 1982, 93-49 & 57
πειρᾶσθαι............
. . Wartelle, 1982, 332
ἀποφαίνειν............Wartelle, 1982, 61
μαρτυρέω............Warteele, 1982, 254

Surprisingly enough, συμβιβάζω is not used.

12. A computer search of the Greek text of the *Rhetoric* via the Ibycus system designed by David Packard produced multiple examples wherein Aristotle used the noun τὸ πιθανόν in the *Rhetoric*, e.g., 1355b10-11; 1355b15; 1355b16 1355b32-33; 1356a20; 1356b28; etc. Of course complete inflexibility in translating any term can lead to confusion. At times τὸ πιθανόν would have to be clarified by inserting prefixing and suffixing words, e.g., "the process of persuasion," "the means of persuasion," and "the state of persuasion resultant in the audience." Wartelle (1982, 332, 337-338) also presented usages of the four grammatical forms of "persuasion." His list compares favorably with the Packard computer search.

13. Ἔστω δὴ ῥητορικὴ δύναμις περὶ ἕκαστον τοῦ θεωρῆσαι τὸ ἐνδεχόμενον πιθανόν. *Rhetoric*, therefore, is in the nature of an investigative process [θεωρῆσαι] which properly applied, will result in good speaking. Cf. 1355b10-11: καὶ ὅτι οὐ τὸ πεῖσαι ἔργον αὐτῆς, ἀλλὰ τὸ ἰδεῖν τὰ ὑπάρχοντα πιθανὰ περὶ ἕκαστον.

14. In Athenian courts, only "relatives of the deceased within the relationship of second cousins could prosecute." (Bonner, 1927, 57) Murder was a family affair, almost like the contemporary feud, except that the family initiated its action in the law courts rather than outside the law. Therefore it seems likely that, with non-professional prosecutors and with family sentiments high, much evidence with highly emotional overtones was offered by the communicators to the Athenians courts, where there was also no judge to challenge the admissibility of such prejudicial evidence.

15. 1355b35-36: τῶν δὲ πίστεων αἱ μὲν ἄτεχνοί εἰσιν αἱ δ' ἔντεχνοι Roberts, 1954, 24)

16. 1355b39-1356a1: ὥστε δεῖ τούτων τοῖς μὲν χρήσασθαι τὰ δὲ εὑρεῖν. As early as 1957, Grimaldi (1957, 188-192) sensed that something was amiss in the way translators were categorizing Aristotle's types of proof, but, instead of electing to label the three types of argument as ἦθος, πάθος, and λόγος, Grimaldi (1957, 189) elected to employ the term πρᾶγμα for the last, giving the word λόγος its proper meaning as "the speech in itself considered in its logical aspect," but hesitating to use the simple term λόγος. By 1980, Grimaldi had adopted for λόγος an evidential aspect, which, from our point of view, was again not intended by Aristotle.

17. In his appendix, Grimaldi expostulated in more detail what he considered to be the position of demonstration in the *Rhetoric*. The discussion, which endeavored to relate a series of passages taken from several sections of the *Rhetoric* presented a more complex position of demonstration than Grimaldi offered earlier and proposed that demonstration forms a category parallel to ἔντεχνοι πίστεις. Although we are impressed with Grimaldi's chain, tying Aristotle's divided thoughts together, we return to our original position, that attempting to reconstruct Aristotle's approach by giving emphasis to isolated specific statements rather than by looking for the sweep of his concepts, can lead to distortion and unnecessarily complicate Aristotle's position.

In the *Prior Analytics* (24a10-24b19), the *Posterior Analytics* (74b5-75b36, and the *Rhetoric* (1355a4-18), Aristotle allowed for a type of reasoning he termed "demonstration." Kennedy, presumably in keeping with the division made in the *Analytics*, placed this category of reasoning parallel to dialectic. Grimaldi (1980, 21) said that "for A[ristotle], there are only two ways by which anything is demonstrated: deduction (this, in rhetoric, is the ἐνθύμημα, 'the syllogism' of rhetoric) and induction (this is παράδειγμα or example)."

In the *Prior Analytics*, Aristotle devoted himself to syllogistic reasoning. In the *Posterior Analytics*, Aristotle dedicated himself to an exposition of scientific reasoning, of which the "demonstration" forms a major part. Whereas the *Prior Analytics* concerned itself for the main part with the decisions about the activities of mankind, the *Posterior Analytics* hoped to broaden that outlook to decisions about things as well, i.e., scientific premises. Since scientific induction had not then achieved the prominence it now enjoys, Aristotle concentrated his efforts on establishing the type of major premises that permit us to say that a given premise had validity and was therefore acceptable in the scientific world.

In the *Posterior Analytics*, Aristotle said that "it is necessary for demonstrative understanding in particular to depend on things which are true and primitive and immediate and more familiar than and prior to and explanatory of the conclusion..." (Barnes, 3,71b19-22) What was "true and primitive and immediate" in Aristotle's time appears to have been more easily acceptable than such premises would be at present. The premises of mathematics, e.g., that the square of the hypotenuse is equal to the sum of the squares of the other two sides of the triangle," something 'demonstrated" in Aristotle's time, encouraged Aristotle to consider that series of premises each based on an obvious truth could lead to the acceptance via "demonstration" of a premise not based upon an obvious truth but based upon premises that were acceptable. Aristotle, therefore, was on the right track in seeking to establish "the nature of scientific knowledge" (Ross, 1980, 507). That he falls short of modern standards is not Aristotle's fault. He had not shared in what has developed since his time. If he were alive today, his *Posterior Analytics* would be written much differently, and would challenge the thinking of the most advanced of our scientists.

An example of a demonstration (not found in Aristotle) would be: "All fish are seafaring animals." If we accept the "truth" of this premise, we have established a scientific demonstration. Present researchers would be much more concerned with gathering specimens and with drawing the major premise based on the findings of their data. Present probability theory would not permit any premises that begin with "all" since probability theory always allows for the possibility of error.

Therefore, what Aristotle referred to briefly in the *Rhetoric* as "demonstration" and what he detailed in the *Posterior Analytics* as "demonstration" involved a use of the term quite different from what many would consider contemporary usage of demonstration. As Barnes explained (1975, xvi), the "demonstration is a species of modal syllogism." That, we observe, is far from a a premise based on scientific experimentation. Barnes (1975, xvi) pointed out that "a demonstrative science can be displayed as a set of demonstrations." The premise of such sets of demonstration, said Barnes (1975, xvi), "is either an axiom (an undemonstratable first principle) or else the conclusion of a prior demonstration." The result is therefore a chain of premises that establishes a scientific fact. Barnes (1975, xvi) concluded that although Aristotle's concept of demonstration has its limitations, it is still "an admirable and astounding invention."

If this is a rough idea of what Aristotle meant by demonstration, how does that meaning enter into rhetorical discourse? Aristotle's references to demonstration in the *Rhetoric* are limited. On 1355a4-5, Aristotle said that rhetorical proof is "a sort of demonstration" (ἡ δὲ πίστις ἀπόδειξίς τις), because people are strongly convinced when they perceive a proof as having the basis of what could amount to a truism. This statement is more in the manner of a passing comment in the *Rhetoric* and is not intended to place demonstration as a major component in rhetorical theory. It could not have been, in Aristotle's manner of thinking, because rhetoric always deals with what is probable, and the demonstration deals with what is "factual."

18. See Eddings v. Oklahoma, 102 S.Ct. 968 (1982) for a recent decision by the United States Supreme Court in which the failure of a state court to consider the faulty environment of a juvenile offender as a mitigating factor to his sentence for killing an officer was considered reversible error.

19. 1356a3-4: αἱ δὲ ἐν τῷ τὸν ἀκροατὴν διαθεῖναί πως, αἱ δὲ ἐν αὐτῷ τῷ λόγῳ, διὰ τοῦ δεικνύναι ἢ φαίνεσθαι δεικνύναι.

20. Taylor, 1818, 2: "...and leave very little to be defined by the judge;" Welldon, 1886, 3: "...and as little as possible left to the discretion of the judges;" Buckley, 1910, 4: "...and to abandon as few as possible to the discretion of the judge;" Jebb, 1909, 2: "...leaving as few points as possible to the discretion of the judges;" Roberts, 1924, 1954, "...and leave as few as may be to the decision of the judges;" Freese, 1926, 5: "...and leave as little as possible to the discretion of the judges," Cooper, 1932, 2 "...leaving as little as possible to the decision of those who judge."

21. A similar passage occurs at 1355a22-23 wherein some translators have inserted the word "judges" when it is not there, and it is apparent that Aristotle did not intend it to be there. ὥστε ἐὰν μὴ κατὰ τὸ προσῆκον αἱ κρίσεις γίγνωνται should be translated "so that if decisions are not made as they should be..."

22. 1354b31-33: ἐν δὲ τοῖς δικανικοῖς οὐχ ἱκανὸν τοῦτο, ἀλλὰ πρὸ ἔργου ἐστὶν ἀναλαβεῖν τὸν ἀκροατήν.

23. 1354b35-1355a1: διδόασι τοῖς ἀμφισβητοῦσιν. Welldon (1886, 5) was not far off when he translated the passage as "...are carried away by the parties instead of judging between them."

24. Jebb, 1909, 3 is closer in translating: "...he indulges the ligitant," while Buckley, 1894, 6 reads "...surrender themselves up to the pleaders" and Taylor, 1818, 4: "...gratify the litigants."

25. 1355a27-28: ἀλλ' ἀνάγκη διὰ τῶν κοινῶν ποιεῖσθαι τὰς πίστεις καὶ τοὺς λόγους ..

26. There is a possibility, even if it is remote, that manuscript distortion took place at 1355a22-29. Perhaps Aristotle's manuscript originally read so that the passage could be translated "the proofs of logic." However, when Aristotle comes close to such phraseology in the *Politics*, 1326a29, the wording is διὰ τῶν λόγων πίστεις, a phrase unlikely to be confused with τὰς πίστεις καὶ τοὺς λόγους.

27. 1356a5-6: The character of the speaker is persuasive when the reasoning is spoken in such a manner as to be worthy of belief. διὰ μὲν οὖν τοῦ ἤθους, ὅταν οὕτω λεχθῇ ὁ λόγος ὥστε ἀξιόπιστον ποιῆσαι τὸν λέγοντα.

28. 1356a19-20: διὰ δὲ τῶν λόγων πιστεύουσιν, ὅταν ἀληθὲς ἢ φαινόμενον δείξωμεν ἐκ τῶν περὶ ἕκαστα πιθανῶν. Although there are variant readings for this passage, the meanings are not sufficiently at variance to distort Aristotle's intent. Parisinus 1741 or the "Ac" manuscript, as Bekker labeled it, reads διὰ τὸν λόγον, and Dufour followed this reading. Cantabrigiensis 1298 or "B" after Bekker reads διὰ τοῦ λόγων. Spengel conjectured that the passage should read διὰ τοῦ λόγου. Freese, Kassel, and Cope followed the Cambridge manuscript; Ross preferred the Spengel conjecture. Cope (1877,I,32,n.6)

came close to the interpretation preferred here by having the text read διὰ τῶν λόγων and translating it as "through the channels or medium...of the speech." However, later in the same footnote to his Greek text, Cope pointed out that there are three kinds of πίστεις or rhetorical proofs: διὰ τοῦ ἤθους; διὰ τῶν ακροατῶν; and "...διὰ τῶν λόγων. "By these λόγοι," continued Cope, "we may understand either the actual words which are the instruments or medium of the reasonings, or better the reasoning or arguments themselves which the words convey. This explanation appears to be sufficiently rational and consistent, and in accordance with the ordinary usages of the language." If we choose the meaning of λόγος which Cope labeled as the better translation, i.e., "the reasoning or arguments themselves which the words convey," we approach the interpretation of λόγος preferred here.

29. Taylor, 1818, 9: "But belief is produced through arguments, when we show what is true, or appears to be true from the probabilities pertaining to the several objects of enquiry;" Welldon, 1886, 12: "Lastly the instrument of proof is the speech itself when we have proved a truth or an apparent truth;" Buckley, 1894, 13: "Men give credit from the force of what is said, when out of the means of persuasion which attach to each subject, we evince the truth, or that which appears so;" Jebb, 1909, 6: "Proof is wrought through the speech itself;" Freese, 1926, 17: "Lastly, persuasion is produced by the speech itself...;" Cooper, 1932, 9: "Thirdly persuasion is effected by the arguments, when we demonstrate the truth, real or apparent, by such means as inhere in particular cases;" and Roberts, 1954, 25: "Thirdly, persuasion is effected through the speech itself when we have proved a truth or an apparent truth by means of persuasive arguments suitable to the case in question." Cooper and Taylor do use the word "argument" which indicates that they were trying to maintain Aristotle's trichotomy of ethos, pathos, and logos. The only problem with their translations is that the term "argument" needs to be reserved for the umbrella term contrapuntal to "evidence" so that the preferred translation here is "logic" or "reasoning" rather than "argument."

30. Roberts' translation here is superior to that of Buckley, Jebb, Freese, and Cooper.

31. Kennedy, 1963, 82-85.

32. Freese, 1926, xxii.

33. 1377b22-23: ἀνάγκη μὴ μόνον πρὸς τὸν λόγον ὁρᾶν, ὅπως ἀποδεικτικὸς ἔσται καὶ πιστός, ἀλλὰ καὶ αὐτὸν ποιόν τινα καὶ τὸν κριτὴν κατασκευάζειν. It is necessary to consider not only to what extent reasoning is convincing and credible, but also to show yourself to be of a certain quality and to put the judge into the proper frame of mind.

34. Federal Rules of Evidence, 1975, Advisory Committee's note, 25: "Exclusion for risk of unfair prejudice, confusion of issues, misleading the jury, or waste of time, all find ample support in the authorities. 'Unfair prejudice' within its context means an undue tendency to suggest decision on an improper basis, commonly, though not necessarily, an emotional one."

35. For one of the modern enlightening expositions of emotion, see Hovland (1953), 56-98.

BIBLIOGRAPHY

Actes du Quatrième Congrès International de Philosophie Médiévale. (1969). Arts Libéraux et Philosophie au Moyan Age, Montreal.

Aristotle. (1984). *The Politics*, tr. Carnes Lord, Chicago. [1319b39-40]

Aristotle. (1966). *The Metaphysics*, tr. Hippocrates Apostle, Grinnell, Iowa. [995a3-6]

Aristotle. (1927). *The Poetics*, tr. W.H. Fyfe, London. [1450b8-12]

Aristotle. (1938). *The Prior Analytics*, tr. Hugh Tiedennick, London. [70a10-11]

Aristotle. (1926). *The Art of Rhetoric*. (see particular translator)

Aristotle. (1952). *The Athenian Constitution*, tr. H. Rackham, London.

Aristotle. (1892). *The Athenian Constitution*, tr. F.G. Kenyon, Oxford.

Aristotle. (1952). *The Eudemian Ethics*, tr. H. Rackham, London.

Aristotle. (1966). *The Topics*, tr. E.S. Forster, London.

Barnes, Jonathan, tr. (1975). *Aristotle's Posterior Analytics*, Oxford.

Bekker, Immanuel & C.A. Brandis, eds. (1831-1870). *Aristotelis Opera*, Edidit Academia Regia Borrussica 5 vols., Berlin.

Black's Law Dictionary. (1933). 3rd ed., St. Paul, Minnesota.

Bonner, Robert J. (1905). *Evidence in Athenian Courts*, Chicago.

Bonner, Robert J. (1927). *Lawyers and Litigants in Ancient Athens*, Chicago.

Bonner, Robert J. and Gertrude Smith. (1930). *The Administration of Justice from Homer to Aristotle*, 2 vols, Chicago.

Buckley, Theodore, tr. [1910 (1833)]. *Aristotle's Treatise on Rhetoric*, London. Originally appeared in 1833.

Cooper, Lane, tr. (1932). *The Rhetoric of Aristotle*, New York.

Cope, Edward M. (1867). *An Introduction to Aristotle's Rhetoric*, London.

Cope, Edward M., ed. (1877). *The Rhetoric of Aristotle*, 3 vols, Cambridge, England.

Crem, T.M. (1957). A Commentary on the Rhetoric of Aristotle, Book I, 31 Chapters 1 & 2, M.A. Thesis, Laval University.

Cronin, James F. (1936). *The Athenian Juror and His Oath*, Chicago.

Dufour, Médéric. (1967). *Aristote Rhétorique*, 3 vols, 3rd ed., Paris.

Eddings v. Oklahoma, 102 S. Ct. 968 (1982).
Federal Rules of Evidence for the United States Courts & Magistrates Effective July 1, 1975, St. Paul, Minnesota.
Freese, John H., tr. (1926). *The "Art" of Rhetoric*, London.
Grimaldi, W.M.A. (1980). *Aristotle, "Rhetoric" I: A Commentary*, New York.
Grimaldi, W.M.A. (1957). "A Note on the ΠΙΣΤΕΙΣ in Aristotle's Rhetoric," *American Journal of Philology* 78, 188-192.
Grimaldi, W.M.A. (1958). "Rhetoric and the Philosophy of Aristotle," *Classical Journal*, 371-375.
Grimaldi, W.M.A. (1972). *Studies in the Philosophy of Aristotle's Rhetoric*, Wiesbaden.
Hovland, Carl. (1953). *Communication and Persuasion*, New Haven, Connecticut.
Jebb, Richard Claverhouse, tr. (1909). *The Rhetoric of Aristotle*, Cambridge, England.
Kennedy, George. (1963). *The Art of Persuasion in Greece*, Princeton.
Kennedy, George. (1980). *Classical Rhetoric and Its Christian and Secular Tradition from Ancient To Modern Times*, Chapel Hill.
Kassel, Rudolf. (1976). *Aristotelis Ars Rhetorica*, Berlin.
Lynch, John P. (1972). *Aristotle's School: A Study of a Greek Educational Institution*, Berkeley.
MacDowell, Douglas M. (1963). *Athenian Homicide Law in the Age of the Orators*, Manchester.
MacDowell, Douglas M. (1978). *The Law in Classical Athens*, Ithaca.
Murphy, James J., ed. (1983). *Renaissance Eloquence*, Berkeley.
Murphy, James J., ed. (1972). *A Synoptic History of Classical Rhetoric*, New York.
Plato. tr. H.N. Fowler. (1960). *The Phaedrus*, London.
Roberts, W. Rhys, tr. (1954). *Aristotle: Rhetoric*, New York.
Roberts, W. Rhys. (1924). "Notes on Aristotle's 'Rhetoric'," *American Journal of Philology* 45, 351-361.
Roemer, Adolph. (1885). *Aristotelis Ars Rhetorica*, Leipsig.
Ross, W.D., ed. (1959). *Aristotelis Ars Rhetorica*, Oxford.
Ross, W.D., ed. (1942). "Introduction," *The Student's Oxford Aristotle*, vol. 1, Oxford.
Smith, Peter, (1985). "Chance Events in Homer (and Aristotle)," paper read at the American Philological Association, Washington, D.C. with an abstract appearing on p. 104 of the proceedings.
Spengel, Leonardi. (1967). *Aristotelis Ars Rhetorica cum adnotatione Leonardi Spengel*, Leipsig.
Taylor, Thomas, tr. (1818). *The Rhetoric, Poetic, and Nichomachean Ethics of Aristotle*, 2 vols, London.
Tovar, Antonio, ed. (1953). *Aristoteles Retorica*, Madrid.
Welldon, J.E.C., tr. (1886). *The Rhetoric of Aristotle*, London.
Wigmore, John H. (1935). *A Students' Textbook of the Law of Evidence*, Brooklyn.

GREEK INDEX

The Greek index was designed as follows:

a. the Greek has been retained just as it appears in the text, including the accent marks in the text, so that the reader can refer to terms without interpolation

b. with long quotations, only the leading words are given, followed by the appropriate Bekker citation

c. When no accent or breathing marks were given in the source, none has been given here.

ἀεί	164
Ἀθηναίων Πολιτεία	183
αἱ δὲ ἐν τῷ τοῦ ἀκροατὸν [1356a3]	205
ἀκροατής	189, 195
ἀλλ' ἀνάγκη διὰ τῶν κοινῶν [1355a27]	205n25
ἅμα	14
ἀμφισβητοῦντες	189
ἀνάγκη μὴ μόνον [1377b22]	206n33
ἀποφαίνειν	204
ἀξιοῦμεν	164
ἀξιοῦσιν	164
ἀπόδειξις	189
Ἄρειος πάγος	179, 185
ἀρἰστοτέλους	29
Ἀριστοτέλους	40n44
αρισΤοΤελους ΤεχΝΗς ρΗΤορικΗς	13
ἀριστοτέλους τέχνης ῥητορικῆς βιβλίον τρίτον γ	25
Ἀριστοτέλους Τέχνης Ῥητορικῆς βιβλία τρία	171
ΑΡΙΣΤΟΤΕΛΟΥΣ ΤΕΧΝΗΣ ΡΗΤΟΡΙΚΝΣ	189
ἀρχῇ	14
ἀρχῆς	14
ἄτεχνοι	168
ἄτεχνοι πίστεις	174, 182, 184-185, 187, 190-192, 195, 203n9, 205n19, 205n21, 205n22, 205n23, 205n25, 205n26, 205n27, 205n28, 206n28, 206n33
ἄτεχνοι πιστέων πέρι	174
βλάβη	34
γίνεται συλλογισμός	14
Γρίλλος	2
δεικνύναι/ἀποδεικνύναι	204n11
διὰ δὲ τῶν λόγων [1356a19]	206n28
διὰ μὲν οὖν τοῦ [τω] ἤθους [1356a5]	205n27
[διὰ] ταῦτα καὶ [1393a3]	15
διὰ τὸν λόγον	205n28
διὰ τοῦ ἤθους, διὰ τῶν ἀκροατῶν	206n28
διὰ τοῦ λόγου	205n28
διὰ τοῦ λόγων	205n28
διὰ τῶν λόγων	205n28
διὰ τῶν λόγων πίστεις	205n26
διδόασι τοῖς ἀμφισβητοῦσιν	205n23
δικανικά	194
δικανικός	194
δικαστής	178, 194

διὸ καί 14, 38n14
διὸ καὶ πολλαχοῦ [1355a1] 203
διὸ κάμνοντες [1379a15] 34

ἐὰν γὰρ ᾖ τι τούτων γνώριμον 14
εἰ 16
[τοῖς ἄλλοις] εἰ δὲ μή [1379a21] 34
εἰ μὴ ἔχοιμεν 16
ἔκλεψε 34
ἔκλεψεν 33
ἑκόντες 15
ἔλαβε 34
ἐμμενοῦμεν 164
ἐμμενοῦσιν 164
ἐν δὲ τοῖς δικανικοῖς [1354b31] 205n22
ἐνδεχόμενον πιθανόν 189
ἐνδέχεται 20
ἔντεχνοι πίστεις 168, 182, 184, 186-187, 190-193, 195, 204n17
ἐν τῇ τέχνῃ 182
ἐνθύμημα 186, 189, 204n17
ἐπαγωγή 189
ἐπεὶ δ' ὅσα [1369b20] 15
ἐπείρασε 39n18
ἐπὶ τοῖς κρίνουσι 193
ἔστιν δ' ἔπαινος λόγος [1367b26] 16
Ἔστω δὴ ῥητορικὴ [1355b26-27] 204n13
εὕρεσις 185
εὑρίσκειν 185

ἤ 16
ἡ δὲ πίστις ἀπόδειξίς τις 205n17
ἤθεα 191
ἦθος 183, 186-187, 190, 195, 204n16
ἢ μὴ ἔχοιμεν 16
[ὑπὲρ τῶν] Ἡρακλει[ω]δῶν 39n19
ἢ τὰ ὑπὲρ τῶν Ἡρακλει[ω]δῶν πραχθέντα 16

θεωρεῖν 20, 185
θεωρῆσαι 204n13
Θεοδέκτεια 1, 2

ίσκου (suffix) 39n25

καὶ δυοῖν 14
καὶ δυοῖν αἰτίοιν τὸ ἀπὸ τοῦ μείζονος αἰτίου μεῖζον 14
καὶ μάλιστα [1363a38-1363b1] 39n28
καὶ ὅτι οὐ τὸ πεῖσαι [1355b10] 204n13
κακόν 14
κοινοὶ τόποι 3
κοινόν 164
κρίνειν 194
κριτής 194

λεχθέντα 16
λόγοι 191, 206n28
λόγος 186-188, 192-195, 204n16, 206n28

μάλιστα 39n28
μάλιστα μέν 34
μᾶλλον 15, 38n18
μαρτυρέω 204n11
μάρτυς 185
μέλειν 15
μελήσει 15
μέλλειν 15
μελλήσε 15
μελλήσει 15
μέλλοντα 15
μέλω 15

νεανίσκου 39n25
νέου μὲν [1361b7] 39n25
νόμος 179, 203n5
νῦν δὲ γελοίως 16

οἰκεῖον 164
οἷον εἴ [1395b7] 15
ὅταν τὸ μὲν κωλῦον τὸ δὲ μὴ κωλῦον μετατεθῇ [1368a10] 16
οὐ γὰρ πολλοὶ ἴσασιν 16
οὐ γὰρ ὥσπερ [1356a10] 203n8
οὐδὲ πάντως [1374a16] 33
οὐκ ἔχοντες 15
οὖν 39n25
οὔχ ἔχοντες 15

πάθη 191
πάθος 183, 186–187, 190, 193, 204n16
παράδειγμα 189, 204n17
παράλογον 39n27
πατέρας . . . υἱούς 170
πείθειν 188
πειρᾶσθαι 204n11
περὶ δὲ τῶν ἀτέχνων 174
περὶ ῥΗτοριΚῆς 29
περὶ ῥητρικῆς 40n44
πιθανός, ή, όν 188
πιθανόν 188, 204n12
πιθανῶς 188
πίστεις 166, 170, 181–182, 186, 188, 190–191, 192–193, 205n11
[τὰς] πίστεις καὶ τοὺς λόγους 194
πίστεις ἄτεχνοι 165, 166, 174
πίστεις ἔντεχνοι 190
πρᾶγμα 187, 189, 204n16
πραχθέντα 16
πρὸς ἀλήθειαν γὰρ τείνει ταῦτα 15

ῥήτωρ 195

συλλογίζεσθαι 189
συλλογισμός 14, 189
συμβιβάζω 204n11
Συναγωγὴ τεχνῶν 2

τὰς πίστεις καὶ τοὺς λόγους 205n26
τείνει 14, 15, 38n17
τεκμήριον τὸ τοιοῦτον τῶν σημείων ἐστίν 38n14
τέχναι 182
τέχνη 181-182, 188-190
τέχνοι 181
τεχνολογία 188
τεχνόλογος 188
τι 15
τινι 14, 15, 38
τις 15
τόποι 4
τριβή 181
τρίτον 39n36
τύχη 181
τῷ 14
τῷ δ' ἀκολάστῳ 38n8
τῷ κοινῷ [νόμῳ] 203n5
τῶν δὲ πίστεων αἱ μὲν ἄτεχνοι εἰσιν αἱ δ' ἔντεχνοι 204n15

φαίνεσθαι 14

χαίρουσιν ἐπιθυμοῦντες 39n28
χιασμός 181

ὡς γὰρ [1393a4] 15
ὥστε δεῖ τούτων τοῖς μὲν χρήσασθαι τὰ δὲ εὑρεῖν 204n16
ὥστε ἐὰν μὴ κατὰ [1355a22] 205n21

LATIN INDEX

credulitas 170
eius, a quo accepit 33
fatuus qui patrem perimens pueros derelinquit 170
fides 170
mens rea 34
patre 170
persuasio 170
si autem non 34

INDEX TO MANUSCRIPTS

The label "MS" does not appear in this index before the manuscript numbers. It appears in the text of this book in the early chapters, where references to manuscripts need to be distinguished from printed books, but it does not appear in later chapters where the confusion of manuscripts and printed books appears unlikely. Authors vary in their usage of "MS," some preferring to make a specific designation and others not. Indexes to manuscripts generally do not include the "MS," since only manuscripts are being listed. See Moraux, Wartelle, Schneider, Kassel, and Lacombe.

Ambrosianus L 76 17
Baroccianus Grec 133 .... 25, 28, 113
Berolinensus Borussica Publica Hamil 43 .... 43, 175
Bologna UB 2400 .... 80n6
Cantabrigiensis Ff.5.8 [1298] 80, 163, 168, 169, 170, 205n28
    compared to Grec 1741 16-17
      date 17

descendants of unrevised	23–24
descendants of revised	23, 24–25, 28–29
location	11
Chicagiensis (Newberry)	29, 33, 170
Chicagiensis (U. of Chicago) 851	80
Dresdensis Da 4	17, 39
Etonensis 129	170
Gulferbytanus Bibl. Ducalis 448.Helmst.	29, 32, 170
Harvardiana Latin 39	40
Laurentianus lxxix 18	81
Laurentianus Pl 86, Codex 19	40
Laurentianus Pl 60, Codexes 10 & 18	40
Laurentianus Pl 31, Codex 14	25, 28, 40
Laurentianus Conv. Sopp. 47	17, 170
Lipsienesis 24	23, 24
Marcianus Grec 200	28, 29, 32, 39, 40, 162, 163, 167, 168, 169
Marcianus Grec 214 [479]	20, 23, 169, 170
Marcianus Grec 215	29, 163
Marcianus Latin VI 64	29, 33
Matritensis 4684	28, 29
Monacensis Graci 90	25, 40, 82
Monacensis Graci 175	40, 69, 82
Monacensis Graci 176	25, 39, 40, 82, 168, 169
Monacensis Graci 234	40
Monacensis Graci 313	20, 23, 39, 168, 169
Monacensis Latin 206	29, 32, 40
Monacensis Latin 8003	29, 32, 40
Palatinus Grec 23 (Vaticanus Grec 23)	23, 24, 163, 167–169
Palatinus Grec 160	29
Palatinus Grec 260	163
Palatinus Latin 1591	80n6
Parisinus Grec 1741	40, 69, 162, 163, 164, 167, 168, 169, 170, 171, 175, 205n28
compared to Monacensis Graci 313	39
corrections by first hand	14
corrections by second hand	15–16
date	5–6
descendants of	17–23
dimensions	13
major lacuna	16
provenance	11–13, 17
topography	13–14
Parisinus Grec 1818	25, 39, 162, 167, 168, 169
Parisinus Grec 1869	25, 39, 162, 167, 168, 169
Parisinus Grec 2038	11, 28, 39, 45, 162, 163, 168, 169
Parisinus Grec 2042	29
Parisinus Grec 2116	28, 39, 162, 167, 168, 169
Parisinus Grec 2346	9, 35
Parisinus Grec 3074	11
Parisinus Latin 1735	43, 175
Parisinus Latin 7695	29, 32, 33, 34, 43
Parisinus Latin 14359	11
Parisinus Latin 14696	29, 32, 33
Parisinus Latin 16097	43, 175
Parisinus Latin 16583	170
Parisinus Latin 16673	29, 33, 38, 43, 170
Parisinus Latin 17917	11
Parisinus Français 5685	11
Parisinus Français 22571	38

Parisinus Nouvelle Acquisition Française 1328 38
Parisinus Nouvelle Acquisition Latin 1876 45
Parisinus Supplementary Grec 1285 .... 24, 39
Toletanus Latin 47.15 .... 33, 170
Tübingensis Mb 15 170
Urbanus Grec 47 .... 17, 23, 163
Vaticanus Grec 23 (see Palatinus Grec 23)
Vaticanus Grec 1340 .... 24, 25, 39, 163, 167–171
Vaticanus Grec 1580 .... 24, 28, 45
Vaticanus Grec 2228 69
Vaticanus Grec 2384 29
Vaticanus Latin 1958 .... 80n6
Vaticanus Latin 4564 43
Vidobonensis 125 170
Wien Latin 2329 80

GENERAL INDEX

Academy 165
adversarial system 183
Aeschlimann, Erhard 41
Agricola, Rudolph 39
Aldine edition of *Rhetoric* (see Greek printings of *Rhetoric*)
Alemannus (see Hermannus Alemannus)
Alexandria 5, 69
Alfarabi 43, 45, 81, 158
Alphabet of the Dead 79
Andronikos of Rhodes 5, 6n
anger 201
Apellicon of Teos 5
Apostolides, Aristoboulus 24
Arabic 38, 43, 44, 81, 171
Arabic-Hebraic culture 9, 35
Arabic translation of the *Rhetoric* 9
archetype 9, 16, 17, 35, 37
Arentin, I. C. de 39
argument 182, 184, 188, 189, 190, 191, 192, 203, 206n28
Ares 182
Aristophanes 182
Aristotle
    biological works 7
    knowledge of law 182–4, 203
    lecture notes, see *Rhetoric*
    library 5, 6
    on rhetoric 1, 178–9, 182, 189, 201–202
    residence in Asia Minor 1, 2
    residence in Athens 1, 2, 3
    school of rhetoric 1, 3, 4–5, 9
Aristotle's works
    Analytics 2, 204n17
    Athenian Constitution 163, 183, 190, 206
    Categories 187
    De Anima 81
    De Caelo 81

    Ethics 57, 74, 81, 83, 184, 206
    Gryllos 2
    Magna Moralis 40
    Metaphysics 178, 179, 206
    Methodics 2
    Physica 81
    Poetics 9, 38, 43, 45, 57, 69, 81, 82, 83, 186, 206
    Politics 4, 40, 74, 81, 179, 204n10, 205, 206
    Posterior Analytics 81, 204n,17, 205n17, 206
    Prior Analytics 195, 204n17
    Theodectea 1, 2-3
    Topics 1, 2, 4, 195, 206
Artz, F.B. 79, 84
Athenaeus 5, 6
Athenian law 178-79, 182, 183, 194, 201, 202, 203, 204
attorneys (see lawyers)
Averroës 33, 38, 45, 81, 158
Avicenne 43

Badawi, Abdurrahman 9, 41
Baluze 28
Bandini, Augiolo M. 160
Barnes, Jonathan 204n17, 205n17, 206
Bedder v. Director of Public Prosecutions 40
Behlen, Ludwig 164
Bekker, Immanuel 6, 36, 41, 162, 163, 167, 170, 172, 174, 206
Bekker edition (see Greek printings of the *Rhetoric*)
Berlin edition (see Greek printings of the *Rhetoric*)
Bessarion, Jean 29, 38
Black's Law Dictionary 203n6, 206
Biponte edition (see Greek printings of *Rhetoric*)
Boggess, W.F. 9, 38, 41, 43, 44, 81, 84, 159
Boivin, Jean 13, 38
Bonitz, Hermann 163, 164, 165, 172
Bonitz Index (see Greek printings of *Rhetoric*)
Bonner Robert 179, 182-185, 189, 200, 202, 203n9, 204n10n14, 206
booksellers 5
Bouhier, Jean 11, 38
Brandes, Paul 6, 84
Brandis, Christian 3, 6, 163, 164, 165, 171, 172
Bradley, John 39, 40, 41
Bubonius, Jacobus 74
Buhle, Theophilus 57, 161, 162, 172
Buhler, Curt 41
Burke, Peter 79, 84
Burnet, John 2, 4, 6

calligraphy 45
Canbini 25
cannons of rhetoric 185
Capelli, Adriano 84
Chalk(c)ondyles, Demetrius 17
Charles IX of France 39
Chartier, Robert 83, 84
Christopher, Henry G.T. 41
Chrysokokkes, Georgios 40
Cicero 4, 5, 6, 162, 185

Colbert 11, 28, 40
Colonna, Aegidio 45, 81, 158
common law 179, 203
commentaria 5
commonplaces 3
Congress of Vienna 39
Constantino, Angelo 25, 39
contracts 91, 95
Convent of Santa Maria Novella 40
Cope, Edward 1, 2, 3, 6, 35, 36, 41, 172, 184, 189, 190, 192-193, 194, 206
Cope edition (see Greek printings of *Rhetoric*)
copyists 5
Corbett, Edward P.J. 3, 6
courts (see law courts)
Cranz, F. Edward 83
Crem, Theresa M. 191, 206
Critias 16
Cronin, James 179, 200, 203, 206
Curtis, Mark 84

Dalberg, Johann 39
d'Ancona, Paola 40
De Boer, Tjite J. 81, 84, 158
deductive reasoning 187, 192
Dejob, Charles 160
de la Treille 82
deliberative oratory 182, 183, 194
Delisle, Leopold 11, 38, 40, 41
Demetrius 17
demonstration 191, 204n17, 205n17
demonstrative oratory 178, 201, 204-5
Demosthenes 2, 164, 178
de Vleechauwer, Herman Jean 5, 6
Diogenes Laerties 201
Dionysius of Halicarnassus 2
discovery 184, 185, 187, 190, 192
Dittmeyer, Leonard 32, 41, 172
Dufour, Médéric 4, 6, 161, 172, 190, 192, 205n28, 206
Düring, Ingemar 1, 6

Eddings v. Oklahoma 205n18, 207
Eisenstein, Elizabeth 8, 41, 42, 57, 83, 84
Elector Philip of the Palatinate 39
emotion 178-179, 182, 183, 191, 193, 195, 201, 202, 203
Emperor Maximillian 23
English translators of the *Rhetoric*
    Buckley, Theodore 14, 41, 177, 189, 192n3, 205n20n24, 206n29n30, 206
    Cooper, Lane 84, 177, 189, 193-194, 196-200, 205n20, 206n28n30
    Freese, John 16, 41, 167, 172, 177, 189, 193-194, 203, 205n20, 206n28n30n32, 207
    Jebb, Richard 34, 41, 177, 189, 193, 205n2024, 206n28, 207
    Roberts, W. Rhys. 7, 14, 39, 41, 177, 181, 184, 188, 189, 190, 192-194, 196-200,
                                                                                   201, 205n20, 206n28n30, 207
    Taylor, Thomas 176, 189, 193, 205n20n28, 206n29, 207
    Welldon, James 176, 189, 192-193, 205n20n23, 206n28, 207
Enos, Richard 180, 181
enthymeme 3, 183, 186, 187, 191, 192, 194, 195
epideictic oratory 178, 182, 183, 194, 201

Erasmus, Desiderius ... 57
Erickson, Keith V. ... 84
Eudemus ... 5
Euripides ... 167
evidence ... 182, 184, 185, 187, 188, 189, 190, 191, 192, 195, 203
example ... 186, 187, 191, 192

fact ... 187, 205n17
Fébry, Nicolas ... 11
Federal Judicial Center ... 203n3
Federal Rules of Evidence ... 203n3, 206n34, 207
Filelfo, Francesco ... 24
forensic oratory ... 178, 179, 182, 183, 194, 201
Francis I of France ... 39
Franck, Adolphe ... 158
Franklin, Alfred ... 158
Franklin, Burt ... 166
Fugger, Ulrich ... 39

Gaisford, Thomas ... 6, 36, 41, 162, 167, 172
Gaisford edition (see Greek printings of *Rhetoric*)
Gardhausen, Victor ... 39, 40, 41
Gazes, Theodore ... 17
Gauthier, Leon ... 158
generic view ... 3, 6
George of Trebizond (see Trapezuntius)
Gnoll, Umberto ... 41
Gorgias ... 183
Graeco-Roman culture ... 6n
Grayeff, Félix ... 6n
Greek printings of the *Rhetoric*
    Aldine ... 45, 57, 69, 79, 164, 168, 175
    Barbaro, Hermolao ... 57, 74, 82-3, 158, 161, 175
    Bekker ... 38, 162-163, 164, 167, 168, 169, 176, 203, 206
        Bekker 2nd edition ... 176
        Bekker third edition (octavo) ... 165, 167, 168, 176
    Biponte ... 161-162, 167, 169, 172, 173, 174, 176
    Bonitz Index ... 163, 165-166, 171, 174, 176, 185, 187
    Buhle (see Biponte)
    Cope ... 164-165, 166, 167, 168, 172, 205n28, 206
    Didot, Firmin ... 167, 176
    Dufour ... 167-168
    Freese ... 205n28
    Gaisford ... 163, 164, 167, 168, 169, 176
    Goulston, Edward ... 161
    Gryphius ... 57, 168, 176
    Isingrinius ... 168
    Kassel ... 169-170, 177, 202-203, 207
    Leipsig (1831) ... 162
    Loeb Library (Freese) ... 167
    Maioragius, Antonius ... 74, 83, 159, 161, 162, 175
    Morel, William ... 162, 167, 168
    Muret, Marc Antoine ... 74, 83, 160, 167, 175
    Oxford (1837) ... 163, 174, 176
    Porto, Emilio ... 74, 79, 83, 162
    Riccobono, Antonio ... 74, 83, 160, 161, 163, 175
    Roemer ... 166-167
    Ross ... 169, 205n28

    Sigonio, Carlo 74, 83, 160, 162, 173, 175
    Spengel 163-164, 169, 177, 205n28
    Sylburg 161, 163, 166, 167, 174, 176
    Tovar 83, 167, 168-169
    Trincavelli, Joannis 39, 57, 69
    Victorius (see Victorius)
Gregoropoulos, Manuel 24
Grynaeus, Simon 57
Grimaldi, William M.A. 84, 177, 183, 186-187, 191, 204n11n16, 207
Gulick, Charles B. 6

Hall, F.W. 33, 41
Hammont, R. 158
Harlfinger, D. 17, 28, 41
Hart, Ignatius 39
Haskins, Charles H. 84
Havet, Ernest 2, 6
hearsay 185
Hebrew 38
Heidelberg 23, 39, 163, 166
helastic jury 185
Henry II of France 38
Henry IV of France 38
Hermannus Alemannus 38, 43, 45, 81, 159
Herrick, Marvin 81, 84
Hill, Forbes I 3, 4, 6n7, 172, 191
Homer 165, 166, 167
Hours, Henri 83, 84
Hovland, Carl 206n35, 207
Hultzen, Lee 84
humanists 79

Ibn Al-Samh 9
Ioannu, Markos 40
impeachment 195
incunabula 42
inductive reasoning 187-188, 190, 192
intent (see *mens rea*)
invent(ion) 184, 185, 190, 191, 192, 203n9
Isocrates 1, 3, 6, 164

Jaeger, Werner 6n, 7, 40
John of Crete (or Rhodes) 29, 40
Joseph, Maximilian 39
Jourdain, l'Abbé 38
Jourdain, Amable 33, 41, 84
judges 178, 184, 190, 191, 192, 193, 202
judicial fact 184, 187
judicial notice 194
jury 178-179, 184, 190, 191, 192, 202, 203

Kantelhardt, Adolf 3-4
Kappas, Matthias 166-172
Kassel, Rudolf 9-11, 16, 17, 20, 24, 25, 28, 32, 34, 35, 36, 39, 40, 41, 47, 69, 80, 82, 84, 161,
                                             169, 172, 195, 202, 203, 205n28, 207
Kassel edition (see Greek editions of *Rhetoric*)
Kearney, Hugo F. 84

Kennedy, George 169, 172, 180-182, 192, 204n17, 206n31, 207
Kenyon, Frederick G. 6n, 7, 183
Kiernan, Thomas 166, 172
Kristeller, Paul O. 74, 84

Lacombe, George 8, 32, 33, 40, 41, 80, 81, 84
lacuna 9, 16, 32, 35, 37, 39
Latin translations of the *Rhetoric*
    Antiqua translation (see Vetusta) 32, 33, 170
    Anonymous 170-171
    Vetusta (Vetus) translation (see Antiqua) 32, 33, 43, 164, 169, 170
    Victorius (see Victorius)
    Moerbeck translation (see William of Moerbeck)
Laemarius, Guillelmus 74, 84
Langkravel, Bernard 165
LaRusso, Dominic 79, 84
law courts 178-179, 181-82, 183, 184, 187, 194, 202
laws 191, 195
lawyers 32, 34-35, 36, 180, 189-190, 192, 193, 194
Lee, M.H.D.P. 1, 7
Lehmann-Haupt, Hellmut 45, 84
Levant 40
Libri Tres 162
Lincy, Leroux de 38n2
Lobel, Edgar 7
Loeb Library (see Greek printings of *Rhetoric*)
logical proof 4, 192
lost manuscripts 11, 20
Louis, Pierre 1, 7
Lowry, Martin 45, 84
Luquet, Georges H. 159
Lyceum 2, 4-5
Lynch, John 6, 207
Lyon 79, 83-84

MacDowell, Douglas 185, 203n2n6, 207
malice 201
Manutius, Aldus 24, 28, 45, 80, 161, 167
marginalia 9, 24, 29, 32, 40, 69, 80
Margoliouth, D.C. 9, 41, 172
Martin, H.J. 83, 84
Mazarin 25
McKeon, Richard 2, 7
Medici, Catherine de 11, 13, 28, 38
Medici, Cosmo de 81
Medici, Francesco 69, 82
Medici, Madeleine 81
Medici library 11
Medieval period 8
Meyer, J.B. 165
Meyer, Wilhelm 22, 23, 82
Moerbeck (see William of Moerbeck)
Monfasani, John 40, 43, 80, 81, 84
Moraux, Paul 2, 7, 8, 39, 41
Morgan, Paul 84
Murphy, James J. 7, 81, 84, 158, 172, 180, 207

Napoleon 39
Neleus 5
Niccolai, Francisco H. 40, 41, 57, 82, 84, 160
Nicéron, Jean Pierre 158, 160
Niebuhr, Barthold G. 3,7, 172

oaths 191, 195
Okko, Adolf 20
Olynthiac War 2
Omont, Henri 41
Organ, Troy 166, 172
Oxford edition (see Greek printings of *Rhetoric*)

Palatinate 23
Palatine library 39
paleological evidence 5
paleography 8
papyri 6n, 7, 8
Paquet, Jean Noël 159
parchment 8
pathos 4
persuasion 178, 181, 182, 183, 185, 188–189, 190, 195, 202, 204
Petrachian Renaissance 84
Phaedrus 181, 207
Phillips' collection 45
Pithou, François 11
Pithou, Pierre 11
Plato 1, 6, 164, 165, 181, 207
Platonic dialogue 4
Plutarch 5, 7
polemic 4, 187
Pope Gregory XII 83
Pope Innocent VIII 83
Pope Leo X 13
Portus(o) of Candia 83
printing press 25, 28, 29, 42, 74, 179
probability 188, 207n17
proofs 4, 178, 183, 188, 189, 191, 192, 194, 195, 206
provocation 34–35
Ptolmys 5
Pucci, Francesco 69

Quintilian 185

Rabe, Hugo 171, 172
Randall, John H. 5, 6, 7
Rashdall, Hastings 84, 85
rational proof 192
real evidence 190, 195
reasoning 187–188, 191, 192, 193–195
Reimer, G. 165
Renaissance 8, 69, 74, 79
Renan, Ernest 158
res judicata 203
rhetoric
    Arabic manuscript 9, 33, 35, 38, 45, 171
    as lecture notes 3, 4, 37, 45, 180–181, 182, 186
    chapters in 13, 37, 43, 166, 174, 175–176

chronological list of printings	42, 79, 90-153
composition, method of	2-4, 6, 8
critical editions	35-37, 41
date of	1-2, 6
demand for	42, 45, 57, 69, 74, 79, 161
earliest Greek MS	5, 6, 9, 16-17, 57
earliest Latin MS	9
earliest printed editions	24, 42, 45
generic theory	3, 4
lacuna	9, 16, 35, 37, 39
lost archetype	9, 11, 16, 23, 35, 37
organization of	3, 4, 6, 37, 39
preservation	4-6
publication	2, 4
title	189

rhetoricians 36, 179-180, 183, 185, 192
Rhodes, Dennis 85
Roemer, Adolph 7, 15, 23, 34, 36, 38, 39, 41, 57, 166, 167, 169, 172, 177, 181, 207
Roemer edition (see Greek printings of *Rhetoric*)
Rome 37
Rose, Valentine 165
Ross, William D. 3, 7, 13, 14, 15, 33, 36, 38, 39, 41, 169, 172, 180, 195, 203, 204n17, 207
Ross edition (see Greek printings of the *Rhetoric*)
Rudolphi, Nicolas 11, 13, 20, 69, 82
Ruediger, Werner 82, 85, 160

Sandys, John E. 1, 3, 7, 158-160, 162, 164-165, 172, 190
Schiolarios, Georgios 28
Schmitt, Christian B. 57, 69, 84, 85
Schneider, Bernd 16, 32, 33, 34, 41, 85, 170-172
scholia 11, 24, 25, 35, 80, 163, 165, 167, 168, 169, 171
Shute, Richard 3, 4, 5
Skepsis 5
Smith, Gertrude 182, 185, 189, 204n10, 206
Smith, J.A. 7, 41
Smith, Peter 207
Socrates 181
Solmsen, Frederick 3, 4, 6, 7, 169, 172
Solon 183
sophistry 182, 189
sophists 6
Sophocles 165
Spengel, Leonard 7, 32, 33, 36, 38, 41, 57, 163, 164, 167, 172, 207
Spengel edition (see Greek printings of the *Rhetoric*)
St. Thomas Aquinas 81
stare decisis 193
Steinschneider, Moritz 158
Stern, S.M. 9, 41
Stevenson, Henry 39
Strabo 5, 6n, 7
Straton 5
Strozzi, Pierre 13, 20
Sturm (Sturmio), John 74, 79, 83
Sulla 5
Sylburg edition (see Greek printings of the *Rhetoric*)
Syriac 9, 39
Syrian 35

Taylor, Alfred E. ... 4, 7
Taylor, Thomas ... 207
terminology (see vocabulary)
Theophrastus ... 5
Theupola, Laurentio ... 40
Thirty Years War ... 23
Thompson, d'Arcy ... 1, 7
Thurot, Carol ... 164, 172
Tilly ... 23
Tkatsch, Jaroslaus ... 9, 41
Toledo ... 33
topics ... 4
torture ... 191, 195
Tovar, Antonio ... 3, 4, 36, 161, 168, 172, 177, 192, 201, 207
Tovar edition (see Greek printings of the *Rhetoric*)
translation
    difficulties of ... 36, 179-180, 201
    legal aspects of ... 193, 195, 196-200, 201
    need for a new ... 180, 201-202
Trapezuntius, George ... 42, 43, 57, 69, 80, 160, 161, 163, 166, 174, 175
Trinity College ... 164
Turks ... 45
Tyrannion ... 5, 37

Usener, Hermann ... 165

Vahlen, Johannes ... 172
Van Gröningen, Bernard A. ... 38, 41
Vater ... 162
Vatican ... 39
velum ... 8
Verbeke, Gerard ... 159
Vergece, Ange ... 28, 39
Victorius, Peter ... 13, 16, 20, 25, 32, 35-36, 38, 40, 41, 57, 69, 74, 79, 81, 82, 160, 161, 162, 164, 167-168, 170, 194
vocabulary ... 8, 180-189, 193, 202
Vogel, Marie ... 39, 40, 41

Wartelle, André ... 8, 40, 41, 85, 166, 167, 172, 185, 187-188, 204n12
Wecklein, Nikolaus ... 172
Wigmore, John ... 203n9, 207
Wilfen, Friedrich ... 39
William of Moerbeck ... 32, 33, 34, 35, 40, 43, 45, 69, 80-81, 159, 164, 167, 168, 169, 170, 175
Winckler, Paul ... 84
witnesses ... 191, 195

Xenophon ... 184

Yūssif, Ali Abdullah A. ... 158

Zeller, Edward ... 2, 3, 4, 7

PN 173 .A73 B73 1989

DATE DUE

PN 173 .A73 B73 1989

AUTHOR

Brandes, Paul D.

TITLE

A History of Aristotle's Rhetoric

DATE DUE	BORROWER'S NAME

PN 173 .A73 B73 1989